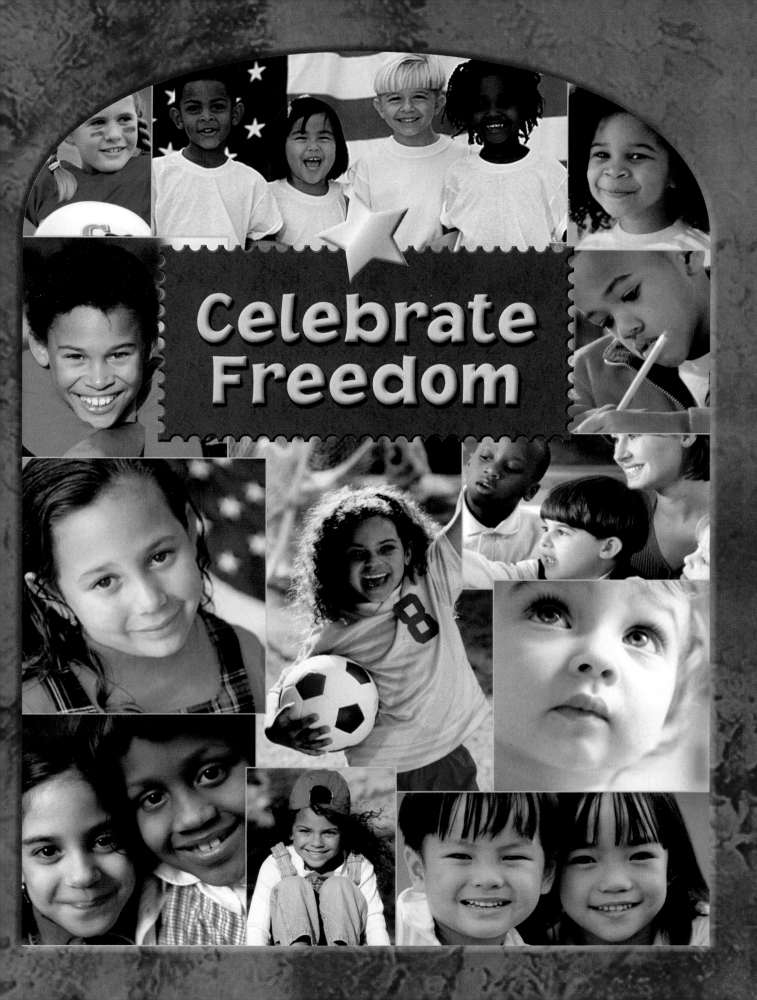

Celebrate Freedom

Three documents are especially important to the United States. These are the Declaration of Independence, the Constitution, and the Bill of Rights. Read parts of these documents. Then answer the questions.

Declaration of Independence, 1776

We hold these truths to be self-evident, that all men are created equal, that they are endowed by their Creator with certain unalienable Rights, that among these are Life, Liberty, and the pursuit of Happiness. That to secure these rights, Governments are instituted among Men, deriving their just powers from the consent of the governed. That whenever any Form of Government becomes destructive of these ends, it is the Right of the People to alter or to abolish it, and to institute new Government . . .

- **What does the Declaration of Independence tell us about American beliefs?**

Constitution of the United States of America, 1789

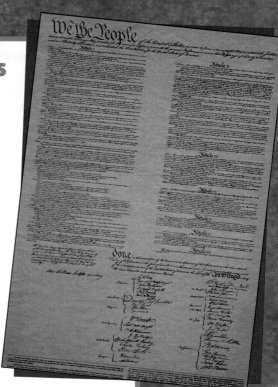

We the People of the United States, in Order to form a more perfect Union, establish Justice, insure domestic Tranquility, provide for the common defense, promote the general Welfare, and secure the Blessings of Liberty to ourselves and our Posterity, do ordain and establish this CONSTITUTION for the United States of America.

- **The first line of the Constitution is "We the People of the United States . . ."
  What does this say about whom the document is for?**

Bill of Rights, 1791

The first ten Amendments (changes) to the Constitution are called the Bill of Rights. They include:

- freedom of religion
- freedom of speech
- freedom of the press
- the right to protest peacefully
- the right to bear arms

- **In what ways might Americans peacefully protest?**

Celebrate Freedom

Independence Day Speech

Independence Hall, Philadelphia, PA.

We celebrate Independence Day on July 4. On this day, we remember the Declaration of Independence. The Declaration was signed on July 4, 1776.

Today, Americans celebrate Independence Day with picnics. We march in parades. We listen to speeches and watch fireworks. We do these things to remember our history. We do these things to celebrate freedom.

Write a speech that explains why Independence Day is important to Americans. Read your speech to the class.

Constitutional Word Search

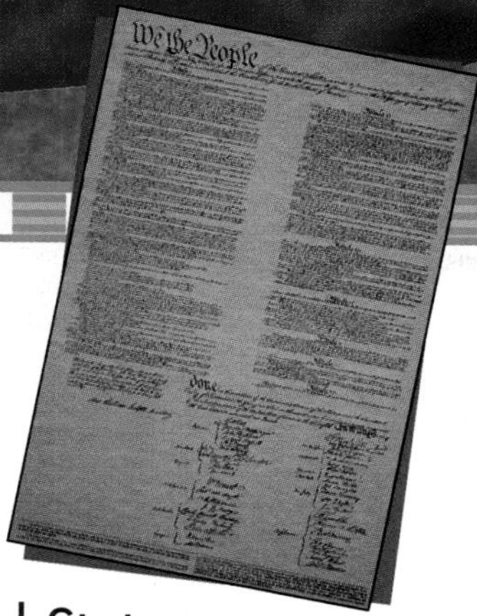

1. Use words from the United States Constitution to make a word grid. Words can be written in every direction.

2. After you have finished making your word grid, trade papers with another student. See if you can find all of the constitutional words in your partner's grid.

Materials:
- Grid Paper
- Pencil
- Eraser

You may include:

Constitution

Union

justice

people

liberty

Celebrate Freedom

Bill of Rights Collage

1. Go through old magazines and cut out pictures that illustrate the Bill of Rights. Choose pictures that show our freedom of speech, freedom of the press, and freedom of religion.

2. Arrange the pictures and paste them onto the paper to create a collage.

3. Beneath your collage, write a paragraph telling what freedom means to you.

Materials:
- Old magazines
- Scissors
- Glue
- Markers
- Construction Paper
- Ruler

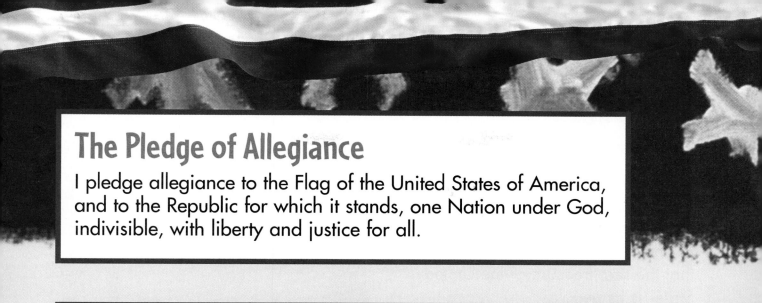

The Pledge of Allegiance

I pledge allegiance to the Flag of the United States of America,
and to the Republic for which it stands, one Nation under God,
indivisible, with liberty and justice for all.

The National Anthem

Oh, say, can you see, by the dawn's early light,
What so proudly we hailed at the twilight's last gleaming?
Whose broad stripes and bright stars, thro' the perilous fight,
O'er the ramparts we watched, were so gallantly streaming.
And the rockets' red glare, the bombs bursting in air,
Gave proof through the night that our flag was still there.
Oh, say, does that Star-Spangled Banner yet wave
O'er the land of the free and the home of the brave?

History

America has always inspired writers and poets. Some write about the majesty of our landforms and the splendor of our cities. Others declare that the real treasure of the United States is its people.

 What do you find impressive about the United States?

Mark Twain
Writer and humorist

The forest about us was dense and cool, the sky above us was cloudless and brilliant with sunshine, the broad lake before us was glassy and clear, or rippled and breezy, or black and storm-tossed, according to Nature's mood; and its circling border of mountain domes, clothed with forests, . . . and helmeted with glittering snow, fitly framed and finished the noble picture.

Mark Twain wrote this description of Lake Tahoe in Roughing It, *a book about his adventures in Nevada and California during the early 1860s.*

Walt Whitman
Poet

The genius of the United States is not best or most in its executives or legislatures, nor in its ambassadors or authors or colleges or churches or parlors, nor even in its newspapers or inventors . . . but always most in the common people.

Whitman wrote this in his introduction to his book of poetry, Leaves of Grass, *in 1855.*

Langston Hughes

Poet and a leader of the Harlem Renaissance, a flowering of African American culture in the 1920s

I, too, sing America.
I am the darker brother.
They send me to eat in the kitchen
When the company comes,
But I laugh,
And eat well,
And grow strong.

Langston Hughes wrote about the experience of African Americans in his poetry. In "I, Too" he wrote about strength in the face of injustice.

Rachel Carson

Writer, marine biologist

The Earth's [plants are] part of a web of life in which there are . . . relations between plants and the earth, between plants and other plants, and between plants and animals.

In 1962, Rachel Carson wrote a book called Silent Spring. *It caused Americans to think about how pesticides affect the environment.*

Geography

Mountains and plains, volcanoes and canyons, forests and swamps, rivers and lakes, islands and seashores, cities and farms—the geography of our country is greatly varied.

 How does Washington, D.C., help tie our country together?

Grand Canyon National Park, Arizona
Over millions of years, the Colorado River cut through layers of limestone, sandstone, and other rock to form the Grand Canyon. Parts of the canyon are one mile deep and 18 miles wide!

Hawaii Volcanoes National Park, Hawaii
Two volcanoes, Mauna Loa and Kilauea, spew lava on the island of Hawaii. Lava from Mauna Loa adds to the size of this 13,600-foot mountain, known as the "Great Builder."

Apostle Islands National Lakeshore, Wisconsin
Twenty islands in Lake Superior off the Bayfield Peninsula form the core of this national lakeshore. Visitors enjoy trout and salmon fishing, sailing, and beautiful views.

Acadia National Park, Maine
Acadia National Park has the highest land along the Atlantic coastline of the United States. The seashore park lies on Mount Desert Island, Isle au Haut, and the Schoodic Peninsula.

Washington, D.C.
Americans look to Washington, D.C., as the center of our government. Our freedom, our liberty, and our laws bring us together as Americans.

Everglades National Park, Florida
Alligators and snakes live in this huge area of shallow water, saw grass, and low hills called hummocks. The Everglades are home to thousands of plants, animals, birds, and insects.

CANADA

Apostle Islands National Lakeshore

Lake Superior

Minnesota

Wisconsin

Michigan

Lake Michigan

Lake Huron

Lake Erie

Lake Ontario

New Hampshire
Vermont
Maine
Acadia National Park

New York
Massachusetts
Rhode Island
Connecticut
New Jersey
Delaware
Maryland

Iowa

Illinois

Indiana

Ohio

Washington, D.C.

West Virginia

Pennsylvania

Virginia

Missouri

Kentucky

Tennessee

North Carolina

South Carolina

Arkansas

Georgia

Alabama

Mississippi

Louisiana

Florida

Ohio River

Mississippi River

Missouri River

as

lahoma

os River

Gulf of Mexico

Everglades National Park

ATLANTIC OCEAN

BAHAMAS

CUBA

Economics

The Mountain States

Our country can be split into regions. States in a region often have landforms, climate, and resources in common. Because of these similarities, states in a region often have similar economies and people work in similar jobs.

 READING CHECK **What jobs do people have in your state?**

The Southwest

The West

The Middle West

The Southeast

The Northeast

Government

A state government is made up of many people who make and carry out laws. Most state governments are set up the same way. The leader of a state's government is called the governor. The group that makes the laws for a state is the legislature. State supreme courts decide if laws are fair.

READING CHECK Who leads the state government?

State capitol building, Phoenix, Arizona

Arizona Governor Jane Dee Hull

Citizenship

In our country people do not wait for someone else to solve problems. During good times and bad, Americans volunteer to help people who are in need. We donate our time and effort in hospitals, nursing homes, and schools. After a fire or tornado, Americans help find housing for people left homeless. We also donate clothes, food, and money.

READING CHECK **What are some ways people volunteer?**

Habitat for Humanity, Austin, Texas

Community tree planting, Long Beach, California

Firefighters raising flag at the ruins of the World Trade Center, New York City, September 11, 2001

Culture

Different regions of the United States have special foods, recreation, art, and music. Forms of music often start in one place and spread to other places. Older forms of music, such as jazz and blues, moved throughout the country as musicians moved. Newer forms, such as Latino and rap, spread more quickly—through radio, music videos, and recordings.

 READING CHECK **How have some forms of music spread from the region of their origin?**

Music Place of Origin

Jazz - New Orleans, Louisiana
Blues - Mississippi River delta
Country - Rural Southern United States
Bluegrass - Appalachian Mountains
Western Swing - Texas and Oklahoma
Cajun - Southwest Louisiana
Polka - Upper Middle West
Latino - South Florida
Tejano - South Texas
Rap - New York City

"King" Oliver's Creole Jazz Band, Louis Armstrong (center of back row), Chicago, Illinois, 1923

Science, Technology, and Society

Technology affects nearly every part of our lives. In the last 100 years, the technology of farming, for example, has changed. New machines and more accurate information about weather and water supply have dramatically increased crop yields.

 READING CHECK How has farming changed in the last 100 years?

Long Ago

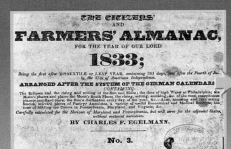

Today

Today

Long Ago

A16

Macmillan/McGraw-Hill

Our Country's Regions

Macmillan/McGraw-Hill

Our Country's Regions

James A. Banks

Richard G. Boehm

Kevin P. Colleary

Gloria Contreras

A. Lin Goodwin

Mary A. McFarland

Walter C. Parker

NATIONAL GEOGRAPHIC

Macmillan
McGraw-Hill

New York

PROGRAM AUTHORS

Dr. James A. Banks
Russell F. Stark University Professor
Director of the Center for
Multicultural Education
University of Washington
Seattle, Washington

Dr. Richard G. Boehm
Jesse H. Jones Distinguished Chair in
Geographic Education and
Director, The Gilbert M. Grosvenor
Center for Geographic Education
Southwest Texas State University
San Marcos, Texas

Dr. Kevin P. Colleary
Curriculum and Teaching Department
Hunter College
City University of New York
New York, New York

Dr. Gloria Contreras
Professor of Education
University of North Texas
Denton, Texas

Dr. A. Lin Goodwin
Associate Professor of Education
Department of Curriculum
and Teaching
Teachers College
Columbia University
New York, New York

Dr. Mary A. McFarland
Social Studies Educational
Consultant, K–12,
St. Louis, Missouri

Dr. Walter C. Parker
Professor and Program Chair
for Social Studies Education
University of Washington
Seattle, Washington

Washington, D.C.

HISTORIANS/SCHOLARS

Dr. Joyce Appleby
Professor of History
University of California, Los Angeles
Los Angeles, California

Dr. Alan Brinkley
Professor of American History
Columbia University
New York, New York

Dr. Nancy Cott
Stanley Woodward Professor of
History and American Studies
Yale University
New Haven, Connecticut

Dr. James McPherson
George Henry Davis Professor of
American History
Princeton University
Princeton, New Jersey

Dr. Donald A. Ritchie
Associate Historian of the United States
Senate Historical Office
Washington, D.C.

PROGRAM CONSULTANTS

Betty Ruth Baker, M.Ed.
Assistant Professor of Curriculum
and Instruction
Early Childhood Specialist
School of Education
Baylor University
Waco, Texas

Dr. Randolph B. Campbell
Regents' Professor of History
University of North Texas
Denton, Texas

Dr. Steven Cobb
Director, Center for
Economic Education
Chair, Department of Economics
University of North Texas
Denton, Texas

Frank de Varona, Ed.S.
Visiting Associate Professor
Florida International University
Miami, Florida

Dr. John L. Esposito
Professor of Religion and International
Affairs, and Director of the Center for
Christian-Muslim Understanding
Georgetown University
Washington, D.C.

READING INSTRUCTION CONSULTANTS

M. Frankie Dungan, M.Ed.
Reading/Language Arts Consultant, K–6
Mansfield, Texas

Antonio A. Fierro
Program Director for the Texas
Reading Initiative, Region 19
El Paso, Texas

Dr. William H. Rupley
Professor of Reading Education
Distinguished Research Fellow
Department of Teaching,
Learning and Culture
College of Education
Texas A&M University
College Station, Texas

GRADE LEVEL CONSULTANTS

Jackie Austin
Instructional Coordinator
Ford Elementary Community
Educational Center
St. Louis, Missouri

William R. Cavins
Fourth Grade Teacher
Lake Mary Elementary School
Lake Mary, Florida

Nancy Cope
Former President
North Carolina Council for the
Social Studies
Sanford, North Carolina

Eloise Dillon
Fourth Grade Teacher
Bateman Elementary School
Chicago, Illinois

Margaret Maddalozzo
Fourth Grade Teacher
Thomas Jefferson Elementary School
Peoria, Illinois

Janie Phelps
Social Studies Supervisor
Orange County Schools
Orlando, Florida

Kathleen Picone
Fourth Grade Teacher
The Willis E. Thorpe School
Danvers, Massachusetts

Dr. Christine Yeh
Child Psychologist
Columbia University
New York, New York

CONTRIBUTING WRITERS

Dinah Zike
Comfort, Texas

Reyna Eisenstark
Ghent, New York

Linda Scher
Raleigh, North Carolina

learning through listening

Students with print disabilities
may be eligible to obtain an
accessible, audio version of the
pupil edition of this textbook.
Please call Recording for the Blind
& Dyslexic at 1-800-221-4792 for
complete information.

Acknowledgments The publisher gratefully acknowledges permission to reprint the following copyrighted material:

From **Magic Windows/Ventanas mágicas** by Carmen Lomas Garza. Copyright © 1999 by Carmen Lomas Garza. Children's Book Press, San Francisco, California. Used by permission. From **Mark Twain and the Queens of the Mississippi** by Cheryl Harness. Copyright © 1998 by Cheryl Harness. Simon & Schuster Children's Publishing Division, New York. Used by permission. From **I Was Dreaming to Come to America** selected by Veronica Lawlor. Copyright © 1995 by Veronica Lawlor. Viking Press, a division of Penguin Putnam Inc., New York. Used by permission. From **Crazy Horse's Vision** by Joseph Bruchac. Copyright © 2000 by Joseph Bruchac. Lee & Low Books Inc., New York. Used by permission. From **Coolies** by Yin. Copyright © 2001 by Yin. Philomel Books, a division of Penguin Putnam Books, New York. Used by permission. From **The Legend of Freedom Hill** by Linda Jacobs Altman. Copyright © 2000 by Linda Jacobs Altman. Lee & Low Books Inc., New York. Used by permission. (continued on page R56)

Macmillan/McGraw-Hill
A Division of The **McGraw·Hill** Companies

Printed in the United States of America
ISBN 0-02-149265-4
5 6 7 8 9 071/043 06 05 04

Contents

Introduction

Unit 5

CHARTS, GRAPHS, & DIAGRAMS

TIME LINES

MAPS

Social Studies Handbook

The Social Studies Strands are a way of thinking about social studies. Social studies is the study of people and the world we live in. This is a very big subject! One way to think about social studies is to break it into parts. We call these parts *strands*.

The pie chart on the next page shows the eight strands of social studies. Each strand teaches us something about the world. Studying all of the strands together leads to an understanding of our world, past and present. The only thing left is the future. That will be up to you!

The Eight Strands
of Social Studies

Economics
Wants and needs, goods and services. Basic human needs are met in a variety of ways.

Citizenship
Rights, responsibilities, pride and hope. Our beliefs and principles help make up our national identity.

Culture
Holidays, traditions and stories. We learn about ourselves and our families through the customs we share and celebrate.

Geography
Location, place, maps and more. People and environments surround us and are ever changing.

Science, Technology, and Society
Inventions, computers and ideas. Technology has changed how people live together in the world.

Social Studies Skills
Many special skills are needed to better understand the world around you.

History
Time and chronology, years and dates. Historical figures and ordinary people help shape our lives.

Government
People work to make the laws that influence our lives. People work with citizens to govern.

Thinking About Reading

Your book examines the geography, history, and economies of different regions in our country. In order to understand the important facts and ideas presented, it is necessary to read your book carefully. The strategies below describe some ways you can become an effective social studies reader.

How to Preview, Ask, Read, and Review:

1. **Preview the lesson.** Read the title, headings, and high-lighted words. Look at the photographs, illustrations, and maps, and read their captions. Think about what you already know about the topic. Form a general idea of what the lesson is about.

2. **Ask yourself questions before you read and as you read.** For example, you might ask, "What is the lesson telling me about the Industrial Revolution?"

3. **Read and reread.** Read the lesson carefully. Figure out the main ideas. Reread a sentence or paragraph if it doesn't make sense to you. Look up the meanings of any unfamiliar words.

4. **Review by summarizing what you have read, either aloud or in writing.** Did you find the answers to your questions?

Communities

A community is a group of people who live and work together. A community may be just one neighborhood, or it may be made up of several neighborhoods near one another.

Cities are made up of many communities. Have you ever visited or lived in **New York City**? It is the largest city in our country. Many people in our country live in large **urban** areas such as Los Angeles, Chicago, and Boston.

Other people prefer **rural** life. Many families have lived on their farms and ranches for a long time. Small towns are also found throughout the rural United States.

Ice skating in New York City

Preview.
The title, the highlighted words, the picture, and its caption tell me this lesson will be about communities in our country.

Ask yourself questions.
One question I might ask is, "What different types of communities will I learn about?"

Read and reread.
I carefully read the paragraphs and think about the main ideas. I look up the meanings of *urban* and *rural*.

Review.
I will say or write the answers to my questions.

Use Visuals

An important way to learn from your reading is to use **visuals**. Visuals are the pictures, maps, charts, and graphs that appear throughout your book. Visuals provide useful information in a clear and easy-to-study form.

Tip!

★ When looking at graphs, maps, or charts, read the legend or key to find out the meanings of special symbols.

★ Look for objects in the picture that might give additional information.

How to Use Visuals

Look closely at the visual. Then ask yourself the following questions:

- What does the picture, map, chart, or graph show?
- How does it help me understand what I have read?
- How does it add to the information I have read?
- What information does the caption or label provide?

Study the picture below. Then read the caption.

Robots build cars in factories.

The caption tells us that today some jobs are done by robots.

Think about the information that is given in the photograph and caption. Then copy and complete the diagram on a separate sheet of paper.

In Colonial Williamburg you can see how newspapers were printed in the 1700s.

Visual:

Caption Information:

The printing press is in Williamsburg. It shows how colonial newspapers were made.

Visual Information:

A printing press is being used.

Keep in Mind

For more help in reading social studies, keep these strategies in mind:

Reread
Make sure you understand what each sentence means before you read further. Reread any sentences that don't make sense to you.

Look up unfamiliar words
Use the glossary in your book or a dictionary to find the meanings of unfamiliar words.

Summarize
In your own words, briefly describe what your reading is about.

Practice Activities!

1. **Use Visuals** Find an interesting photograph in your book. Write a caption for it.
2. **Create a Visual** Create a visual by making an illustration of something you like. Write a caption for it. Then exchange visuals with a classmate and discuss them.

Context Clues

You can often figure out the meaning of an unknown word by using **context clues**. A context clue can come before, after, or in the same sentence as the unknown word. Using context clues will help you to become a better reader.

★ Have you heard this word before? Think about how it was used.

★ Write down the context clues you used to find the meaning of the new word.

★ After you find its meaning, use the new word in a sentence of your own to help you remember it.

How to Use Context Clues

Ask yourself the following questions:

- Are any parts of this word familiar?

- Are there other words, phrases, or sentences in the paragraph that can help me figure out the meaning of the word?

- What information do the other words, phrases, or sentences provide?

- Do the pictures give me any information about the word?

Read the paragraph below. What context clues would you use to identify the meaning of the word *immigrants*?

Today, people from almost every country in the world live here. Starting in the 1600s, **immigrants** (IHM ih gruntz) began to arrive. Most immigrants came here to find a better way of life.

Context Clue: people from almost every country in the world live here

Context Clue: came here to find a better way of life

Context Clue: began to arrive

Try It!

Read the paragraph below about American colonists. Then copy and complete the chart to find context clues for the word *boycott*.

The colonists held a town meeting to protest the new taxes by Britain. The colonists made a list of all the British goods they would **boycott**. They refused to buy tea and other goods that came from Britain. Women held "spinning bees" to spin thread so they would not have to buy clothes from Britain.

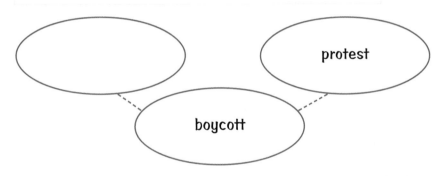

protest

boycott

- What steps did you take to find the meaning of *boycott*?

For more help in reading social studies, keep these strategies in mind:

Reread
Make sure you understand what each sentence means. Reread any sentences that do not make sense to you.

Find the main idea
As you read, think about the topic and the main idea in each paragraph or section.

Summarize
In your own words, briefly describe what you are reading about.

Practice Activities!

1. **Read** Look in your book for an unfamiliar word or term. Then look for context clues to help you figure out the meaning of the word.

2. **Write** Choose an unfamiliar word from the dictionary. Write a short paragraph using the new word and one or two context clues.

WELCOME TO Washington, D.C.

Physical Systems

People enjoy sunlight, trees, and water at city parks.

Places and Regions

Every Spring people fly kites by the Washington Monument.

The World in Spatial Terms

This aerial view shows buildings, streets, and green spaces surrounding the Mall. The Mall can be seen between the Capitol Building and the Washington Monument.

Human Systems

Transportation routes, such as roads, are built to carry people and goods to and from the city.

Uses of Geography

Riders on Washington's underground trains use the subway map to find their way.

Environment & Society

Kayakers use the natural environment that surrounds Washington, D.C. for recreation.

Using Globes

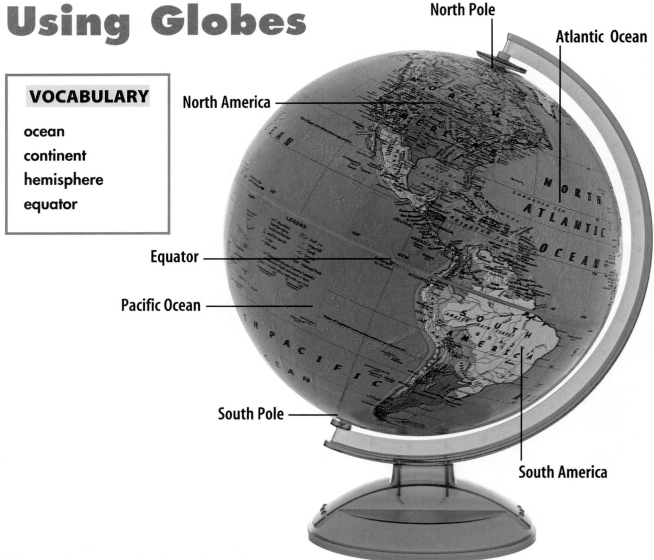

VOCABULARY

ocean
continent
hemisphere
equator

Labels on the globe:
- North Pole
- Atlantic Ocean
- North America
- Equator
- Pacific Ocean
- South Pole
- South America

What does a globe show?

- A globe is a model of Earth. Like Earth, a globe is a round object, or sphere. A globe is a useful tool for showing what Earth looks like.

- Globes show the parts of Earth that are land and the parts that are water. Which does Earth have more of, water or land?

- Earth's largest bodies of water are called **oceans**. There are four oceans—the Atlantic, Arctic, Indian, and Pacific.

- Look at the globe above. What color is used on the globe to show oceans?

- Globes also show the large bodies of land called **continents**. The seven continents are Africa, Antarctica, Asia, Australia, Europe, North America, and South America. Find North America and South America on the globe above. Which oceans do you see bordering these continents?

The Hemispheres

NATIONAL GEOGRAPHIC

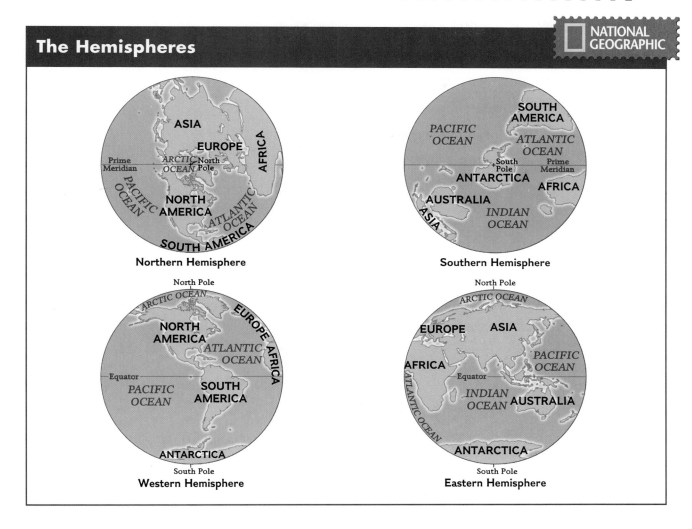

Northern Hemisphere

Southern Hemisphere

Western Hemisphere

Eastern Hemisphere

What are the four hemispheres?

- Look again at the globe on the previous page. You can see only half of the globe or sphere at one time. A word for half a sphere is **hemisphere**. The word "hemi" means half. Geographers divide Earth into four different hemispheres.

- Earth is divided into the Northern Hemisphere and Southern Hemisphere by the **equator**. The equator is an imaginary line that lies halfway between the North Pole and the South Pole. Look at the maps of the hemispheres above. Which continents are located on the equator? On which continent is the South Pole shown?

- Earth can also be divided into two other hemispheres. What are the names of these hemispheres?

Using Maps

VOCABULARY

cardinal directions	relative location
compass rose	map symbol
intermediate directions	map key
	scale
	locator

What are cardinal directions?

- Directions describe the way you face or move to get somewhere. North, east, south, and west are the main directions, or **cardinal directions**.

- If you face the North Pole, you are facing north. When you face north, south is directly behind you. West is to your left. What direction will be to your right?

How do you use a compass rose?

- A **compass rose** is a small drawing on a map that can help you find directions.

- The cardinal directions are written as N, E, S, and W. Find the compass rose on the map above. In which direction is Cleveland from Coshocton?

What are intermediate directions?

- Notice the spikes between the cardinal directions on the compass rose. These show the **intermediate directions**, or in-between directions.

- The intermediate directions are northeast, southeast, southwest, and northwest. The direction northwest is often written as NW. What letters are used for the other intermediate directions?

- Intermediate directions help us describe **relative location**. When we use relative location we describe one place in relation to another. For example, using the map on this page you can say that Mansfield is southwest of Cleveland.

Why do maps have titles?

- When using a map, first look at the map title. The title names the area the map shows. It may also tell you the kind of information shown on the map. Look at the maps below. What is the title of each?

Why do maps include symbols?

- A **map symbol** is something that stands for something else.

- Many maps use the color blue to stand for water, for example. What do dots sometimes stand for?

How can you find out what map symbols stand for?

- A **map key** gives the meaning of each symbol used on the map.

- When you look at a map, you should always study the map key. Look at the maps on this page. What symbol marks places of interest on the map of San Francisco?

- Draw your own map of place where you live. Put in the streets. Use symbols to show where you live, your school, a store, a friend's house, a stop sign, and a park or playground. Finally, don't forget to insert a compass rose.

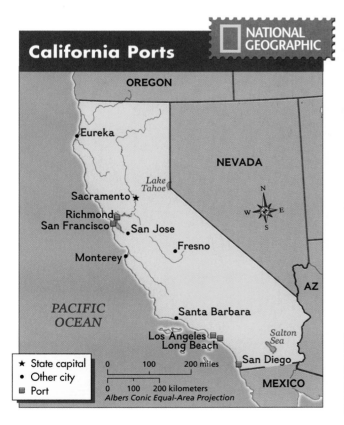

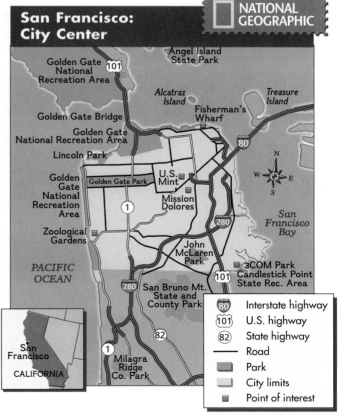

What is a map scale?

- All maps are smaller than the real area that they show. So how can you figure out the real distance between places? Most maps include a **scale**. The scale shows the relationship between distances on a map and real distances on the ground.

- The scales in this book are drawn with two lines. The top line shows distance in miles. What unit of measurement does the bottom line use?

How do you use a map scale?

- You can also make a scale strip like the one shown on this page. Place the edge of a strip of paper under the scale lines on the map of below. Mark the distances in miles.

- Use your scale strip to measure the distance between the ranger station and Observation Tower. Place the edge of the strip under the two points. Line the zero up under the ranger station. What is the distance to the Observation Tower in miles?

What do locators show?

- A **locator** is a small map set onto the main map. It shows where the area of the main map is located. Where on the map below is the locator?

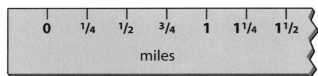

| 0 | 1/4 | 1/2 | 3/4 | 1 | 1 1/4 | 1 1/2 |

miles

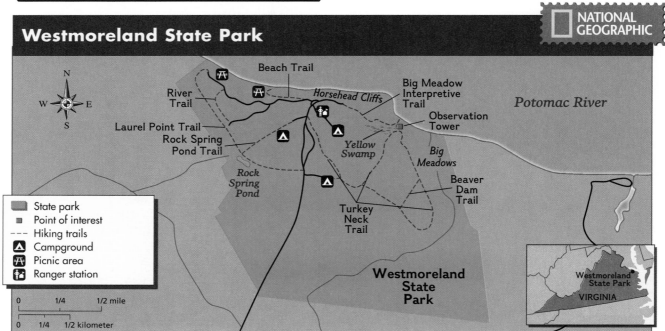

Westmoreland State Park

NATIONAL GEOGRAPHIC

Beach Trail
River Trail
Big Meadow Interpretive Trail
Horsehead Cliffs
Potomac River
Laurel Point Trail
Rock Spring Pond Trail
Observation Tower
Yellow Swamp
Big Meadows
Rock Spring Pond
Beaver Dam Trail
Turkey Neck Trail

Westmoreland State Park

- State park
- Point of interest
- - - Hiking trails
- Campground
- Picnic area
- Ranger station

| 0 | 1/4 | 1/2 mile |
| 0 | 1/4 | 1/2 kilometer |

Westmoreland State Park
VIRGINIA

Different Kinds of Maps

VOCABULARY

political map	transportation map
physical map	
landform map	historical map

What is a political map?

- A **political map** shows information such as cities, capital cities, states, and countries. What symbol is used to show state capitals on the map below? What city is the capital of your state? What is the symbol for our nation's capital?

- Political maps use lines to show borders. The states or countries are also shown in different colors.

- Use the map on this page to answer these questions. Are states bigger in the west or the east? Which states border Canada? Which states border Mexico?

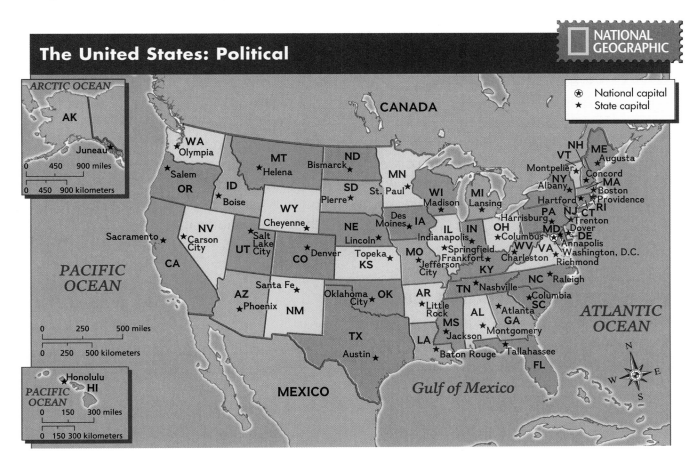

The United States: Political

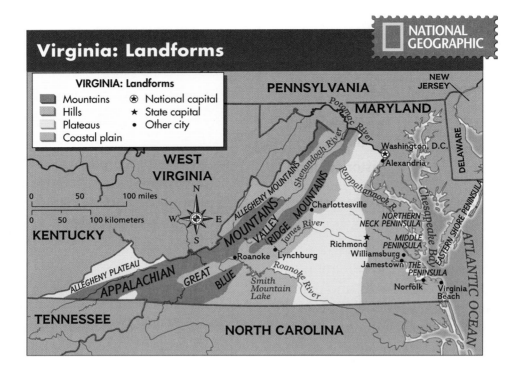

What are physical maps?

- There are different kinds of **physical maps** in this book. One kind of physical map shows landforms, or the shapes that make up Earth's surface. These maps are called **landform maps**. Mountains, hills, and plains are all examples of landforms.

- Look at the map above. What kinds of landforms are found in Virginia? What mountain ranges are found in the state?

What is a transportation map?

- A **transportation map** is a kind of map that shows how you can travel from one place to another.

- Some transportation maps show roads for traveling by car, by bike, or on foot. Other transportation maps may show bus, train, ship, or airplane routes. Look at the map of Indianapolis on the next page. What kinds of routes are shown on the map of Indianapolis?

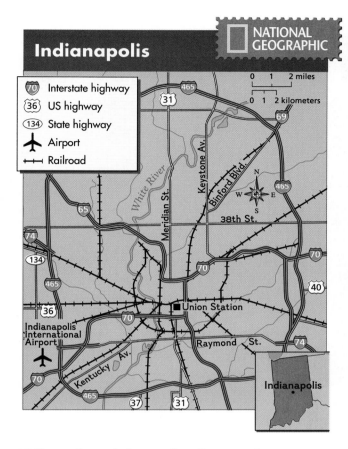

Indianapolis

NATIONAL GEOGRAPHIC

70	Interstate highway
36	US highway
134	State highway
✈	Airport
⊢—⊦	Railroad

0   1   2 miles

0   1   2 kilometers

White River · Keystone Av. · Binford Blvd. · Meridian St. · 38th St.

31 · 465 · 69 · 465 · 70 · 40 · 65 · 74 · 134 · 465 · 36 · 70 · 70 · 465 · 37 · 31

Union Station

Indianapolis International Airport

Kentucky Av. · Raymond St. · 74

Indianapolis

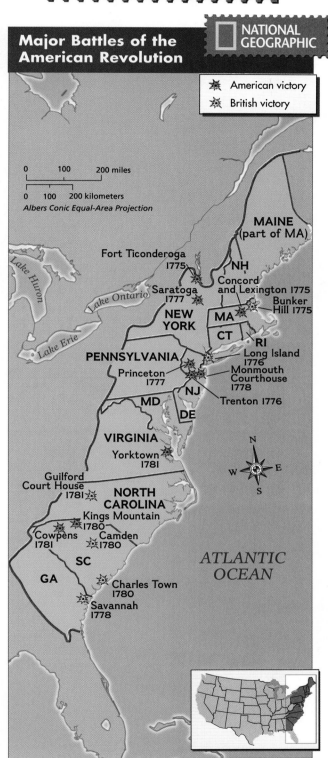

Major Battles of the American Revolution

NATIONAL GEOGRAPHIC

✸	American victory
✸	British victory

0   100   200 miles

0   100   200 kilometers

Albers Conic Equal-Area Projection

MAINE (part of MA)

Lake Huron · Lake Ontario · Lake Erie

Fort Ticonderoga 1775

NH

Concord and Lexington 1775

Saratoga 1777

Bunker Hill 1775

NEW YORK

MA

CT

RI

PENNSYLVANIA

Long Island 1776

Princeton 1777

Monmouth Courthouse 1778

NJ

Trenton 1776

MD

DE

VIRGINIA

Yorktown 1781

Guilford Court House 1781

NORTH CAROLINA

Kings Mountain 1780

Cowpens 1781

Camden 1780

SC

GA

ATLANTIC OCEAN

Charles Town 1780

Savannah 1778

What is a historical map?

- A **historical map** is a map that shows information about past events and where they occurred. When you look at a historical map, first study the map title. What information do you think you would find on the historical map on this page?

- Historical maps often show dates in the title or on the map. Study the map. What historical dates does it show?

- The map key tells you what the symbols stand for on the map. What is the symbol for a battle? What do the colors of the symbols tell you? Who won more major battles in the American Revolution?

The United States:
Its Land
and People

On a visit to Arizona's famous Grand Canyon, President Theodore Roosevelt exclaimed, *"The Grand Canyon fills me with awe. It is beyond comparison—beyond description . . . [it] is the one great sight which every American should see."*

The Grand Canyon is one of many spectacular sights found in our country. In this Introduction you will learn about the places and the people that make the United States special.

The Western Hemisphere

Do you know how the United States fits into the world? It is part of the **Western Hemisphere**, which stretches from the North Pole to the South Pole.

Between the North and South Poles are three continents. Look at the map. If you traveled through the Western Hemisphere, you would learn a lot about its **geography** (jee AHG ruh fee). Geography is the study of Earth. It is also the way that people live on it and use it. Land and water, plant and animal life, and human activities are all part of geography.

On your trip, you would see many different **landforms**. Landforms are the shapes that make up Earth's surface. One kind of landform is a **plain**. It is a large area of nearly flat land.

Your trip begins at the North Pole. Your first stop is the **tundra**, a huge plain that is frozen for most of the year.

South of the tundra are the **Rocky Mountains**. They stretch from **Canada** to **Mexico**.

Heading farther south, you pass through Central America into South America. In Brazil, you

The Western Hemisphere

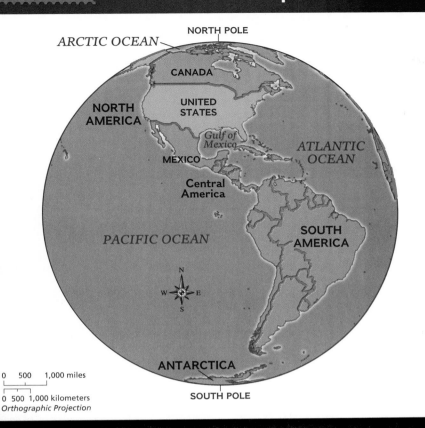

NORTH POLE

ARCTIC OCEAN

CANADA

NORTH
AMERICA

UNITED
STATES

Gulf of
Mexico

MEXICO

ATLANTIC
OCEAN

Central
America

PACIFIC OCEAN

SOUTH
AMERICA

N
W E
S

0   500   1,000 miles

0 500 1,000 kilometers
Orthographic Projection

ANTARCTICA

SOUTH POLE

1. Which continents are located in the Western Hemisphere?

2. What ocean is located between Canada and the North Pole?

3. Where is the South Pole located?

4. Name the areas that make up North America.

find the **Amazon Rain Forest**. It is home to a variety of plants and animals.

Along the western part of South America, you find the high **Andes Mountains**. Among them is the tallest mountain in the Western Hemisphere, Mt. Aconcagua (ak un KAUG wuh).

Continuing south, you reach the South Pole. It is covered mostly by a huge sheet of ice.

READING CHECK

What does the study of geography include?

Our Country's Land

Walt Whitman celebrated America in "Leaves of Grass," a famous poem. He wrote:

"Land of coal and iron! land of gold! land of cotton, sugar, rice! Land of the ocean shores! land of sierras and peaks!"

Whitman's words describe our country well. The geography of the United States is full of variety. Our country has deep lakes, huge fields, and mountains that seem to touch the sky.

Thick swamps and marshes, like the **Everglades** in Florida, can be found in the southern part of the United States. These are also known as **wetlands**, where the ground is very wet or covered with water.

On the **Coastal Plain** of the Atlantic Ocean, you'll find sandy beaches and rocky shores. A coast is the land along an ocean.

Another kind of plain is found inland. The **Interior Plains** are made up of the Great and Central Plains. They cover much of the middle part of our country.

You have already read about the Rocky Mountains. They are the longest chain of mountains found in the United States.

Unusual rock formations are found along the **Columbia Plateau**. A plateau is a high, flat landform. It rises steeply above the surrounding land. The Columbia Plateau is located in Washington, Idaho, and Oregon.

READING CHECK ✓ Name three landforms found in the United States.

United States Geography

The map shows some of the natural features that make our country a special place to live. Use it to answer the following questions.

QUESTIONS:

1. What is the highest point?
2. What is the lowest point?
3. Which river forms a border between Indiana and Kentucky?
4. What states do the Rocky Mountains cross?

ALASKA
Mt. McKinley
▲ 20,320 ft.
(6,194 m)

0   250   500 miles
0 250 500 kilometers

WASHINGTON

COLUMBIA PLATEAU

COAST RANGES

CASCADE RANGE

OREGON

IDAHO

Snake Riv

SIERRA NEVADA

CENTRAL VALLEY

NEVADA

Great Salt Lake

U

Death Valley ▼
282 ft. (86 m)
below sea level

Grand

CALIFORNIA

ARIZON

⊛ National capital
▲ Highest peak
▼ Lowest point

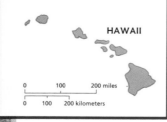

HAWAII

0   100   200 miles
0   100   200 kilometers

FIND THESE PLACES

Grand Canyon

Rocky Mountains

Interior Plains

Coastal Plain

The Everglades

Columbia Plateau

Appalachian Mountains

Death Valley

Coast Ranges

Cascade Range

The United States

NATIONAL GEOGRAPHIC

Missouri River

MONTANA

NORTH DAKOTA

MINNESOTA

Lake Superior

MAINE

VERMONT

NEW HAMPSHIRE

SOUTH DAKOTA

WISCONSIN

Lake Michigan

MICHIGAN

Lake Huron

Lake Ontario

NEW YORK

MASSACHUSETTS

RHODE ISLAND

WYOMING

NEBRASKA

IOWA

Lake Erie

PENNSYLVANIA

CONNECTICUT

NEW JERSEY

INTERIOR PLAINS

Platte River

ILLINOIS

INDIANA

OHIO

Ohio River

WEST VIRGINIA

DELAWARE

MARYLAND

Washington, D.C.

COLORADO

KANSAS

MISSOURI

KENTUCKY

VIRGINIA

Arkansas River

MOUNTAINS

APPALACHIAN MOUNTAINS

NORTH CAROLINA

N

W   E

S

OKLAHOMA

ARKANSAS

TENNESSEE

SOUTH CAROLINA

COASTAL PLAIN

NEW MEXICO

Mississippi River

MISSISSIPPI

ALABAMA

GEORGIA

TEXAS

Rio Grande

LOUISIANA

FLORIDA

The Everglades

0	150	300 miles
0	150	300 kilometers

To learn more, visit our Web site:
www.mhschool.com

Reading Elevation Maps

On a trip across the United States, you would fly over different landforms. Suppose you wanted to land near mountains and go hiking. How would you know which would be easy to climb? For this kind of information, you would need an **elevation** (el uh VAY shun) map. Elevation is the height of the land above the level of the sea. Elevation at sea level is 0 feet.

Feet		Meters
10,000		3,000
7,000		2,000
3,000		1,000
700		200
0		0
Below sea level		Below sea level

LEARN THE SKILL

Look at the map on the next page. Use it to follow the steps below to learn how to read an elevation map.

1. **Locate the map's title.**
   The title of the map is United States: Elevation.

2. **Locate the map key.**
   An elevation map uses colors to show different heights. A map key tells you what each color stands for. For example, all the places in yellow on the map are between 3,000 feet and 7,000 feet above sea level.

3. **Use elevations to understand rivers.**
   Elevation maps tell us about more than mountains. You can also use them to understand rivers. Have you ever wondered why rivers flow in one direction? The answer has to do with elevation. Every river begins at a higher elevation than where it ends. Gravity pulls the water downhill. You can use an elevation map to help you find out in which direction a river flows.

TRY THE SKILL

Let's try using the elevation map to trace the path of a river. The Rio Grande begins in western Colorado. This is high in the Rocky Mountains. What color is the area where the river begins? Now check the map key. You can see that the river begins at an elevation of 7,000 to 10,000 feet above sea level.

Follow the river's path. It flows through areas of lower and lower elevation. Finally, it empties into the Gulf of Mexico, which is at sea level.

Now answer the following questions.

1. What is elevation?

2. How can a map key help you read an elevation map?

3. How does an elevation map tell us which way a river flows?

4. In what color would this map show a plateau 700 to 3,000 feet high?

EXTEND THE SKILL

Now use the elevation map to trace the path of the Mississippi River. First, locate the river on the map. Follow its path to where the river empties. Then answer the questions below.

- How high is the elevation where the river begins?

- Where does the river empty?

- How can an elevation map help you learn about geography?

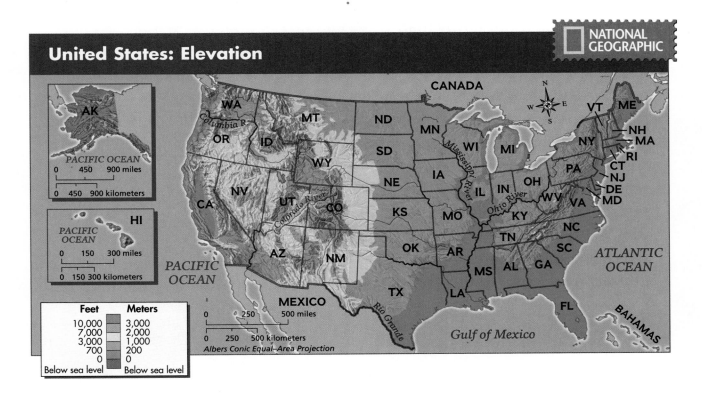

United States: Elevation

Weather and Climate

Every place has a pattern of weather over many years. This is its **climate** (KLIGH mit). Different parts of our country have very different climates.

Climate has two parts. The first part is **temperature** (TEM pur uh chur). It is a measure of how hot or cold the air is. The temperature in Arizona stays warm all year. This is because it is closer to the equator than other parts of our country. The closer to the equator you are, the warmer the temperature. Alaska, which is far north of the equator, is cold all year.

Oceans also affect temperature. Water heats up more slowly than air, so oceans stay cool during the summer. Breezes off the ocean keep the land nearby cool, too.

During winter, oceans get cold more slowly than land. Ocean breezes bring warmer air to nearby land. This keeps the temperatures mild. But ocean breezes do not reach far inland. Those places tend to get hotter in the summer and colder in the winter.

Did you realize that elevation also affects temperature? The higher a place is above sea level, the colder its climate usually will be.

The other part of climate is called **precipitation** (prih sihp ih TAY shun). Precipitation is the moisture that falls to the ground. It may be in the form of rain, snow, sleet, or hail.

READING CHECK

What are the two parts of climate?

Climate of the United States

People who live in warm climates may not own a single jacket. In colder climates, people have heavy coats, boots, and wool hats. As you study the map and charts, think about how climate affects our lives. Then answer the following questions.

QUESTIONS:

1. Which states have the warmest temperatures in January?
2. Which has the coldest?
3. How does the sun help form rain?
4. Look at the table on rainfall and find those cities on the map.

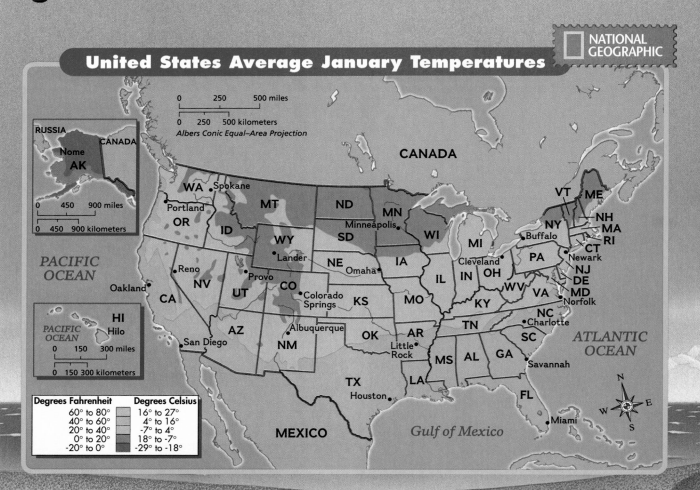

United States Average January Temperatures

NATIONAL GEOGRAPHIC

Degrees Fahrenheit	Degrees Celsius
60° to 80°	16° to 27°
40° to 60°	4° to 16°
20° to 40°	-7° to 4°
0° to 20°	18° to -7°
-20° to 0°	-29° to -18°

How Rain Is Made

— Sun

Cool air changes water vapor back into water

Sun's heat causes evaporation

Some water goes into the air as water vapor

Water falls back to Earth as rain

Precipitation in United States Cities

CITY	RAINFALL (in rounded inches)	CITY	RAINFALL (in rounded inches)
Albuquerque, NM	9	Norfolk, VA	45
Buffalo, NY	39	Portland, OR	36
Cleveland, OH	37	Reno, NV	8
Houston, TX	46	San Diego, CA	10
Lander, WY	13	Savannah, GA	49

Source: World Almanac 2001/
National Climate Data Center

To learn more, visit our Web site: www.mhschool.com

Natural Resources

We are greatly affected by our **environment** (en VIGH run munt). Environment is the surroundings in which people, plants, and animals live. It includes landforms and the **natural resources** (REE sor sez) of a place. A natural resource is a material found in nature that people use.

Our country is rich in natural resources. However, many of them will not last forever and we must use them wisely. Some resources are **renewable** (rih NOO uh bul). Renewable means that we can renew, or replace, them. Trees, for example, are renewable resources because they can be replanted. Water is another renewable resource. Every time it rains, water is returned to our rivers.

Other kinds of resources are **nonrenewable**. This means there

is a limited supply. When we have used them up, they will be gone forever. **Minerals** are nonrenewable resources. A mineral is a natural substance found in the earth that does not come from plants or animals. Workers dig pits to find minerals such as iron, silver, and copper.

Fuels (FYOO ulz) such as oil, natural gas, and coal are also nonrenewable. They are sources of heat or energy. With fuels, we heat our homes, plow our fields, and cook our meals. Fuels also power cars, buses, and airplanes.

Someday these fuels will be gone. Scientists are trying to develop new sources of energy. Solar power is one possibility. Wind power is another.

There is one other important resource: people. People are the key that makes our country work. Farmers plant crops. Miners and oil workers produce fuels. Factory workers make cars, books, and a thousand other products. Natural resources could not be used without human resources.

READING CHECK

What is the difference between renewable and nonrenewable resources?

Changing the Land

Our environment shapes us, but we also shape it. One way we shape the land is by finding and using natural resources. We drill for oil and dig for minerals. We plant crops in soil. We also cut down trees for wood.

How we use another resource, water, also changes the land. Some parts of our country get very little rainfall. In those places, people have built dams. A dam is a wall built across a river to control the flow of water. Dams hold water so that the water can be sent to dry areas for drinking, washing, and watering crops. Water can also be used to make electricity.

As people settle in new areas, they build houses and offices. They also pave roads and construct bridges. Towns and cities form, bringing more newcomers and greater changes. Where and how we live is one of the biggest ways we shape the land.

With all these changes, it is important that we keep our environment safe. We can fight **pollution** (puh LOO shun), or anything that dirties the air, soil, or water. Reusing cans and

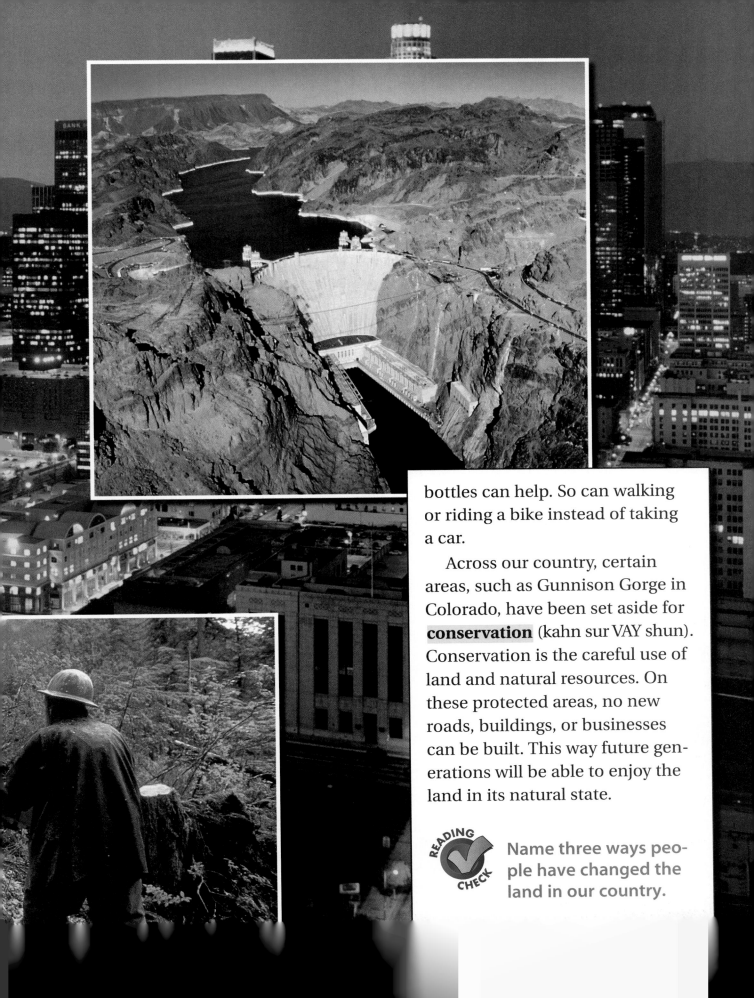

bottles can help. So can walking or riding a bike instead of taking a car.

Across our country, certain areas, such as Gunnison Gorge in Colorado, have been set aside for **conservation** (kahn sur VAY shun). Conservation is the careful use of land and natural resources. On these protected areas, no new roads, buildings, or businesses can be built. This way future generations will be able to enjoy the land in its natural state.

READING CHECK

Name three ways people have changed the land in our country.

Resources of the United States

As you study the maps and chart, think about how people in different areas make use of the land and resources around them. Then answer the questions.

QUESTIONS:

1. In which states is copper found?
2. Are gold and silver found in the eastern or western part of the United States?
3. Which two states share one of our country's major dams?
4. In which state are three of the largest cities located?

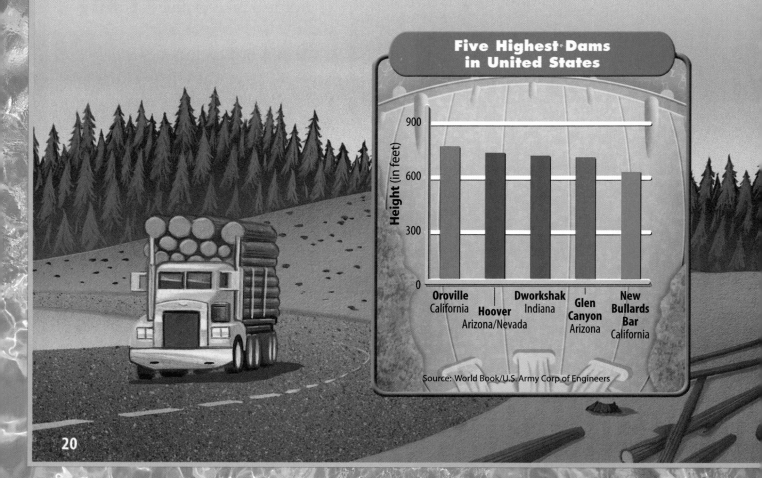

Five Highest Dams in United States

Height (in feet)

Oroville	California
Hoover	Arizona/Nevada
Dworkshak	Indiana
Glen Canyon	Arizona
New Bullards Bar	California

Source: World Book/U.S. Army Corp of Engineers

United States Land Use and Resources

Legend:
- Farming
- Forest
- Grazing
- Little-used land
- Manufacturing
- Coal
- Copper
- Fishing
- Gold
- Iron
- Limestone
- Oil/natural gas
- Silver
- Uranium
- Zinc
- National capital
- Major city

Lambert Azimuthal Equal-Area Projection

Top Ten United States Cities

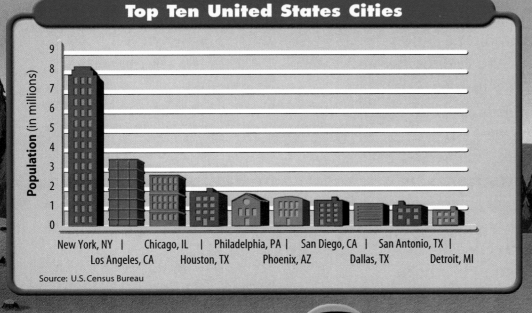

Population (in millions)

New York, NY | Chicago, IL | Philadelphia, PA | San Diego, CA | San Antonio, TX
Los Angeles, CA | Houston, TX | Phoenix, AZ | Dallas, TX | Detroit, MI

Source: U.S. Census Bureau

To learn more, visit our Web site:
www.mhschool.com

We, the People

Many people in the United States come from countries all over the world. They are **immigrants** (IHM ih gruntz), or the children of immigrants. An immigrant is a person who comes to live in a new land from another place. Look at the graphs on the opposite page. Compare the immigrants between 1978–1998 with those who came between 1900–1920.

Most immigrants came here to find a better life. However, early in our country's history, around 600,000 Africans were brought here against their will in **slavery**. Slavery is the practice of making one person the property of another. Enslaved people were forced to work without pay and had no freedom. Slavery ended in the United States in 1865.

Before immigrants arrived, people lived in our country for thousands of years. They were the **ancestors** (AN ses turz) of the Native Americans living today. Beginning with your parents and grandparents, your ancestors are all those in your family born before you.

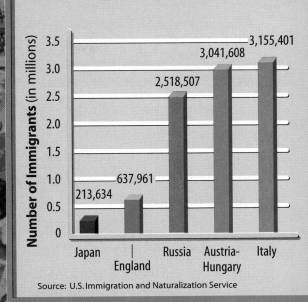

Immigrants 1900–1920

Number of Immigrants (in millions)

- Japan: 213,634
- England: 637,961
- Russia: 2,518,507
- Austria-Hungary: 3,041,608
- Italy: 3,155,401

Source: U.S. Immigration and Naturalization Service

Immigrants 1978–1998

Number of Immigrants (in millions)

- Turkey: 60,821
- Japan: 115,748
- India: 606,796
- China*: 748,778
- Mexico: 3,788,920

*1976–1985 (includes Taiwan)

Today, the **population** of the United States is more than 284 million people. Population means the number of people who live in an area. New Americans are born or arrive here every day.

READING CHECK

Who are your ancestors?

Chart Skill

1. How many immigrants arrived from India from 1978–1998?

2. Based on these charts, did more immigrants come to the United States from 1900–1920 or from 1978–1998?

Our Cultures and Customs

One way to better understand the people of our country is to study their different **cultures**. Culture is the way of life of a group of people.

Culture includes many things people share. People speak languages. They observe holidays. They practice religions. All these things are part of culture. Culture even includes music, sports, clothing, and food.

Customs are an important part of any culture. A custom is the special way a group of people does something. Each culture has its own customs.

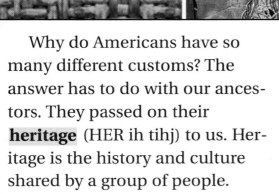

Why do Americans have so many different customs? The answer has to do with our ancestors. They passed on their **heritage** (HER ih tihj) to us. Heritage is the history and culture shared by a group of people.

Playing steel drums is part of the heritage of people from Trinidad, an island in the West Indies. People with a common heritage form an **ethnic group**. This is a group of people whose ancestors are from the same country or area.

Today, the United States is made up of many rich and interesting cultures. As Americans we respect the differences in each other's customs and history. Respect for others is part of our country's heritage.

READING CHECK

What is included in a group's culture?

Our Constitution

"I pledge allegiance (uh LEE juhns) to the flag of the United States of America, and to the Republic for which it stands, one Nation under God, indivisible, with liberty and justice for all."

When you say the Pledge of Allegiance, you are promising to support our country's **government**. A government is the laws and people that run a country, state, or city.

In 1787 our country's first leaders wrote the **Constitution** (kahn stih TOO shun). The Constitution is the plan for our country's government.

The Constitution promises rights to all Americans. Every American has the right to say what he or she believes about our country. We all have the right to practice our own religion. We all must be treated fairly under the law.

The Constitution also states that our country is a **democratic republic** (dem uh KRAT ihk ree PUB lihk). In a democratic republic, people pick represen-tatives to run the government. Democracy means that the power to rule comes from the people.

Citizens choose the people who will represent them by vot-ing. A citizen is a person who was born in a country or has earned the right to become a member of that country.

Voting is not just a right, it is also a responsibility. So is paying **taxes**. A tax is money people pay to the government. Taxes pay for schools, roads, and other things provided by the government.

READING CHECK What is the Constitution?

Our Government

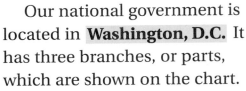

Our national government is located in **Washington, D.C.** It has three branches, or parts, which are shown on the chart.

Congress is the legislative branch. It creates laws for the whole country. It is made up of the Senate and the House of Representatives. Voters of each state elect two senators to the United States Senate. The number of representatives depends on how many people live in the state. If a state has few people, it sends fewer representatives. Senators serve for six years and representatives for two.

The **President** is elected every four years. This person is head of the executive branch of government. The President makes sure that laws passed by Congress are carried out. The President also meets with the leaders of other

Three Branches of the National Government

EXECUTIVE
President
• Carries out laws
• Meets with leaders of other countries
• Leads military

LEGISLATIVE
Congress
(100 Senators, 435 Representatives)
• Makes laws for our country
• Decides how much money to spend

JUDICIAL
Supreme Court
(9 Justices)
• Makes sure our laws follow the Constitution

⦿ Chart Skill

1. How many senators does Congress have?

countries and is in charge of our military forces.

The President also selects the justices, or judges, of the **United States Supreme Court**. The Supreme Court is the highest court in our country. It is the judicial branch, the third branch of our government. This branch makes sure that our laws follow the Constitution.

Each branch also keeps watch over the other two. This is known as the system of **checks and balances**. It makes sure that no branch gains too much power.

READING CHECK

Name the three branches of our country's government.

29

Writing an Outline

You have just learned about our country's government. It might seem difficult at first to organize all the information you have read. Writing an **outline** helps you to group facts and see how they are related. An outline is a plan that presents ideas about a subject in an organized way. It can also help you better understand what you have read.

VOCABULARY

outline

OUR COUNTRY'S GOVERNMENT

I. Constitution
   A. Plan for running our government
   B. Written in 1787
   C. Makes our country a democratic republic
II. Citizens
   A. Vote for representatives
   B. Pay taxes
III. Three Branches of Government
   A. Legislative
   B. Executive
   C. Judicial

LEARN THE SKILL

Use the following steps when you create an outline, such as the one above.

1. **Identify the topic.**
   The topic of this outline is "Our Country's Government."

2. **Identify the main ideas.**
   The main ideas are "Constitution," "Citizens," and "Three Branches of Government."

3. **Include supporting details and facts.**
   Look back at pages 26–29. There are several details and facts that support the main ideas. "Plan for running our government," for example, is a fact that supports "Constitution." Details and supporting facts should be included in an outline.

4. **Organize the information.**
   When you create an outline, start with Roman numerals to show the sequence of the main ideas. Then, under each of your main ideas, group the facts that support it. Place a capital letter beside each fact.

TRY THE SKILL

Read the passage about Supreme Court Justice Sandra Day O'Connor.

Sandra Day O'Connor grew up on a cattle ranch in Arizona. A disagreement over her family's ranch sparked her interest in law. In 1952, she graduated from Stanford Law School.

O'Connor's career as a judge began in 1974. She was elected to Arizona's Superior Court. In 1981, President Ronald Reagan chose her to be the first woman to serve on the United States Supreme Court. Sandra Day O'Connor was sworn in on September 25, 1981.

Now, create an outline organizing the information found in the passage. Then use your outline to answer the following questions.

1. What is the topic of the passage?

2. What are the main ideas?

3. What are the facts related to O'Connor's career as a judge?

4. How can writing an outline help you better understand what you read?

EXTEND THE SKILL

An outline can also help you write a report. Read the outline below about the home of the United States President. Identify the topic and main ideas. Write a short report based on the outline. Then answer the questions below.

- How can an outline help you to write a report?

- How can an outline help you to **compare** and **contrast** information that you read?

THE WHITE HOUSE
  I. Construction
      A. Competition held to choose design
      B. Architect James Hoban won
      C. White House built 1792–1800
  II. Naming
      A. First called the "President's Palace"
      B. Officially named "Executive Mansion" in 1810
      C. Changed to "White House" by President Theodore Roosevelt

Our Economy

Americans work together to keep our **economy** strong. An economy is the way a country uses resources. It's also the way a country produces goods and **services**. Services are jobs people do to help others. Doctors and teachers are two examples of service workers.

Our economy is based on the **free-enterprise system**. This means people are free to start and run their own businesses. The free-enterprise system lets Americans make their own economic decisions.

Over ten years ago, 39 students at Crenshaw High School in Los Angeles decided to become **entrepreneurs**. An entrepreneur is a person who starts and runs his or her own business. The students began to sell vegetables and herbs they grew near the school's football field. They called their business "Food From the 'Hood."

The students used the **profit** they made to help pay for college. Profit is money earned after paying salaries, tools, and other costs. The students thought of a new product. They decided to sell salad dressing made from their

garden vegetables. Several community groups became **investors** to help the business grow. An investor is a person or group who puts money into a business. Usually, investors receive a share of the profit. However, these investors wanted the profits to go toward the college fund.

By 2001, "Food From the 'Hood" had earned more than $170,000. Over 80 students received money to help pay for their college education.

The free-enterprise system also benefits **consumers**. Consumers are the people who buy a product or use a service. The system of free-enterprise gives consumers choices between products and prices. Every time you spend or earn money, you are taking part in our country's economy.

READING CHECK ✓ What is an entrepreneur?

Regions of the United States

Geographers, or people who study geography, find it useful to divide our country into **regions** (REE junz). A region is an area with common features that set it apart from other areas.

The United States has six regions. They are the Southwest, the Southeast, the Northeast, the Middle West, the Mountain States, and the West. Each is shaped by its environment, people, and history. Look at the map. Which region do you call home?

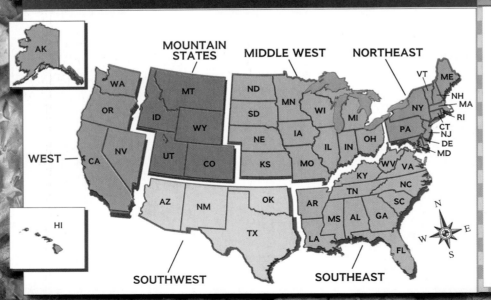

NATIONAL GEOGRAPHIC **Regions of the United States**

AK

MOUNTAIN STATES

MIDDLE WEST

NORTHEAST

WA

MT

ND

MN

SD

WI

MI

VT ME

NH

MA

NY

RI

CT

NJ

DE

MD

OR

ID

WY

NE

IA

IL

IN

OH

PA

WEST

CA

NV

UT

CO

KS

MO

WV

VA

HI

KY

TN

NC

AZ

NM

OK

AR

SC

MS

AL

GA

TX

LA

FL

N

W — E

S

SOUTHWEST

SOUTHEAST

Map Skill

1. Find Idaho. What region is it in?

2. Which region has the fewest states?

The Southwest has a history that makes it different from other regions. It was once part of the country of Mexico. Today, people of Mexican heritage still live in the Southwest.

The ways people earn a living can also make a region special. The Southeast sits along the Atlantic Ocean and the Gulf of Mexico. Fishers of the region have great success catching shrimp and other shellfish.

The ways that people use and change the land can shape a region. Newcomers from all over the world came to live in the Northeast. They built many towns and cities throughout the region. Today, the Northeast has several busy cities, such as Philadelphia.

The people of a region help to form its culture. In the Middle West several towns hold Oktoberfests, a German harvest festival. Many people in the region have ancestors who came from Germany, Sweden, Norway, or Poland. Their heritage is remembered in celebrations and events.

The Mountain States are known for tall slopes. Some are rugged and covered with heavy snow. Others have thick forests that provide a wealth of lumber. They make the region's environment different from other areas.

Location can also shape a region. States in the West border the Pacific Ocean. Immigrants from China, Japan, the Phillippines, and other countries along the Pacific are some of the groups that have moved into the region. They built communities that draw from their cultures.

The regions of our country are **interdependent**. That means people in one region depend on those in other regions to help meet their needs.

Interdependence works because the regions stay connected. **Transportation** plays a big part in connecting the regions. Transportation means moving goods or people from one place to another. Cars, trucks, buses, trains, airplanes, and ships are all used for transportation in our country. Technology and communication also help regions stay connected.

What are the six regions of the United States?

Americans, One and All

In this Introduction, we have looked at our country's land, climate, and resources. We have studied its people, economy, and government.

You have also learned about the six regions of the United States. In the rest of this book, we will take a closer look at each one of these regions.

Katharine Lee Bates traveled across the United States about a hundred years ago. Her trip inspired the lyrics to "America, the Beautiful," with music by Samuel Ward.

America, the Beautiful

Music by Samuel Ward
Words by Katharine Lee Bates

1. O beau-ti-ful for spa-cious skies, for am-ber waves of grain.
2. O beau-ti-ful for pil-grim feet, whose stern im-pass-ioned stress
3. O beau-ti-ful for he-roes proved in lib-er-at-ing strife,
4. O beau-ti-ful for pa-triot dream that sees be-yond the years,

For pur-ple moun-tain maj-es-ties a-bove the fruit-ed plain.
A thor-ough-fare for free-dom beat a-cross the wil-der-ness.
Who more than self their coun-try loved, and mer-cy more than life.
Thine al-a-bas-ter cit-ies gleam un-dim'd by hu-man tears.

A-mer-i-ca! A-mer-i-ca! God shed His grace on thee,
A-mer-i-ca! A-mer-i-ca! God mend thine ev'-ry flaw,
A-mer-i-ca! A-mer-i-ca! May God thy gold re-fine,
A-mer-i-ca! A-mer-i-ca! God shed His grace on thee,

And crown thy good with broth-er-hood, from sea to shin-ing sea.
Con-firm thy soul in self-con-trol, Thy lib-er-ty in law.
Till all suc-cess be no-ble-ness, and ev'-ry gain di-vine.
And crown thy good with broth-er-hood, from sea to shin-ing sea.

Introduction REVIEW

VOCABULARY REVIEW

Number a sheet of paper from 1 to 5. Beside each number write the term from the list below that best completes the sentence.

culture   tundra

Constitution   Western Hemisphere

natural resource

1. Something in the environment that people can use is a ___.

2. The ___ states that our country is a democratic republic.

3. An ethnic group has its own ___, or way of life.

4. A huge plain that is frozen for most of the year is called a ___.

5. North America and South America are two of the continents found in the ___.

TECHNOLOGY

For more resources to help you learn more about the places you read about, visit www.mhschool.com and follow the links for Grade 4 Regions, Introduction.

◯ SKILL REVIEW

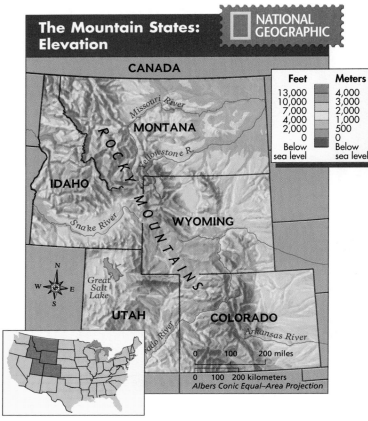

NATIONAL GEOGRAPHIC

The Mountain States: Elevation

CANADA

Feet	Meters
13,000	4,000
10,000	3,000
7,000	2,000
4,000	1,000
2,000	500
0	0
Below sea level	Below sea level

MONTANA

Missouri River

Yellowstone R.

IDAHO

ROCKY MOUNTAINS

Snake River

WYOMING

Great Salt Lake

UTAH

Colorado River

COLORADO

Arkansas River

0   100   200 miles

0   100   200 kilometers

Albers Conic Equal–Area Projection

6. **Geography Skill** Look at the map on this page. Find the Snake River. How high is the elevation where it begins?

7. **Geography Skill** In which direction does the Snake River flow?

8. **Geography Skill** Why might it be helpful to have an elevation map on a trip across the United States?

9. **Study Skill** Read the section on culture on pages 24–25. Then write an outline, using the main ideas "Culture" and "Heritage."

10. **Study Skill** How can writing outlines help you organize information?

Activities

Language Arts

- Work together in teams to create a weather report for the local news. In the report, describe the weather for the past week. Also describe the overall climate for the current year.

- Next, make a poster about your local climate. Show the kind of clothing a person would wear during each of the four seasons in your area.

- Check your local newspaper or the Internet for articles on the weather and climate in your area. You might also find pictures to illustrate your poster. Consider using glitter, paints, and colored paper to make your poster special.

Plant Life

- Make a map showing the plant life in your community. Are there parks and forests in your area? Are you in a wetlands area?

WRITING ACTIVITIES

Writing to Inform Suppose you have a pen pal in another country. Your pen pal knows very little about the United States. **Write** him or her a description of our country. Be sure to include information about the environment, the people, and the heritage of the United States.

Writing to Persuade Choose a region of our country and write your own travel brochure. **Write** a description that persuades tourists to visit. Mention any interesting sites or locations.

Writing to Express Describe a special celebration you have attended in your state. Include descriptions of any costumes people wore or any special food that was served. Also mention any activities held at the celebration. Include as many details as you can.

LITERATURE

MAGIC WINDOWS
Ventanas mágicas
by Carmen Lomas Garza

Introduction

Cut-paper art (papel picado) has a long history in Mexico. Banners made from tree bark thousands of years ago were followed by the tissue paper cutouts you see today.

My grandmother taught me how to cut paper for **embroidery** designs when I was little. She's also the first person I saw making paper cutouts. I've been making them myself for twenty-seven years now. I started by cutting out simple designs with scissors. Later I began using a craft knife to create **intricate** designs like the pieces you see in this book.

These pieces are like magic windows. When you look through them, you can see into another world.

Introducción

El papel picado tiene una larga historia en México, desde los estandartes de amate o papel de corteza de árbol de hace miles de años hasta el papel picado que vemos hoy.

Mi abuela me enseñó cómo recortar papel para diseños de **bordado** cuando yo era pequeña. También fue la primera persona que vi hacer papel picado. Ahora ya

---

embroidery (em broi′ də rē) detailed designs on cloth or cut out on paper

intricate (in′ tri kit) very involved or complicated

bordado diseños detallados hechos en tela o papel

llevo haciéndolos yo misma por veintisiete años. Comencé recortando diseños sencillos con tijeras. Después empecé a usar un estilete con navaja para crear diseños **intrincados** como las piezas que vemos en este libro.

Estas piezas son como ventanas mágicas. Cuando miramos a través de ellas, podemos ver otro mundo.

---

intrincados diseños con mucho detalles o complejos

Offering for Antonio Lomas

This is my grandfather, Antonio Lomas, watering the corn in his garden. There's also squash and garlic, chile, and **nopales**. He always had vegetables growing, and he would always share what he had grown with his sons and daughters and grandkids.

This paper cutout is big. It measures five feet by eight feet and has ten sections. I tied them to a stick, and hung the stick from the ceiling.

---

nopales (nō pə' les) prickly pear cactus

I used to love helping my grandfather water his garden at the end of the day. It gave me a chance to be really close to him. If he wanted to talk to me, I was right there to listen to him. If I wanted to ask questions, he was there for me.

Ofrenda para Antonio Lomas

Éste es mi abuelo, Antonio Lomas, regando su maizal en su jardín. También hay plantas de calabazas, ajos, chiles y **nopales**. Mi abuelo todo el tiempo plantaba verduras que cultivaba para luego siempre compartirlas con sus hijos e hijas y todos sus nietos.

Este papel picado es grande, mide cinco pies por ocho pies. Tiene diez secciones que uní al conectarlas a una vara que colgué del techo.

Me gustaba ayudar a mi abuelo a regar su jardín al final del día. Esto me daba la oportunidad de estar de veras muy cerca a él. Si él quería hablar commigo, yo estaba ahí mismo para escucharlo. Si yo le quería preguntar algo, ahí estaba él para mí.

---

nopales cactos

Write About It!

Write a paragraph that explains why you think cut-paper art is important to Carmen Lomas Garza. Then tell about a craft that you would like to learn and why it is important to you.

Unit 1

The Southwest

TAKE A LOOK

How is the Southwest different from other regions?

The Southwest is famous for its sunny climate and unusual landforms, such as Arizona's Monument Valley.

Explore more about southwestern landforms at our Web site www.mhschool.com

1

THE Big IDEAS ABOUT...

Environment of the Southwest

Arizona, New Mexico, Oklahoma, and Texas are the four states of the Southwest region. The Southwest is known for colorful canyons, beautiful deserts, and gushers of oil. In this chapter, you will read more about the region's geography, climate, and natural resources.

FROM COAST TO CANYONS

From the Gulf Coast to the Grand Canyon, the Southwest has a variety of landforms and water.

DESERTS AND OIL

The hot, dry Southwest has a limited amount of water but is rich in oil and other natural resources.

WELLS FOR WATER AND OIL

Wells dug to reach water and oil have changed the land in the Southwest.

Foldables

Use your Foldable to record what you learn about "The Environment of the Southwest."

1. Place two sheets of paper one inch apart, forming a one-inch tab across the top.
2. Roll the bottom of the two sheets up to make three tabs the same size. Fold and staple.
3. Write the title of the chapter on the large tab, and the three lesson titles on the small equal-sized tabs.

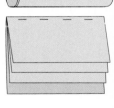

Lesson 1

From Coast to Canyons

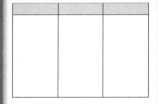

VOCABULARY

canyon
mesa
butte
erosion

READING STRATEGY

Draw a chart like this. Write one fact about each land-form found in the Southwest.

What are the major natural features of the Southwest?

Lesson Outline

• Land and Water
• Plateaus, Canyons, Mesas
• The Roaring Rapids

BUILD BACKGROUND

The Southwest is made up of four states: Oklahoma, Texas, New Mexico, and Arizona. That's fewer states than any other region in our country. However, these states cover more area than the twelve states of the Southeast. These four states also include a wide variety of land-forms and environments.

Rio Grande

LAND AND WATER

Flat lowland covers the Coastal Plain in Texas. Moving north, the vast Great Plains reach into Oklahoma, Texas, and New Mexico. As you head west, the geography changes. The tall Rocky Mountains tower above parts of New Mexico and Arizona.

Flowing out of the Rocky Mountains, the **Rio Grande** river forms part of the border between the United States and Mexico. At the end of its journey, the river empties into the **Gulf of Mexico**. Find these and other natural features of the Southwest on the map on this page.

What two major plains can be found in the Southwest?

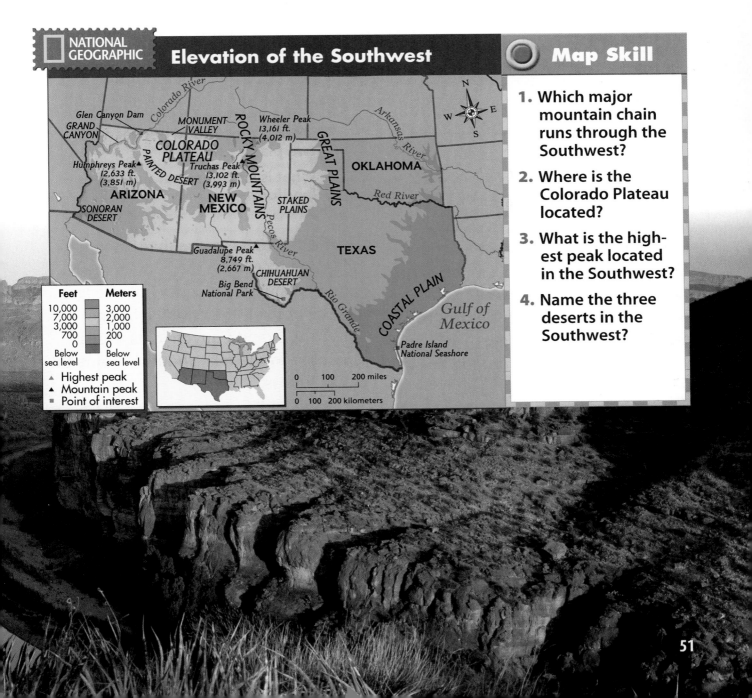

Elevation of the Southwest

NATIONAL GEOGRAPHIC

Glen Canyon Dam
GRAND CANYON
Colorado River
MONUMENT VALLEY
ROCKY MOUNTAINS
Wheeler Peak 13,161 ft. (4,012 m)
Arkansas River
COLORADO PLATEAU
PAINTED DESERT
Humphreys Peak 12,633 ft. (3,851 m)
Truchas Peak 13,102 ft. (3,993 m)
GREAT PLAINS
OKLAHOMA
ARIZONA
NEW MEXICO
STAKED PLAINS
Red River
SONORAN DESERT
Pecos River
Guadalupe Peak 8,749 ft. (2,667 m)
CHIHUAHUAN DESERT
Big Bend National Park
TEXAS
COASTAL PLAIN
Rio Grande
Gulf of Mexico
Padre Island National Seashore

Feet **Meters**
10,000	3,000
7,000	2,000
3,000	1,000
700	200
0	0
Below sea level	Below sea level

▲ Highest peak
▲ Mountain peak
■ Point of interest

0 100 200 miles
0 100 200 kilometers

Map Skill

1. Which major mountain chain runs through the Southwest?

2. Where is the Colorado Plateau located?

3. What is the highest peak located in the Southwest?

4. Name the three deserts in the Southwest?

51

Plateau, Mesa, Butte

PLATEAU

CANYON

MESA

BUTTE

Diagram Skill

1. **What can be found between the two plateaus?**

2. **What is similar about the three landforms?**

PLATEAUS, CANYONS, MESAS

The **Colorado Plateau** is the major plateau found in the Southwest. It is located in part of northern Arizona and New Mexico. Much of the Colorado Plateau is one mile above sea level. The area is famous for its **canyons**. A canyon is a deep, narrow valley with steep sides. Among the deepest is the **Grand Canyon**.

A **mesa** (MAY suh) is another landform found in the Southwest. A mesa is a hill with a flat top. It is smaller than a plateau. The region also has **buttes** (BYOOTS), which are like mesas, but are even smaller.

The Grand Canyon

The Grand Canyon stretches 217 miles through northern Arizona. In some places it is more than one mile deep! At its widest, the canyon measures 18 miles from one rim, or edge, to the other. If there were a bridge over the Grand Canyon at its widest point, it would take about six hours to walk across.

Look at the photograph on the next page. At the bottom of the canyon is the **Colorado River**. It flows southwest out of the Rocky Mountains. As the river rushed downhill, over millions of years, it cut a deep path into the plateau. The path gradually grew deeper and deeper. The river also carved the walls of the canyon into fantastic shapes.

This process is known as **erosion**. It is the slow wearing away of the land by water, wind, or ice. Canyons, mesas, and buttes are all formed by erosion.

Into the Canyon

Each year about four million people visit the Grand Canyon, which is a national park. In fact, the canyon is one of our country's most famous natural features. Many people admire the sights from the rim of the canyon. Others make their way down into the canyon itself.

There are several ways to explore the canyon. Visitors can hike along trails to the foot of the canyon. People can also ride mules instead of walking. One of the most exciting ways to explore the Grand Canyon is to go "white water" rafting down the Colorado River.

Suppose you wanted to see the canyon by raft. First you need to get to the Colorado River. A long hike is ahead of you from the South Rim of the canyon.

You begin by going down a steep trail. Far below you can see the Colorado River. From here it looks like a narrow stream. Actually, the river is 300 feet across.

Hours pass as you make your way down the trail. As you stop and look around, you can see the beauty of the canyon. The walls drop in terraces, or

steps. As you get closer to the river, you see rocks in different shades of blue, gold, purple, and brown in the walls.

When you reach the bottom, you find the river is ice cold. It's much too fast to swim in, but you can dunk your feet to cool off.

How was the Grand Canyon formed?

The Grand Canyon is vast—whether you are at the top looking down or riding into it.

THE ROARING RAPIDS

At the bottom of the canyon, you climb into a rubber raft with a guide and three other people. You are now ready to "ride the rapids."

What is a rapid? A rapid is where a river flows very swiftly as elevation drops. As the Colorado River flows through the Grand Canyon, it falls more than 1,000 feet in elevation. Most of this drop takes place as the river flows over small waterfalls.

"Do you hear that roar?" your guide asks. "We're approaching Granite Rapids." Cold water splashes into the raft as it shoots downward. You feel as if you're on a roller coaster. Then, in less than a minute, the water is calm again. There is so much water in the raft that everyone helps to bail it out. Now you know what it is like to be a "river runner"!

"River runners" enjoy white water rafting on Granite Rapids.

Camping In the Canyon

Suddenly the river is calm again. Colorful rock walls slowly pass by on either side. A green lizard clings to the underside of a rock. Desert bighorn sheep make their way down a steep slope.

At night your group sets up camp on a sandbar. Moonlight on the rock makes the canyon look black and gray. Far above, stars shine in the night sky.

Your trip down the river takes several more days. Sometimes you stop to hike or climb in the smaller side canyons.

Finally the Grand Canyon's high walls become less steep. The water of the Colorado River is now calm and blue. You have reached the end of the Grand Canyon.

What can you see on a trip down the rapids of the Grand Canyon?

Bighorn sheep live in the Grand Canyon.

PUTTING IT TOGETHER

Natural features such as the Grand Canyon amaze us with their beauty and wildlife. They also teach us important lessons about the geography and history of the United States. Americans in every region can take pride in our country's natural features.

Review and Assess

1. Write one sentence using each of the vocabulary words:

   butte   erosion
   canyon   mesa

2. Where is the Colorado Plateau located?

3. Describe the major natural features of the Southwest.

4. What effect has the Colorado River had on the **geography** of the Southwest?

5. **Compare** and **contrast** mesas and buttes.

Look at the map on page 51. Which river forms part of Arizona's border? Using the elevation key, find the direction in which it flows.

• •

Write a paragraph describing a visit to the Grand Canyon.

Lesson 2

Deserts and Oil

Find! Out!

How does the climate affect life in the Southwest?

Lesson Outline

- The Dry Southwest
- Life in a Dry Climate
- Black Gold

VOCABULARY

desert
adapt
drought
petroleum

READING STRATEGY

Draw a word web like this. Fill in four ways people, animals, and plants survive desert life.

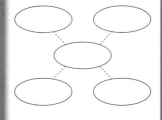

BUILD BACKGROUND

The **Painted Desert** in northern Arizona is named for its colorful rocks. Sunlight and minerals in the soil seem to "paint" the rocks red, yellow, orange, blue, and purple.

THE DRY SOUTHWEST

The Coastal Plain in Texas is warm and rainy. As a result, the area has thick forests. Eastern Texas and Oklahoma get more than 40 inches of rain a year. Farmers there grow cotton, peanuts, and other crops.

High up in the Rocky Mountains, the climate is very different. Temperatures there can drop far below the freezing mark.

Deserts

Many parts of the Southwest are covered by **deserts**—dry lands where little rain falls. A desert gets less than 10 inches of precipitation each year.

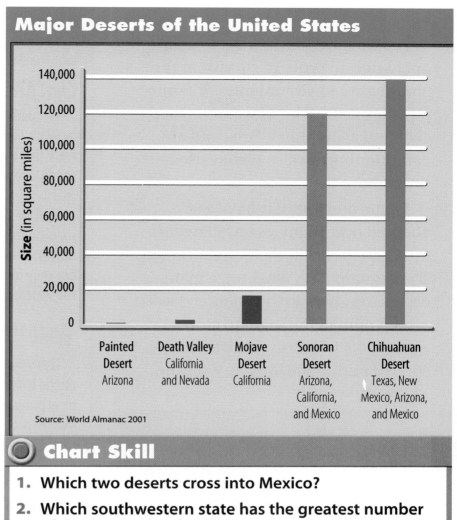

Major Deserts of the United States

Source: World Almanac 2001

⬤ **Chart Skill**

1. **Which two deserts cross into Mexico?**
2. **Which southwestern state has the greatest number of deserts on the chart?**

The Southwest is also closer to the equator than other parts of the country. The temperatures are high all year. The heat and dry air affect the region's land.

The **Sonoran** (suh NOR uhn) **Desert** covers over 120,000 square miles and is about the size of the entire state of New Mexico! The chart above shows five of the major deserts found in the United States.

Natural Resources

The Southwest has many kinds of natural resources, including minerals and rich soil. Sometimes, a single resource can play a big role in shaping a region. In the Southwest, this resource is oil.

 **Why are deserts found in the Southwest?**

LIFE IN A DRY CLIMATE

People have found ways to **adapt**, or change, in order to survive in the Southwest's environment. For example, they drink a lot of water to keep cool and avoid thirst. Fans and air conditioning are also widely used throughout the region.

Plants and animals have also adapted over many years, allowing them to survive in their environment. The saguaro (suh WAH ro), a giant cactus tree, lives in the Sonoran Desert. After a rainfall the saguaro stores water in its trunk. In this way, it can survive during the long, dry season.

Exploring
TECHNOLOGY

Cool Air in a Hot Climate

Air conditioners were invented in 1902 by Willis Carrier of Buffalo, New York. They were first used in factories and theaters. Air conditioners draw in hot air from a room, cool it off, and blow it back out. Today, central air systems have replaced single air conditioning units in many homes and businesses. They use technology that is similar, but they can heat or cool the air. They also conserve energy.

Activity

Use your school library or the Internet to learn how people stayed cool before air conditioning.

Most desert animals, such as rabbits, are light colored. Light colors reflect the sun, and as a result do not get as hot. This helps the animals stay cooler. The kangaroo rat, a common desert animal, hardly drinks at all. It gets most of the water it needs from the seeds it eats.

The saguaro can grow to be 60 feet tall and weigh as much as 20,000 pounds.

The Dust Bowl

Until the 1930s, the Great Plains area had been fertile wheat-growing country. However, in 1932, there was almost no rainfall in parts of Texas, Oklahoma, and states in the Middle West. The **drought** continued through most of the 1930s. A drought is a period of little or no rain.

At the same time, enormous dust-storms blew across the region. Why? Farmers had plowed up thick prairie grasses to plant wheat. They didn't realize that the wild grasses held the soil in place better than wheat could. Wind blew the dried out soil right off their fields.

As a result of the Dust Bowl, thousands of families lost their homes and farms. Many of them moved to California to find jobs on other people's farms. It took many years for the region to recover.

One of the worst storms of the Dust Bowl occurred on April 14, 1935. Read the following account from a Texas newspaper.

What was the Dust Bowl?

excerpt from
Amarillo Daily News
— *April 15, 1935*

Darkness settled swiftly after the city had been enveloped in the stinking, stinging dust, carried by a 50-mile-an-hour wind. Despite closed windows and doors, the **silt** *crept into buildings to deposit a dingy, gray film. Within hours the dust was a quarter inch in thickness in homes and stores.*

Why do you think people later named the storm the "Black Blizzard"?

silt: rock and soil particles

This pump jack brings **petroleum** to the surface from deep within the ground.

BLACK GOLD

Although the Southwest has little rainfall, it is rich in natural resources. Fields produce large amounts of cotton, wheat, and sorghum. The Gulf of Mexico offers a supply of shrimp and other fish. Grasses provide food for cattle.

Those resources, along with many others, can be found above ground. However, two of the most important southwestern resources are found beneath Earth's surface. Minerals such as copper, silver, and uranium are mined from below ground. People of the Southwest also drill to find oil, a resource that is so valuable it has been nicknamed "black gold."

Drilling for Oil

Oil is a common name for **petroleum** (puh TROH lee um). Petroleum can be difficult to find because it is underground. Scientists study rocks in an area to determine if oil is present. Then workers use an enormous steel bit to drill. They sometimes drill a hole a mile or more deep! If they strike oil, special pipes are lowered into the ground. These pipes bring the oil to the surface.

Texas and Oklahoma are two of our country's largest producers of oil, a fuel. The oil found in the Southwest is used throughout the United States.

What are the major natural resources found in the Southwest?

60

PUTTING IT TOGETHER

Today southwestern farmers better understand how to work with the soil to avoid dust storms. However, they still search the skies for the promise of rain.

Petroleum is an important resource in the Southwest. "Black gold" helped build the region's economy and the way of life in our country. In Lesson 3, you will read more about the search for these two precious resources— water and oil—in the dry Southwest.

These workers are checking to make sure the oil pump equipment is in good condition.

Review and Assess

1. Write one sentence for each of the vocabulary words:

   adapt   **drought**
   desert   **petroleum**

2. How do scientists look for petroleum?

3. Analyze how the climate affects life in the Southwest.

4. How has the saguaro cactus adapted to its **environment**?

5. **Classify** these resources: petroleum, copper, silver, and uranium.

Use an encyclopedia, almanac, or other source to find the three largest deserts in the world.

• •

Write a page in a diary describing what it might have been like to live through a dust storm.

Working with Latitude and Longitude

Every place on Earth has an absolute, or exact, location. Imaginary lines that cross each other like a tic-tac-toe grid can help you describe that location. They provide an "address" for the location.

This is different from the relative location of a place. If you say that the Painted Desert is near Flagstaff, Arizona, you are describing its location in relation, or connection, to something else. Relative location does not give an exact "address," like the absolute location.

Pilots use this system of lines and "addresses" to keep track of where they are. Up among the clouds a pilot must be sure of a plane's location at all times. Pilots also need an exact way to explain where they are going.

VOCABULARY

latitude

parallel

degrees

longitude

prime meridian

meridian

global grid

USING LATITUDE

Look at the map on this page and place your finger on the equator. This is the starting point for measuring **latitude**. Latitude is a measure of how far north or south a place is from the equator.

Lines of latitude are also called **parallels** because they are parallel lines. Parallel lines always remain the same distance apart and never cross each other.

Each line of latitude has a number. You can see that the equator is labeled 0°, meaning zero **degrees**. Degrees are used to measure the distance on Earth's surface. The symbol ° stands for degrees.

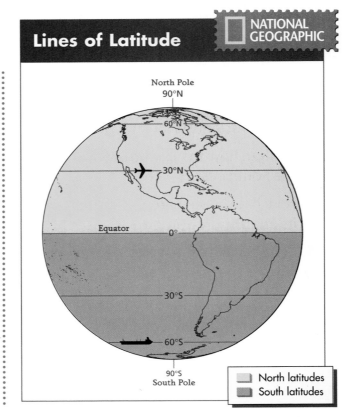

Lines of Latitude

NATIONAL GEOGRAPHIC

North Pole
90°N

60°N

30°N

Equator   0°

30°S

60°S

90°S
South Pole

North latitudes
South latitudes

Now look at the lines of latitude north of the equator. Notice that these parallels are labeled N for "north." The North Pole has a latitude, too, which is 90°N. The parallels south of the equator are labeled S for "south." The latitude of the South Pole is 90°S.

Look again at the map on the previous page. Find the ship, which is sailing west. It is located at 60°S. Now find the small airplane on the map. Along which parallel is it flying?

USING LONGITUDE

Now look at the map on this page. It shows lines of **longitude**. Like parallels, these are imaginary lines on a map or globe. But instead of measuring distance north or south, they measure distance east or west of the **prime meridian**. Prime means "first." Lines of longitude are also called **meridians**. The prime meridian is the starting place for measuring lines of longitude. That's why the prime meridian is marked 0° on the map. Put your finger on the prime meridian. It runs through the western parts of Europe and Africa.

Look at the meridians to the west of the prime meridian. These lines are labeled W for "west." The lines to the east of the prime meridian are labeled E for "east." Longitude is measured up to 180° east of the prime meridian and up to 180° west of the prime meridian. Since 180°E and 180°W fall on the

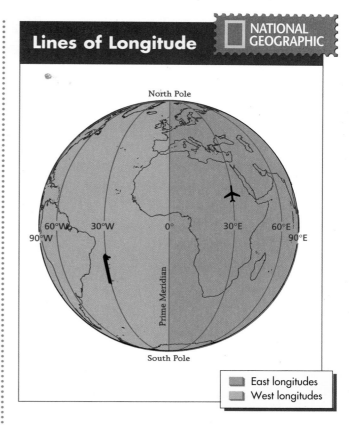

Lines of Longitude

North Pole

60°W   30°W   0°   30°E   60°E

90°W   90°E

Prime Meridian

South Pole

■ East longitudes
■ West longitudes

same line, this line is marked neither E nor W. This line runs through the Pacific Ocean.

Unlike lines of latitude, meridians are not parallel to one another. Look at the map on this page again. As you can see, the meridians are far apart at the equator. They meet, however, at the North Pole and the South Pole.

Find the ship on the map. It is traveling along longitude 30°W. Now look at the airplane on the same map. It is flying over the continent of Africa. Which line of longitude is the airplane traveling along? In which direction is it flying?

Geography Skills

Global Grid

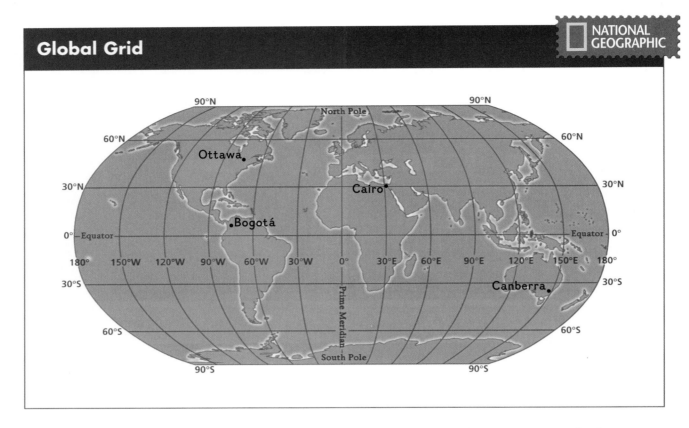

NATIONAL GEOGRAPHIC

LEARN THE SKILL

The lines of latitude and the lines of longitude cross to form a grid. A grid is a set of crisscrossing lines. The grid on this map is called a **global grid** because it covers the entire Earth.

1. **Locate the equator.**
    Remember that lines of latitude measure degrees north and south from the equator. Now find Canberra, Australia, and Bogotá, Colombia, on the map. Which of these two cities is closer to the equator? How can you tell?

2. **Locate the prime meridian.**
    Remember that lines of longitude measure degrees east and west from the prime meridian. Now find Ottawa,

Canada, and Cairo, Egypt. Which city is east of the prime meridian and which city is west?

3. **Identify the degrees to find the "address."**
    Find Canberra again. As you can see, it is located at about 30°S latitude. It is also located at 150°E, so, we say that its location—or its "address"—is 30°S, 150°E.

    When you locate a place on a map, always give latitude first and longitude second. You must also remember to give north or south for the latitude, east or west for the longitude. To describe a place that is not exactly at the point where two lines cross, use the closest lines or estimate in between them.

TRY THE SKILL

On the map below, find two cities, using the latitude and longitude "addresses." What is the name of each?

- 40°N, 120°W
- 40°N, 90°W

Describe the location of these two cities, using latitude and longitude.

- Columbia
- Portland

Now answer the following questions.

1. How can the equator and prime meridian help you find lines of latitude and longitude?

2. Which two cities on the map are both near 35°N latitude?

3. How can using latitude and longitude help you in your daily life?

EXTEND THE SKILL

Trace the map of the United States. Place these cities on your map, using their nearest latitude and longitude "addresses."

- Jacksonville, 30°N, 80°W

- Las Vegas, 35°N, 115°W

Now compare the map of the United States to the Global Grid.

- How are the lines of latitude different?

- How are the lines of longitude different?

- What types of people might use latitude and longitude in their work?

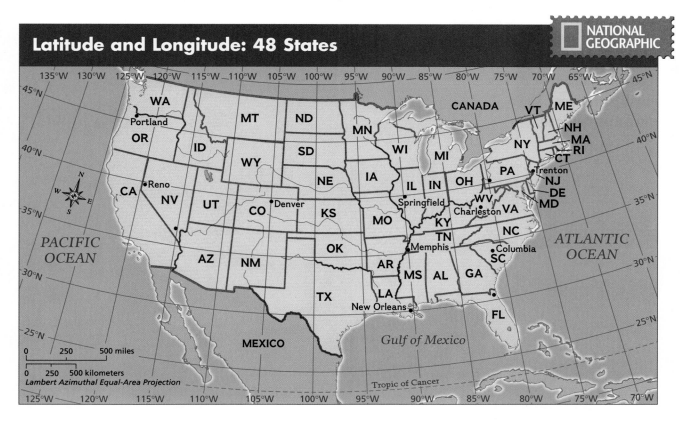

Latitude and Longitude: 48 States

NATIONAL GEOGRAPHIC

Wells for Water and Oil

Find Out!

How has the search for water and oil changed the Southwest?

VOCABULARY

aquifer

spring

aqueduct

dry farming

crude oil

refinery

petrochemical

READING STRATEGY

Copy the main idea pyramid. Fill in the supporting details about finding oil and water underground as you read.

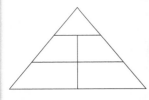

Lesson Outline

• Aquifers and Aqueducts

• Gusher at Spindletop

BUILD BACKGROUND

The search for two valuable resources—water and oil—has shaped the Southwest. Workers drill deep into the ground to find petroleum. People also dig wells and build dams to find the water they need. All of these have changed the region's environment.

Oil refinery in West Texas

AQUIFERS AND AQUEDUCTS

Much of the water people of the Southwest use comes from **aquifers** (AK wuh furz). Aquifers are underground layers of rock or sand that trap rainwater. Sometimes they form rivers. In the Southwest, these layers are made of limestone. It is a soft rock that absorbs rain like a sponge. These layers are shown on the diagram on this page.

One way to get water from an aquifer is to find a natural **spring**. A spring is a place where underground water comes to the surface. The other way is to dig a well.

People can also get water by building a dam across a river. A dam acts as a wall to hold back part of the river to form a lake. A canal or pipe called an **aqueduct** (AK wuh dukt) carries the water to cities and farms.

Many farmers rely on water from aqueducts to help grow their crops. Others use **dry farming**. Dry farming is a way to grow crops with only a small amount of rainwater. Some farmers plant crops every other year to store up moisture in the soil.

READING CHECK

Why do people in the Southwest dig wells and build dams?

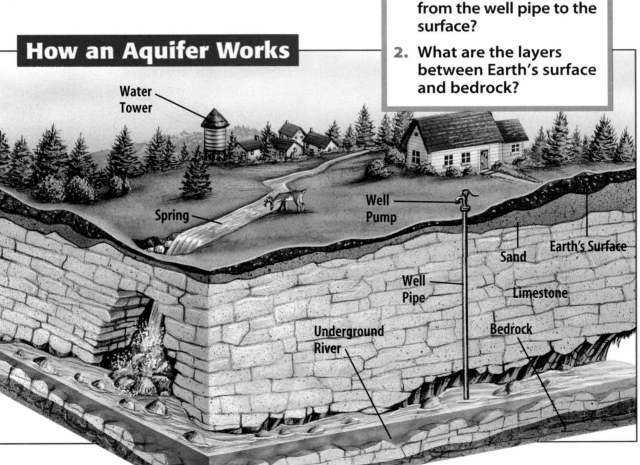

How an Aquifer Works

Water Tower

Spring

Well Pump

Well Pipe

Sand

Earth's Surface

Limestone

Underground River

Bedrock

Diagram Skill

1. **How does water get from the well pipe to the surface?**

2. **What are the layers between Earth's surface and bedrock?**

By 1903, thousands of people were drilling for oil at Boiler Avenue, Spindletop.

GUSHER AT SPINDLETOP

In 1901, a crew was drilling for oil on a hill called Spindletop near **Beaumont, Texas**. Suddenly a huge stream of oil burst high into the air! This "gusher" of oil was shooting up at the rate of 75,000 barrels a day.

From Well to Refinery

The oil boom changed many businesses. Soon this fuel powered ships, locomotives, and factory machines. A new product—gasoline—made automobiles run.

The petroleum that bubbles up from the ground is called **crude oil**. Crude oil is not very useful. It must be taken to a factory called a **refinery** (ri FI nuh ree). There the crude oil is refined, or separated into parts. These parts include gasoline and heating oil.

Exploring ECONOMICS

Supply and Demand

Before Spindletop, there was not much of a demand for oil in the United States. Demand is the willingness of people to buy something and the ability to pay for it. The price of oil in the early 1900s was one dollar per barrel. Soon after Spindletop, however, the supply of oil increased. Supply is the willingness and ability to sell something in the market. But the price did not remain very high. In fact, with so much oil being produced, the price quickly dropped to 25 cents. Later, it fell to 3 cents per barrel.

Activity

There are 42 gallons in one barrel of oil. Look up the price of a barrel of oil in a newspaper. Then figure out how much one gallon of oil costs today.

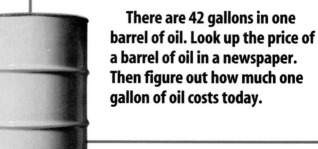

Petrochemicals

Refineries in the Southwest also produce **petrochemicals** (pet roh CHEM ih kulz), or chemicals made from petroleum. Look around your classroom. The paint on the walls is probably made from petrochemicals. If you write with a pen, it may be made from these chemicals too. Even your classmates' clothing or sneakers may be made of petrochemicals!

Why is crude oil taken to refineries?

PUTTING IT TOGETHER

Today, more people are moving to the Southwest than ever before. A larger population, however, can be a problem in dry areas. As the region continues to grow, people must find and protect an important natural resource—water.

Review and Assess

1. Write one sentence for each of the vocabulary words:

aqueduct	**petrochemical**
aquifer	**refinery**
crude oil	**spring**
dry farming	

2. When was oil discovered in the Southwest?

3. Analyze some of the changes to the region's environment in the search for oil and water.

4. What are some techniques farmers use to deal with the Southwest's difficult **environment**?

5. **Compare** and **contrast** how people find water and oil in the Southwest.

Activities

Draw a chart that shows some of the products made from petrochemicals.

• • • • • • • • • • • • • • • • • • • •

Write a one-paragraph newspaper report describing what it might have been like when oil was discovered at Spindletop.

69

VOCABULARY REVIEW

Number a sheet of paper from 1 to 6. Beside each number write the word or term from the list below that matches the description.

aqueduct	degree
canyon	desert
crude oil	drought

1. a pipe that carries water to cities and farms

2. a deep, narrow valley with steep sides

3. a period of little or no rain

4. a form of petroleum when it is drilled out of the ground

5. dry land where little rain falls

6. used to measure the distance on Earth's surface

CHAPTER COMPREHENSION

7. Which river forms the southwestern border of Texas?

8. How are mesas different from buttes?

9. What happened in Beaumont, Texas, in 1901?

10. What happens to crude oil in a refinery?

11. What are petrochemicals?

12. **Write** a paragraph that describes the natural features of the Southwest.

SKILL REVIEW

Arizona: Latitude and Longitude

NATIONAL GEOGRAPHIC

★ State capital
• Other city
■ Point of interest

13. **Geography Skill** What are lines of latitude and longitude?

14. **Geography Skill** How many degrees apart are the lines of latitude on this map?

15. **Geography Skill** Which city is closest to the 32°N line of latitude?

16. **Geography Skill** How many degrees apart are the lines of longitude shown on this map?

17. **Geography Skill** Using latitude and longitude, give the address for Phoenix.

18. **Geography Skill** Why is it important to understand latitude and longitude?

USING A MAP

19. Which plateau lies north of the Grand Canyon? Which is south?

20. Name two bodies of water that run through the Grand Canyon area.

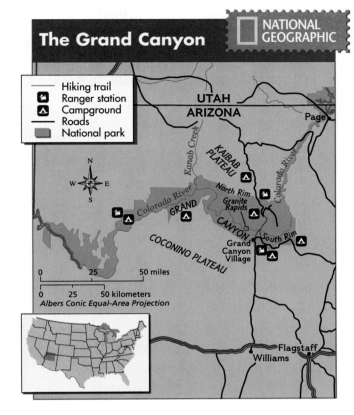

The Grand Canyon — NATIONAL GEOGRAPHIC

Hiking trail
Ranger station
Campground
Roads
National park

UTAH
ARIZONA
Page

KAIBAB PLATEAU
Kanab Creek
Colorado River
North Rim
Granite Rapids
GRAND
CANYON
South Rim
Grand Canyon Village
COCONINO PLATEAU

Colorado River

0   25   50 miles
0   25   50 kilometers
Albers Conic Equal-Area Projection

Flagstaff
Williams

Activity

Learning About Geography Suppose you took a trip to the Painted Desert during your summer vacation. **Write** a travel article about your trip for the school paper. You can use magazines, encyclopedias, or the Internet to research your article.

Foldables

Use your Foldable to review what you have learned about the environment of the Southwest region of the United States. As you look at the lesson titles on the tabs of your Foldable, mentally recall what you learned in each lesson, then review your notes under the tabs of your Foldable to check your memory and responses. Record any questions that you have on the back of your Foldable, and discuss them with class-mates, or review the chapter to find answers.

The Southwest
• the Grand Canyon stretches 217 miles long and 18 miles wide
• rapids form where river elevation drops
Canyons to Coast
Deserts and Oil
Wells: Oil and Water

THE Big IDEAS ABOUT...

History and Economy of the Southwest

The first people to live in the Southwest were Pueblo Native Americans. The Spanish arrived later, bringing their culture and customs. Other newcomers soon joined them. Today the Southwest is a growing region with a rich heritage.

THE HOPI

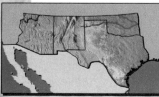

The Hopi people are Pueblo Native Americans who have adapted to life in the desert.

ARRIVAL OF THE SPANISH

Spanish explorers and other newcomers brought changes to the Southwest that are still felt today.

THE RISE OF RANCHING

A new industry, ranching, helped the region's economy grow.

THE SOUTHWEST TODAY

With a rising population and new industries, the Southwest remains strong.

Foldables

Use your Foldable to record what you learn about the "History and Economy of the Southwest."

1. Fold a two-inch tab along the long side of a sheet of 8 ½" x 11" paper.

2. Fold the paper in half like a hamburger with the tabs inside.

3. Open to discover two pockets. Glue the ends of the pockets together to hold index cards or quarter sheets of notebook paper.

The Hopi

How does the past affect the present for the Hopi people?

Lesson Outline

• People of the Desert
• Hopi Life
• Reservation Life Today

VOCABULARY

pueblo
adobe
reservation

READING STRATEGY

Draw a word web like this one. Fill in four things that are a part of Hopi culture.

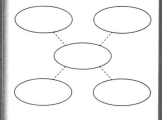

BUILD BACKGROUND

Today, the Southwest has the largest population of Native Americans of all the regions. The area is home to different groups, including the Navajo, Apache, and Hopi.

PEOPLE OF THE DESERT

Pueblo Native Americans have lived in the Southwest for more than 1,000 years. *Pueblo* is the Spanish word for town or village. Pueblo groups living in the region include the Zuñi, the Santa Clara, and the Hopi of Arizona.

The Hopi People

Many Hopi are farmers. They grow beans, squash, melons, and corn, their most important crop. Hundreds of years ago, Hopi ancestors learned how to grow crops in the difficult southwestern climate. Today, Hopi farmers plant in canyons and valleys that become naturally flooded with rainwater each year. They also plant seeds twelve inches deep to use moisture trapped in the soil.

Rain is an important resource for Hopi farmers, as it is for all farmers in the Southwest. In the Hopi culture, they pray to kachinas (kuh CHEE nahz), or spirits, for rain. Every two years in August, dancers perform the Snake Dance to ask for rain. This ceremony attracts thousands of visitors to Arizona.

The Hopi carry on the traditions of their ancestors, such as farming (left), making kachina dolls (right), and performing special dances, such as the Rainbow Dance (above).

READING CHECK

How have the Hopi people adapted to life in the desert?

HOPI LIFE

About 1,000 years ago, the Hopi began to build villages made of **adobe** (uh DOH bee). Adobe is clay and straw that has been baked in the sun and used as building materials. Adobe kept the houses cool in the summer and warm in the winter.

There were no doors on the ground floor of an adobe house. To get inside, ladders were used to climb to the second level. If there was any danger, the ladders were pulled up, keeping the people inside safe. Many Hopi people live in adobe houses today.

Road to Reservations

During the 1800s, southwestern lands became a part of land claimed by the United States. Newcomers began to settle in Native American areas. Disagreements soon followed. The United States sent soldiers to the Southwest to protect the settlers. They also fought many battles with Native Americans. As a result, the United States created **reservations**. A reservation is land set aside by the government for Native Americans.

This home at Acoma **Pueblo**, New Mexico was built of **adobe** many years ago.

The Hopi Reservation was created in 1882. The Hopi were forced onto this much smaller area of land. They were also urged to drop their traditions, such as their religion, and take on the ways of the settlers. However, many Hopi fought to keep their old customs and culture.

Land Disagreements

The Navajo and Hopi people have different ways of life. Since the 1700s both groups have had disagreements over how to use the same land.

Navajo moved from area to area. Looking for more grass, they moved their animals onto Hopi lands.

In 1974, Congress divided up the Hopi Reservation between the two groups. This was called the Navajo-Hopi Land Settlement Act. Today, the Hopi and Navajo both claim land in the "Four Corners" area. The Four Corners is the place where the borders of four states—Arizona, Colorado, Utah, and New Mexico—meet. Look at the map below and find where these and other Native American reservations are located today.

The Navajo were herders with tens of thousands of sheep. Their flocks needed wide, grassy areas to feed. To keep the grass from running out, the

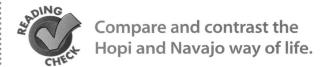

Compare and contrast the Hopi and Navajo way of life.

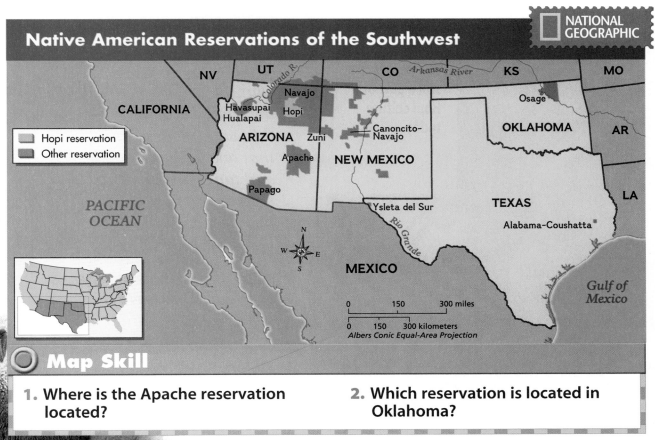

Native American Reservations of the Southwest

NATIONAL GEOGRAPHIC

Hopi reservation
Other reservation

Map Skill

1. **Where is the Apache reservation located?**

2. **Which reservation is located in Oklahoma?**

RESERVATION LIFE TODAY

Today, about 10,000 people live on the Hopi Reservation in northeastern Arizona. The reservation is made up of villages on or near three high mesas, known as First Mesa, Second Mesa, and Third Mesa. **Old Oraibi** (ohr IGH bee), located on Third Mesa, is one of our country's oldest villages. It was established over 800 years ago.

Some Hopi follow the way of their ancestors and earn a living as farmers. Others make and sell traditional baskets, pottery, and silver jewelry.

Preserving a Way of Life

While thousands live on the reservation, other Hopi people have moved to cities and towns throughout Arizona and the Southwest. Though they are spread out, many consider the three mesas in Arizona home. The area has shaped their traditions and way of life. Read the excerpt by poet Wendy Rose. She describes the connection she feels between her Hopi ancestors and the southwestern environment.

READING CHECK Where do many Hopi people live today?

Creating pottery and baskets are still a part of Hopi culture today.

Primary Source:

excerpt from
"To Some Few Hopi Ancestors"
— *by Wendy Rose, 1977*

*No longer the drifting
and falling of wind
your songs have changed,
they have become
thin willow whispers
that take us by the ankle
and tangle us up
with red mesa stone
that keep us turned
to the round sky.*

What do you think she means by "your songs have changed"?

PUTTING IT TOGETHER

Like many Native Americans, the Hopi people respect the heritage of their ancestors. Their traditions are shaped by the desert they have called home for over a thousand years. They also have modern ways shared by most Americans. For the Hopi, life is a mix of traditional customs and newer ways.

The Hopi girls (above) are dressed for a celebration in Flagstaff, Arizona. This Hopi jar (right) was made to hold seeds.

Review and Assess

1. Write one sentence for each of the vocabulary words:

   adobe   **reservation**
   pueblo

2. What Pueblo groups currently live in the Southwest region?

3. Analyze how the past affects the present for the Hopi. How might life for the Hopi be different if they did not have to move to a reservation?

4. Describe how Hopi farmers grow crops in the dry Southwest.

5. **Compare** and **contrast** the life of Hopi ancestors with Hopi who are living in the Southwest today.

Activities

Look at the map on page 77. Which state has set aside the most acreage of land for reservations?

• •

Write a poem describing what it might be like to live in a home made of adobe.

**READING
STRATEGY**

Draw a main idea
pyramid. Fill in the
main idea of the
lesson and four
supporting details.

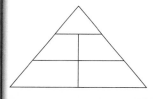

Herders of the Gobi Desert

Find out! *How did the people of Mongolia adapt to the Gobi Desert?*

Lesson Outline
• The Gobi Desert
• Culture of the Desert

BUILD BACKGROUND

Mongolia is a large country in Northern Asia. The **Gobi Desert** covers the southern third of the land. The climate is dry and dust storms blow across the desert. Like the Hopi people of the Southwest, the people of **Mongolia** have adapted to their environment in order to survive.

A man rides a camel through the Gobi Desert.

THE GOBI DESERT

The central and northern parts of Mongolia are located on the Siberian **steppe**. A steppe is dry, flat grassland. Mongolia's climate is harsh. The long, cold winter lasts from October to April. The average temperature in January is 15°F below zero. Summer days can be hot. This is especially true in the Gobi Desert where temperatures often reach 100°F. But even in the summer the temperature can become quite cold due to winds from the north. These winds often cause dust storms.

A Nomadic Way of Life

The people of Mongolia adapted to the harsh climate over thousands of years. Traditionally, Mongolians lead a **nomadic** way of life. *Nomadic* means moving from place to place.

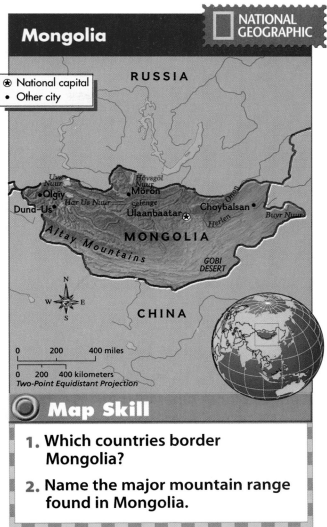

Mongolia

NATIONAL GEOGRAPHIC

⊛ National capital
• Other city

RUSSIA

Uvs Nuur
•Olgiy
Dund-Us•
Har Us Nuur
Hövsgöl Nuur
•Mörön
Selenge
Ulaanbaatar ⊛
Orhon
Choybalsan •
Herlen
Buyr Nuur

Altay Mountains

MONGOLIA

GOBI DESERT

CHINA

0   200   400 miles
0   200   400 kilometers
Two-Point Equidistant Projection

Map Skill

1. **Which countries border Mongolia?**

2. **Name the major mountain range found in Mongolia.**

Most Mongolians, like the Navajo, are herders. Families move with the seasons to find food for their animals. The animals they raise include cattle, sheep, goats, horses, and camels. The meat, wool, and hides of the animals are brought to local markets and are also sold to other countries. About one third of the world's **cashmere** comes from Mongolia. Cashmere is wool from goats.

READING CHECK

Describe the climate of the Gobi Desert.

81

top of the morin-khuur is carved in the shape of a horse's head. A Mongolian legend explains that the instrument was invented after the death of a winged horse.

Festivals

Each year in July, Mongolians hold the *Naadam Festival*. This festival hosts a series of sporting events featuring wrestling, archery, and horse racing. To Mongolians these sports represent wisdom, courage, and strength.

The other main festival is called *Tsagaan Saar*, or "White Month." Tsagaan Saar celebrates the new year. During this time, Mongolians gather with relatives, friends, and neighbors for lavish meals.

CULTURE OF THE DESERT

Most Mongolians live in homes called *gers* (gurz). A ger is a large circular tent made of felt. No matter where it is, the door of the ger always faces south. The ger is designed to be warm in the winter and cool in the summer. It can withstand the fierce winds of the Gobi Desert. Yet, it can also be easily lifted and taken apart when herders move to their winter grazing grounds. *Gers* are also known as *yurts*.

Important Traditions

The most popular instrument in Mongolia is the *morin-khuur.* This is a stringed instrument played only by men. The

 READING CHECK What is a *ger*?

Colorful rugs cover the walls and floor inside a ger (top). This camp of gers (middle) is set up on the edge of the Gobi Desert. A member of the Mongolian Folk Ensemble plays the morin-khuur (left).

In Ulaanbaatar, a father and daughter stand on the platform of a railroad station (above). A Mongolian artist designed this necklace of coral and jade stones (right).

Courtesy of the Division of Anthropology, American Museum of Natural History

PUTTING IT TOGETHER

Today Mongolia's population has grown to roughly two and a half million people. About one third of the total population live in the capital city of **Ulaanbaatar** (oo lahn BAH tor). Ulaanbaatar is the largest city in the country. Even in cities, many Mongolians live in gers.

Review and Assess

1. Write one sentence for each of the following vocabulary words:

   cashmere   nomadic   steppe

2. Why do the herders of Mongolia move from place to place?

3. Describe how the people of Mongolia have adapted to the environment of the Gobi Desert.

4. Describe two elements of Mongolian **culture** and traditions.

5. **Compare** and **contrast** Mongolians to the Hopi people of the Southwest.

Activities

Make a Venn diagram listing the similarities and differences between the climates of the Gobi Desert and the Southwest.

• •

Write a story set in the Gobi Desert. Be sure to include such details as the weather, animals you might see, and a description of the homes you see.

Lesson 3

Arrival of the Spanish

How did Spanish settlers change the Southwest?

VOCABULARY

conquistador

mission

rancho

PEOPLE

Christopher Columbus

Francisco Coronado

Eusebio Francisco Kino

Davy Crockett

READING STRATEGY

Draw a main idea pyramid like this one. Fill in the main idea and supporting details as you read.

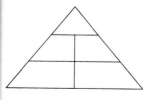

Lesson Outline

• The Search for Gold

• Missions and Ranchos

• Conflicts in the Southwest

BUILD BACKGROUND

In 1492 an Italian explorer named **Christopher Columbus** sailed from Spain across the Atlantic Ocean. He landed in the Bahama Islands. More explorers and settlers soon followed.

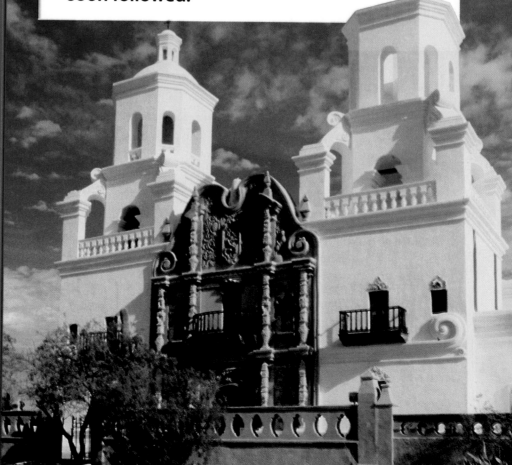

THE SEARCH FOR GOLD

In the 1500s, the Spanish explored Mexico, Central America, and South America. There they found huge supplies of gold and silver. They wondered if the Southwest contained similar riches.

In 1540 **Francisco Coronado** organized an army to march into the area. About 300 Spanish, African, and Native American soldiers made up his army. Coronado was a Spanish **conquistador** (kohn KEE stah dohr). This word means "conqueror" in Spanish.

San Xavier del Bac **Mission** (left) is near Tucson, Arizona. The mural of Coronado (above) hangs in the Panhandle-Plains Museum in Texas.

His army marched north from Mexico. They hoped to find great wealth. They visited several Pueblo communities, including those of the Hopi. However, none of the towns had any gold or silver. After traveling thousands of miles, Coronado's army returned to Mexico empty-handed.

 READING CHECK Why did Coronado explore the Southwest?

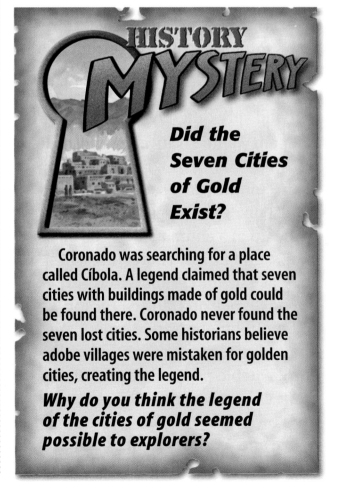

HISTORY MYSTERY

Did the Seven Cities of Gold Exist?

Coronado was searching for a place called Cíbola. A legend claimed that seven cities with buildings made of gold could be found there. Coronado never found the seven lost cities. Some historians believe adobe villages were mistaken for golden cities, creating the legend.

Why do you think the legend of the cities of gold seemed possible to explorers?

85

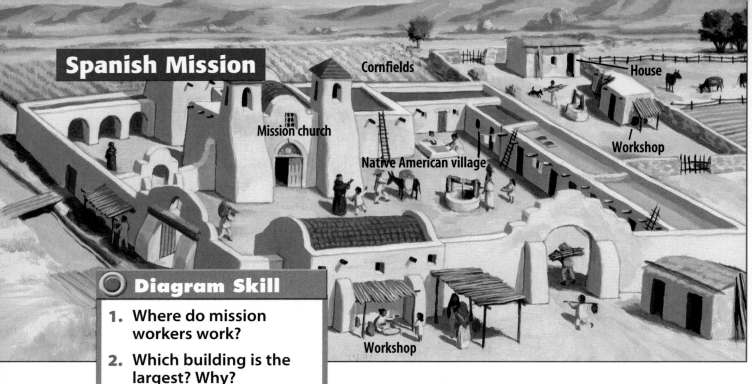

Spanish Mission

Cornfields

House

Mission church

Native American village

Workshop

Workshop

Diagram Skill

1. **Where do mission workers work?**

2. **Which building is the largest? Why?**

MISSIONS AND RANCHOS

Coronado claimed southwestern lands for Spain. Spanish settlers soon followed him into the region. There they came across Native Americans, who led very different lives.

Spain wanted Native Americans to become Christians. Priests were sent to the Southwest to set up **missions** (MISH unz). These settlements were made up of a church, houses, workshops, and farms. There, priests such as **Eusebio Francisco Kino** (eh oo SE bee oh frahn SEES koh KEE noh) taught Native Americans about the Roman Catholic religion. Some Pueblo people became Christians. Others continued to practice their own religion. Many were forced to live and work at the missions, which were built throughout the Southwest.

Ranching

The Spanish also introduced horses and ranching to North America. Coronado led not only an army, but also a herd of 500 cattle into the Southwest. These Spanish "longhorns" quickly adapted to their new environment. On huge farms called **ranchos**, settlers raised thousands of cattle. *Rancho* is Spanish for ranch. By the early 1600s, raising cattle had become a way of life in the Southwest.

READING CHECK **Why did Spanish settlers build missions?**

BIOGRAPHY

Focus On: **Leadership**

Eusebio Francisco Kino was an explorer of the Southwest. He was also an Italian priest who worked as a missionary throughout the region from 1681 to 1711.

Kino founded over 20 missions, including **San Xavier del Bac** (Sahn HAH vee ayr del BAK) near present-day **Tucson** (TU sahn), Arizona. He also brought cattle, horses, goats, and sheep to the region. Kino introduced ranching to the Pueblo Native Americans.

Eusebio Francisco Kino was a strong leader. He opened up the Southwest to new settlers and he created ties with Native Americans. Kino also drew a map of the region that was in use for more than 100 years.

Link to Today Make a list of three qualities a leader of our times should have. Describe why each is important.

THE LIFE OF EUSEBIO FRANCISCO KINO	1645 Kino is born in Italy	1681 Spain sends Kino to North America	1700 Mission San Xavier del Bac is founded	1705 Kino creates a map of the Southwest area	1711 Kino dies in Mexico

1640　　　1660　　　1680　　　1700　　　1720

LIFE AROUND THE WORLD	1643 Louis XIV becomes king of France at age four	1647 English gain control of present-day New York City from the Dutch	1675 Issac Newton studies the science of gravity	1706 Benjamin Franklin is born in Boston

CONFLICTS IN THE SOUTHWEST

After living under Spanish rule for more than 100 years, Pueblo Native Americans staged a revolt. In 1680, they attacked Spain's post in **Santa Fe, New Mexico**, and drove the Spanish out. But the peace did not last long. Twelve years later, the Spanish army returned. They again seized the Pueblo villages.

By the 1700s, Spain claimed a large area of North America. In time, however, the Spanish settlers began to dislike being ruled by a European country far away. They won their independence in 1821. The Southwest became part of the new country, Mexico.

Fight for Texas

In the 1830s, Texas was part of Mexico. About this time, newcomers began to move there from the United States. Although they had promised to be loyal to Mexico, many saw themselves as Texans first. They did not want to be ruled by Mexico. In 1835, the settlers rebelled.

A major battle was fought at **The Alamo**, a mission in San Antonio. The Mexican army had marched into the area. Led by **Davy Crockett** and others, a group of settlers refused to give in. The army attacked and the settlers were defeated. Although they lost the battle, they later won the war. Texas finally joined the United States in 1845 as a state.

Spanish and Mexican influences continue to be a part of life in the Southwest. This group of dancers entertains people at the Mexican market in San Antonio, Texas.

PUTTING IT TOGETHER

Spanish explorers were the first Europeans to settle the Southwest. They brought many changes that helped shape the region's heritage. Today Native American and Spanish cultures can be seen in the language, customs, and buildings of the Southwest region.

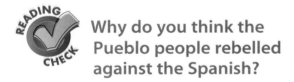 **READING CHECK** Why do you think the Pueblo people rebelled against the Spanish?

You can visit **The Alamo** where David Crockett and many others fought for Texas's independence.

Review and Assess

1. Write one sentence for each of the vocabulary words:

   conquistador   rancho mission

2. Where was an important battle fought in Texas?

3. Analyze how Spanish settlers changed life in the Southwest.

4. Why did settlers in Texas rebel against the Mexican government?

5. **Summarize** the reasons explorers traveled to the Southwest.

 **Activities**

Using the information in this lesson, create a time line of events in the history of the Southwest.

. . . .

Suppose you were on Coronado's expedition through the Southwest. **Write** a letter home describing your journey through the region.

Reading Time Lines

To understand history, you need to know when things happened. You also need to know in which *order* they happened. For example, did Coronado set off on his expedition before or after Eusebio Francisco Kino created a map of the area?

A **time line** can answer this question. A time line is a diagram that shows when events took place. It also shows the amount of time that passed between events. In this way, a time line helps to give a sense of sequence, or order, to history.

VOCABULARY

time line

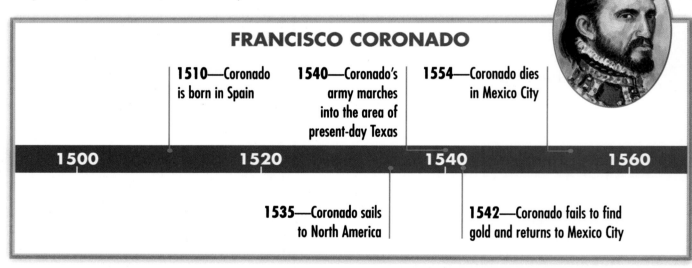

FRANCISCO CORONADO

1510—Coronado is born in Spain

1540—Coronado's army marches into the area of present-day Texas

1554—Coronado dies in Mexico City

1500　　1520　　1540　　1560

1535—Coronado sails to North America

1542—Coronado fails to find gold and returns to Mexico City

LEARN THE SKILL

In the last lesson you read about explorer Eusebio Francisco Kino. At the bottom of page 87, a time line shows important dates in his life. The time line above shows events in the life of conquistador Francisco Coronado.

1. **Identify the title of the time line.**
   The title of this time line is "Francisco Coronado." It charts events in his life. For example, Francisco Coronado was born in 1510.

2. **Note how much time each part represents.**
   Like most time lines, this one is divided into equal parts. Each part represents a certain number of years. On Coronado's time line, each part represents 20 years.

3. **Read from left to right.**
   The earliest event—Coronado's birth—is on the left side. The most recent—Coronado's death—is on the right.

TRY THE SKILL

As you can see, time lines can show events from a person's life. They can also be used for other kinds of topics. The time line below charts important events in the exploration of the Southwest.

1. What is the title of the time line?

2. How much time does each part represent?

3. Did French explorers or Spanish explorers reach the Southwest first?

4. Compare this time line to the one on the previous page. Which event appears on both?

5. In what other subjects would a time line be useful?

EXTEND THE SKILL

Time lines not only help you understand events from history, they can also help you examine events from your life. Suppose that you went to a new school in September, got an A in music class in December, joined the soccer team in October, and played a pilgrim in the Thanksgiving play in November. Create a time line that shows these events in the order that they happened.

- How can a time line help you in your daily life?

EXPLORERS OF THE SOUTHWEST

1520—Spanish explorer Alonso Alvarez de Piñeda sails along the Pánuco River in Mexico

1685—French explorer La Salle builds a colony along the coast of what is today Texas

1500	1550	1600	1650	1700

1538—Fray Marcos de Niza explores the Southwest

1540—Coronado's army marches into the area of present-day Texas

1700—Mission San Xavier del Bac is founded

The Rise of Ranching

Find Out!

How did ranching change the way of life in the Southwest?

VOCABULARY

vaquero
cattle drive
barbed wire

PEOPLE

Nat Love
Lizzie Johnson
  Williams

READING STRATEGY

Draw a chart like this one. Compare cowboys in the past to cowboys today.

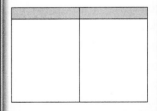

BUILD BACKGROUND

There was a lot of work to do on a ranch. Native American workers known as **vaqueros** (vah KE ros), or cowboys, rode on horseback to herd the cattle. Later the herding was done by Spanish-speaking colonists. Vaqueros were experts with horses. They could also guide a large herd from one grazing spot to another. Today, cowboy skills remain an important part of south-western ranching and culture.

ON THE RANGE

When the Southwest became part of the United States, many people moved there. Some new settlers hoped to grow crops. Others wanted to work on ranches. The men who herded the cattle became known as cowboys.

Cowboys

Who were the cowboys? Many were Mexicans who already lived in the region. Others came from different parts of the United States. About one-fourth of all cowboys were African Americans from the Southeast. Born into slavery in 1854 in Tennessee, **Nat Love** later became one of the best-known cowboys.

By the 1830s, millions of cattle roamed the range because there were no fences dividing the land. Ranchers hired cowboys to keep track of their herds. Those called "line riders"

patrolled the boundaries of the ranch. They protected cattle from thieves and wild animals. A cowboy spent many nights in the saddle, guarding the herd.

What work did cowboys do on the range?

James Walker painted *Vaqueros in a Horse Corral* (left) in 1877. Nat Love (right) was one of the Southwest's most famous cowboys.

93

CATTLE DRIVES

By the middle 1860s there was great demand for beef in the Northeast. However, there were not enough cattle in the Northeast to feed that region's cities.

In Texas, cattle sold for $4 each. The same animal was worth $40 in the Northeast! How could ranchers get their cattle to those northern cities?

The answer was the **cattle drive**. In a cattle drive, cowboys herded the cattle north from Texas. Cattle trails led to railroad lines outside of the region. From there the cattle were carried east by train.

Lizzie Johnson Williams (above) was called "the cattle queen of Texas." She traveled on the **Chisholm Trail** (below).

More than 4 million cattle traveled north in the cattle drives!

The Chisholm Trail

Many ranchers drove their herds up the **Chisholm** (CHIHZ um) **Trail**. This route stretched nearly 1,000 miles, from **San Antonio, Texas**, to **Abilene, Kansas**. Look at the song about this famous trail on the next page.

A cattle drive was hard, dangerous work. A small number of cowboys would guide thousands of longhorns across plains, hills, and rivers. Usually a herd could cover only 10 miles each day. As a result, the cattle drive lasted three months or more. The herders faced droughts and thunderstorms. Sometimes the herd was attacked by outlaws.

During the 1880s, **Lizzie Johnson Williams** was one of the few women to travel the Chisholm Trail. Williams ran a ranch in Driftwood, Texas. She rose early each morning to count her herd.

What route did the Chisholm Trail take?

The Old Chisholm Trail

Cowboy Song

Verse

1. Come a - long boys, and lis - ten to my tale.

I'll tell you of my trou - bles on the old Chis - holm trail.

Refrain

Come a ti yi yip - py, yip - py ay, yip - py ay,

Come a ti yi yip - py, yip - py ay.

2. I woke one mornin' on the old Chisholm trail,
A rope in my hand and a cow by the tail. *Refrain*

3. I started up the trail on October twenty-third,
Started up the trail with the old cow herd. *Refrain*

4. On a ten dollar horse and a forty dollar saddle,
I'm gonna punch those Texas cattle. *Refrain*

5. It's bacon and beans 'most ev'ry day,
I'd as soon be a-eatin' prairie hay. *Refrain*

6. It's cloudy in the west and it looks like rain, and I
left my old slicker in the wagon again. *Refrain*

7. I'm gonna see the boss, gonna get my money,
Goin' back home to see my honey. *Refrain*

RANCHING TODAY

During the late 1800s, changes began to occur in the ranching business. An Iowa farmer named Joseph Glidden invented **barbed wire** in 1874. Using this sharp metal wire, farmers could fence off huge areas of land using very little wood.

Fences caused a big problem for cowboys. They could not drive cattle across fenced lands. This made it hard for herds to reach grass and water.

By 1890, railroad lines went into Texas and Oklahoma. There was no longer a need for cattle drives.

Today, ranching is still big business in the Southwest. However, modern

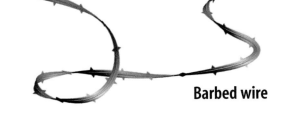

Barbed wire

ranchers use helicopters to round up a herd. They are also more likely to drive trucks than ride horses.

Even with all of these changes, much of the cowboy spirit remains. Rodeos are shows that feature men, women, and children competing in roping, riding, and other cowboy skills. This is one way that cowboy culture is kept alive today.

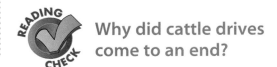

Why did cattle drives come to an end?

In 1910, this woman worked as a ranch hand herding cattle on horseback. Some ranches in the Southwest are so large that helicopters are used to herd cattle.

PUTTING IT TOGETHER

Ranching has long been a big business in the Southwest. Ranchers depend on cowboys to look after their cattle. These workers use many skills, including herding and roping. Until the 1880s, cowboys brought cattle to market on long drives. The spread of railroads and new inventions changed ranching and cowboy culture forever. But the cowboy way of life is still an important part of the region's culture.

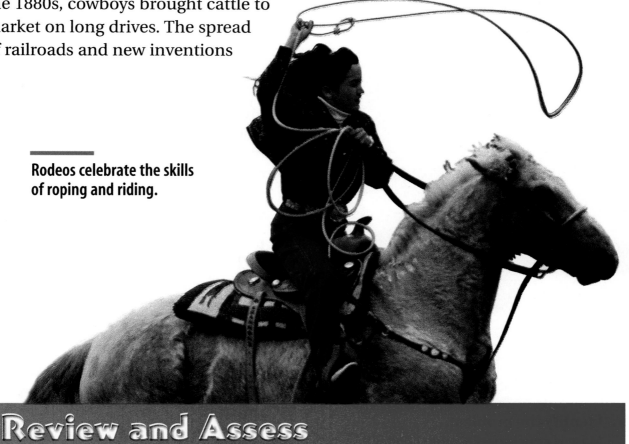

Rodeos celebrate the skills of roping and riding.

Review and Assess

1. Write one sentence using each of the vocabulary words:

   **barbed wire   vaquero
   cattle drive**

2. Who was Lizzie Johnson Williams?

3. Analyze how ranching affected life in the Southwest.

4. What was the effect of barbed wire and railroads on the ranching business?

5. What is the **main idea** of this lesson?

Activities

You read that cattle were worth $4 each in Texas and $40 in the north in the 1800s. How much could a rancher earn by selling 200 cattle in the north? In Texas?

• •

Suppose you are a cowboy guarding a herd. **Write** the words to a short song or poem describing your job.

Problem Solving

Every day you face problems. Problem solving is a process you can use to find solutions. It can help you figure out how to open a stuck window, find a lost book, or end an argument with a friend.

> **VOCABULARY**
>
> consequence
> evaluate

LEARN THE SKILL

Follow these steps to solve a problem.

1. **Identify the problem.**
   Marc is concerned about the election for class president at his school. Last year, only a few students voted. He decides to make sure this year's election is different. First he identifies the problem. More students need to be encouraged to vote.

2. **Gather information.**
   Marc finds students who did not vote in the last election. He asks them why they decided not to participate. Most say they did not know enough about the candidates to pick one.

3. **Identify the options.**
   Marc thinks of a couple of ways to solve the problem. Maybe the candidates could hand out flyers that explain what they would do as president. Or they could hold a debate.

4. **List the possible consequences.**
   Each choice has a **consequence**, or result. Flyers might not give enough information. A debate would give the students a chance to see and hear the candidates and learn more.

5. **Ask your parents, teacher, or other adults to help you choose the best solution.**
   Marc decides to hold a debate. He asks his parents what they think about his solution. They agree with him. Marc also asks the two candidates running for office if they would participate. Both agree. Marc then checks with the school principal to arrange a time and place.

6. **Evaluate the solution.**
   Most of Marc's class attends the debate. A week later, there is a high turnout at the election. Based on this final result, Marc **evaluates**, or judges the value of, his solution. Holding a debate was the best solution to the problem.

TRY THE SKILL

The Music Club at Elmwood Elementary School has a problem. It does not have enough money for all the club members to attend a national elementary school parade in Washington, D.C.

Marcy suggests waiting until next year, when the club will have more money. Jamal suggests sending three students and their parents on behalf of the entire club. Li suggests holding a bake sale to raise money so all members can participate and some parents can accompany the group.

Follow the steps on the previous page, to help the Music Club solve their problem.

1. How would you identify the problem?

2. What information would help solve the Music Club's problem?

3. What are the possible options and consequences they face?

4. Will the school and parents approve of the solutions reached?

EXTEND THE SKILL

Understanding how to solve problems can also help you to understand history. People in the past needed to solve problems, just as we do. The problems may have been different, but the problem-solving process was the same. In the last lesson, you read that there was a great demand for beef in the Northeast. However, the cattle were far away in the Southwest.

- How did ranchers solve their problem?

- How can understanding problem solving help you understand history?

The Southwest Today

Why has the population grown in the Southwest?

VOCABULARY

industry
high technology
astronomer
NAFTA

READING STRATEGY

Draw a word web like this one. Fill in some of the Southwest's important industries.

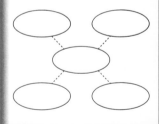

Lesson Outline

- The Oil Industry Today
- High Technology and Trade
- The Sun Belt

BUILD BACKGROUND

Today, the Southwest oil industry reaches into new areas. Workers can be found on land and on the water. Offshore rigs in the Gulf of Mexico bring up oil from beneath the sea.

THE OIL INDUSTRY TODAY

During the early 1900s, the petroleum **industry** brought many newcomers to the region. An industry is all the businesses that make one kind of good or provide one kind of service. Many workers were needed to drill oil, refine it, and ship it. Newcomers flocked to the region to take these and other jobs.

Other Industries

In the 1940s, the United States was fighting in World War II. Before this war, there was little manufacturing in the Southwest. However, the war created a need for new products. Southwest factories built airplanes, tanks, and bridges. Many companies still build these products today. Other

Southwest industries include health care, farming, and as you have read, ranching.

READING CHECK Name three goods produced in the Southwest.

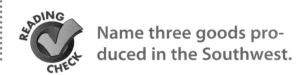

Peanut farming and the manufacturing of aircraft are two important industries in the Southwest.

101

HIGH TECHNOLOGY AND TRADE

In recent years, two industries have become strong in the region, trade and **high technology**. High technology is the use of new scientific ideas and special tools to meet people's needs. One high technology industry in the Southwest is aircraft production.

Science In the Southwest

Astronomers are scientists who study planets and stars. The Southwest, as you have read, has little precipitation. The dry air makes it a good place for telescopes. On **Kitt Peak**, near Tucson, Arizona, astronomers study the Milky Way. Earth, the sun, and the planets of our solar system are found in this galaxy.

Trade

In 1993 the United States, Canada, and Mexico entered into a trade agreement called **NAFTA**, or North American Free Trade Agreement. The goal of NAFTA is to strengthen trading ties among North American countries.

Mexico is our country's largest trading partner. Many goods are shipped into the United States through the Southwest region.

READING CHECK What high technology industry can be found in the Southwest?

At Kitt Peak National Observatory, **astronomers** can view the Milky Way.

DATAGRAPHIC

The Growing Southwest

Booming industries have brought many newcomers to the Southwest. Study the map and graph. Then answer the questions.

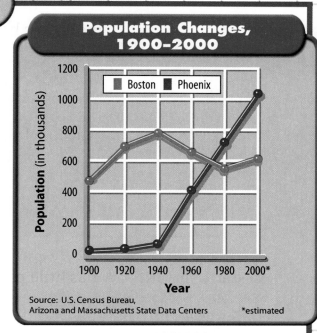

Population Changes, 1900–2000

Population (in thousands)

■ Boston ■ Phoenix

1200
1000
800
600
400
200
0

1900 1920 1940 1960 1980 2000*

Year

Source: U.S. Census Bureau, Arizona and Massachusetts State Data Centers   *estimated

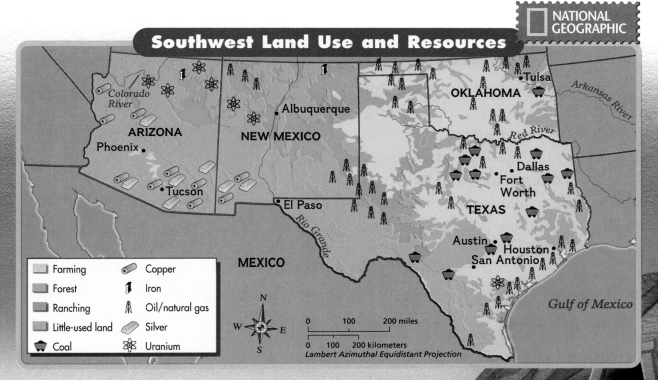

NATIONAL GEOGRAPHIC

Southwest Land Use and Resources

Colorado River

ARIZONA

Phoenix

Tucson

NEW MEXICO

Albuquerque

El Paso

Rio Grande

MEXICO

OKLAHOMA

Tulsa

Arkansas River

Red River

Dallas
Fort Worth

TEXAS

Austin
Houston
San Antonio

Gulf of Mexico

Legend:
- Farming
- Forest
- Ranching
- Little-used land
- Coal
- Copper
- Iron
- Oil/natural gas
- Silver
- Uranium

N
W   E
S

0   100   200 miles
0   100   200 kilometers
Lambert Azimuthal Equidistant Projection

QUESTIONS:

1. In how many states is copper mined?
2. What is the change in Boston's population from 1900 to 2000? The change in Phoenix?

To learn more, visit our Web site: **www.mhschool.com**

Many people enjoy horseback riding in the Sun Belt (above). Some families in the Southwest plant cactus gardens (below).

THE SUN BELT

The populations of Houston, Dallas, and Oklahoma City are growing fast. These cities are located in an area called the Sun Belt. This term describes the part of our country that has a warm, sunny climate all year. The Southeast, Southwest, and parts of the West are in the Sun Belt.

Why do so many people move to the Sun Belt? Some want to escape crowding in the Northeast and the Middle West cities. Others are looking for jobs in the region.

Conserving Resources

Sudden population growth can put a strain on the environment of a place. This is especially true in the Southwest, where resources such as water are in short supply.

To save water, some citizens in **Phoenix** (FEE niks), **Arizona**, and other cities have stopped growing lawns which must be watered. Instead they plant cactus gardens in their yards. Perhaps they hope to learn a lesson about using resources from these desert plants!

As you have read, air conditioners help people adapt to high temperatures. However, they can use a lot of electricity. This puts a strain on the region's supply.

As the Southwest grows, it is important to conserve these and other resources. This will protect the environment and save the resources for future generations.

READING CHECK How do people in the Southwest conserve water?

PUTTING IT TOGETHER

The oil industry today continues to be a big business in the Southwest. High technology and trade industries have also helped the Southwest grow. As the population rises in the Sun Belt, it is important to conserve resources.

Houston, Texas is the tenth largest metropolitan area in the United States.

Review and Assess

1. Write one sentence for each of the vocabulary words:

   astronomer   **industry**
   high technology   **NAFTA**

2. Which country is the leading trading partner with the United States?

3. Analyze why the number of people in the Southwest has grown.

4. Why does the **environment** of the Southwest need to be protected?

5. What is the **main idea** of this lesson?

Look at the map on page 103. In which state are most of the Southwest's oil deposits found?

Suppose you are a worker in the Southwest. **Write** a paragraph describing the kind of work that you do.

Points of View

How should water be conserved?

In the dry Southwest, water is a precious resource. Many people want to have a say in how it is used and conserved. Read and think about these different points of view. Then answer the questions that follow.

DIANN SHEARER

Cotton grower, Casa Grande, Arizona
Excerpt from an interview, 2001

66 Water needs to be distributed as needed among the various users such as farmers and ranchers. Consumers must know that if they want to have food and fiber grown in America at a low cost, farmers must have water. We have become very efficient in irrigating the land through leveling fields, ditch lining, and drip irrigation. All of these practices conserve water. 99

JIM BACA

Mayor, Albuquerque, New Mexico
Excerpt from an interview, 2001

66 As a population grows, water use will increase. Here in Albuquerque we have been able to increase our water supply in several ways. Many people use higher efficiency washing machines, water-saving toilets, and other technology. Unless the Southwest becomes a wetter place, there will have to be limits on growth. The only new source of water is conservation. 99

KEN KRAMER
Executive Director, Lone Star Sierra Club
Austin, Texas
Excerpt from an interview, 2001

❝The population of water birds, such as ducks and pelicans and fish, may shrink because there isn't enough water flowing into rivers and streams. We should protect our fish and wildlife resources by conserving water and avoiding water projects that could hurt the environment, such as dams and pipelines.❞

Thinking About the Points of View

1. With more than 400,000 people, Albuquerque is New Mexico's largest city. How might this influence mayor Jim Baca's point of view?

2. Diann Shearer depends on irrigation to grow cotton, alfalfa, and wheat on 3000 acres of land. How might this affect her opinion?

3. Ken Kramer is the head of a group that works to protect wildlife in the parks and nature preserves of Texas. How might this affect his opinion?

4. What other points of view might people have on this issue?

 Building Citizenship

Leadership

Some people join groups that share their point of view. A few people become leaders in these groups. Choose an issue and research a group that you might join. What leadership roles does the group have?

 Write About It!

Make a list of the different groups in the Southwest who share the region's water resources. Write a short skit in which members of two different groups describe what their needs are. They should also talk about how they can conserve water.

Chapter 2 REVIEW

VOCABULARY REVIEW

Number a sheet of paper from 1 to 6. Beside each number write the word or term from the list below that best matches the description.

adobe	cattle drive
astronomer	industry
barbed wire	pueblo

1. scientist who studies planets and stars
2. sun-baked brick made of clay and straw
3. all the businesses needed to produce one kind of good or one kind of service
4. Spanish word for town or village
5. sharp metal wire used to make a fence
6. cowboys herd cows along trails to northern railroads

CHAPTER COMPREHENSION

7. Where is the Hopi Reservation?
8. Look at the map on this page. Which regions did the cattle trails connect?
9. How did barbed wire change ranching in the Southwest?
10. Where do scientists study astronomy in the Southwest?
11. What is high technology?
12. Write a paragraph that describes the skills cowboys use.

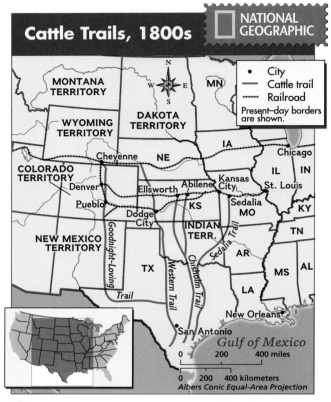

Cattle Trails, 1800s

NATIONAL GEOGRAPHIC

- City
— Cattle trail
······ Railroad
Present–day borders are shown.

SKILL REVIEW

13. **Study Skill** What is a time line?
14. **Study Skill** How can time lines help you understand history?
15. **Study Skill** Draw a time line that begins with the year you were born and ends with this year. Place three events on the time line.
16. **Reading/Thinking Skill** What are the steps to solving a problem?
17. **Reading/Thinking Skill** What is a consequence?
18. **Reading/Thinking Skill** Why do you think it is important to know how to solve problems?

USING A TIME LINE

1500	1600	1700	1800	1900	2000

1540
Francisco Coronado marches into Southwest

1705
Eusebio Francisco Kino maps the Southwest

1800s
Cowboys drive herds on cattle trails

1845
Texas becomes a state

1882
Hopi Reservation created

1902
Willis Carrier invents air conditioner

1993
NAFTA is signed by the United States, Canada, and Mexico

19. How many years passed between Coronado's arrival in the Southwest and Kino's map of the area?

20. How many years were there between the invention of air conditioning and the signing of the NAFTA agreement?

Learning About Culture Suppose you had a pen pal who was a Hopi Native American. **Write** a letter to him or her describing your life. Include some of the customs of your family and community. Ask your pen pal about his or her life and culture.

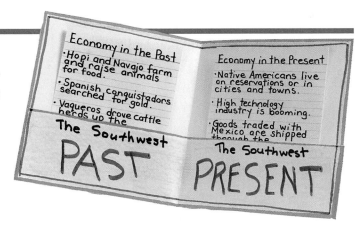

Use your Foldable to review what you have learned about the history and economy of the Southwest. Remove your note cards from the "Past" and "Present" pockets of your Foldable. Sort the cards into stacks—distant past, recent past, and present. Arrange the sorted cards—edge to edge—to form a time line of sequential information.

VOCABULARY REVIEW

Number a sheet of paper from 1 to 5. Beside each number write the term from the list below that best completes the sentence.

adapt   **petroleum**

conquistador   **pueblo**

high technology

1. To survive in the dry Southwest, people have learned to ___.

2. The use of new scientific ideas and methods is known as ___.

3. ___, or oil, is a valuable resource found in the Southwest region.

4. Francisco Coronado was a well-known ___ who explored the Southwest.

5. Many Hopi Native Americans still live in ___ villages.

TECHNOLOGY
For more resources to help you learn more about the places you read about, visit **www.mhschool.com** and follow the links for Grade 4 Regions, Unit 1.

⦿ SKILL REVIEW

6. **Geography Skill** Explain the difference between latitude and longitude.

7. **Geography Skill** Look at the map of Texas below. How many degrees apart are the lines of latitude? How about the lines of longitude?

8. **Geography Skill** What is the line of latitude for San Antonio? Which city shares this latitude line, Houston or Dallas?

9. **Geography Skill** Remember that the equator can affect temperatures and its location is 0°. Which city do you think might have a warmer climate, Amarillo or Laredo? Why?

10. **Geography Skill** What kinds of people might use latitude and longitude in their work?

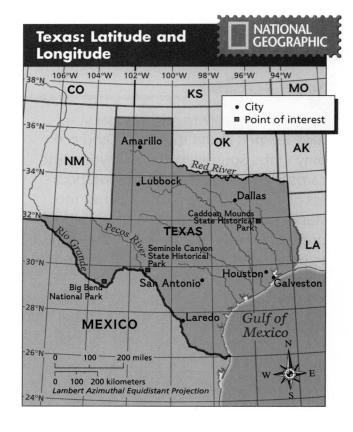

Texas: Latitude and Longitude

NATIONAL GEOGRAPHIC

• City
■ Point of interest

1   Sudden population growth can put a strain on the environment of a place. This is especially true in the Southwest, where resources such as water are in short supply.

2   To save water, some citizens have stopped growing lawns that must be watered. Instead they plant cactus gardens. Perhaps they hope to learn a lesson about using resources from these desert plants!

3   Air conditioners help people adapt to high temperatures. How-ever, they can use a lot of electricity. This puts a strain on the supply.

4   As the Southwest grows, it is important to conserve these and other resources. This will protect the environment and save the resources for future generations.

1   Using an air conditioner puts a strain on the environment by—

   A   taking up too much space
   B   producing too much noise
   C   using large amounts of water to cool a home
   D   using large amounts of electricity

2   What is one way that people in the Southwest conserve water?

   F   They grow desert plants instead of grass in their yards.
   G   They use air conditioning to cool their homes.
   H   They grow cactus plants inside their homes.
   J   They get water from nearby lakes and streams.

WRITING ACTIVITIES

Writing to Inform Use your textbook, school library, or the Internet to learn more about the Dust Bowl. **Write** a short article that explains the difficulties farmers faced during that time.

Writing to Persuade **Write** a travel brochure about the Grand Canyon. Include a description that persuades tourists to visit. Mention any interesting sites and activities they can see or do there.

Writing to Express Suppose you are a cowboy or cowgirl during the 1800s. **Write** a short story about life on the cattle trail. Describe what you might see along the way. Include details about how you would spend a typical day.

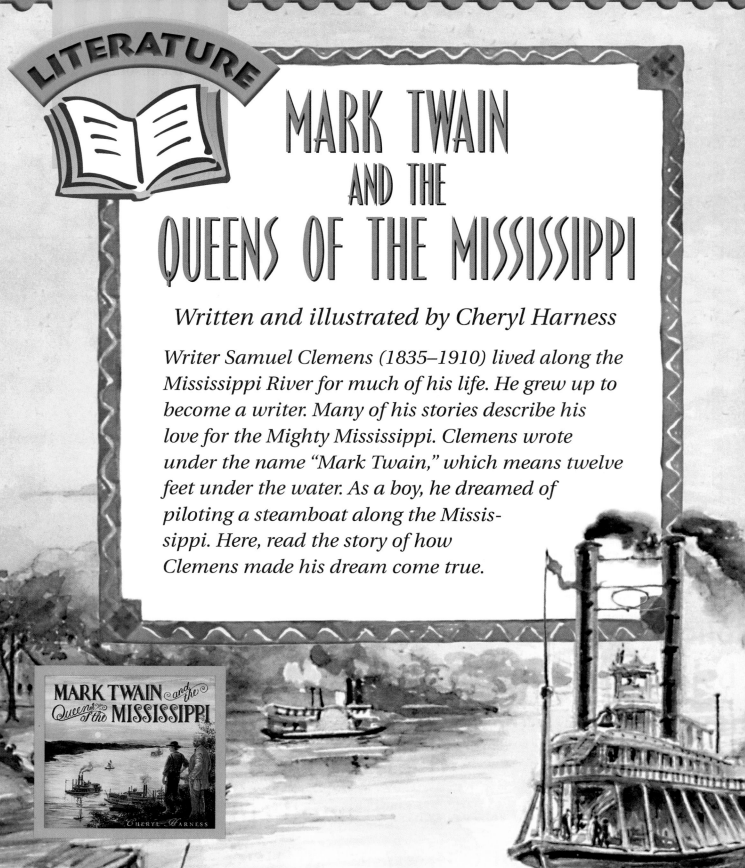

MARK TWAIN AND THE QUEENS OF THE MISSISSIPPI

Written and illustrated by Cheryl Harness

Writer Samuel Clemens (1835–1910) lived along the Mississippi River for much of his life. He grew up to become a writer. Many of his stories describe his love for the Mighty Mississippi. Clemens wrote under the name "Mark Twain," which means twelve feet under the water. As a boy, he dreamed of piloting a steamboat along the Mississippi. Here, read the story of how Clemens made his dream come true.

MARK TWAIN *and the* Queens *of the* MISSISSIPPI

CHERYL HARNESS

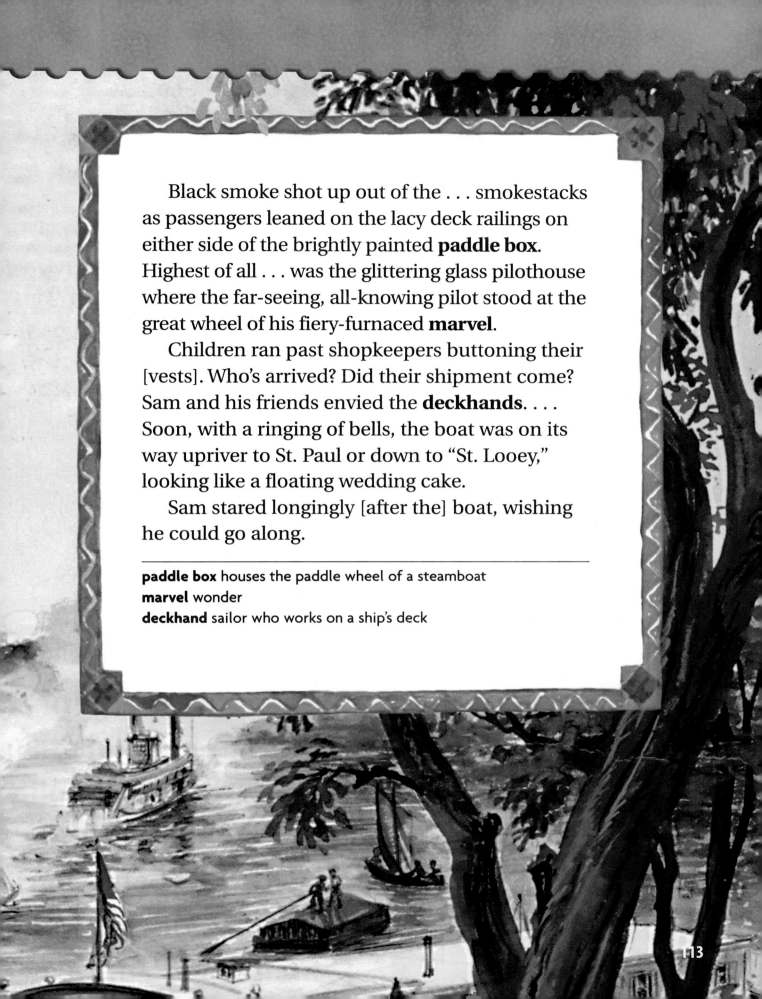

Black smoke shot up out of the . . . smokestacks as passengers leaned on the lacy deck railings on either side of the brightly painted **paddle box**. Highest of all . . . was the glittering glass pilothouse where the far-seeing, all-knowing pilot stood at the great wheel of his fiery-furnaced **marvel**.

Children ran past shopkeepers buttoning their [vests]. Who's arrived? Did their shipment come? Sam and his friends envied the **deckhands**. . . . Soon, with a ringing of bells, the boat was on its way upriver to St. Paul or down to "St. Looey," looking like a floating wedding cake.

Sam stared longingly [after the] boat, wishing he could go along.

---

paddle box houses the paddle wheel of a steamboat
marvel wonder
deckhand sailor who works on a ship's deck

Before the *Paul Jones* steamed back upriver to St. Louis, Sam had talked the pilot, Horace Bixby, into "learning" him the river. Young Sam Clemens would be a **cub-pilot**, a steamboatman at last.

---

cub-pilot pilot-in-training

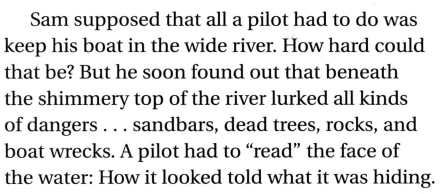

Sam supposed that all a pilot had to do was keep his boat in the wide river. How hard could that be? But he soon found out that beneath the shimmery top of the river lurked all kinds of dangers . . . sandbars, dead trees, rocks, and boat wrecks. A pilot had to "read" the face of the water: How it looked told what it was hiding.

Sam learned all 1,300 miles of the lower Mississippi, all the way from St. Louis to New Orleans. To be a pilot, Sam thought proudly, was to be the only . . . independent human being on earth.

Write About It!

Samuel Clemens fulfilled his dream of piloting a riverboat. What do you dream of doing? **Write** a one-page story in which you reach your goal.

The Southeast

TAKE A LOOK

What is special about the Southeast's environment?

The region's waters provide shipping routes, a resource for farmers, and a home for roseate spoonbills and other animals.

Explore more about the waters of the Southeast at our Web site www.mhschool.com

3

THE Big IDEAS ABOUT...

Environment of the Southeast

In the twelve Southeast states there are mountain ranges, rolling hills, powerful rivers, and marshy wetlands. The region is known for its fertile soil that allows many plants and crops to grow. There are also valuable natural resources throughout the region.

ROLLING DOWN THE RIVER

One of our country's most important rivers, the Mississippi, flows through the western part of the Southeast.

WARM WEATHER AND CASH CROPS

A long growing season makes the Southeast region a source of many fruits, vegetables, and grains.

MINING FOR COAL

The states of West Virginia and Kentucky produce most of the coal used in our country.

Foldables

Make this Foldable study guide and use it to record what you learn about "The Environment of the Southeast."

1. Fold a sheet of paper like a hot dog, but make one side 1" longer than the other.
2. On the short side of the paper, make two cuts, equal distances apart to form three tabs.
3. Label the 1" tab with the chapter title. Label the small tabs with the name of each lesson.

Rolling Down the River

How have rivers helped to shape the Southeast?

VOCABULARY

source
tributary
river basin
mouth
port
delta

READING STRATEGY

Copy the main idea pyramid. As you read, fill in the main idea of this lesson. Add supporting details.

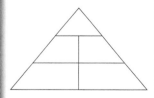

Lesson Outline

• The Mighty Mississippi
• Along the River
• At River's End

BUILD BACKGROUND

Before highways were built, rivers were one of the easiest and fastest ways to travel in some parts of our country. Early explorers used boats to travel through North America. By the 1700s, boats carried people up or down the river, stopping at towns along the way. By the middle 1800s, the river was filled with steamboats and barges loaded with grain, rice, and furs.

Steamboat *Natchez* on the Mississippi

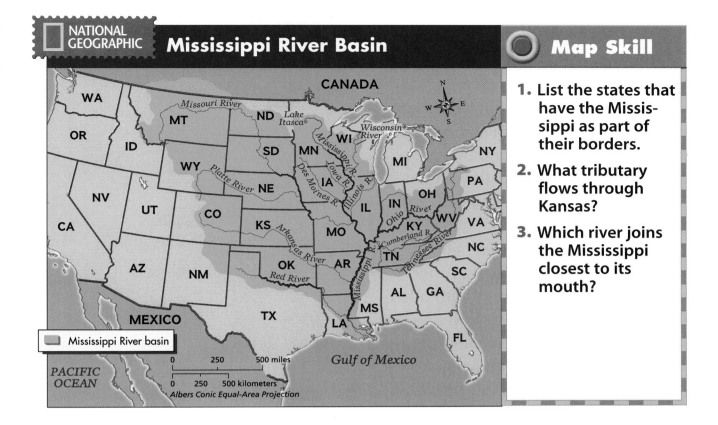

1. List the states that have the Mississippi as part of their borders.

2. What tributary flows through Kansas?

3. Which river joins the Mississippi closest to its mouth?

THE MIGHTY MISSISSIPPI

The **Mississippi River** was named by Algonkian-speaking Native Americans. Their words *Misi Sipi* mean "big water" or "father of waters." It is the longest river in North America.

The starting point, or **source**, of the Mississippi is the tiny Lake Itasca in Minnesota. Here the river is the size of a shallow creek. However, as it flows south it grows wider and deeper as more water flows into the river.

Nearly 250 smaller rivers, called **tributaries**, flow into the Mississippi. Some of the tributaries, such as the Missouri and Ohio rivers, are actually large rivers. They carry water from states as far away as Montana to the Mississippi. All the land drained by a river and its tributaries is called the **river basin**. Use the map on this page to find out how many states are in the Mississippi River basin.

The water from the Mississippi's enormous river basin flows down to the **mouth** of the river. The mouth is the place where a river empties into an ocean or other large body of water. The mouth of the Mississippi is located in Louisiana, where it empties into the Gulf of Mexico.

What is the source of the Mississippi River?

121

ALONG THE RIVER

Although it does not flow very quickly, the river carries large amounts of silt, or fine dirt. As it flows, the silt is picked up from some places and dropped off in others. Over time, silt changes the shape of the river as it is formed into islands, sandbars, and river bends.

For centuries, people and goods have traveled by river. Native Americans used the river to trade with other groups. Later, settlers used river barges to bring supplies to their growing communities. Steering large boats on the Mississippi River has never been easy. Today, skilled pilots spend years learning to safely steer through the muddy Mississippi waters. Even experienced captains must pay close attention to the many changes in the river so their boats are not damaged

or sunk. Special boats are also used to make the center of the river safer. These boats check the river depth and remove silt that has built up on the river bottom.

Engineers also play an important role in keeping the river safe for the people who live near its banks. They build special walls of earth, called levees, next to the river. These walls make it harder for the river to flood the land in seasons of heavy rain or melting snow.

READING CHECK How does silt change the river?

A barge moves along the Mississippi at New Orleans (above). A levee protects the town of Bayou Sorrel, Louisiana (left).

DATAGRAPHIC

Moving Goods in Our Country

In the United States, it is a big job to get food and other goods to every region. Use the charts below to compare different ways to ship goods around our country.

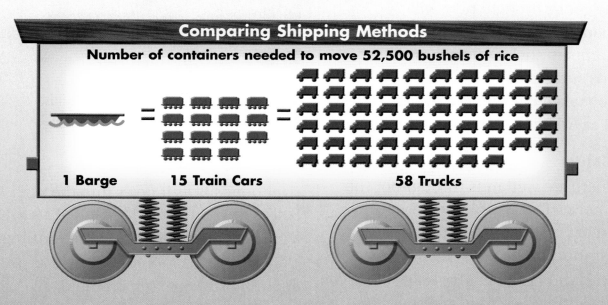

Comparing Shipping Methods

Number of containers needed to move 52,500 bushels of rice

1 Barge = 15 Train Cars = 58 Trucks

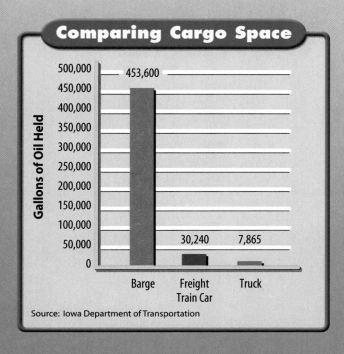

Comparing Cargo Space

Gallons of Oil Held

- Barge: 453,600
- Freight Train Car: 30,240
- Truck: 7,865

Source: Iowa Department of Transportation

QUESTIONS:

1. How many trucks would it take to carry 52,500 bushels of rice?
2. How many more gallons of oil can a barge hold than a train car?
3. Why might people use the river instead of roads to ship goods?

To learn more, visit our Web site: **www.mhschool.com**

AT RIVER'S END

For riverboats and barges, travel begins and ends at a **port**. A port is a place where ships load and unload goods. In Missouri's Port of St. Louis, ships are loaded with grain, coal, or salt for the trip down the Mississippi.

At the end of the river is the Port of New Orleans in Louisiana. Some goods brought here will be loaded onto ships that will travel to countries such as Russia and Brazil. Goods such as coffee, rubber, and steel, will be taken back up the river to states such as Arkansas, Missouri, and Illinois.

Snowy egrets (above) live in the wetlands. A Russian ship takes on a load of grain in New Orleans (below).

Wetlands

There are wetlands throughout the Southeast. The **Okefenokee Swamp** in Georgia and the Florida Everglades are two important ones.

The land near the Mississippi River's mouth is almost as low as sea level. Here the river creates a **delta**. A delta is land formed by the soil the river deposits as it flows into the sea. Soil in the delta near the Gulf of Mexico is rich, black, and good for farming.

Read what Captain Lawrence says about his life working on the river.

READING CHECK What is a delta?

124

excerpt from

Captain Milford Lawrence, pilot of the Mississippi Queen

— *from* **Discover! America's Great River Road** *published in 1992*

The people living ashore are so interesting. They love their river, their boats, the fish, the recreation. They feel so much ownership of the river and its valleys. Those of us who work on the river feel this appreciation, too; a strong sense that this river belongs to all of us.

Who do you think is responsible for taking care of the river environment?

PUTTING IT TOGETHER

The Mississippi has been at the heart of travel and trade in our country for hundreds of years. Ports along the river have helped many of our cities to grow. Next you will learn how the rich land of the Southeast makes this region a center for agriculture.

A pilot uses modern technology to steer a towboat along the river.

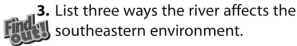
Review and Assess

1. Write one sentence for each of the vocabulary words:

delta	**port**	**source**
mouth	**river basin**	**tributary**

2. What body of water is at the mouth of the Mississippi River?

3. List three ways the river affects the southeastern environment.

4. Describe some ways the Mississippi is now safer for boats to travel.

5. How do rivers help people to **solve** the **problem** of transporting goods across our country?

Activities

Using the map on page 121, choose a tributary of the Mississippi River. List each state it passes through on its way to join the Mississippi.

• •

Use your textbook, school library, or the Internet to learn more about the wetlands in the Southeast. **Write** a description of the plants and animals you might find on a visit there.

Comparing Maps at Different Scales

The map on this page shows the major bodies of water of the Southeast, including the Mississippi. If you were writing a report on rivers found just in the state of Mississippi, this map might not give enough information. You would need Map B, on the next page, to see more details. It shows a smaller area with greater details.

Map A: Water of the Southeast

LEARN THE SKILL

No map can be as large as the area it shows, so all maps are drawn to scale. The scale can be large or small. Follow the steps below to compare maps of different scales.

1. **Locate the map scales.**
   First, find the **map scale** on each map that you are comparing. Remember that a map scale uses a unit of measurement to show a real distance on Earth. Find the scale on Map B, on the next page. How many miles does each inch represent? The scale for each map depends on the size of the area it shows. The number of details on a map can also determine the scale.

2. **Identify small-scale versus large-scale.**
   Map A is a **small-scale map**. It shows few details on a large area. A **large-scale map** shows a lot of details on a smaller area. What kind of a map is Map B? How can you tell?

3. **Compare the maps.**
   Comparing maps at different scales can help you see both the "big picture" and important details. Map A shows the rivers and lakes of the Southeast. Map B shows the major rivers and lakes found in Mississippi.

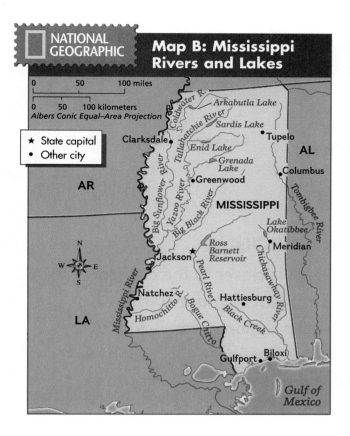

Map B: Mississippi Rivers and Lakes

0 50 100 miles
0 50 100 kilometers
Albers Conic Equal–Area Projection

★ State capital
• Other city

AR

Coldwater R.
Arkabutla Lake
Tallahatchie River
Sardis Lake
Clarksdale
Enid Lake
• Tupelo
Grenada Lake
AL
• Greenwood
• Columbus
Big Sunflower River
Yazoo River
Big Black River
MISSISSIPPI
Tombigbee River
Lake Okatibbee
Ross Barnett Reservoir
• Meridian
Jackson ★
Chickasawhay River
Pearl River
• Natchez
Homochitto R.
Hattiesburg
Bogue Chitto
Black Creek
Mississippi River
LA
Gulfport • Biloxi
Gulf of Mexico

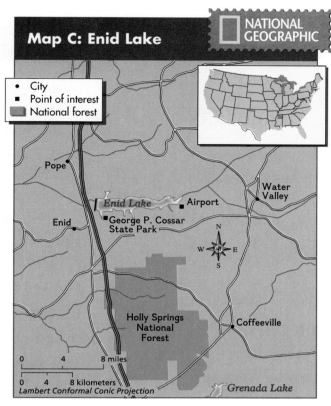

Map C: Enid Lake

NATIONAL GEOGRAPHIC

• City
■ Point of interest
National forest

Pope
Water Valley
Enid Lake
• Airport
Enid
■ George P. Cossar State Park
Holly Springs National Forest
Coffeeville
0 4 8 miles
0 4 8 kilometers
Lambert Conformal Conic Projection
Grenada Lake

TRY THE SKILL

Look again at Map A and Map B. Use them to answer the following questions.

1. What is a map scale?

2. Which map shows the path of the Pearl River?

3. Which map shows the path of the Cumberland River?

4. If you wanted to find out more about Grenada Lake would you need a large-scale or small-scale map?

EXTEND THE SKILL

Now look at Map C. It shows Enid Lake in northern Mississippi. Use it to answer the following questions.

• Is it a small-scale map or a large-scale map? How can you tell?

• When might you need to compare maps of different scales in your own life?

Lesson 2

Warm Weather and Cash Crops

VOCABULARY

agriculture
growing season
cash crop
irrigation
tourist

READING STRATEGY

Copy the main idea chart. Write the main idea of this lesson at the top. Add supporting details as you read.

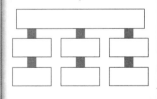

Lesson Outline
• The Growing Season
• Working with the Climate

BUILD BACKGROUND

The Southeast is closer to the equator than many other parts of our country. This location gives the region a warm climate for much of the year. Heavy rainfall and rich soil also help southeastern farmers grow a variety of crops. Many of the fruits and vegetables you eat every day come from the Southeast. Closer to the coast, the region's warm climate makes it a popular place to vacation.

THE GROWING SEASON

Plentiful water and good soil are just two reasons why **agriculture** (AG rih kul chur) is a large part of the region's economy. Agriculture is the business of growing crops and raising animals. All regions support some agriculture, but in the Southeast it's a booming business.

Although many crops can be grown in cooler climates, the warm Southeast region is the only place where certain crops can be grown. This is because the Southeast has a longer **growing season** than some other regions of our country. A growing season is the number of days in a year when the weather is warm enough for crops to grow.

Some crops, like wheat, need only 90 days without frost to grow. Others require longer amounts of time. Cotton needs 180 frost-free days, while oranges cannot grow if there are more than a few days of frost in a year.

Peaches, tomatoes, rice, beans, and peanuts are just a few crops that grow in this region. Peaches and onions grow well in the state of Georgia. Mississippi and Louisiana are two of the largest rice producers in our country. The region also grows soybeans, sugarcane, and sweet potatoes.

READING CHECK What is a growing season?

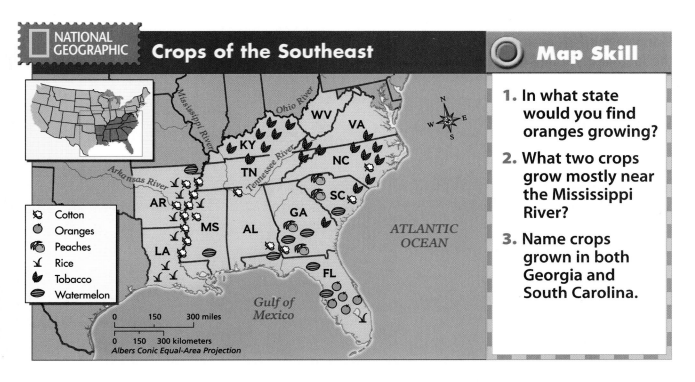

NATIONAL GEOGRAPHIC

Crops of the Southeast

Map Skill

Legend:
- Cotton
- Oranges
- Peaches
- Rice
- Tobacco
- Watermelon

0   150   300 miles
0   150   300 kilometers
Albers Conic Equal-Area Projection

States shown: WV, VA, KY, TN, NC, AR, SC, MS, AL, GA, LA, FL

Mississippi River, Ohio River, Tennessee River, Arkansas River, ATLANTIC OCEAN, Gulf of Mexico

1. **In what state would you find oranges growing?**

2. **What two crops grow mostly near the Mississippi River?**

3. **Name crops grown in both Georgia and South Carolina.**

WORKING WITH THE CLIMATE

The rich soil in most of the Southeast allows many farmers to grow **cash crops**. A cash crop is grown to be sold for money.

One of the first cash crops in the Southeast was tobacco. English settlers in Virginia saw Native Americans there growing tobacco plants. The Virginia settlers planted their own tobacco and began to sell it to England. Settlers in Georgia began growing peanuts as a cash crop, while South Carolina grew rice from seeds brought by a ship traveling from Africa.

Water from Irrigation

In some parts of the Southeast, such as Florida and Georgia, there isn't enough rain to grow certain crops. Farmers there water their crops by irrigation. This is the use of ditches or pipes to bring water to fields. The water is drawn from nearby rivers, lakes, and wetlands. However, farmers must be careful not to drain too much water from these places.

Following the Sun

The warm climate of the Southeast brings many **tourists**, or people on vacation. They swim at the beaches, camp in national parks, and enjoy

Oranges (right) are an important **cash crop** in the Southeast. Farmers use **irrigation** to water their fields (below).

sports such as golf and tennis. Many tourists decide to move to the Southeast when they get older and retire.

 What are some cash crops grown in the Southeast?

PUTTING IT TOGETHER

A warm climate and long growing season in the Southeast make it easy to grow many different kinds of cash crops. Selling crops and providing services to tourists are two important parts of the Southeast economy.

GREETINGS FROM FLORIDA!

Review and Assess

1. Write one sentence for each of the vocabulary words:

   agriculture   **irrigation**
   cash crop   **tourist**
   growing season

2. List some crops that require a long growing season.

3. How does the climate affect the activities of the Southeast?

4. Using what you know, describe the types of jobs you would expect to find in the Southeast **economy**.

5. Make a **prediction** about what might happen if the Southeast had an unusually early and cold winter.

Activities

Choose one cash crop you learned about in the lesson. Use your school library or the Internet to find out more about it. List some uses for the crop you chose and whether the crop was found in North America or was brought here from another country.

. . . .

Suppose you wanted to plan a snack for your family. Use the map on page 129 to **write** a menu. Use only foods that are grown in the Southeast.

Mining for Coal

Find Out!

How does the Southeast provide coal to the country?

Lesson Outline
- Buried Treasure
- Dangerous Work

VOCABULARY

coal
labor union

READING STRATEGY

Copy the word web. As you read the lesson, use it to describe coal mining.

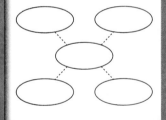

BUILD BACKGROUND

Natural resources in the Southeast take many different forms. Pine trees are one natural resource. They are used to make paper and other products. In North Carolina, the trees are also used in the furniture industry. **Coal**, another natural resource of the Southeast, is dug out of the ground by miners. Coal is a black or brown mineral found in the ground. You will learn more about it in this lesson.

BURIED TREASURE

Much of the coal used in our country comes from states in the Southeast. Plants turn into coal after millions of years in the ground. Look at the diagram on this page to see how coal is formed.

Coal can be burned to produce heat and light. It can also be burned to create other forms of energy, such as electricity.

For at least 3,000 years, people have used coal as fuel. In the last unit, you learned about the Hopi. They used coal for heat to bake pottery.

Until the 1830s, though, the coal industry grew slowly. When railroads were built, trains began to carry coal across the country. Demand for this fuel increased rapidly. By the 1890s, Americans were using almost 200 million tons each year.

READING CHECK What are some uses for coal?

African American coal miners in Kentucky in the 1920s (far left). This miner's lamp (left) was fueled by kerosene.

How Coal Is Formed

Plants in swamps die and decay. They sink to the bottom and form peat.

SWAMP
PEAT
UNDERCLAY

Layers of sediments—sand and soil—pile up on top of the peat, pressing it into a thinner layer.

SEDIMENTS
PEAT
UNDERCLAY

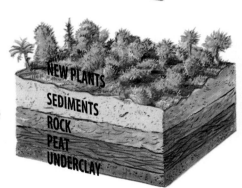

Sediments turn into rock. This rock puts more pressure on the peat and heats it, turning it into coal.

NEW PLANTS
SEDIMENTS
ROCK
PEAT
UNDERCLAY

Diagram Skill

1. In what layer would you find decaying plants?

2. What is the name for the layers of sand and soil that build up?

3. What two things does the rock layer cause that forms coal from peat?

DANGEROUS WORK

During the 1800s and early 1900s, coal miners used shovels and picks to remove coal from underground tunnels. Sometimes explosives were used to blast through the rock so miners could reach the coal.

Coal mining tunnels were dark, cramped, and dangerous. Tunnels could cave in, trapping miners inside. Dust made it hard for the miners to breathe. Gases from the earth could also fill the tunnels and cause explosions. Many miners died while working in coal mines.

Exploring TECHNOLOGY

Digging Machines

Today, machines make mining faster and safer. The Continuous Miner machine can unearth 1,000 tons of coal in just 8 hours. However, human miners are still needed to run the machine. They operate it, make sure the cables are kept clear, and build supports to keep the tunnel from caving in.

Activity

What are some other ways that machines could improve the mining industry?

Working for Change

Until 1940, young children worked in the mines sorting coal from other rocks. The children worked so they could earn money to help support their families. In 1940 a law was passed to stop young children from doing dangerous work such as mining.

In 1890, miners in the United States formed a **labor union**. A labor union is a group of workers who try to get better working conditions. The union got the miners better pay and safer working conditions. Over the years the miners' union convinced the government to pass laws to protect workers. The laws forced companies to build safer mines. The companies also had to provide medical care to miners with lung damage from years of breathing in coal dust.

READING CHECK What were some dangers faced by miners?

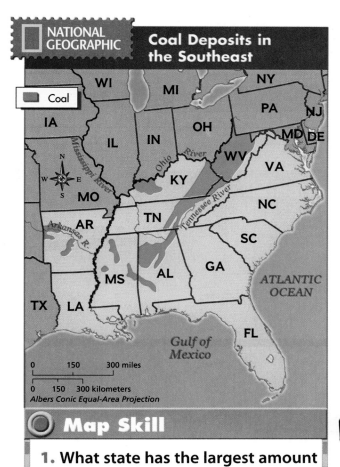

NATIONAL GEOGRAPHIC

Coal Deposits in the Southeast

Coal

Map Skill

1. **What state has the largest amount of coal deposits?**

2. **How many states in the Southeast have no coal deposits at all?**

PUTTING IT TOGETHER

More than half of our country's electricity comes from power plants that burn coal. Coal is also a big part of our country's economy. The United States earns around $3.5 billion each year by selling coal to countries such as Canada, Italy, and Japan.

Miners today wear helmets combined with lights.

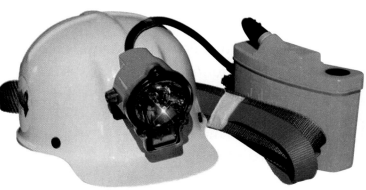

Review and Assess

1. Write one sentence for each of the vocabulary words:

   coal   labor union

2. What is peat and how does it form?

3. How does the Southeast supply the country with coal?

   Find Out!

4. What role did the railroads play in changing the demand for coal?

5. Describe the conditions that **caused** miners to form a labor union and the **effects** it had on mining.

Using the map on this page, list the states in the Southeast where coal deposits are found. How do you think these areas looked millions of years ago before coal was formed?

• •

Write a paragraph describing the reasons why you might join a labor union if you worked in a coal mine.

135

VOCABULARY REVIEW

Number a sheet of paper from 1 to 5. Beside each number write the word or term from the list below that matches the description.

agriculture	tourist
coal	tributary
delta	

1. land formed by the soil that a river deposits as it flows into a larger body of water
2. any river that flows into a larger river
3. a mineral found under Earth's surface that is burned as fuel
4. the business of growing crops and raising animals
5. a person traveling on vacation

CHAPTER COMPREHENSION

6. Where would you find the beginning of the Mississippi River?
7. How does a delta form?
8. How does irrigation help farmers in the Southeast?
9. Why is the growing season in the Southeast longer than in some other parts of the country?
10. List two cash crops that are grown in the Southeast.
11. What are some uses for coal?
12. What is a labor union?
13. How has mining changed since the middle 1800s?

SKILL REVIEW

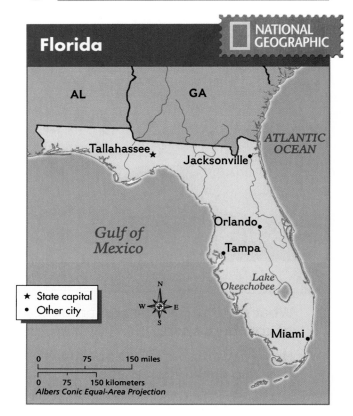

14. **Geography Skill** What is a map scale?
15. **Geography Skill** Why would you want maps drawn at different scales?
16. **Geography Skill** How does a scale strip help you to measure distances on a map?
17. **Geography Skill** What is the distance between Jacksonville and Miami?
18. **Geography Skill** Use the map scale to estimate distance. From Jacksonville, is it a farther trip to Tallahassee or Orlando?

USING A CHART

19. What quantity of oranges was harvested in the 1994 growing season?

20. In what year were the fewest oranges harvested? What might have happened in that year?

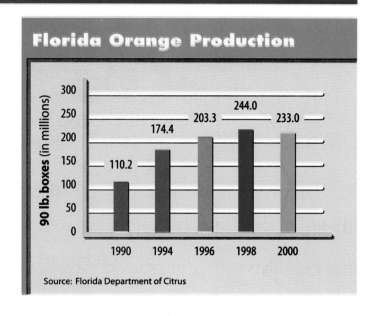

Florida Orange Production

Source: Florida Department of Citrus

Activity

Writing About Tourism Suppose you were a tourist in the Southeast traveling by riverboat. Use your textbook, school library, or the Internet to learn more about the area around the Mississippi River. Then write a letter about your vacation to a friend. Include the states you passed through, places you visited, and what you saw on the trip.

Foldables

Use your Foldable to review what you have learned about the environment of the Southeast. As you look at the tabs of your Foldable, mentally recall environmental features of land and water that influence the 12 states in this region. Rank these environmental features in order of how many states they affect directly. Review your notes under the tabs of your Foldable to check your memory and responses. Record any questions that you have on your Foldable, and discuss them with classmates, or review the chapter to find answers.

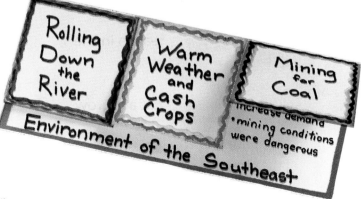

THE Big IDEAS ABOUT...

History and Economy of the Southeast

Early Native Americans farmed and hunted in the Southeast.

Settlers from England built communities on the coast of the

Atlantic Ocean. Later, the Southeast would be the home to

many conflicts over issues such as slavery and civil rights.

Today, the region is still growing and changing.

THE CHEROKEE

These Native Americans of the central Southeast region preserve their culture in their own written language.

COLONIAL WILLIAMSBURG

Once the capital of Virginia, Williamsburg is one place where English settlers met and talked about forming a free country.

A COUNTRY DIVIDED

The Civil War brought an end to slavery in our country. After the war the Southeast had to rebuild.

CIVIL RIGHTS AND THE SOUTHEAST TODAY

The struggle for civil rights in the Southeast paved the way for many of the region's leaders today.

Foldables

Use this Foldable study guide to record what you learn about the "History and Economy of the Southeast."

1. Fold 3 sheets of paper in half like hamburgers, leaving one side 1" longer than the other.

2. Fold the 1" tab forward over the short side, then fold it back the other way.

3. Glue the straight edge of each sheet onto the tab of another. This will result in a six-section timeline.

4. As you read the chapter, record information from past to present.

The Cherokee

What did Sequo-yah contribute to the Cherokee culture?

Lesson Outline
• Cherokee Culture
• Sequoyah's Gift
• A Terrible Trail

VOCABULARY

council
syllabary
Trail of Tears

PEOPLE
Sequoyah

READING STRATEGY

Copy the flowchart below. List the sequence of events that happen in this lesson.

BUILD BACKGROUND

Many groups of Native Americans lived in the Southeast. The Cherokee were one of these groups. They called themselves *Aniyunwiya* (anh uh YEWN wee yah) or "first people." They first lived in the area of the Great Lakes. Later, they moved to an area in the Southeast.

Cherokee lodge

CHEROKEE CULTURE

Boys and girls learned different skills. The men taught boys to fish and to hunt deer, rabbits, and squirrels. They also learned how to trade goods with other communities. Girls were taught how to farm, cook, and make clothing. They also learned the art of weaving baskets used to store and carry food and goods.

Both men and women participated in the village **council**. A council is a group of people who meet to talk and make decisions.

Cherokee shirt

Each village was governed by a council.

Once a year the leaders of these councils traveled to their capital, **Echota** (e CHAH tuh), located in what is now Tennessee. The council leaders discussed trade, farming, and relations with other Native American groups.

READING CHECK What was life like for the Cherokee in the Southeast?

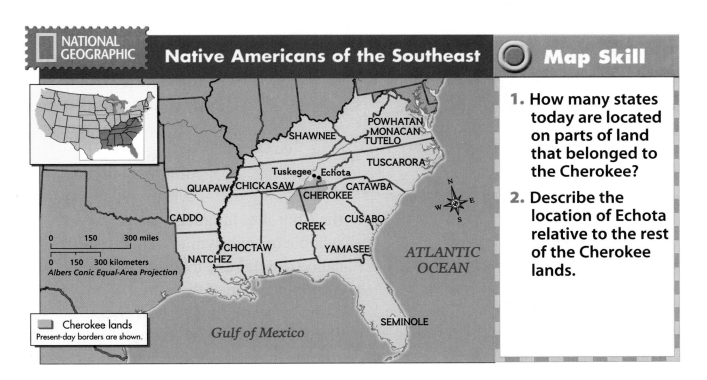

NATIONAL GEOGRAPHIC
Native Americans of the Southeast
Map Skill

SHAWNEE
POWHATAN
MONACAN
TUTELO
TUSCARORA
Tuskegee Echota
QUAPAW CHICKASAW
CATAWBA
CHEROKEE
CADDO
CUSABO
CREEK
CHOCTAW
YAMASEE
NATCHEZ
ATLANTIC OCEAN

0   150   300 miles
0   150   300 kilometers
Albers Conic Equal-Area Projection

SEMINOLE
Gulf of Mexico

Cherokee lands
Present-day borders are shown.

1. **How many states today are located on parts of land that belonged to the Cherokee?**

2. **Describe the location of Echota relative to the rest of the Cherokee lands.**

The young Sequoyah was very interested in the stories his grandfather and the village storytellers told. He loved to hear about the adventures they described. They also told stories about the world in which they lived.

As Sequoyah grew older, he saw how the Cherokee culture was changing. His people were quickly adopting the ways of European settlers. He worried that the old stories and ways of doing things would be lost. He wanted to find a way to help people remember these things.

A New Alphabet

Sequoyah had seen the settlers using an alphabet to write to each other and to remember important events. However, the letters and sounds of their language were not the same as the Cherokee language.

In 1809 he decided to create a written language for his own people. He began by noting each of the different sounds, or syllables, used in the Cherokee language. He gave each syllable its own symbol. This system is called a **syllabary** (SIH luh bayr ee). Although some of the symbols he used came from the English and Greek alphabets, they represented different sounds in the Cherokee syllabary.

Charles Banks Wilson painted this picture of Sequoyah that hangs in the state capitol building in Oklahoma City, Oklahoma. Cherokee Syllabary (right).

SEQUOYAH'S GIFT

Around 1760, a boy named **Sequoyah** (sih KOY uh) was born in the Cherokee village of Tuskegee (tus KEE gee) in what is now Tennessee. It was one of more than 40 Cherokee villages in the Southeast.

Gaining Acceptance

Sequoyah tried many different systems for writing the words of the Cherokee language. He visited a nearby school to watch how children learned to read and write in English. He even borrowed spelling books so that he could learn more about how written languages worked.

When he finished his syllabary in 1821, some Cherokee did not know what to think of his work. Sequoyah had to work hard to convince his people that his alphabet was useful. He taught his daughter, Ahyokah, the alphabet and brought her before the council. Sequoyah had the council give him a message to write down. Then he brought his daughter to read it back to them. The council was amazed, but thought it might be a trick.

Front page of the first edition of the *Cherokee Phoenix* (above). Cherokee artist Bob Annesley created this sculpture (below) of Sequoyah and Ahyokah.

The council sent for young men from other Cherokee villages. They came and learned the alphabet. Then the council tested each of them to see if they could read messages written by the other young men. This convinced them that Sequoyah's system worked.

The Cherokee quickly realized how useful the writing system was. It was easy to learn and could be used to share news among all the Cherokee. By the late 1820s, a printing press was created with Cherokee symbols. It was used to print the first newspaper written in the Cherokee language. The newspaper was called the *Cherokee Phoenix* and is still read today.

READING CHECK What is a syllabary?

143

A TERRIBLE TRAIL

In the 1700s, there were about 12,000 Cherokee people. In the early 1800s, some states began to pass laws to limit the rights of the Cherokee. Finally, the United States government decided to remove Native Americans from their land to make room for European settlers.

Most Cherokee wanted to stay near their homeland in the Southeast. Some fled into the Great Smoky Mountains. However, at the order of President Andrew Jackson, most of them were forced to leave in 1838.

Almost 15,000 Cherokee had to journey hundreds of miles to what is now Oklahoma. Many made the four-month-long trip on foot or horseback.

They could not bring many supplies in the few wagons they had and were not prepared for traveling in the harsh weather.

About 4,000 Cherokee died of illness, hunger, or exhaustion. Those who survived remembered it as the **Trail of Tears**. When they arrived at their new land, they worked hard to build a new life for themselves. Soon there was a new Cherokee capital at **Tahlequah** (TAH lah kwah), Oklahoma, where it remains today.

READING CHECK What was the Trail of Tears?

Robert Lindneux painted this picture of the **Trail of Tears** in 1942. United States soldiers are wearing blue coats and tall hats.

PUTTING IT TOGETHER

The Cherokee passed on their culture and history through story-telling. Sequoyah's syllabary helped the Cherokee preserve their history and culture. Today, over 165,000 Cherokee live in Oklahoma. More than a million live across the United States. Though they all speak English, many still use Cherokee writing.

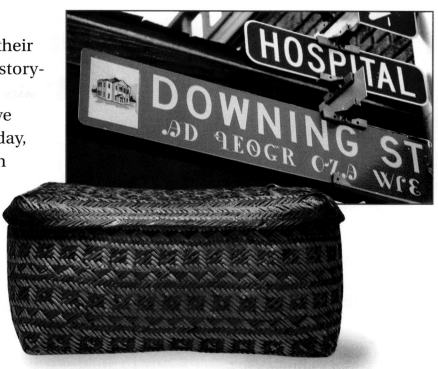

Cherokee culture is seen in artifacts such as this basket, and modern street signs in Tahlequah, Oklahoma.

Review and Assess

1. Write one sentence for each of the vocabulary words:

   **council   Trail of Tears
   syllabary**

2. How did Sequoyah's daughter help him to prove that his alphabet worked?

3. What were the **effects** of Sequoyah's contribution to Cherokee culture?

4. On the Trail of Tears, the Cherokee traveled west. Use the map on page 141 to list Native American groups living to the west of the Cherokee lands.

5. **Compare** and **contrast** life in a Cherokee village with life in your community.

Activities

Create a two-column chart on a sheet of paper. In each column, list the ways that Cherokee men and women contributed to their community. Put skills done by both groups in both columns.

• •

Suppose you were writing for the *Cherokee Phoenix*. **Write** a news story about the Trail of Tears.

Colonial Williamsburg

How did Thomas Jefferson help to win independence for America?

Find Out!

VOCABULARY

colony

House of Burgesses

Declaration of Independence

PEOPLE

Thomas Jefferson

Lesson Outline

- An English Colony
- Jefferson's Williamsburg
- Steps to Independence

READING STRATEGY

Copy the flowchart. Use it as you read to identify the flow of events in this lesson.

BUILD BACKGROUND

For thousands of years, Native Americans were the only people in the Southeast. In 1565 people from Spain settled in Florida. People from England built a colony they called **Jamestown**, Virginia in 1607. A **colony** is a place that is ruled by a distant country. By 1699, colonists chose **Williamsburg** as the capital of their colony. You can see their capitol building below.

AN ENGLISH COLONY

Virginia was England's first permanent colony in North America. As the colony grew, Jamestown became its first capital. However, the Jamestown settlement was in a low and swampy area. The water at the mouth of the river near the **Chesapeake Bay** was often too salty to use. The colonists, or settlers, decided to move the capital to another location in Virginia.

In 1699, they chose a town called Williamsburg, located farther up the James River. The center of Williamsburg was its main road, named for the Duke of Gloucester. It was about a mile long. There were many shops and taverns. Farmers came into the town to buy and sell goods. Craftworkers such as weavers, printers, blacksmiths, and cabinetmakers worked in shops along the street.

At one end of the main road was the capitol building. Although the colony was ruled by England, the colonists handled some governing tasks themselves. Four times a year people from all over the colony came to Williamsburg. These were "public

Many women in Williamsburg sewed their own clothing and made their own hats.

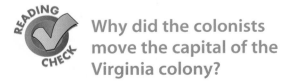

times" when the colony's courts were open to the people.

In the center of town were the Bruton Parish Church and the Governor's Palace. The main road ended at the gates of the College of William and Mary. This was the second oldest college in the colonies.

READING CHECK

Why did the colonists move the capital of the Virginia colony?

JEFFERSON'S WILLIAMSBURG

Thomas Jefferson was born in central Virginia in 1743. His parents were wealthy and wanted him to have a good education. Jefferson attended the College of William and Mary in Williamsburg. After finishing college, Jefferson went on to study law.

Although Jefferson worked hard at his studies, he enjoyed the colonial community of Williamsburg. He attended concerts and dances in the capital. He became interested in how government works. He also met other people who had new ideas about how the colonies should be governed.

The House of Burgesses

In Williamsburg, Jefferson observed the work of the **House of Burgesses** (BUR jihs ez). *Burgess* is an old English word for citizen. The House of Burgesses was a group of Virginia citizens who made laws for the colony.

The House of Burgesses was not the kind of democracy we have today. Only white men with property were allowed to vote. Women, African Americans, Native Americans, and the poor could not vote. The Burgesses could also be overruled by the Royal Governor. The governor was sent by the king of England to rule the colony.

Thomas Jefferson came to Williamsburg as a young man to attend college. His telescope can be seen at his home in Monticello, Virginia.

A painting of the **House of Burgesses**

An Angry Colony

Jefferson began serving in the House of Burgesses in 1769. People in Virginia and other colonies were forced to pay taxes to England on items they used every day, such as tea and stamps. The colonists did not have any representatives in the English Parliament, or legislature. This made many colonists angry.

Several members of the House of Burgesses complained about the laws and taxes of the colony. Jefferson said, "the British Parliament has no right to exercise [use] authority over us."

These ideas upset the Royal Governor. He decided to close the House of Burgesses in 1774. He wanted to put an end to the colonists' making decisions for themselves.

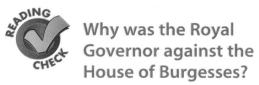 **Why was the Royal Governor against the House of Burgesses?**

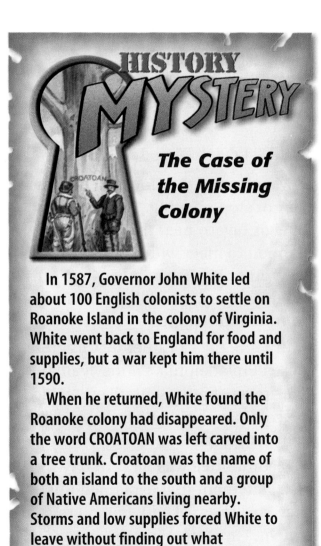

HISTORY MYSTERY

The Case of the Missing Colony

In 1587, Governor John White led about 100 English colonists to settle on Roanoke Island in the colony of Virginia. White went back to England for food and supplies, but a war kept him there until 1590.

When he returned, White found the Roanoke colony had disappeared. Only the word CROATOAN was left carved into a tree trunk. Croatoan was the name of both an island to the south and a group of Native Americans living nearby. Storms and low supplies forced White to leave without finding out what happened to the colony.

What do you think might have happened to the colonists?

Members of the **House of Burgesses** met at Raleigh Tavern when the governor drove them out of the Capitol.

STEPS TO INDEPENDENCE

Members of the House of Burgesses did not stop meeting. They met in the Raleigh Tavern near the capitol. They planned to meet with representatives from other English colonies in North America. They called the meeting the Continental Congress.

In 1775, the Continental Congress met in Philadelphia, Pennsylvania. The group of representatives decided the colonies should be independent, or free, of English rule.

A committee was picked to work on a statement that explained this decision. They asked Jefferson to write it. His statement, the **Declaration of Independence**, was approved by the Congress on July 4, 1776. You can read part of this important document on this page.

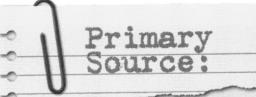

Primary Source:

excerpt from the
Declaration of Independence
— approved by the Continental Congress in 1776

*We hold these truths to be self-evident; that all men are created equal; that they are **endowed** by their Creator with certain **unalienable** rights; that among these are life, liberty, and the pursuit of happiness; that, to secure these rights, governments are **instituted** among men, **deriving** their just powers from the **consent** of the governed.*

Why do you think Jefferson wrote that governments require the consent of the people governed?

endowed: given
unalienable: basic
instituted: founded
deriving: getting
consent: agreement

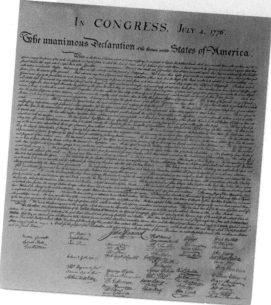

Williamsburg Today

Today you can visit stores, work-shops, and other businesses that are almost exactly as they were in Jefferson's time. The people there show how weavers, printers, and other towns-people made their living.

How do you think the Continental Congress got its name?

Tourists in Williamsburg watch a demonstration of 18th century wig making.

PUTTING IT TOGETHER

Thomas Jefferson's Declaration of Independence was not enough to free the colonies from English rule. That took years of fighting in the American Revolution. After the war, the country's citizens remembered Jefferson's leadership. They elected him the third President of the United States.

Review and Assess

1. Write one sentence for each of the vocabulary words:

   colony
   Declaration of Independence
   House of Burgesses

2. What might have happened if the colonists had been allowed to have representatives in Parliament?

3. How did Jefferson participate in the decision to declare independence?

4. What **economic** problem did colonists have with the English government?

5. **Compare** and **contrast** the House of Burgesses with our democracy today.

Activities

Jefferson and other leaders often talked about whether the colonies should be free or remain under English rule. With a partner, prepare arguments for and against independence for the colonies. Present both points of view to the class.

• • • • • • • • • • • • • • • • • • • •

Suppose you had been asked to write the Declaration of Independence. **Write** a statement explaining why the colonists wanted to be free from English rule.

Building a New Government

VOCABULARY

apartheid

township

PEOPLE

Nelson Mandela

Frederik Willem de Klerk

READING STRATEGY

Copy the main idea pyramid. Fill in the main idea of this lesson. Add supporting details as you read.

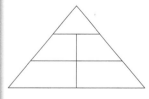

How did South Africa build a new government?

Lesson Outline

- South African Independence
- The End of Apartheid

BUILD BACKGROUND

South African leader **Nelson Mandela** wrote, "When I walked to the voting station, my mind dwelt on the heroes who had fallen so that I might be where I was that day. . . . I did not go into that voting station alone on April 27 (1994); I was casting my vote with all of them."

South Africans line up to vote in 1994.

SOUTH AFRICAN INDEPENDENCE

In the country of **South Africa**, democracy once seemed like a dream. Europeans had ruled much of this country since the 1700s. Dutch settlers first formed a colony at **Cape Town**. In 1814, the British took control of South Africa from the Dutch.

A Country Divided

In 1948, the white leaders created a system of laws called **apartheid** (uh PAHR tighd). This means "apartness." Apartheid took away the rights and freedoms of blacks in South Africa.

Under apartheid, millions of blacks had to give up their land to whites. They were forced to live in **townships**. Townships are crowded areas for blacks in or near cities. They could not vote, own land, or move freely in the country. Even though South Africa won independence from Britain in 1961, apartheid continued.

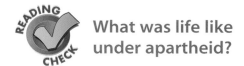

READING CHECK What was life like under apartheid?

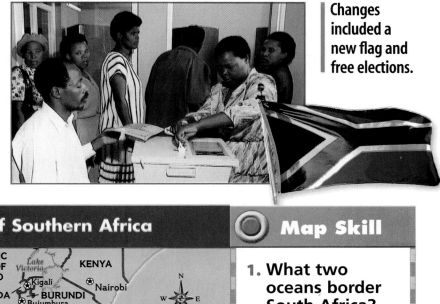

Changes included a new flag and free elections.

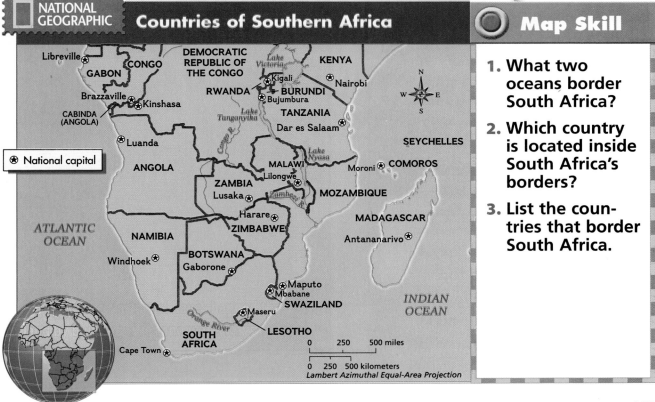

NATIONAL GEOGRAPHIC
Countries of Southern Africa

Libreville
GABON
CONGO
Brazzaville
Kinshasa
CABINDA (ANGOLA)
DEMOCRATIC REPUBLIC OF THE CONGO
Lake Victoria
RWANDA
Kigali
BURUNDI
Bujumbura
Lake Tanganyika
TANZANIA
KENYA
Nairobi
Dar es Salaam
Luanda
ANGOLA
National capital
ATLANTIC OCEAN
NAMIBIA
Windhoek
ZAMBIA
Lusaka
Zambezi R.
MALAWI
Lilongwe
Lake Nyasa
MOZAMBIQUE
SEYCHELLES
COMOROS
Moroni
MADAGASCAR
Antananarivo
INDIAN OCEAN
BOTSWANA
Gaborone
Harare
ZIMBABWE
Orange River
Maseru
LESOTHO
SOUTH AFRICA
Cape Town
Maputo
Mbabane
SWAZILAND
0   250   500 miles
0   250   500 kilometers
Lambert Azimuthal Equal-Area Projection

Map Skill

1. What two oceans border South Africa?

2. Which country is located inside South Africa's borders?

3. List the countries that border South Africa.

THE END OF APARTHEID

Nelson Mandela was a black lawyer who became a leader in the fight against apartheid. To stop his protests, the government put him in prison.

In 1989, **Frederik Willem de Klerk** became president of South Africa. De Klerk thought it was time for change in South Africa. In 1990, he released Nelson Mandela from prison. Mandela had been locked up for 27 years. The next year, De Klerk ended most apartheid laws.

Even greater changes followed. Mandela, De Klerk, and other leaders called for national elections to be held in 1994. It was the first time all South Africans, black and white, had the right to vote. The voters elected Nelson Mandela to be their new president.

A New Constitution

After the elections, the people of South Africa began writing a Constitution. It was signed into law on December 10, 1996. The Constitution created a government with executive, legislative, and judicial branches.

Like the United States Constitution, the South African Constitution has a Bill of Rights. For most South Africans,

Mandela with de Klerk (above) and signing the new constitution (below). Schools (right) are no longer segregated by **apartheid**.

this is the most important part of the Constitution. The Bill of Rights protects the rights of all people in the country. It promises to uphold the values of equality and freedom.

What is important about the South African Constitution?

PUTTING IT TOGETHER

South Africa still faces many challenges to its government and economy. Overcoming the effects of apartheid will take years, but the victory in South Africa has given many people hope.

The changes in South Africa have helped people in other African countries work toward democratic governments. These people now believe they can shape their own futures by gaining, protecting, and practicing new rights and freedoms.

Review and Assess

1. Write one sentence for each of the vocabulary words:

   apartheid   township

2. In what year did all South Africans have the right to vote in a national election?

3. Describe how South Africa built a new government after apartheid.

4. What part of the Constitution refers to the rights of citizens in South Africa?

5. What was the **effect** of apartheid on black South Africans?

Activities

Look at the map of South Africa on page 153. Make a list of the countries that surround it and each country's capital city.

• •

Suppose you were a South African voting for the first time. **Write** a letter to a friend in the United States explaining how it felt.

Making Decisions

Making **decisions** is a skill that people use every day. Making a decision is the same as making a choice. Decisions may be simple, like deciding what clothes to wear, or more difficult, like deciding where to live. Whether simple or difficult, to make a good decision you have to know what your goal is.

> **VOCABULARY**
>
> decision

LEARN THE SKILL

Follow these steps to make a decision.

1. **Identify a goal.**
   Here is an example. Jimmy wants to join a school club. His goal is to learn a new skill. Students are starting a chess club and a poetry club. Jimmy must decide which club to join.

2. **Gather information.**
   Jimmy asks students from each group what activities they plan to hold. The chess club will practice twice a week during lunch hour. They will also attend competitions in different cities around the state. The poetry club meets after school. They promise to print a book of poems and hold readings at the local library.

3. **Identify the options.**
   If Jimmy joins the chess club he could learn more about the game, meet new people at competitions, and travel to other cities. If he joins the poetry club he could have his poems printed and read them in front of audiences at the library.

4. **Predict the consequences of each option.**
   Each option has a consequence, or result. Playing chess is a skill Jimmy would like to learn. However, it would mean a lot of practice. Also, he is not sure if he can travel to all the competitions.

   Jimmy likes to write poetry and would enjoy seeing his poems in a book. But the club meets after school and he might miss the bus home. Also, he is

nervous about reading aloud in front of an audience.

5. **Make the decision that best helps you reach your goal.**
Although Jimmy enjoys writing poetry, his goal is to learn a new skill. He decides to sign up for the chess club and attend as many competitions as he can.

TRY THE SKILL

Suppose your family is planning a vacation somewhere in the Southeast. Where would you go? One possible choice is Colonial Williamsburg in Virginia. There you can visit historic buildings and see how people lived during colonial times. Your other choice is the Everglades in Florida. On this trip, you can canoe, hike, or watch wildlife, such as alligators.

One thing to keep in mind is the weather. It has been rainy in the Southeast lately. You might have to cancel a trip to the Everglades. But if it rains on your visit to Colonial Williamsburg, you can go inside the different buildings.

Follow the steps on the previous page to make your decision. Then answer the questions below.

1. What is your goal?

2. What are the possible options and their consequences?

3. What is the best choice and why?

4. How can decision-making skills help you in your daily life?

EXTEND THE SKILL

Understanding how to make decisions can also help you to understand history. People in the past needed to make decisions, just as we do. The choices may have been different, but the process was the same. In Lesson 2, you read about the House of Burgesses. Look back at pages 148–150 to answer these questions.

- What decision did representatives make at the Continental Congress in 1775?

- What consequences do you think resulted from their decision?

- How can understanding the decision-making process help you better understand history?

A Country Divided

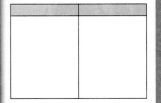

What led to the Civil War?

READING STRATEGY

Copy the chart. Use it as you read to describe the two sides of the Civil War.

Lesson Outline

• Life on a Plantation
• Reacting to Slavery
• A Nation at War

BUILD BACKGROUND

By the 1850s, much of the land used by Native Americans was taken over to create **plantations**. A plantation is a large farm where crops such as cotton or sugarcane are grown. Plantation owners in the Southeast grew cash crops they could sell to make money. In the South, cotton was the most important cash crop grown. A popular saying during the 1850s was "Cotton Is King."

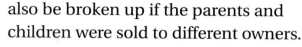
LIFE ON A PLANTATION

Each plantation was like a small town. Some of the enslaved people were blacksmiths, carpenters, and weavers, but most worked in the cotton fields. These enslaved workers were not paid for the work they did.

They worked from dawn to dusk filling burlap sacks with cotton. Even children worked in the fields. Some of the women did the housework, fixed meals, and cared for the owner's children. Only on Sundays and some holidays were they free from work.

Some slave owners were cruel. The few laws that protected enslaved workers were rarely enforced. Families could

Frederick Douglass

also be broken up if the parents and children were sold to different owners.

One of the country's best-known speakers and writers on slavery was **Frederick Douglass**. Read what he wrote about his childhood in slavery in the 1820s:

I never saw my mother . . . more than four or five times in my life . . . She was hired by a Mr. Stewart, who lived about twelve miles from my home. She made her journeys to see me in the night, traveling the whole distance on foot, after . . . her day's work. She was a field hand, and a whipping is the penalty of not being in the field at sunrise.

Slaves attempted to rebel many times. Some stole crops or destroyed property. Others escaped to the northern states, Canada, or Mexico. By the 1850s, about 1,000 people escaped every year.

READING CHECK What is a plantation?

Enslaved African Americans planted and harvested cotton on **plantations** (left).

159

REACTING TO SLAVERY

Harriet Tubman was one woman who escaped from slavery. She made her way to the home of Thomas Garrett in Wilmington, Delaware. Garrett was part of the **Underground Railroad**. This was not really a railroad, but a group of people who helped slaves escape to freedom. They often hid slaves in their homes and provided them with food for their journey.

With Garrett's help, Tubman crossed the border into Pennsylvania, where she could be free. She lived for two years in Philadelphia before she decided to try and bring other enslaved people to freedom.

Harriet Tubman

Tubman became a "conductor," or leader, for the Underground Railroad. She made as many as 19 trips back into the slave states to lead people to freedom.

As Tubman's fame spread, a group of plantation owners offered a $40,000 reward for her capture. By the time of her last trip in 1860, she had led almost 300 people to freedom.

Many other people took part in the Underground Railroad to help enslaved African Americans escape. Together they helped more than 50,000 African Americans gain their freedom.

NATIONAL GEOGRAPHIC

The Underground Railroad

Map Skill

Legend:
- Free states
- Slave states
- Territories
- Major routes of the Underground Railroad

1. What free states shared borders with slave states?

2. Which slave state had an Underground Railroad route that did not go north?

3. What geographic feature did many routes in the Middle West follow?

Debate Between States

In most Northern states, slavery was illegal. Some Northerners believed slavery was wrong and should be ended everywhere in the United States. They called for **abolition**, or an end to slavery. Abolitionists, such as Frederick Douglass and the Grimke sisters, worked to end slavery.

Many people in the Southeast believed they needed to use enslaved people to make money from their crops. Many slave owners claimed that they provided enslaved African Americans with proper food, clothing, and shelter. They argued that their enslaved workers were well cared for.

They also believed that each state, not the national government, should have the right to decide about slavery and other issues. This view was called states' rights.

Southerners began to talk about leaving the **Union**. The word *Union* describes the group of states that make up the United States. In 1861, **Abraham Lincoln** became President of the United States. Lincoln was not an abolitionist, but he believed no more slave states should be added to the Union. Some white Southerners thought he would use his position as President to end slavery everywhere.

READING CHECK ✓

What does the word *abolition* mean?

Angelina Emily and Sarah Moore Grimke (left) spoke out against slavery. Abraham Lincoln (above) became the 16th President of the United States.

A NATION AT WAR

Shortly after Lincoln became President, 11 Southern states began to form a new country called the Confederate States of America, or the **Confederacy**. Lincoln tried to persuade these states to return to the Union, but the Confederacy chose **Jefferson Davis** of Mississippi as its president. The map on this page shows how the states were divided between the Union and the Confederacy.

In April of 1861, Confederate soldiers in South Carolina fired on Union troops at Fort Sumter. This marked the begin-

Jefferson Davis

ning of war. The **Civil War**, or the "War Between the States," lasted more than four years.

Since most of the battles of the Civil War were fought in the Southeast, the Southerners knew the land better. They were also led by one of the best generals of the time, **Robert E. Lee** of Virginia.

The North had many more people, so it had a larger army. It also had more factories to make guns, uniforms, and other supplies.

On January 1, 1863, President Lincoln announced that all slaves in the

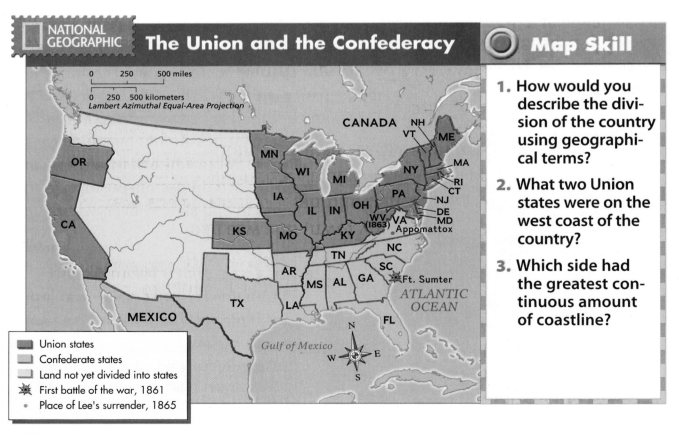

NATIONAL GEOGRAPHIC **The Union and the Confederacy** ◯ **Map Skill**

0   250   500 miles
0   250   500 kilometers
Lambert Azimuthal Equal-Area Projection

CANADA
OR
CA
MEXICO
MN WI MI IA IL IN OH
KS MO KY
TN
AR
MS AL GA SC
TX LA
FL
NH VT ME
NY MA
PA RI CT
NJ
WV (1863) VA DE MD
Appomattox
NC
Ft. Sumter
ATLANTIC OCEAN
Gulf of Mexico

N W E S

■ Union states
▢ Confederate states
▢ Land not yet divided into states
☀ First battle of the war, 1861
• Place of Lee's surrender, 1865

1. How would you describe the division of the country using geographical terms?

2. What two Union states were on the west coast of the country?

3. Which side had the greatest continuous amount of coastline?

Confederate states would be freed. This was called the **Emancipation Proclamation** (e man sih PAY shun prahk luh MAY shun). More than 180,000 freed African Americans began to fight on the side of the Union to end slavery.

Lincoln's announcement marked a turning point in the war. The Union began to win more and more battles under General **Ulysses S. Grant**. In April 1865, Lee surrendered to Grant at Appomattox Court House, Virginia.

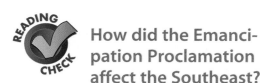

How did the Emancipation Proclamation affect the Southeast?

PUTTING IT TOGETHER

By the end of the Civil War more than 620,000 Americans had been killed. The war brought slavery to an end. However, for African Americans it was not the end of the struggle for freedom.

Confederate officer's cap

Union forage cap

Review and Assess

1. Write one sentence for each of the vocabulary words:

   abolition   Emancipation
   Civil War   Proclamation
   Confederacy   plantation
                   Union

2. What was the Underground Railroad?

3. What were some of the issues that caused the people of the United States to fight against each other?

4. Using geographical terms, describe how the country was divided during the Civil War.

5. Suppose you lived in the Southeast in the 1860s. How would you have **decided** whether your state should side with the Confederacy or the Union?

Activities

Suppose you were a conductor on the Underground Railroad. Use the maps on pages R18 and R20 to plan a route from Mississippi to New York. Describe the landforms you would find along the route.

Write a paragraph explaining how you think enslaved workers felt when they heard about the Emancipation Proclamation.

Summarizing

In the last lesson, you read about slavery and plantation life during the 1800s. Stories from history are usually filled with information. In order to understand what you read, it is helpful to summarize the information. In a **summary**, you briefly tell the most important information in your own words.

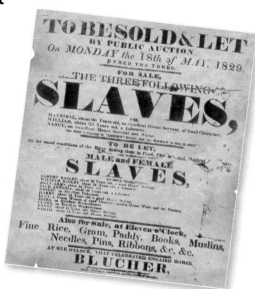

> **VOCABULARY**
>
> summary

LEARN THE SKILL

Read the passage below then follow the steps to create a summary.

Slavery became a central part of life in the Southeast. In all of the Southern states, the hard labor of enslaved African American workers kept the plantations booming. Southern plantations grew crops such as cotton, tobacco, sugar, and rice. By 1860, one-quarter of all families in the South had enslaved workers.

1. **Identify the topic.**
   As you read, look for the topic of a paragraph or section. In the paragraph above, the topic is underlined. It reads: *"Slavery became a central part of life in the Southeast."*

2. **Identify the most important information.**
   Look for facts that support the topic. Titles, headings, and key words can help you find important information. In the paragraph above, important information includes *"enslaved African American workers kept the plantations booming"* and *"By 1860, one-quarter of all families in the South had enslaved workers."*

3. **Organize the information.**
   Organize the most important information in a clear way. Only include facts that relate to the topic. The sentence *"Southern plantations grew crops such as cotton, tobacco, sugar, and rice"* does not tell you enough about the topic. Therefore, it should not be included in a summary.

4. **Write a summary in your own words.**
   Remember to keep your summary brief. A summary on the passage would read:

   "Slavery was an important part of life in the South. Plantations kept growing due to the work of enslaved African Americans. One-fourth of all Southern families had enslaved workers by 1860."

TRY THE SKILL

Read the following paragraph about the history of cotton in the Southeast.

Cotton has long been an important cash crop in the South. Early explorers found that Native Americans made clothing from cotton. During the 1700s, American colonists began to grow the crop. It was grown on both large plantations and small farms. Cotton became so important it was known as "King Cotton." A popular song was written about it.

Write a brief summary. Use your summary to answer the following questions.

1. What is the topic?

2. What is the most important information?

3. What facts are not useful to include in a summary on the history of cotton?

4. How can writing a summary help you in your studies?

EXTEND THE SKILL

The summary below is about Harriet Tubman's work on the Underground Railroad. However, it contains information that does not relate to the topic. Rewrite it, using only the most important information.

Harriet Tubman was one of the "conductors" of the Underground Railroad. She escaped from slavery, then later helped others find freedom in the North. When Tubman was a child, her father taught her about the woods. By 1860, she had led almost 300 people to freedom. A postage stamp with her picture was issued in 1978.

Use your summary to answer the following questions.

• What is the topic?

• What facts should not be included in a summary?

• How can writing a summary help you find the **main idea** when you read?

Civil Rights and the Southeast Today

VOCABULARY

segregation
civil rights
boycott

PEOPLE

Martin Luther
King, Jr.
Rosa Parks
Condoleezza Rice

READING STRATEGY

Copy the main idea
pyramid. Fill in the
main idea of this
lesson. Add sup-
porting details as
you read.

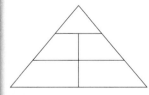

How did the struggle for civil rights change the Southeast?

Lesson Outline
• A Separate Southeast
• Fighting for Rights
• Leading to the Future

BUILD BACKGROUND

After the Civil War, African Americans still did not have the same rights as white citizens. Some continued to struggle to make a living by farming. Others moved to big cities for jobs in manufacturing and services. Throughout the region, African Americans faced **segregation**. Segregation means to set a group of people apart. Segregated cities such as **Atlanta**, Georgia and **Montgomery**, Alabama were among the first places where the struggle for equality began.

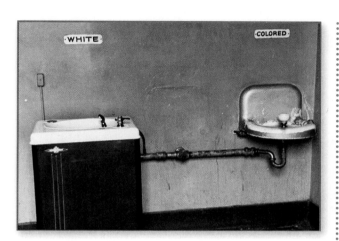

Under **segregation**, laws separated black and white Americans (above). African American children (below) stage a "sit-in" in a luncheonette in 1958. This woman (left) explains the Supreme Court's decision to her daughter.

A SEPARATE SOUTHEAST

In many Southeastern cities, African Americans were denied **civil rights**. These are the rights of people to be treated equally under the law. Under segregation, African Americans had to use separate restaurants, schools, and even water fountains. African Americans were forced to attend schools that often did not have enough teachers or books. They also had to sit in separate sections on trains and buses.

In 1954, the United States Supreme Court decided that segregation in schools broke the laws of the United States Constitution. The court said public schools must accept students of all races. However, some people still wanted to keep blacks and whites apart.

Strong community leaders would have to keep working for equal rights. One such leader was **Martin Luther King, Jr.** He was born in Atlanta in 1929. As a young man, King went to Morehouse College, an African American college in Atlanta.

The civil rights movement grew after a woman named **Rosa Parks** was arrested in 1955. Parks was arrested because she broke a law by refusing to give up her seat on a crowded bus to a white person.

What are civil rights?

Martin Luther King, Jr. led the March on Washington in 1963. The **civil rights** movement brought Americans with a common goal together.

FIGHTING FOR RIGHTS

Rosa Parks's arrest angered citizens in Montgomery, Alabama. A teacher named Jo Ann Robinson organized a **boycott**. In a boycott, people refuse to buy or use something if they disagree with the company that sells it.

For almost a year, African Americans did not ride city buses to work or school. They walked or shared cars. The boycott led to a Supreme Court decision that made the city change its law. In 1956, African Americans were allowed to sit anywhere they wanted on the buses.

The civil rights movement brought together many black and white Americans. In 1963, Dr. Martin Luther King, Jr. led the March on Washington. More than 250,000 Americans went to our country's capital to ask that all people be treated equally. King made a famous speech about his dream of equality for all people.

In 1964, King won the Nobel Peace Prize. Four years later he was killed by James Earl Ray, who disagreed with his views. In 1986, our government declared a national holiday in King's honor.

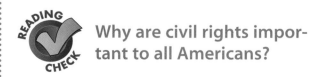 **Why are civil rights important to all Americans?**

BIOGRAPHY

Focus On: Courage

Rosa McCauley Parks was born in Tuskegee, Alabama in 1913. She was married to Raymond Parks and worked as a seamstress in Montgomery, Alabama. In 1955, she was riding home on a bus and decided she shouldn't have to give up her seat just because she was African American. The driver had her arrested and the Montgomery bus boycott began.

Parks lost her job during the boycott and many people were angry with her. She moved to Detroit and worked for congressman John Conyers. She founded the Rosa and Raymond Parks Institute for Self-Development and received many honors and awards. Today the Rosa Parks Library and Museum is located on the spot where she was arrested.

Link to Today Using a newspaper or the Internet, find a person in the news today who shows courage. Write a short report on this person's life.

THE LIFE OF ROSA PARKS	1913 Born in Tuskegee, Alabama	1955 Parks is arrested for not giving up her bus seat	1980 Parks receives Martin Luther King, Jr. Non-violent Peace Prize	2000 Rosa Parks Library and Museum opens in Montgomery
1900	**1925**	**1950**	**1975**	**2000**
LIFE AROUND THE WORLD	1920 Gandhi leads non-violent protests in India	1952 Mandela leads non-violent resistance in South Africa	1956 Supreme Court rules segregation on city buses is illegal	1963 March on Washington, D.C.	1989 People in China rally for democracy

LEADING TO THE FUTURE

Today, many government leaders in the Southeast are African American, including the mayors of almost three hundred Southeastern cities. Leaders of many ethnic groups continue to work together to protect the civil rights of all citizens. They also work to improve the region by encouraging new businesses, improving schools, and promoting tourism.

African American mayors (above) meet at an annual national conference. National Security Advisor Condoleezza Rice (below) speaks before a business council.

An Advisor to the President

One Southerner who is making a difference is **Condoleezza Rice**. She grew up under segregation in **Birmingham**, Alabama. She worked hard and did well in school. In college, Rice studied politics and relationships between countries.

President George W. Bush chose Rice to be his National Security Advisor in 2000. She gives the president advice on decisions that will affect our nation's relationship with other countries. She also studies events that occur in foreign countries and how they might affect the United States.

READING CHECK   Who is Condoleezza Rice?

170

PUTTING IT TOGETHER

Many years after the Civil War ended, African Americans still had to struggle for their rights as American citizens. In the Southeast, they led protests and boycotts to fight for their civil rights. Today, African Americans in the Southeast are leaders in government and business. They help make their communities stronger and better.

Review and Assess

1. Write one sentence for each of the vocabulary words:

   boycott   **segregation**
   civil rights

2. Who is Rosa Parks?

3. Identify some ways the Southeast was changed by the civil rights movement.

4. What role did individual citizens have in helping the bus boycott work?

5. Describe the **cause** and **effects** of the Montgomery bus boycott.

Activities

Using the map on page R18, estimate the distance people from the cities of Atlanta, Georgia and Montgomery, Alabama had to travel to join the March on Washington in 1963.

• •

Using your school library or the Internet, research Martin Luther King, Jr.'s speech *I Have a Dream*. Then **write** your own speech about the importance of protecting civil rights.

Being a Good Citizen
Helping Fight Fires

A television news show helped convince 10-year-old Braden Snyder that he could help save lives. From the show, he learned about a special camera that allows firefighters to see through thick smoke. The camera makes finding people and pets in burning buildings safer and easier. Braden decided to raise money to buy one of these machines for his local fire department.

"Firefighters save people's lives every day," says Braden. "I wanted to support that." He asked his friend, Cate Crittenden, to help him. They talked first with the Henrico County fire chief. The chief welcomed their help, but warned that it would be hard to raise the $16,000 needed to buy the camera.

Braden and Cate were not discouraged. They began by sending more than 1,000 letters to families and businesses in the community asking for money. At first only a few donations came in. Then a local newspaper and a TV station aired stories about the project. "After that," explains Braden, "more people wanted to help us."

66...It was a great honor for us to help people ...**99**

Braden and Cate went to community events, shopping malls, and school carnivals. "We talked to as many people as we could. We carried a poster with a picture of the camera and explained how it could help fight fires."

It took Braden and Cate 18 months to reach their goal. They felt very proud when they presented the camera to the fire department. Cate explains, "It was a great honor for us to help people as important as firefighters, to do their job."

Richmond, Virginia

Be a Good Citizen

Making Connections

- **What jobs in your community help protect the people there?**

- **Does your community have a fire safety program for young people? What kinds of information does it provide?**

Talk About It!

- **How did the TV show appearance affect Braden and Cate's project?**

- **What are some ways volunteers in your city or town support firefighters, police officers, and other community workers?**

Act On It!

In the Classroom

Imagine that you have been asked to write a speech for Cate and Braden. Working in small groups, choose one person to give the speech. The rest should help write the speech, explaining the importance of firefighters' safety equipment.

In the Community

Identify a safety issue in your community. Write a letter to your local fire or police department explaining what you would do to help solve the safety problem.

VOCABULARY REVIEW

Number a sheet of paper from 1 to 5. Beside each number write the word or term from the list below that matches the description.

boycott   **council**   **segregation**
colony   **plantation**

1. a place ruled by a distant country

2. large farm where crops such as sugar-cane and cotton are grown

3. refusing to buy or use a company's product or service if you disagree with the company that sells it

4. the practice of setting one group apart from another by law

5. a group of people who meet to talk and make decisions

CHAPTER COMPREHENSION

6. Who was Sequoyah and how did he help preserve the Cherokee culture?

7. What was the Trail of Tears?

8. What was the purpose of the House of Burgesses?

9. Who was Thomas Jefferson and how did he participate in early American government?

10. Describe life for enslaved plantation workers in the South.

11. What were the causes and effects of the Civil War?

12. What was life like for African Americans after the Civil War?

13. Choose one leader in the civil rights movement and describe his or her contributions.

 ## SKILL REVIEW

14. **Reading/Thinking Skill** Predict three possible results Harriet Tubman might have considered when she decided to help other enslaved workers escape.

15. **Reading/Thinking Skill** Describe a decision you had to make and the steps you took to make it.

16. **Reading/Thinking Skill** Why do you think Rosa Parks decided to break the segregation laws?

17. **Study Skill** What is a summary?

18. **Study Skill** Summarize the reasons why a written language was created for the Cherokee.

USING A TIME LINE

1600	1700	1800	1900	2000

1619
Founding of House of Burgesses

1776
Thomas Jefferson writes the Declaration of Independence

1838–1839
Trail of Tears

1860
Harriet Tubman makes her last Underground Railroad trip

1865
Civil War ends

1955
Montgomery bus boycott begins

1963
Martin Luther King, Jr., leads March on Washington

2000
Condoleezza Rice named National Security Advisor

19. How many years passed between the founding of the House of Burgesses and the Declaration of Independence?

20. How many years were there between the end of the Civil War and the March on Washington?

Activity

Writing an Alphabet Suppose you wanted to create your own language. Write out the alphabet. Then design your own symbols to replace some or all of the letters. Write a message using your new alphabet. Trade messages and codes with a classmate and decode the message you have been given.

Foldables

Use your Foldable to review what you have learned about the history and economy of the Southeast. Without looking at the events and information recorded on your Foldable time line, see if you can mentally recall the events that occurred in this region before, during, and after the Civil War. Review your notes on the inside of your Foldable to check your responses. Record any questions that you have on the back of your Foldable and discuss them with classmates, or review the chapter to find answers.

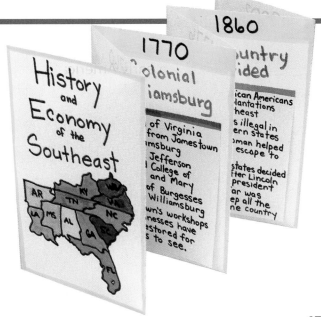

VOCABULARY REVIEW

Number a sheet of paper from 1 to 5. Beside each number write the term from the list below that best completes the sentence.

agriculture   segregation

boycott   tourist

council

1. ____ prevented African Americans from using many of the same facilities as whites.

2. A ____ might stay in a hotel while visiting a city on vacation.

3. Cash crops were one part of the Southeast's ____ industry.

4. Native Americans gathered to talk and make decisions with other groups in a ____.

5. Organizing a ____ is one way to show a company you do not agree with its activities.

TECHNOLOGY

For more resources to help you learn more about the places you read about, visit **www.mhschool.com** and follow the links for Grade 4 Regions, Unit 2.

⦿ SKILL REVIEW

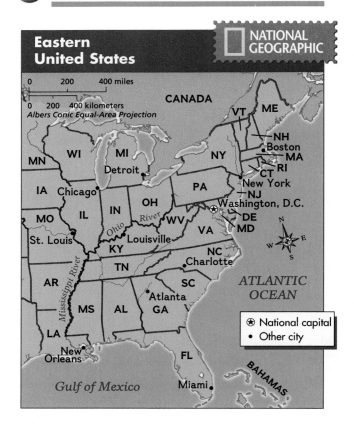

Eastern United States

0   200   400 miles

0   200   400 kilometers
Albers Conic Equal-Area Projection

NATIONAL GEOGRAPHIC

CANADA

⊛ National capital
• Other city

ATLANTIC OCEAN

Gulf of Mexico

6. **Geography Skill** Using the map scale, measure the distance escaping slaves had to travel to get from Atlanta to New York.

7. **Reading/Thinking Skill** List the steps you would use to make a decision.

8. **Reading/Thinking Skill** What are some of the other possible results that could have happened when Rosa Parks decided not to give up her seat.

9. **Study Skill** Summarize the conditions for African Americans living under slavery.

10. **Study Skill** Why might it be useful to write a summary of each lesson you read in your textbook?

1 Around 1760, a boy named Sequoyah was born in the Cherokee village of Tuskegee in what is now Tennessee. The young Sequoyah was very interested in the stories his grandfather and the village story-tellers told.

2 As Sequoyah grew older, he saw how the Native American culture was changing. His people were adopting the ways of European settlers. He worried that the old stories and ways of doing things would be lost.

3 Sequoyah had seen the settlers using an alphabet to write to each other and to remember important events. However, the letters and sounds of their language were not the same as the Cherokee language.

4 In 1809 he decided to create a written language for his own people. He began by noting each of the different sounds, or syllables, used in the Cherokee language. He gave each syllable its own symbol.

1 Which word best describes Sequoyah?

A talkative
B intelligent
C polite
D impatient

2 Sequoyah's goal in creating a written language was to—

F communicate with the settlers
G teach his language to the settlers
H preserve the culture of his people
J learn his grandfather's language

WRITING ACTIVITIES

Writing to Express Suppose you are a Cherokee who must leave the land you live on in the Southeast. **Write** a letter telling what life was like on the Trail of Tears and how it feels to be forced to leave your home.

Writing to Persuade African Americans boycotted the Montgomery buses to win their civil rights. **Write** a speech to per-suade white people to join the boycott. Explain why civil rights are important to everyone in the community.

Writing to Inform Use your textbook, school library, or the Internet to learn more about African Americans in government. Choose one person and **write** a report about his or her work in government.

LITERATURE

I WAS DREAMING TO COME TO AMERICA

Selected by Veronica Lawlor

Newcomers who came to America once had to pass through Ellis Island in New York. Between 1892 and 1954, more than 12 million immigrants stepped through its doors. In 1973, the Ellis Island Oral History Project was started. It gave immigrants the chance to describe their experiences. To date, more than 1,200 people have been interviewed. Here are some of their stories.

"Going to America then was almost like going to the moon. . . . We were all bound for places about which we knew nothing at all and for a country that was totally strange to us."

  —Golda Meir, Russia,
  Arrived in 1906,
  Age 8

I Was Dreaming
to Come to America

Memories from the Ellis Island Oral History Project
Selected and illustrated by Veronica Lawlor
Foreword by Rudolph W. Giuliani, Mayor, New York City

"When I was about 10 years old I said, 'I have to go to America.' Because my uncles were here already, and it kind of got me that I want to go to America, too. . . . I was dreaming about it. I was dreaming to come to America. . . . And I was dreaming, and my dream came true."
—Helen Cohen, Poland, Arrived in 1920, Age 20

"I never saw such a big building [Ellis Island]—the size of it. I think the size of it got me. According to the houses I left in my town, this was like a whole city in one, in one building. It was an enormous thing to see, I tell you. I almost felt smaller than I am to see that beautiful [building], it looked beautiful.

"My basket, my little basket, that's all I had with me. There was hardly any things. My mother gave me the *sorrah* [a kind of sandwich], and I had one change of clothes. That's what I brought from Europe."
—Celia Adler, Russia, Arrived in 1914, Age 12

"Unless you saw it, you couldn't **visualize** the misery of these people who came to the United States from Europe. . . . They were tired; they had gone through an awful lot of hardships. It's impossible for anyone who had not gone through the experience to imagine what it was."

—*Edward Ferro*, **Inspector**, *Ellis Island, Italy, Arrived in 1906, Age 12*

"And then we settled at Ellis Island there, we stayed there . . . My sister took sick, I took sick, my other sister took sick. . . . I had a low-grade temperature and my eyes were red. I wasn't used to the electric lights, I suppose. Different environment, you know.

"We got oatmeal for breakfast, and I didn't know what it was, with the brown sugar on it, you know. So I couldn't get myself to eat it. So I put it on the windowsill [and] let the birds eat it."

—*Oreste Teglia, Italy, Arrived in 1916, Age 12*

---

visualize (vizh′ u ə līz′) picture or imagine
inspector (in spek′ tər) an official who examined the
   immigrants

"Coming to America had meaning. I was a kid of seven and in contrast to what I had gone through, Ellis Island was like not a haven, but a heaven. I don't remember any fright when I got to Ellis Island.

"My father's dream and prayer always was 'I must get my family to America.' . . . America was a paradise, the streets were covered with gold. And when we arrived here, and when we landed from Ellis Island and [went] to Buffalo, it was as if God's great promise had been fulfilled that we would eventually find freedom."
—*Vartan Hartunian, Turkey (Armenian), Arrived in 1922, Age 7*

Write About It!

Write a paragraph that describes your experience going to a new place, for example, starting a new school or visiting a new city.

Unit 3

The Northeast

TAKE A LOOK

What is special about the climate of the Northeast?

The four seasons of the Northeast include snowy winters, rainy springs, hot summers, and colorful falls.

Explore more about the climate
of the Northeast at our Web site
www.mhschool.com

THE Big IDEAS ABOUT...

Environment of the Northeast

The Northeast may be the smallest region of our country, but its landforms and features are recognized across the United States. The seasonal climate has made it a good place for people to farm and build communities.

FROM THE MOUNTAINS TO THE COAST

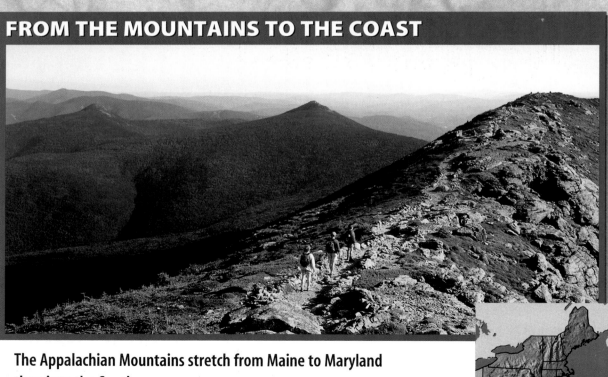

The Appalachian Mountains stretch from Maine to Maryland then into the South.

FORESTS AND FARMS

The growing season in the Northeast is shorter than in some regions, but there is plenty of land for dairy and maple syrup farms.

SEAWAYS AND CITIES

People in the Northeast have changed the land by building cities and waterways.

Make this Foldable study guide and use it to record vocabulary words and geographic locations you study in "The Environment of the Northeast."

1. Fold a sheet of notebook paper in half like a hot dog.
2. On one side only, cut along every third line to make about 10 tabs.
3. Fold a sheet of construction paper in half like a hot dog, and store your vocabulary Foldable inside.
4. Write the chapter title on the outside cover.

1

Along the Atlantic Coast

VOCABULARY

harbor
bay
glacier
fall line
broadleaf
needleleaf

What are the major landforms of the Northeast?

Lesson Outline

• The Atlantic Coastal Plain
• Mountain Ranges
• Trees and Forests

READING STRATEGY

Copy the diagram below. Fill in the similarities and differences between the Northeast and Southwest.

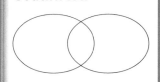

BUILD BACKGROUND

Ships loaded with goods pass through this deep **harbor** in Boston. A harbor is a sheltered place along a coast where ships can dock. This harbor makes this port in Massachusetts one of the region's busiest.

THE ATLANTIC COASTAL PLAIN

The Northeast is divided into two subregions. The New England states are Maine, Vermont, New Hampshire, Massachusetts, Rhode Island, and Connecticut. The states belonging to the Middle Atlantic subregion are New York, New Jersey, Pennsylvania, Delaware, and Maryland.

The **Atlantic Coastal Plain** is one of the landforms the Northeast shares with the Southeast. This flat land along the Atlantic coast has many deep harbors. Cities, such as New York and Philadelphia, can easily trade with other regions and countries. This has helped to make the Northeast an important trading center.

There are many **bays** that border the jagged Atlantic coast. A bay is a part of an ocean or lake that cuts deeply into the land. Find **Delaware Bay** on the map below. Clams, oysters, and crabs are found in this and other bays along the Atlantic.

READING CHECK ✓ What features make up the Atlantic Coastal Plain?

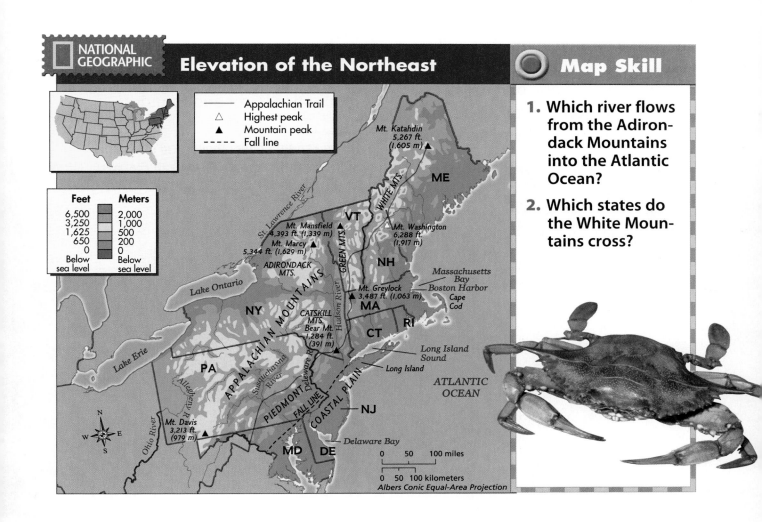

Elevation of the Northeast

NATIONAL GEOGRAPHIC

Appalachian Trail
△ Highest peak
▲ Mountain peak
----- Fall line

Feet	Meters
6,500	2,000
3,250	1,000
1,625	500
650	200
0	0
Below sea level	Below sea level

Mt. Katahdin 5,267 ft. (1,605 m) ▲
ME
WHITE MTS.
St. Lawrence River
VT
Mt. Mansfield ▲ 4,393 ft. (1,339 m)
Mt. Marcy ▲ 5,344 ft. (1,629 m)
△ Mt. Washington 6,288 ft. (1,917 m)
GREEN MTS.
ADIRONDACK MTS.
NH
Lake Ontario
Hudson River
Mt. Greylock 3,487 ft. (1,063 m) ▲
Massachusetts Bay
Boston Harbor
Cape Cod
NY
CATSKILL MTS.
Bear Mt. 1,284 ft. (391 m) ▲
MA
RI
APPALACHIAN MOUNTAINS
CT
Long Island Sound
Lake Erie
PA
Susquehanna River
Long Island
ATLANTIC OCEAN
Allegheny R.
PIEDMONT
COASTAL PLAIN
Delaware R.
FALL LINE
NJ
Ohio River
Mt. Davis 3,213 ft. (979 m) ▲
MD DE
Delaware Bay

N W E S

0   50   100 miles
0   50   100 kilometers
Albers Conic Equal-Area Projection

Map Skill

1. Which river flows from the Adirondack Mountains into the Atlantic Ocean?

2. Which states do the White Mountains cross?

MOUNTAIN RANGES

The **Appalachian Mountains** are a long chain of mountains that runs through both the Northeast and the Southeast. These mountains are found in almost every state of the Northeast.

The Appalachian Mountains are made up of several smaller groups of mountains. In the Northeast, these include the Green Mountains of Vermont, the White Mountains of New Hampshire, the Catskill Mountains of New York, and Pennsylvania's Allegheny Mountains.

The Appalachians are one of the oldest mountain ranges in the world. They were formed about 250 million years ago, when Earth's thick crust moved, causing parts of it to sag and bend. This movement pushed some of the land high above the surface. Some

scientists think that these peaks once rose miles into the sky. Yet today, the Appalachians are not very high. Wind, water, and ice have worn them down.

Thousands of years ago part of the Northeast was covered with **glaciers** (GLAY shurz). A glacier is a huge sheet of ice that slowly moves across the land. For thousands of years, glaciers moved over some of the Appalachian Mountains. The ice sheets carried tons of rock and soil away from the land over which they moved. This made the mountains lower and rounder.

Hikers can spot deer (above) and other animals along the Appalachian Trail (below).

The Appalachian Trail

All year long, people can be found hiking the **Appalachian Trail**. It stretches from Springer Mountain in Georgia to Mt. Katahdin in Maine. The trail is the longest marked footpath in the world.

Winding over peaks, rivers, and green valleys, the trail covers more than 2,000 miles. Suppose you are hiking the Appalachian Trail. How long would it take if you walked ten miles a day?

The Fall Line

East of the Appalachian Mountains lies a low plateau. This plateau meets the Atlantic Coastal Plain at the **fall line**. This line is where the hard rock of the mountains and the low plateau meet the softer rock of the

The Great Falls mark the **fall line** of the Passaic River in New Jersey (above).

Atlantic Coastal Plain. Water wears away the soft rock faster than the hard rock. This creates a drop. The diagram on this page shows a waterfall at the fall line.

READING CHECK Which mountain ranges are located in the Northeast?

A Waterfall at the Fall Line

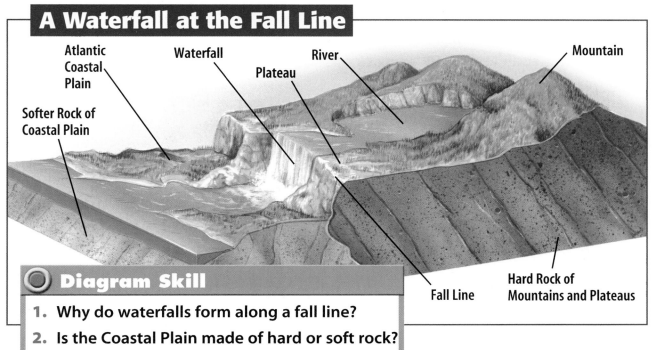

Atlantic Coastal Plain

Waterfall

Plateau

River

Mountain

Softer Rock of Coastal Plain

Fall Line

Hard Rock of Mountains and Plateaus

Diagram Skill

1. Why do waterfalls form along a fall line?
2. Is the Coastal Plain made of hard or soft rock?

Maples and oaks are **broadleaf** trees.

TREES AND FORESTS

Trees need a great deal of water to grow. The Northeast is near the ocean and gets plenty of precipitation all year.

The forests in the Northeast have two types of trees. One is the **broadleaf** tree, which has fairly wide leaves. The leaves of this tree change color in autumn. Hickories, oaks, and maples are examples.

The other kind of tree is the **needleleaf**. These leaves are long and thin, like needles. Needleleaf leaves do not change color in autumn. That is why these trees are also called evergreens. Pines, firs, and spruces are all examples of needleleaf trees.

People have been enjoying the forests of the Northeast for centuries. Read how one writer described the woods near his cabin outside of Boston.

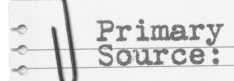
Primary Source:

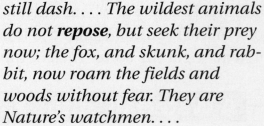

excerpt from
Walden
— *by Henry David Thoreau, 1854*

*Though it is now dark, the wind still blows and roars in the wood, the waves still dash. . . . The wildest animals do not **repose**, but seek their prey now; the fox, and skunk, and rabbit, now roam the fields and woods without fear. They are Nature's watchmen. . . .*

Why do you think Thoreau called the animals of the forest "watchmen"?

repose rest

READING CHECK

Name the two kinds of trees found in the Northeast.

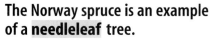
The Norway spruce is an example of a **needleleaf** tree.

PUTTING IT TOGETHER

The Atlantic Coastal Plain and mountain ranges are the Northeast's major landforms. Many of the thirteen colonies were located in the Northeast, where the Atlantic Ocean helped support the area's economy. Natural waterways are still very important to the people and businesses of the busy Northeast.

A lighthouse stands on the shores of Cape Elizabeth near Portland, Maine.

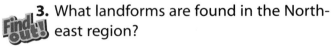
Review and Assess

1. Write one sentence using each of the vocabulary words:

bay	**glacier**
broadleaf	**harbor**
fall line	**needleleaf**

2. Where do waterfalls form?

3. What landforms are found in the Northeast region?

4. How has the Atlantic Ocean affected the **economy** in the Northeast?

5. **Compare** and **contrast** the two kinds of trees found in the Northeast.

Activities

Look at the map on page 187. Name all the harbors and bays found along the Atlantic Coastal Plain of the Northeast.

• •

Suppose you spent an afternoon hiking through a northeastern forest. **Write** a diary entry describing the trees you saw and other sights along the way.

A Colorful Environment

What is special about the environment of the Northeast?

Lesson Outline
• Why Four Seasons?
• Natural Resources

VOCABULARY

foliage
granite
quarry

READING STRATEGY

Copy the word web below. Fill in four resources found in the Northeast.

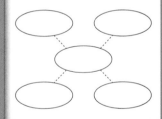

BUILD BACKGROUND

The Northeast has four seasons. They are rich and varied. The summer can be as hot and humid as a Florida summer. Some winters are as cold as winter in Alaska. In spring, millions of people visit Washington, D.C., to see cherry trees in bloom. But autumn is thought by many to be the most beautiful season in the region.

Autumn in the White Mountains in New Hampshire

WHY FOUR SEASONS?

Why does the Northeast have four seasons? One reason is that Earth spins on a tilt as it circles the sun. In July, the Northern hemisphere is tilted toward the sun, making it warmer. In December, the Northern hemisphere is cold because it is tilted away from the sun.

In autumn and winter, terrible storms called "northeasters" may hit this region. Read the following newspaper account from the *Gloucester Daily Times* in Massachusetts. A movie was later made about this same storm.

Primary Source:

excerpt from
"Storm Blindsides Cape Ann"
—by Gail McCarthy, October 1991

*A northeaster's giant tides and . . . winds **blindsided** Cape Ann on October 30, 1991, leaving a path of destruction that **demolished** homes, **devoured** waterfront property and sank a local fishing vessel with all six **hands** lost at sea.*

How does the writer describe the force of this storm?

---

blindsided: struck without warning
demolished: completely destroyed
devoured: eaten or washed away
hands: workers

Fall Foliage

Colorful **foliage** (FOH lee ihj), or leaves, are a well-known feature of the Northeast's forests during September and October. As the temperature falls with the arrival of autumn, the leaves stop making green pigment. Pigment is a substance that gives a plant its color. Without this green pigment, other colors in the leaves begin to show through. After a few weeks the leaves die and drop off the branches.

 How do seasons affect the Northeast?

Scene from the movie "The Perfect Storm"

Holstein Friesian cows are raised on this farm.

NATURAL RESOURCES
Soil

The Northeast region is rich in natural resources. The best soil for growing crops is found in the Middle Atlantic states. There farmers grow such crops as lettuce, sweet corn, onions, cabbages, and tomatoes.

In the New England states, the soil is thinner and rockier. This makes farming difficult. Though some farmers here grow crops, many more raise dairy cows, chickens, and other animals.

Trees

As you have read, the climate of the Northeast is good for trees. The trees here are not only beautiful, they are also an important natural resource. Paper, pencils, and many other products you use may have come from the trees of a Northeast forest.

Water

In the last lesson, you read about the importance of the Atlantic Ocean to life in the Northeast. There are also thousands of freshwater lakes and underground springs inland. These areas supply water for people to drink and use.

Rock and Stone

Vermont and New Hampshire have large deposits of rock, such as **granite** (GRAH nit), and stone, such as marble. Granite is a very hard rock that is used to build buildings. Rocks and stones are mined from **quarries** (KWAH reez). Quarries are places where stone is cut or blasted out. Northeastern quarries provide granite and other minerals to people all over the world.

Why do many New England farmers raise animals instead of crops?

194

Marble like the kind cut from a **quarry** in Vermont (above) was used to build the Supreme Court Building in Washington, D.C. (right).

PUTTING IT TOGETHER

The four seasons in the Northeast affect the people who live there throughout the year. The natural resources are varied and provide different ways to make a living. From rocks and stone, to trees and water, the natural resources help people of the Northeast meet their needs.

Review and Assess

1. Write one sentence for each of the vocabulary words:

   **foliage   quarry
   granite**

2. How does the soil differ in New England and the Middle Atlantic states?

3. What makes the environment of the Northeast special?

4. How do Earth and the sun affect the climate of the Northeast?

5. **Summarize** this lesson in two paragraphs in your own words.

Activities

Make a chart listing four natural resources from this lesson. Then explain at least one way each resource is used.

• •

Write a paragraph describing your favorite season. Explain why you made that choice.

Identifying Cause and Effect

In the last lesson, you read that in New England the land is rocky and the soil is thin. This can make it difficult to grow crops. The thin soil is a **cause**. A cause is something that makes something else happen.

As a result of the thin soil, New England farmers tend to raise dairy animals. This is an **effect**. An effect is what happens as a result of something else. Identifying cause and effect allows you to connect facts and events in a meaningful way. It helps explain why things happen.

LEARN THE SKILL

Read the passage below.

Fourth-grader Enrique just got a poor grade on his science test. However, he is doing well in math. His friend Natasha got a low score on the math quiz, but she understands science. So, the two friends decide to help each other out. They meet one afternoon a week to study. As a result, Enrique's science grade goes up, and so does Natasha's math grade.

Follow these steps to identify cause and effect and learn how they work together.

1. **Identify the cause of an event.**
   In the example, Enrique and Natasha's low grades are the cause. It leads them to meet once a week to study.

2. **Identify the effect.**
   Their study meetings are the effect. They are what happens as a result of the low scores.

3. **Look to see if an effect becomes a cause.**
   Often, an effect causes something else in turn. Because Enrique and Natasha studied together, both of their grades went up. In this way, the study meetings are now the cause and the higher grades are the effect.

4. **Identify clue words.**
   Clue words can help you find causes and effects. Clue words that show causes include "because," "as a result of," and "since." Clue words that show effects include "so," "therefore," and "as a result."

TRY THE SKILL

Read another passage.

Tina has trouble finding her way around because her family just moved into a new neighborhood. Therefore, she asks some of the kids on her block to help her map out the area. Several kids agree and the group gets together for a map-making party. As a result, Tina gets a map and makes some new friends.

1. What is the cause and what are the effects?

2. Which fact might be seen as both a cause and an effect?

3. What clue words are found in the passage?

4. How might identifying cause and effect help you in your daily life?

EXTEND THE SKILL

Identifying cause and effect can also help you understand geography. It can help you understand how land changes over time. In Lesson 1, you read about the Appalachian Mountains. You may wish to look back at the lesson for help in answering the following questions.

• What caused the mountain peaks to wear down?

• How can identifying cause and effect help you understand geography?

Lesson 3

Seaways and Cities

VOCABULARY

canal
lock
suburb
urban
metropolitan area
commute

READING STRATEGY

Copy the chart below. List the ways people have changed the region's land and water.

How has the land changed in the Northeast?

Lesson Outline

- The St. Lawrence River
- Cities Rise in the Northeast

BUILD BACKGROUND

Have any buildings been constructed in your community recently? Are any new tunnels or bridges under development? Those are some of the ways people change the land to meet their needs. People have made the Northeast a region of busy waterways and bustling cities, such as **Baltimore**, Maryland.

198

THE ST. LAWRENCE RIVER

In 1959, the St. Lawrence Seaway was completed. It made it possible for ships to travel from the Atlantic Ocean to the **Great Lakes**. The cost was shared between the United States and Canada. Follow the route on the map.

A system of **canals** was built along the St. Lawrence River. A canal is a waterway dug across the land. This made it easier for large ships to travel the river. **Locks** help ships move from one level to another. A lock is a part of a canal that is closed off by gates. The water in the lock can be raised or lowered. The St. Lawrence Seaway con-

Some ships travel more than 1,000 miles along the St. Lawrence Seaway.

nects northeastern cities, such as **Buffalo**, New York, to cities in Canada, like **Montréal, Quebec**.

 READING CHECK Why were canals built on the St. Lawrence River?

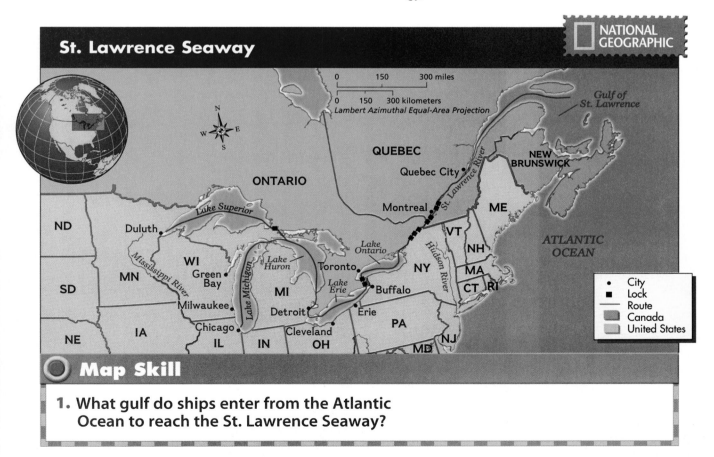

St. Lawrence Seaway

NATIONAL GEOGRAPHIC

0   150   300 miles
0   150   300 kilometers
Lambert Azimuthal Equal-Area Projection

QUEBEC

ONTARIO

Quebec City

Gulf of St. Lawrence

NEW BRUNSWICK

Montreal

St. Lawrence River

ME

Lake Superior

ND

Duluth

Lake Ontario

VT

NH

ATLANTIC OCEAN

Hudson River

WI

Green Bay

Lake Huron

Toronto

NY

MA

MN

Mississippi River

Lake Michigan

Lake Erie

Buffalo

CT RI

SD

MI

Milwaukee

Detroit

Erie

PA

IA

Chicago

Cleveland

NJ

NE

IL

IN

OH

MD

Legend:
- City
- Lock
- Route
- Canada
- United States

Map Skill

1. What gulf do ships enter from the Atlantic Ocean to reach the St. Lawrence Seaway?

CITIES RISE IN THE NORTHEAST

Perhaps the greatest change in the Northeast has been the creation of large cities. Buildings, highways, bridges, and tunnels were constructed as newcomers came to the region. Today, Boston, New York, Philadelphia, and Washington, D.C., are some of the largest cities in the Northeast and the country.

These cities are so large, **suburbs** have been created around them. A suburb is a community that is located just outside a city. People began moving to suburbs in the 1920s when **urban** areas, or cities, grew more crowded.

Metropolitan Areas

An urban area and its suburbs make up a **metropolitan area**. The Northeast has more metropolitan areas than any other region.

New forms of transportation made growth of metropolitan areas possible. Subways, railroads, and cars could carry travelers in and out of cities quickly. People no longer needed to live close to where they worked. Instead they could **commute**, or travel back and forth, each day.

Solving a Problem

In 2001, New York City leaders faced the problem of what to do with worn-out subway cars. Delaware leaders offered to sink about 400 of the old cars into the waters off their coast.

Some people are concerned that the subway cars will leak dangerous mineral fibers into the water. Others note the cars were cleaned before they were dumped. They believe the cars are not a threat to the environment.

READING CHECK Why do suburbs develop?

The George Washington Bridge connects New York City to New Jersey.

PUTTING IT TOGETHER

Great changes have affected the land in the Northeast. Waterways were enlarged to increase shipping and trade. Homes, stores, and offices were built as urban areas developed. High-ways connected cities to suburbs. With all these changes, the people of the Northeast must care for their land and conserve natural resources as metropolitan areas increase.

Off the Delaware coast, these subway cars serve as a reef, or shelter, where fish can live.

Review and Assess

1. Write one sentence for each of the vocabulary words:

   canal   **metropolitan area**
   commute   **suburb**
   lock   **urban**

2. Name the seaway that connects the Atlantic Ocean to the Great Lakes.

3. How have people changed the land in the Northeast?

4. How can seaways and canals help the **economy** of a region?

5. How did New York City leaders **solve** the **problem** of what to do with old, unused subway cars?

Activities

Look at the map on page 199. Using the map scale, find out how many miles a ship would travel along the seaway from Erie, Pennsylvania to Quebec City, Canada.

• •

Suppose you are a farmer who lives near a growing city. **Write** a letter to a friend describing how you feel about this rapid growth.

VOCABULARY REVIEW

Number a sheet of paper from 1 to 5. Beside each number write the word or term from the list below that matches the description.

fall line   **metropolitan area**

foliage   **suburb**

harbor

1. a city and its surrounding towns
2. a sheltered place along a coast
3. a community located just outside a city
4. the place where waterfalls form
5. the leaves of a tree

CHAPTER COMPREHENSION

6. What states make up the Northeast of the United States?
7. What is a bay?
8. How did the Appalachian Mountains form in the Northeast?
9. What footpath stretches more than 2,000 miles from Maine to Georgia?
10. How do waterfalls form?
11. What are the two main types of trees found in the Northeast?
12. How do locks help ships move through one level of a canal to another?
13. Name two ways people have changed the land of the Northeast.

 ## SKILL REVIEW

14. **Reading/Thinking Skill** What caused the Appalachian Mountains to be lower and rounder than most mountains?
15. **Reading/Thinking Skill** What effect did harbors and canals have on trade?
16. **Reading/Thinking Skill** What causes some leaves to change colors?
17. **Reading/Thinking Skill** How did the St. Lawrence Seaway affect the Great Lakes?
18. **Reading/Thinking Skill** What effect was caused by people moving out of urban areas?

USING A CHART

19. Where did the fewest people live in the years 1990 and 2000?

20. Which city had the largest increase in population between 1990 and 2000?

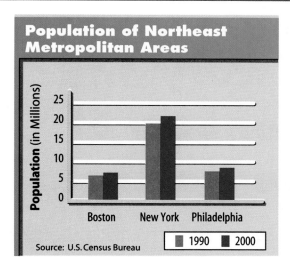

Population of Northeast Metropolitan Areas

Source: U.S. Census Bureau

Activity

Writing About the Economy The land, environment, and natural resources of the Northeast all contribute to the region's economy. Research the dairy farming industry, and **write** a paragraph explaining its importance to this region.

Foldables

Use your Foldable vocabulary book to review what you have learned about the environment of the Northeast. Use your vocabulary book to quiz yourself. Look at the words on the tabs of your Foldable and see if you can remember something about each word, then apply them to the Northeast region of the U.S. Look under the tab to check your answers. Record any questions that you have on the back of your Foldable, and discuss them with classmates, or review the chapter to find answers.

glacier
harbor
broadleaf
foliage
suburb
bay
fall line
commute
needleleaf
quarry

6

THE Big IDEAS ABOUT...

History and Economy of the Northeast

Before European settlers arrived, the Northeast was home to dozens of Native American groups. Later colonies formed, immigrants arrived, and new industries expanded. Today, the Northeast is still changing.

A NATIVE AMERICAN NATION

Descendents of Northeastern Native Americans preserve their heritage.

SETTLERS FIGHT FOR FREEDOM

George Washington leads troops during the American Revolution.

NEW PEOPLE AND INDUSTRIES

Many immigrants to the United States arrived at Ellis Island.

FOCUS ON THE FUTURE

Transportation is one of the important issues for the Northeast's future.

Foldables

Make this Foldable study guide and use it to record what you learn about the "History and Economy of the Northeast."

1. Fold a sheet of 8 $\frac{1}{2}$" x 11" paper in half like a hamburger, but leave one side of the paper 1" longer than the other.

2. Make one cut in the middle of the short side, dividing it into two equal sections.

3. Write "Northeast" on the 1" tab, and label the two large tabs "History" and "Economy."

The Iroquois Confederacy

Find Out!

How did Native Americans of the Northeast live and work together?

Lesson Outline
- Uniting the Iroquois
- Life Among the Iroquois
- The Iroquois Today

VOCABULARY

Iroquois
  Confederacy
longhouse
clan
Great Law of
  Peace
sachem

PEOPLE

Deganawida
Hiawatha

READING STRATEGY

Copy the word web you see below. Use it as you read to describe the Iroquois culture.

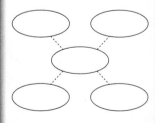

BUILD BACKGROUND

For hundreds of years, the natural resources of the Northeast supported many Native American groups. They lived off the land by fishing, hunting, and farming. They traveled the region's many rivers and lakes by canoe. One of the most powerful groups of Native Americans lived mostly in what is now the state of New York. This group was known as the Iroquois.

NATIONAL GEOGRAPHIC
Native Americans of the Northeast

0   50   100 miles
0   50   100 kilometers
Albers Conic Equal-Area Projection

▢ Iroquois Land
• City
Present-day borders are shown.

CANADA

ABENAKI

MAHICAN

HURON

MOHAWK
Lake Ontario
Onondaga
ONEIDA
MASSACHUSET
WAMPANOAG

SENECA
ONONDAGA
CAYUGA
PEQUOT

TUSCARORA
Lake Erie

ERIE

Susquehanna River
Delaware River

ATLANTIC OCEAN

SUSQUEHANNA

DELAWARE

NANTICOKE

◉ **Map Skill**

List the Native American groups that formed the Iroquois Confederacy.

UNITING THE IROQUOIS

Look at the map on this page to see where each group lived. As the region became crowded, the groups disagreed over land and natural resources. In the late 1500s, **Deganawida** (day gahn un WEE duh) a Huron Native American, tried to persuade people to stop fighting. However, they would not listen.

Deganawida decided to join with a Mohawk leader named **Hiawatha** (hi uh WAH thuh). Hiawatha called members of five groups together. He convinced them to form the **Iroquois Confederacy**. A confederacy is a union of people who join together for a common goal. Around 1722, a sixth group joined the confederacy. Read what Hiawatha said to these leaders.

READING CHECK **Why was the Iroquois Confederacy formed?**

```
Primary
Source:
```

excerpt from **a speech by Hiawatha**
— *as told by Iroquois Chief Elias Johnson-Tuscarora, published in 1957*

We must unite ourselves into one common band of brothers. We must have but one voice. Many voices make confusion. We must have one fire, one pipe and one war club. This will give us strength.

What images are used to encourage the groups to join together?

This diorama shows how the Iroquois built longhouses. Today, longhouses are only used for special ceremonies.

LIFE AMONG THE IROQUOIS

Iroquois villages were usually built near a river or lake. Small villages might have 100 people in them. Larger villages had as many as 1,000 people.

Each village was made up of **longhouses**. These were rectangular buildings made from the wood and bark of elm trees. Some were more than 200 feet long. The longhouse buildings were so important that the Iroquois called themselves the *Hodenosaunee* (hoh den oh SAH nee), or "people of the longhouse."

Dozens of families lived in each longhouse. Each family had its own living space along the sides of the longhouse. The families stored food and supplies above their living area. A center aisle ran down the length of the longhouse. Here the families built fires for cooking and heating.

Most of the villages were connected to each other by well-used trails. One trail, called the Hodenosaunee Trail, stretched more than 250 miles. It connected the villages of five of the six Iroquois groups.

Clan Leaders

Women had a great deal of power in Iroquois villages. They were the leaders of the **clans**. A clan is a group of families who share the same ancestor. Women owned the longhouses and everything in them. They also owned the land. No important decision could be made without their support. Women also chose which of the men would lead the villages.

Governing the Confederacy

Deganawida the "Peace Maker," and Hiawatha helped organize the Iroquois Confederacy around 1570.

The Confederacy leaders had to agree on a way to govern such a large group of Native Americans. The leaders outlined their new government in the **Great Law of Peace**. Under this law, council members promised that "their hearts shall be full of peace and good will, and their minds filled with a yearning for the welfare [well being] of the people."

A Grand Council of 50 men ruled the Iroquois Confederacy. Each of the groups had a set number of council members, or **sachems** (SAY chumz). Sachems were chosen by the powerful women of each group. If the sachem did not make good decisions as part of the Grand Council, the women could replace him.

The capital of the Iroquois Confederacy was **Onondaga**, in what is now New York state. The Grand Council met there every summer to discuss war,

Iroquois moccasin and bag (above). An Iroquois council meeting held in the late 1800s (below).

peace, and trade with other Native American groups. Although each Iroquois group made its own decisions, decisions made by the Grand Council affected all Iroquois groups.

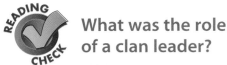

What was the role of a clan leader?

209

THE IROQUOIS TODAY

Today, there are approximately 70,000 Iroquois living in the United States. Most still live in the Northeast region, but their way of life has changed. Instead of farming and hunting, they hold many different types of jobs in the community.

Instead of longhouses, the Iroquois now live in modern houses. However, longhouses are still used for special ceremonies. Some Iroquois also speak the language of their ancestors.

The Grand Council still meets each year in Onondaga, New York, to discuss issues that affect the Iroquois.

An Enduring Game

One lasting part of Iroquois culture is now shared across the Northeast. It is the game of lacrosse. Players carry wooden sticks with nets attached at the top. They use them to shoot a small ball at a goal to score points.

Native Americans originally played this game for recreation and to settle disagreements between groups. Today lacrosse is played between groups of Native Americans, as well as at many high schools and colleges around the country and world. Players now wear helmets, gloves, and shoulder pads to protect themselves.

READING CHECK Why do you think the Iroquois carry on the traditions of their ancestors?

Traditional Mohawk (top) and Seneca (right) dances are performed at ceremonies today.

PUTTING IT TOGETHER

The Iroquois Confederacy brought six different Native American groups together. In a similar way, the 50 states of the United States form one country. Some historians think that the Iroquois Confederacy may have provided a model for our country's government.

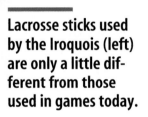

Lacrosse sticks used by the Iroquois (left) are only a little different from those used in games today.

Review and Assess

1. Write one sentence for each of the vocabulary words:

   clan　　　　　　　　**longhouse**
   Great Law of Peace　**sachem**
   Iroquois Confederacy

2. What was the Iroquois Confederacy?

3. List some of the ways the Native Americans of the Northeast worked together.

4. **Describe** the role women played in the Iroquois culture.

5. **Compare** and **contrast** the life of the Iroquois today and in the time of Hiawatha.

Activities

Use the map on page 207 to describe the relative locations of each of the Native American groups that made up the Iroquois Confederacy.

• •

Suppose you were a reporter covering the council meeting between Hiawatha and the other Native American leaders. **Write** a news story about the meeting and what it meant for the different groups.

Lesson 2

The American Revolution

Find Out!

What role did the Northeast play in the American Revolution?

Lesson Outline
• Protests in Boston
• Preparing to Fight
• The American Revolution

VOCABULARY

import
export
Patriot
Boston Massacre
Boston Tea Party
Minutemen
American
  Revolution

PEOPLE

Crispus Attucks
John Adams
Paul Revere
William Dawes
George Washington

READING STRATEGY

Copy the chart you see below. Use it to follow the sequence of events in this lesson.

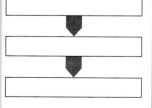

BUILD BACKGROUND

Like colonists in Virginia, settlers were unhappy in the Massachusetts colony of the Northeast. English colonists, known as Pilgrims, started the Massachusetts colony at Plymouth in 1620. They left England to seek freedom to practice their religion. By the middle 1700s, more than 16,000 people lived in Boston, the colony's largest city. Boston would play an important role in the fight for independence from Great Britain.

Reconstruction of Plimoth Plantation, Massachusetts, today

212

PROTESTS IN BOSTON

Boston's location on Massachusetts Bay made it a center for trade. Docks, ship-yards, and warehouses lined the shore. The deep water made it possible for even the largest ships to dock in the harbor. Long Wharf stretched 2,000 feet out into the water to allow ships to load and unload.

The Sons of Liberty group staged many public protests against taxes.

The colonies **imported** goods, such as tea and cloth, from England. Imported goods are bought from another country. The colonies also **exported** raw materials, such as lumber, to Britain. Exported goods are sold to another country.

British Military in Boston

By the middle 1700s, Boston was a bustling city crowded with sailors, craftsmen, and merchants. There were also many British soldiers. Britain sent them after colonists began to protest the colony's taxes. The colonists were angry that some of the goods from Britain were taxed. Colonists thought the taxes were unfair.

The colonists boycotted goods taxed by the British. They refused to drink tea from Britain. Women spun wool for clothing so they would not have to buy imported fabric. Some colonists even chased the tax collectors out of town. Colonists who protested British rule were called **Patriots**.

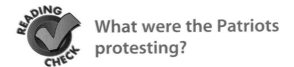

What were the Patriots protesting?

213

HISTORY MYSTERY

Do Pictures Tell the Truth?

An engraving by Paul Revere shows his view of the Boston Massacre. Does it show what really happened? Today we know the engraving did not tell the truth. The colonists were part of an angry mob armed with sticks and muskets. Many of them also threw snowballs at the soldiers. Revere did not show this because he wanted to build support for the colonists.

How do you think his engraving helped to win more support for the colonists?

PREPARING TO FIGHT

In March of 1770, a group of colonists at the Boston Custom House charged at British soldiers. The soldiers fired on the crowd. Five men were killed, including **Crispus Attucks** a former slave who was a seaman in Boston. The attack became known as the **Boston Massacre**. A massacre is the killing of many people who cannot defend themselves.

The soldiers were arrested and charged with murder. **John Adams**, a lawyer from Massachusetts, agreed to defend the soldiers.

Colonists Protest

In 1773 colonists, dressed as Native Americans, boarded a British ship and threw thousands of pounds of tea into the harbor. As a result, the British government closed the port of Boston until the colonists paid for the tea. The closed port ruined Boston's economy.

People in the other British colonies heard about the massacre and about the **Boston Tea Party**. They sent food and money to help the people of Boston. Some Patriots began gathering weapons outside of Boston and training to fight. They were known as **Minutemen** because they promised to be ready to fight at a minute's notice.

READING CHECK How did the colonists protest British taxes?

BIOGRAPHY

Focus On: Justice

John Adams was born in the Massachusetts Bay colony in 1735. He attended Harvard and taught school for several years before becoming a lawyer. Adams often took unpopular cases because he thought everyone deserved a just trial.

After the Boston Massacre, the British soldiers were arrested and brought to trial in court. Several lawyers refused to take their case, but Adams agreed to represent them. He was so successful that six of the soldiers were found innocent. The other two were released after a punishment the next day.

Adams went on to serve in the Continental Congress. During the revolution, he went to other countries to ask for help fighting Britain. Adams was the first Vice President and became the second President of the United States.

Link to Today

Use your school library or the Internet to learn about symbols used to represent justice. Choose one symbol and prepare a drawing and explanation of what it stands for.

THE LIFE OF JOHN ADAMS		1735 Born in Braintree, Massachusetts		1770 Defends British soldiers of the Boston Massacre	1789 Becomes Vice President	1797 Becomes President	1826 Dies at the age of 90
1650	**1700**		**1750**		**1800**		**1850**
LIFE AROUND THE WORLD	1699 The French settle in Louisiana		1754 French and Indian War in North America		1803 United States buys Louisiana Territory	1825 First passenger railroad in England	

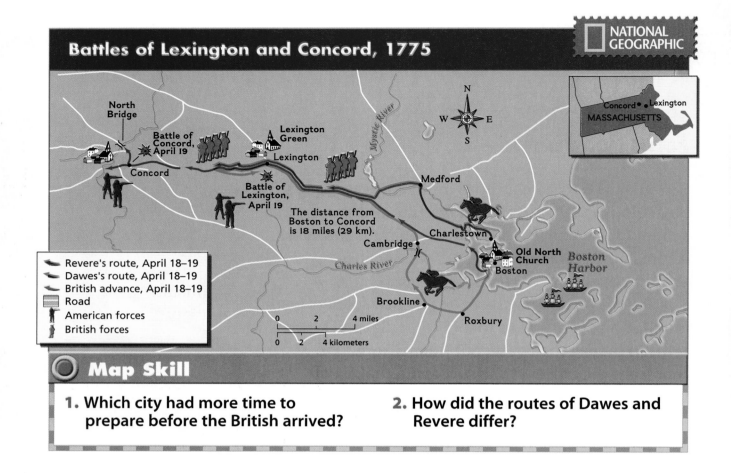

Battles of Lexington and Concord, 1775

NATIONAL GEOGRAPHIC

North Bridge

Battle of Concord, April 19

Concord

Lexington Green

Lexington

Battle of Lexington, April 19

The distance from Boston to Concord is 18 miles (29 km).

Mystic River

Medford

Charlestown

Cambridge

Charles River

Old North Church

Boston

Boston Harbor

Brookline

Roxbury

Concord • Lexington
MASSACHUSETTS

N
W E
S

Revere's route, April 18–19
Dawes's route, April 18–19
British advance, April 18–19
Road
American forces
British forces

0   2   4 miles
0   2   4 kilometers

Map Skill

1. Which city had more time to prepare before the British arrived?

2. How did the routes of Dawes and Revere differ?

THE AMERICAN REVOLUTION

The Minutemen stored muskets, gunpowder, and cannonballs in the town of Concord. On April 18, 1775, the British army decided to take the weapons away from the colonists. **Paul Revere** and **William Dawes** knew of the plan and rode to **Lexington** to alert the Minutemen.

When the British arrived, the Minutemen stood their ground. At Lexington, eight Americans died and one British soldier was wounded. By the time the British reached Concord, the supplies had been hidden and the Minutemen were better prepared.

They fired on the British, killing 73 British troops. This marked the beginning of the **American Revolution**. The war between the thirteen colonies and Great Britain had started.

An Army Forms

The colonists would now have to fight against one of the best armies in the world. Few colonists were trained as soldiers, but many volunteered to fight. In 1775, the Continental Congress asked **George Washington** to lead the army of colonists.

The army was made up of farmers, craftworkers, and merchants. They did not have fancy uniforms or even enough shoes and horses at times. Many battles were lost, but for six years, the colonists kept fighting.

In 1781, Washington's army won an important victory over the British in Yorktown, Virginia. The British were outnumbered and forced to surrender. The war went on for two more years. In 1783, at a meeting in Paris, France, Britain agreed to recognize the United States as an independent country.

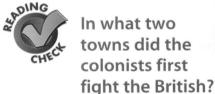

In what two towns did the colonists first fight the British?

George Washington

PUTTING IT TOGETHER

In 1787, state delegates met to discuss a new Constitution. Almost a year later the states made the new Constitution a law. The country elected Washington as its President, and each state elected representatives to Congress.

The fight for freedom from Britain was long and difficult. After the revolution, a new form of government was created for the country. Today our country is still governed by the Constitution.

Review and Assess

1. Write a sentence for the vocabulary words:

   American Revolution   **import**
   Boston Massacre   **Minutemen**
   Boston Tea Party   **Patriot**
   export

2. Who was John Adams, and what role did he play in the American Revolution?

3. What part did the Northeast play in the American Revolution?

4. What **economic** reason did the colonists have for their protests?

5. Using what you know about the army of colonists, would you have **predicted** that they would win? Why or why not?

Activities

Paul Revere is famous for having a spy use lanterns to signal whether the British were traveling from Boston by land or water to reach Lexington. Using the map on page 216, describe why this information was important.

• •

Suppose you were a newspaper reporter at the Boston Massacre. **Write** an article to let other colonies know what happened.

Drawing Inferences

Suppose you have a friend named Eddie who is not feeling well. Eddie tells you he has sniffles, a cough, and a fever. What's wrong? Based on Eddie's clues, you figure out he has a cold.

Sometimes meanings or connections are not always made clear. It can be helpful to draw **inferences** when you read or study. An inference is something you figure out based on clues and information that you already know. Making inferences can help you better understand what you read. It can also help you make sense of new information.

VOCABULARY

inference

LEARN THE SKILL

Follow the steps below to draw an inference.

1. **Identify clues.**
   Suppose a family has just moved into the house next door to yours. When you go over to introduce yourself, you find them unpacking their things. In one box, they have a baseball bat, balls, and a glove. In another box, they have packed in-line skates and tennis rackets. The family tells you they plan to put up a basketball hoop in their yard. They ask if you would like to play sometime.

2. **Compare the clues to information you already have.**
   You know that bats, balls, gloves, skates, rackets, and hoops are all sports equipment. You also know that people often own items based on their interests.

3. **Make an inference.**
   You figure out that your new neighbors enjoy playing sports. To make this inference, you put the clues together with the information you already had. Drawing inferences is like "reading between the lines."

TRY THE SKILL

In the last lesson, you also read about events leading up to the American Revolution. Read the following passage. Then answer the questions below.

Colonists in Massachusetts wanted to have a say in how they were governed. They wanted to make their own decisions about taxation. The people of Boston also did not like having the British army in their city. A group of colonists staged a protest against the British. It became known as the Boston Tea Party.

1. What inference can you make about the colonists and British rule?

2. What clues did you use?

3. What information did you already have that helped you make the inference?

4. How can drawing inferences help you better understand what you read?

EXTEND THE SKILL

Knowing how to draw inferences can also help you understand history. It helps connect facts and events from the past. Read the following passage about the Minutemen. Make an inference and answer the questions below.

Minutemen were volunteer soldiers who fought in the American Revolution. They had to be ready to fight at a moment's notice. They were farmers, craftworkers, and businessmen. The Minutemen did not have fancy uniforms or even enough shoes and horses.

• What inference can you make about the Minutemen and their experience as soldiers?

• How can drawing inferences help you better understand history?

The Industrial Revolution

How did the Industrial Revolution change the Northeast?

Lesson Outline
- A Growing Revolution
- From Farms to Factories
- Coming to America

VOCABULARY

Industrial Revolution
invention
telegraph
tenement
sweatshop

PEOPLE

Samuel Slater
Hannah Wilkinson Slater
Samuel Morse

READING STRATEGY

Copy the chart below. Fill in the main ideas at the top, then add supporting details below.

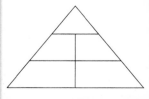

BUILD BACKGROUND

In 1783, the United States gained its independence. A new nation rose out of the American Revolution. Many people wanted our country to grow quickly. They looked to new methods of manufacturing and transportation. A different kind of revolution began to develop. It was a revolution of machines that changed our country forever.

Slater Mill in Pawtucket, Rhode Island

A GROWING REVOLUTION

In the middle 1700s, most Americans lived and worked on farms. One hundred years later, many people lived in towns and cities. They worked in factories and stores. They had better ways to travel and new products to buy.

What happened during those hundred years? The **Industrial Revolution**. From the late 1700s to the middle 1800s, new power-driven machines replaced hand tools. Goods were produced faster and in greater numbers. New industries were created and our economy expanded.

The Industrial Revolution began in England. New methods and machines changed factory work and travel. Coal was used instead of wood as a source of energy. Steam engines powered boats and railroads.

Samuel Slater

By the late 1700s, changes began to develop in the United States too. **Samuel Slater** was called the "Father of the American Industrial Revolution." Born in England, Slater settled in Rhode Island to live and work.

Samuel Slater

There he built the Northeast's first successful textile, or cloth, mill in 1793.

Hannah Wilkinson Slater, Samuel's wife, also played an important role in the Industrial Revolution. She created a new way to spin thread. Her **invention**, cotton sewing thread, made it easier to sew cloth. An invention is something that is created for the first time.

Other mills were built across the region. Hundreds of young women from nearby farms took jobs spinning cloth. Waterfalls were used to power the machines they operated. These machines allowed one person to make as much cloth in one day as many people would make working by hand. The growing textile industry helped the United States remain independent from Great Britain.

READING CHECK Why was the Industrial Revolution important?

Yarn was wound on spindles and used to make cloth.

221

FROM FARMS TO FACTORIES

Factories soon became as important as farms. By the middle 1800s, factories across the Northeast produced goods of all kinds—from shoes to tools to furniture.

Buyers of these goods were not always close by. Americans realized they needed faster ways to travel and ship goods around the country.

Exploring TECHNOLOGY

Riding the Rails

In 1831, Robert Livingston Stevens returned from a business trip to England with very special cargo. He brought back America's first steam locomotive. This was a locomotive with an engine powered by steam. On November of that year, his train, the *John Bull*, made a trial run in New Jersey.

Stevens spent the next few years laying tracks for a railroad line. He designed the inverted T rail. It was soon used throughout the world. Stevens's line, the Camden and Amboy Railroad, became one of the first successful railways in the country.

Activity

Write a newspaper article that describes how witnesses might have reacted during the trial run of *John Bull*.

Morse invented a code (above) for his **telegraph** (right).

Improvements and Inventions

The Erie Canal was completed in 1825. It linked Lake Erie to the Hudson River. In 1837 **Samuel Morse** of Charlestown, Massachusetts, invented the **telegraph**. This machine sends electrical signals through wires. It allowed people to communicate over long distances.

Why was the telegraph important?

DATAGRAPHIC

Waves of Change

As the Industrial Revolution spread across our country, new inventions brought Americans closer together. Study the time line and map below. Then answer the questions.

Inventions of the Industrial Revolution

1780 — 1810 — 1840

1793 — Samuel Slater opens textile mill

1825 — Erie Canal completed

1831 — *John Bull* makes its first run

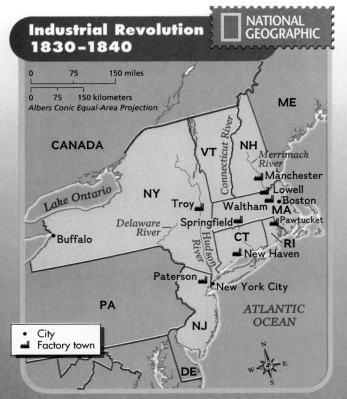

Industrial Revolution 1830–1840

NATIONAL GEOGRAPHIC

0   75   150 miles
0   75   150 kilometers
Albers Conic Equal-Area Projection

CANADA
Lake Ontario
NY
Troy
Buffalo
Delaware River
Springfield
Paterson
PA
NJ
DE
ME
VT
NH
Connecticut River
Merrimack River
Manchester
Lowell
Waltham
Boston
MA
Pawtucket
CT
RI
New Haven
Hudson River
New York City
ATLANTIC OCEAN

• City
⚒ Factory town

QUESTIONS:

1. Which state had the greatest number of factory towns in 1840?
2. The Lowell factory was built near which river?
3. Did the *John Bull* make its first run before or after the Erie Canal was completed?

TECHNOLOGY
To learn more, visit our Web site: **www.mhschool.com**

223

COMING TO AMERICA

The growth of factories and businesses meant that more workers were needed. Immigrants looking for new opportunities came to our country in large numbers. Between 1820 and 1920, about 36 million people entered the United States.

Many immigrants crossed the Pacific Ocean and landed in the West. Many more sailed across the Atlantic Ocean to New York City. From 1892 to 1954, **Ellis Island** in New York Harbor was their first stop.

Tenement Life

Most newcomers arrived in New York with little money. Often they lived in crowded neighborhoods lined with **tenements**. A tenement is a poorly built apartment building. Usually these buildings were cramped and unsafe.

Tenement life was hard. The buildings had few windows. There was little light or air in the apartments. Often five or six people would sleep in one small room. Outside the streets were dirty with coal dust.

Earning a Living

Immigrants did all sorts of jobs to support themselves. Some sold goods from carts in the streets. Others worked in the garment, or clothing, industry.

During the late 1800s and early 1900s, New York City became the center of the country's garment industry. The Industrial Revolution made this possible. Instead of sewing a shirt or dress by hand, workers used sewing machines. Even immigrants who spoke

Many immigrants sailed past the Statue of Liberty when they arrived (right). Some went on to work in crowded **sweatshops** (below).

no English could be taught to use a sewing machine quickly. Garment workers were men, women, and even children. Their jobs included sewing, cutting, tailoring, and pressing.

Sweatshops

Clothing factories became known as **sweatshops**. In the summer, the temperature inside the sweatshops could reach 120°F. Sweatshop workers labored for 12 to 14 hours a day for very low pay. Although the conditions were terrible, most immigrants were determined to make a better life for themselves in their new country.

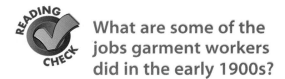

What are some of the jobs garment workers did in the early 1900s?

The Tenement Museum in New York City shows what life was like for many immigrants.

PUTTING IT TOGETHER

By 1900, the United States was a leader in manufacturing with the help of new machines and immigrant workers. Today people still come to the United States looking for opportunities. These new Americans enrich our country and way of life.

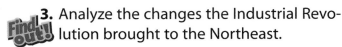

Review and Assess

1. Write one sentence for each of the vocabulary words:

   Industrial Revolution   **telegraph**
   invention   **tenement**
   sweatshop

2. Who was Samuel Morse?

3. Analyze the changes the Industrial Revolution brought to the Northeast.

4. How did **technology** aid the Industrial Revolution in the 1800s?

5. Name three **effects** of the Industrial Revolution in the Northeast.

Make a chart listing the people and inventions from the lesson. Explain the importance of each.

• •

Suppose you are an immigrant who arrives in New York City in 1900. **Write** a letter home describing your experience.

225

The City of Mumbai

VOCABULARY

migrate

Why did workers move to Mumbai in the 1800s?

Lesson Outline
- Island City
- Mumbai Today

READING STRATEGY

Copy the chart you see here. Use it to fill in events from Mumbai's history.

BUILD BACKGROUND

Architect John Begg described the city of Bombay, **India**, now known as **Mumbai** (moom BIGH), this way in 1920: "Bombay is energetic, exuberant [lively], sparkling, and has building stones of many kinds and colors. . . ."

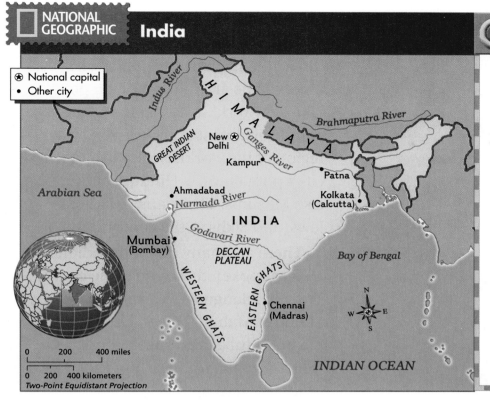

National capital
Other city

Indus River

HIMALAYA

Brahmaputra River

GREAT INDIAN DESERT

New Delhi

Ganges River

Kampur

Patna

Arabian Sea

Ahmadabad

Narmada River

Kolkata (Calcutta)

INDIA

Mumbai (Bombay)

Godavari River

DECCAN PLATEAU

Bay of Bengal

WESTERN GHATS

EASTERN GHATS

Chennai (Madras)

INDIAN OCEAN

0   200   400 miles
0   200   400 kilometers
Two-Point Equidistant Projection

1. **Mumbai is on the coast of what body of water?**

2. **Using the map scale, find the distances from Mumbai to New Delhi and to Kolkata.**

ISLAND CITY

Look at the map to find the city of Mumbai. Bridges connect the city to India. Mumbai was founded as a trading post by Portuguese traders in the 1530s. The city was originally called Bombay from the Portuguese words for "fair bay."

In 1995, the city's name was officially changed to Mumbai after the Hindu goddess Mumba. Hinduism is the major religion of India.

Trade Center

Mumbai has been a major shipping and trading center for most of its history. The country's first cotton mill was built in 1854. Many people **migrated** or moved to the city in hopes of finding a job at the mill. By 1860, Mumbai had become the largest cotton market in India.

The American Civil War, which you read about in Chapter 4, helped the cotton market in Mumbai. During the Civil War, the Union prevented the Confederacy from selling their cotton crops to other countries. As a result, Mumbai became the main supplier of cotton to the rest of the world.

A *sari* is a style of dress worn by women in India. Colorful cloth is draped around the body.

READING CHECK **Why did many people migrate to Mumbai?**

Automobile manufacturing is one of the city's industries.

MUMBAI TODAY

Today the cotton industry is still important in Mumbai. Other major industries in the city include automobile manufacturing, engineering, publishing, and food processing. Mumbai is also the center of India's high-technology industry. Factories there produce parts such as electronic chips, which are used in computers and other high-tech products.

Another booming industry for the city is entertainment. Mumbai produces the second highest number of films in the world each year, after the United States. Because of this, Mumbai is sometimes known as the "Hollywood of India."

Many People, Many Languages

Mumbai is the sixth-largest city in the world. Its current population is estimated to be around 15 million people. Like New York City, Mumbai is home to people of almost every religion and region of the world. Nearly half of the city's population is Hindu, but there are also Muslims, Christians, Buddhists, Jews, and Sikhs in the community.

There are many different Indian languages spoken throughout the country. The main language of Mumbai is Marathi (Mah RUH tee). However, people in Mumbai also speak Hindi, as well as Arabic, Chinese, English, and other languages.

READING CHECK ✓ What are the major industries in Mumbai today?

Many people arrive by train to work and shop.

228

PUTTING IT TOGETHER

Mumbai has tried to reduce overcrowding and the problems that result from it. Recently, the government set up a new plan to manage the city's land use, housing, and transportation. The government hopes this plan will improve life in this big city.

Exotic spices, such as curry, are bought and traded in outdoor markets.

Review and Assess

1. Write one sentence for the following vocabulary word:

   migrate

2. Why did Mumbai become the world's main supplier of cotton in the 1860s?

3. Explain why workers migrated to Mumbai in the middle 1800s.

4. How has the **economy** of Mumbai changed over time?

5. **Compare** and **contrast** Mumbai with New York City.

Activities

Using an almanac, research the populations of Mumbai, New York City, and Tokyo, Japan. Make a bar graph that compares the number of people in each city.

Suppose you are a historian. **Write** a brief history of Mumbai from the 1800s to the present.

Using Special Purpose Maps: Distribution Maps

So far, you have studied physical and political maps of different parts of the United States. These are common kinds of maps that tell us about the land, water, and cities of our country. Other maps in the book serve a special purpose. They focus on specific kinds of information, such as rainfall or population.

Distribution maps are one kind of special purpose map. They show how something is spread out over an area. Some of the things distribution maps can feature include language, climate, and products.

LEARN THE SKILL

Study Map A on this page. Then follow the steps below to read distribution maps.

1. **Identify the title of the map.**
   The title of this map is Map A: New York Population, 1900. In the last lesson, you read about immigrants settling in New York during the early 1900s. Map A shows how people were spread across the state at that time.

2. **Locate symbols and a map key.**
   Dots appear on the map. The map key explains that each dot represents 5,000 people. They show exactly how people were distributed across New York.

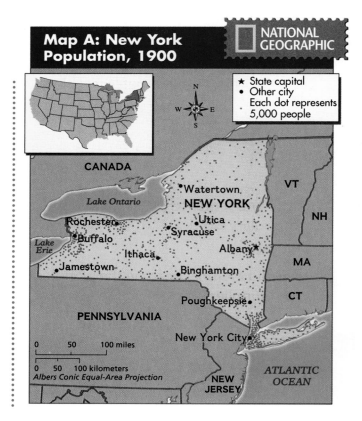

Map A: New York Population, 1900

NATIONAL GEOGRAPHIC

★ State capital
• Other city
· Each dot represents 5,000 people

CANADA

Lake Ontario

•Watertown

NEW YORK

VT

NH

Rochester•

Lake Erie

•Buffalo

•Utica

Syracuse

Albany★

MA

Ithaca

•Jamestown

•Binghamton

CT

Poughkeepsie•

PENNSYLVANIA

New York City•

0   50   100 miles

0   50   100 kilometers
Albers Conic Equal-Area Projection

NEW JERSEY

ATLANTIC OCEAN

TRY THE SKILL

Map B shows how the population of New York is spread out today. Use Maps A and B to answer the following questions.

1. Why is this a distribution map?

2. What symbol on the map is used to show population? What does it represent?

3. Where was most of the population located in 1900?

4. Where is most of the population located today?

5. **Compare** and **contrast** Maps A and B.

6. How can distribution maps help you better understand history?

EXTEND THE SKILL

Draw a population distribution map for your school. First outline the classrooms in your school. Then use dots to show how many students are in each classroom. Use one dot for every four students. Then answer the following questions.

- How many students are in your school?

- How are they spread out across the different classrooms?

- What other kinds of subjects could you show on a distribution map for your area?

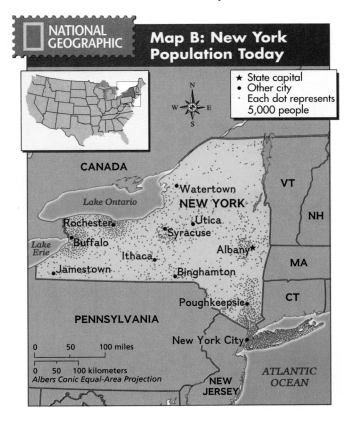

NATIONAL GEOGRAPHIC

Map B: New York Population Today

★ State capital
● Other city
· Each dot represents 5,000 people

N W E S

CANADA

Lake Ontario

VT

NEW YORK

•Watertown

•Utica

•Syracuse

Rochester•

Lake Erie

•Buffalo

Ithaca•

Albany★

NH

MA

•Jamestown

•Binghamton

CT

Poughkeepsie•

PENNSYLVANIA

0   50   100 miles

0   50   100 kilometers
Albers Conic Equal-Area Projection

New York City•

NEW JERSEY

ATLANTIC OCEAN

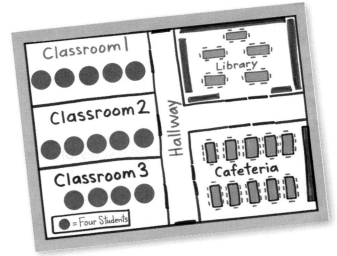

Lesson 5

The Northeast Today

What challenges face the Northeast today?

VOCABULARY

megalopolis
Boswash
terrorism

PEOPLE

George W. Bush

READING STRATEGY

Copy the chart below. Write the main idea of this lesson. As you read, add supporting details.

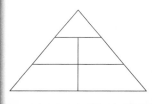

Lesson Outline

• One of Many Gateways

• Growing Cities and Suburbs

• Terrorists Strike

BUILD BACKGROUND

Based on size, the Northeast is the smallest area of our country. However, it is big in many other ways. In the 2000 Census, three of the ten largest metropolitan areas by population were located in the Northeast. The Northeast continues to grow in many other ways as well.

232

ONE OF MANY GATEWAYS

Today immigrants to the United States arrive in many cities across our country. However, cities such as New York and Boston are still among the top ten places to welcome newcomers into the country. More than one million immigrants moved to New York City between 1990 and 2000.

Most immigrants to the Northeast today come from different places than earlier generations of immigrants. Hispanic and Asian people are the most common immigrants to the Northeast. The Dominican Republic, Ecuador, China, and Korea are just some of the places they come from.

Like earlier groups, these newcomers retain parts of their heritage while trying to fit into their new home. Many build communities with other immigrants where they can shop, speak their language, and get news about their former home.

The work done by immigrants has changed over time as well. Some still take low-paying jobs, but today they

Immigrants from the Dominican Republic (top) and Muslim countries (above) celebrate their cultures with parades.

may also come to attend school, work in the technology industry, or get jobs that use their experience with other cultures and languages.

READING CHECK What are some countries where immigrants today are likely to come from?

233

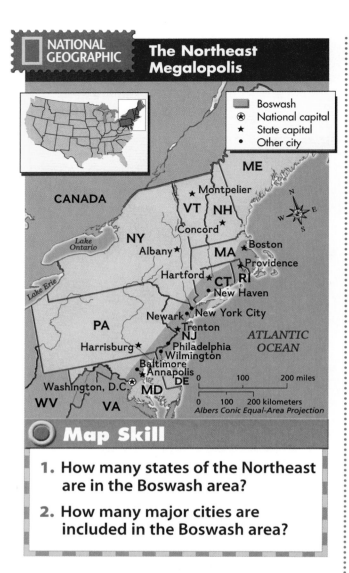

NATIONAL GEOGRAPHIC

The Northeast Megalopolis

Boswash
⊛ National capital
★ State capital
• Other city

CANADA

ME

★ Montpelier

VT   NH

Concord ★

NY

Lake Ontario

Albany ★

MA

Boston

Hartford ★   CT   RI

Providence

New Haven

Newark   New York City

Trenton ★

NJ

PA

Harrisburg ★

Philadelphia

Wilmington

Baltimore

★ Annapolis

ATLANTIC OCEAN

Washington, D.C. ⊛   DE

MD

WV   VA

0   100   200 miles

0   100   200 kilometers

Albers Conic Equal-Area Projection

◯ Map Skill

1. **How many states of the Northeast are in the Boswash area?**

2. **How many major cities are included in the Boswash area?**

GROWING CITIES AND SUBURBS

Many of our country's largest and oldest cities are located along the Northeastern Atlantic Coast. These cities had a head start on growth during the Industrial Revolution. Today, they continue to grow and change.

Most of the cities are close together and have large populations. As the cities became crowded and conditions changed, more people began moving to the suburbs. Today, many businesses have grown up around these suburbs. Smaller towns have encour-

High speed trains can help reduce traffic by carrying more people at faster speeds than cars.

aged companies to move there because the towns are close to major cities, but do not cost as much.

As homes and companies spread out from the center of large cities, they also spread closer to other cities along the coast. As they grew closer, these cities formed a **megalopolis**. A megalopolis is a group of cities so close together that they can be thought of as one huge community.

In the Northeast, people can go from one city to another quickly and easily. Some people even call the area of the Northeast between Boston and Washington **Boswash**. Use the map on this page to explain why they use this nickname.

Managing a Megalopolis

People who live in Philadelphia, Pennsylvania may work in Newark,

person in them. Buses, vans, and carpools can use these lanes to travel through traffic faster.

Cities also charge tolls on roads, bridges, and tunnels. Some of these fees are higher during the busiest times of day to persuade people to use mass transit. The cities sometimes charge less money for drivers who use small electronic cards to automatically pay the tolls instead of using cash.

 Why is transportation a concern in cities today?

Traffic around Boston is heaviest during rush hours.

New Jersey or in New York City. Companies with many employees often have offices in several cities and even states. This makes transportation one challenge the Northeast faces.

One solution to this challenge is mass transit. Hundreds of buses and light-rail trains carry suburban residents to their jobs in large cities. High-speed trains travel between large cities such as Boston and New York. These trains can go more than 150 miles per hour and make very few stops along the route.

Cities are also trying to change people's attitudes about commuting by car. Some highways have lanes set aside for vehicles with more than one

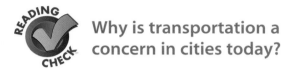

The Cost of Commuting

Some experts think charging different fees on roads will encourage the use of mass transit and new technology to reduce traffic. At the George Washington Bridge, drivers entering New York City with electronic cards pay $5 during rush hours and $4 at other times. Drivers who pay cash are always charged $6.

Activity

Suppose you drove across the bridge to the city five times a week. Compare the costs of paying with cash and with the electronic card for four weeks. Would this convince you to use the new technology?

President George W. Bush addresses Congress.

TERRORISTS STRIKE

Terrorism is the use of fear and violence to gain political goals. Many countries have lived with terrorism for years, but the United States had few attacks until the 1990s.

On February 26, 1993, terrorists set off a bomb under the World Trade Center in New York City. Six people were killed, but the buildings reopened.

In 1995, a government building in Oklahoma City was bombed and 168 people were killed.

A smaller bomb exploded at the 1996 Summer Olympic Games in Atlanta. In the next four years, bombs in foreign countries hit two United States embassies and a military ship.

September 11, 2001

On the morning of September 11, 2001, terrorists at major American airports hijacked four planes. They flew the first two planes into the World Trade Center towers. Both buildings collapsed and 2,830 people were killed.

The third plane hit the Pentagon, our country's military headquarters in Washington D.C. Nearly 200 people died in the attack. The fourth plane crashed in a field when passengers fought back against the hijackers.

Americans were horrified by the attacks. A total of 3,063 people were lost on this day. President **George W. Bush** and the government immediately resolved to stop terrorist groups around the world. Americans prepared for another long struggle in their history.

Summarize the information on this page.

Rescue workers search the World Trade Center rubble.

PUTTING IT TOGETHER

The Northeast today is one of the busiest and most populated parts of our country. Immigrants continue to come to the Northeast from countries around the world. As the cities grow, they draw closer together.

This spread of cities can make the Northeast seem like just one big city. This growth is mostly good for the region, but it also presents challenges. The growing cities must continue to work together to solve problems such as transportation and safety.

Oriole Park in downtown Baltimore

Review and Assess

1. Write one sentence for each of the vocabulary words:

   Boswash   **terrorism**
   megalopolis

2. What two groups of immigrants in the Northeast are growing the fastest?

3. What are two challenges the Northeast faces today?

4. **Outline** some of the ways cities in the Northeast are trying to solve transportation problems.

5. **Summarize** the effects of terrorism on the United States.

Activities

Using the map on page 234, group the cities included in the Northeast megalopolis by state.

• •

Using your school library or the Internet, research mass transit systems in your town or a nearby city. Make a list of each form of transportation offered. Include the cost of each and information about available routes.

Points of View

How can traffic problems be solved?

From Boston to Baltimore, the Northeast has some of the most congested, or crowded, highways. Read and think about these different points of view, then answer the questions that follow.

MARY JOHNSON
Educational Consultant, Andover, Massachusetts
Excerpt from an interview, 2001

66 Many roads need to be modernized. Some need more lanes or wider lanes. Others need to have exits spaced farther apart. On some highways we need to change the way cars come on and off. This will help traffic flow more smoothly. When cars are too close together, fender benders and car crashes occur. When they do, traffic piles up. 99

VALERIE BURNETTE EDGAR
Director of Communications
Maryland Department of Transportation
State Highway Administration
Baltimore, Maryland
Excerpt from an interview, 2001

66New technologies now allow many people to work at home instead of commuting to work. People might take buses or trains to work two days a week and telecommute the rest of the time. In southern Maryland, some federal government agencies have teleworking centers where workers go to work at computers instead of going into the nation's capital each day. 99

LYNN WILKINS
Central Division Transportation Director
New Jersey Transit
Maplewood, New Jersey
Excerpt from an interview, 2001

66 We need to find ways to get people to take mass transit. It has to be easy and convenient. We need to have stops near the places where people live and work. Some buses can carry as many as 100 people. Think about how many cars that would take off the road. Taking public transportation helps with traffic and reduces air pollution. 99

Thinking About the Points of View

1. Mary Johnson is an ordinary citizen who lives outside of Boston. She commutes into the city for her work. How do you think this influences her point of view?

2. Valerie Burnette Edgar works for an agency that supervises the airport and the state's roads and highways.

   What reasons might she have for her opinion?

3. Lynn Wilkins oversees buses, trains and other light rail in an area of New Jersey. How do you think this may have affected his opinion?

4. What other points of view might people have on this issue?

 Building Citizenship

Justice

Not everyone in this country can afford to have a car. This is one reason why some people think it is unfair to spend money on roads. They want to improve mass transit systems. Do you think the systems need to be improved to serve people who do not have cars?

 Write About It!

Do most people in your community travel by car or by mass transit? Are there certain times of day when the traffic is very heavy or very light? Write a paragraph describing a trip across your community by car or public transportation.

VOCABULARY REVIEW

Number a sheet of paper from 1 to 5. Beside each number write the word or term from the list below that matches the description.

longhouse   Patriot

megalopolis   sweatshop

Minutemen

1. volunteer colonial soldiers who served against the British
2. a factory where workers are employed at poor wages and in unhealthy conditions
3. a long wooden building in an Iroquois village that housed many families
4. a colonist who was opposed to British rule
5. a group of cities close together that can be thought of as one community

CHAPTER COMPREHENSION

6. What was Hiawatha's role in forming the Iroquois Confederacy?
7. Describe the Iroquois government.
8. Why was the harbor important to the city of Boston?
9. Why did the British decide to march on the towns of Lexington and Concord?
10. What is a tenement?
11. Describe the working conditions for immigrants in sweatshops.
12. What countries are today's immigrants to the Northeast likely to come from?
13. How is the Northeast solving transportation problems?

SKILL REVIEW

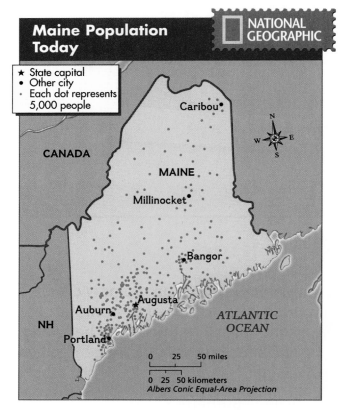

Maine Population Today — NATIONAL GEOGRAPHIC

★ State capital
● Other city
· Each dot represents 5,000 people

CANADA, MAINE, Caribou, Millinocket, Bangor, Augusta, Auburn, Portland, NH, ATLANTIC OCEAN

0   25   50 miles
0   25   50 kilometers
Albers Conic Equal-Area Projection

14. **Geography Skill** What does a distribution map show?
15. **Geography Skill** What does the distribution map on this page show?
16. **Geography Skill** How do you think this map is different from one that would have been made in the 1700s?
17. **Reading/Thinking Skill** What steps are used to draw an inference?
18. **Reading/Thinking Skill** What inference can you make about life under British rule using this chapter's description?

USING A TIME LINE

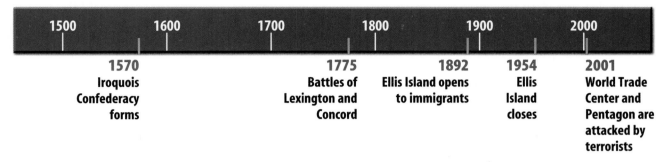

1500	1600	1700	1800	1900	2000

1570
Iroquois
Confederacy
forms

1775
Battles of
Lexington and
Concord

1892
Ellis Island opens
to immigrants

1954
Ellis
Island
closes

2001
World Trade
Center and
Pentagon are
attacked by
terrorists

19. How many years after the Iroquois Confederacy formed were the first battles of the American Revolution fought?

20. How many years did Ellis Island serve as the gateway for immigrants to the United States?

Activity

Writing About Immigration Suppose you were an immigrant coming to the United States. **Write** a paragraph describing the things you would want to bring with you and what you would have to leave behind. Include your thoughts about the journey and what you hope to do in the new country when you arrive.

Foldables

Use your Foldable to review what you have learned about the history and economy of the Northeast. As you look at the front of your Foldable, ask yourself questions and see if you can answer them without looking under the tabs. Try to mentally recall what you learned in each lesson about the Northeast. Record any questions that you can't answer on the back of your Foldable and discuss them with classmates, or review the chapter to find answers.

VOCABULARY REVIEW

Number a sheet of paper from 1 to 5. Beside each number write the term from the list below that best completes the sentence.

foliage	**sweatshop**
harbor	**suburb**
longhouse	

1. Immigrants to the United States often had to work in a ___.

2. ___s grew as people moved to areas outside of the cities.

3. Boston's economy was built around the ships that arrived and left from its ___.

4. In autumn, the ___ changes color.

5. Several Iroquois families lived in each ___ in a village.

TECHNOLOGY

For more resources to help you learn about the places you read about, visit **www.mhschool.com** and follow the links for Grade 4 Regions, Unit 3.

● SKILL REVIEW

6. **Geography Skill** What does the map tell you about how the population of Pennsylvania is distributed?

7. **Geography Skill** How might you identify suburban areas from the population distribution map?

8. **Reading/Thinking Skill** What can you infer about population and land use from the map?

9. **Reading/Thinking Skill** What are some of the causes and effects of changing the land in the Northeast?

10. **Reading/Thinking Skill** Identify the causes and effects of the colonists' protests against British rule.

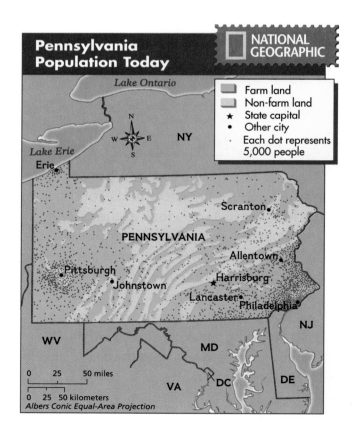

Pennsylvania Population Today

NATIONAL GEOGRAPHIC

Legend:
- Farm land
- Non-farm land
- ★ State capital
- • Other city
- · Each dot represents 5,000 people

Lake Ontario

Lake Erie

Erie

NY

Scranton

PENNSYLVANIA

Allentown

Pittsburgh

Johnstown

Harrisburg

Lancaster

Philadelphia

NJ

WV

MD

0 25 50 miles
0 25 50 kilometers
Albers Conic Equal-Area Projection

VA   DC   DE

1   During the late 1800s and early 1900s, New York City became the center of the country's garment, or clothing, industry. The Industrial Revolution made this possible. Instead of sewing a shirt or dress by hand, workers used sewing machines. Many garment workers were immigrants. They were men, women, and even children. Their jobs included sewing, cutting, tailoring, and pressing.

2   Clothing factories became known as sweatshops. In the summer the temperature inside the sweatshops could reach 120°F. Workers labored for 12 to 14 hours a day for very low pay. Although the conditions were terrible, most immigrants were determined to make a better life for themselves in their new country.

1 The word *garment* means—

A factory
B workers
C sewing
D clothing

2 What inference can you make about some immigrant workers?

F They were paid well for working long hours in sweatshops.
G They were willing to work in terrible conditions to live in America.
H They were not affected by the Industrial Revolution.
J They used the money they earned to return to their home countries.

WRITING ACTIVITIES

Writing to Inform Suppose you are a member of the Iroquois. **Write** a journal entry describing a day in the life of your village. Include the work you do, food you might eat, and other activities you might do.

Writing to Persuade Suppose you were John Adams during the American Revolution. **Write** a letter to persuade the governments of European countries to help the colonists fight against England.

Writing to Express **Write** a report on the events leading up to the American Revolution. Include the feelings of the colonists and the events that helped them decide to fight for independence.

Crazy Horse's Vision

By Joseph Bruchac
Illustrated by S. D. Nelson

*For hundreds of years, the **Lakota** people have lived on the Great Plains of the Middle West. One of their leaders, Crazy Horse (1849?–1877), was one of the best-known Native American heroes. Yet many people do not know he was called Curly as a boy. This story describes his early years and life on the plains. You will learn more about Crazy Horse and the Lakota in this unit.*

Lakota (Lə Kō tə) Native American group, often called Sioux

Crazy Horse, they say, was always different. Many children cry when they are born, but not Crazy Horse. He studied the world with serious eyes.

"Look at our son," his mother said. "How brave he is!"

"See how curly his hair is," said his father, Tashunka Witco.

"We will call him Curly," said his mother.

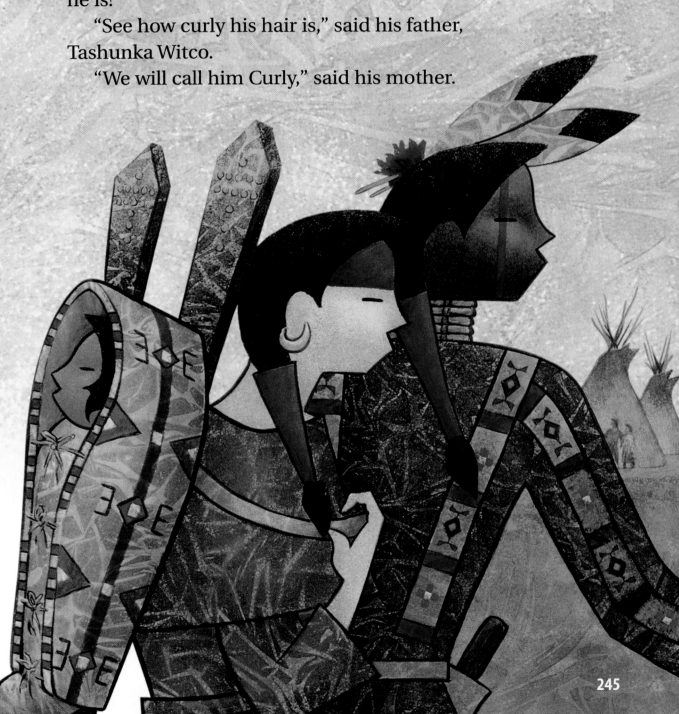

Seasons passed. The boy named Curly grew strong and wiry, but would never be tall. Though small, Curly was a leader. When others spoke, he was quiet. When others hesitated, he acted.

"Follow me," he would say, and the other boys would follow. A Lakota boy could go wherever he wanted and Curly wanted to go everywhere. He led his friends to swim in the river and ride far over the plains. They followed him up the highest cliffs where eagles nested.

"Be brave," he told them. "If we're brave, we can help our people."

. . . Summers later, Curly joined the men on a buffalo hunt for the first time. Hunting buffalo was dangerous. If your horse stumbled and you fell, you could get trampled to death. To strike a running buffalo with an arrow was difficult. Even the best hunters often had to shoot several arrows to bring down a buffalo.

As the hunters rode down the hill, the buffalo began to run. Their hooves sounded like thunder. Curly's swift horse carried him ahead of the others. Soon he was in the midst of the herd, next to a huge buffalo. Guiding his horse with his knees, Curly drew back the arrow and let it loose. It went straight and the buffalo fell. When the others caught up to him, Curly was standing by his first buffalo.

"I give this buffalo to all those in our camp who have no one to hunt for them," he said.

Write About It!

What important leadership qualities did Curly have? **Write** a paragraph that explains why it is important for a leader to have these qualities.

247

Unit 4

The Middle West

TAKE A LOOK

How is the Middle West growing and changing today?

The Middle West is known for farming, yet bustling cities such as St. Louis, Missouri, are part of the region, too.

Explore more about the cities of the Middle West at our Web site **www.mhschool.com**

THE *Big* IDEAS ABOUT...

Environment of the Middle West

When settlers began moving across the northern Appalachian Mountains, they arrived in the Middle West. Today the region is made up of 12 states in the heart of our country. In this chapter you will explore the land, climate, and natural resources of the Middle West.

ACROSS THE PLAINS

The Middle West region's rich soil and flat land make it a world-leading producer of corn, wheat, and other grains.

AN INLAND CLIMATE

Hot summers, cold winters, and sudden storms make weather an important part of daily life in the Middle West.

INTO THE HILLS

Iron deposits are a valuable natural resource found in this region.

Foldables

Make this Foldable study guide and use it to record what you learn about the "Environment of the Middle West."

1. Fold a sheet of paper like a hot dog, but make one side 1" longer than the other.
2. Make two cuts on the short side, dividing it into three equal sections.
3. Write the title of the chapter on the 1" tab, and write "Across the Plains," "Inland Climate," and "Into the Hills" on the three cut tabs.

Across the Plains

Lesson Outline
• Plains, High and Low
• Farming the Prairie

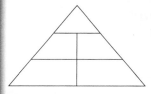

BUILD BACKGROUND

In the past, people thought of the land between the Appalachian and Rocky Mountains as the "middle" of the West. That is why this region is called the Middle West. The major landform is the Interior Plains. Most of the Middle West is made up of these low, flat lands. They seem to stretch out as far as the eye can see.

Corn farm on the Central Plains

252

PLAINS, HIGH AND LOW

The map on this page shows the natural features of the Middle West. The Interior Plains are made up of two parts. To the east are the **Central Plains**. To the west are the **Great Plains**. There is no sharp border between them.

The geography of these two areas is different. The Central Plains are low—not much higher than sea level in some places. Gentle slopes cover much of the land.

West of the Mississippi River, the land begins to rise. On the western edge of the Great Plains, the land is higher than 3,000 feet above sea level. These plains are mostly made up of dry grassland.

Rivers and lakes can also be found throughout the region. Four of the Great Lakes are in the Middle West. They are Lakes Superior, Michigan, Huron, and Erie. Together, with Lake Ontario, all five form the largest body of freshwater in the world.

READING CHECK Which two areas make up the Interior Plains?

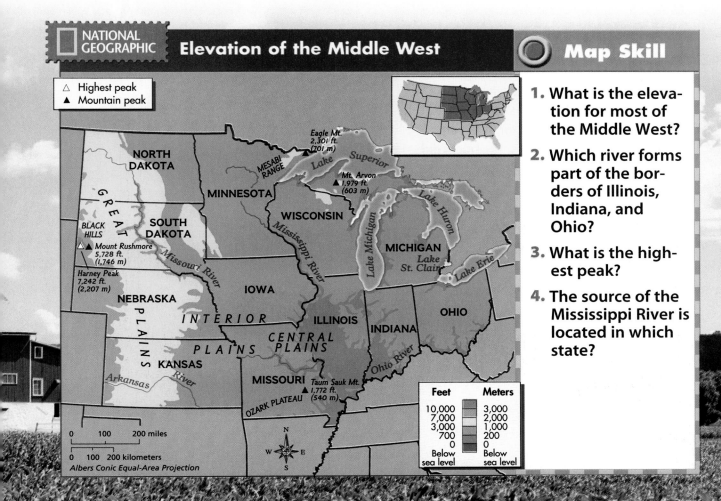

NATIONAL GEOGRAPHIC

Elevation of the Middle West

Map Skill

△ Highest peak
▲ Mountain peak

NORTH DAKOTA

Eagle Mt. 2,301 ft. (701 m)

MESABI RANGE

Lake Superior

Mt. Arvon 1,979 ft. (603 m)

MINNESOTA

GREAT

BLACK HILLS

SOUTH DAKOTA

WISCONSIN

Mississippi River

Lake Huron

Lake Michigan

MICHIGAN

Lake St. Clair

Lake Erie

△▲ Mount Rushmore 5,728 ft. (1,746 m)

Missouri River

Harney Peak 7,242 ft. (2,207 m)

NEBRASKA

P L A I N S

I N T E R I O R

IOWA

ILLINOIS

INDIANA

OHIO

P L A I N S

CENTRAL PLAINS

KANSAS

Arkansas River

MISSOURI

Taum Sauk Mt. 1,772 ft. (540 m)

Ohio River

OZARK PLATEAU

0   100   200 miles
0   100   200 kilometers
Albers Conic Equal-Area Projection

N W E S

Feet	Meters
10,000	3,000
7,000	2,000
3,000	1,000
700	200
0	0
Below sea level	Below sea level

1. What is the elevation for most of the Middle West?

2. Which river forms part of the borders of Illinois, Indiana, and Ohio?

3. What is the highest peak?

4. The source of the Mississippi River is located in which state?

FARMING THE PRAIRIE

Until about 100 years ago, much of the Central Plains was **prairie**. A prairie is a flat area covered with tall grasses and wildflowers. The soils of the prairie are naturally very fertile. Farmers have plowed up most of the prairie to plant crops. Huge farm fields stretch across the flat plains.

Crops of the Plains

On the Central Plains, corn is the main crop. Farmers in Iowa can produce more than a billion bushels of corn in one year! Much of it is fed to farm animals. Some of this corn is shipped to markets across the country and around the world. Soybeans are also grown in this area.

Wheat is the major crop on the Great Plains. Kansas and North Dakota are our country's biggest wheat producers. **Livestock**, or farm animals, also graze in this area. Raising cattle, pigs, and chickens is important to the agriculture in much of the Middle West.

READING CHECK What are the region's major crops?

Exploring TECHNOLOGY

Tractors

In 1904, Benjamin Holt developed the first successful tractor. It was called the "caterpillar," or crawler tractor. It ran on tracks looped around wheels. The tracks did not get bogged down in heavy soil. Holt later set up a tractor manufacturing plant in Peoria, Illinois. Today, tractors are used not only in farming, but also construction, mining, and other industries.

Activity

Research modern tractors and write a paragraph describing how they are used today.

PUTTING IT TOGETHER

The Middle West is a region of wide plains, mighty rivers, and huge lakes. Its flat lands and fertile soil make it an important center for farming. In the next lesson, you will learn how the region's climate also plays a part in its agriculture.

Cows graze on a dairy farm in Wisconsin (left). Other **livestock** raised in the Middle West include sheep (above) and pigs (below).

Review and Assess

1. Write one sentence for each of the vocabulary words:

   livestock   prairie

2. Who was Benjamin Holt?

3. Describe the geography of the Middle West region.

4. How does the **geography** of the Middle West affect agriculture in the region?

5. **Compare** and **contrast** the Central Plains with the Great Plains.

Activities

Using the map on page 253, list all the natural features found in the Middle West.

. . . .

Suppose you are a farmer on the Great Plains. **Write** a diary entry describing the kinds of crops you grow or animals you raise.

255

Reading Circle and Line Graphs

VOCABULARY

graph
circle graph
line graph

Suppose you wanted to study how much wheat the Middle West produces compared to other regions. A **graph** could help you compare information. Graphs are special diagrams that show information in a clear way. By presenting facts in a picture, they tell you a lot with only a few words.

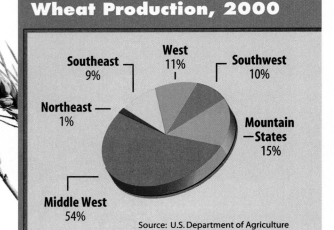

Wheat Production, 2000

Southeast 9%
West 11%
Southwest 10%
Northeast 1%
Mountain States 15%
Middle West 54%

Source: U.S. Department of Agriculture

LEARN THE SKILL

Look at the graph on this page as you follow the steps.

1. **Identify the type of graph.**
   The graph on this page is a **circle graph**. This kind of graph can show you how the parts of something make up or fit into the whole. Because each part looks like a slice of pie, a circle graph is some-times called a pie graph.

   The graph on the next page is a **line graph**. It shows how information changes over time. A line graph often shows an increase or decrease in number.

2. **Identify the graph's title.**
   The title of the circle graph on this page is "Wheat Production, 2000."

3. **Study any labels on the graph.**
   Labels on the circle graph include "Middle West," "Southeast," and all the other regions. This tells you that the graph's "slices" show how much wheat was produced in each region.

4. **Compare facts and figures.**
   You can tell that the most wheat was produced in the Middle West because this is the largest "slice" of the graph. The number 54 means that 54 percent of our country's wheat was produced in that region in 2000. How does the circle graph help you to compare this amount to wheat produced in other regions?

Indiana Corn Production, 1995-2000

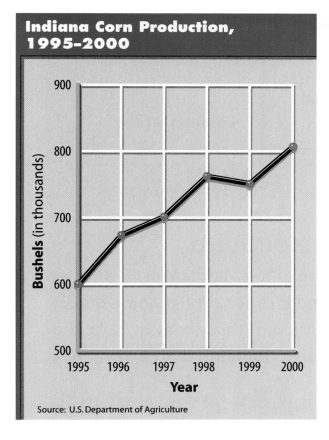

Source: U.S. Department of Agriculture

TRY THE SKILL

Look at the graph on this page. Trace the line on the graph with your finger. Then study the labels. Use the graph to answer the following questions.

1. What kind of graph is it?

2. What time period does the graph show?

3. What does each dot show?

4. How did the production of corn in the state of Indiana change?

EXTEND THE SKILL

Suppose that the number of students in your school is 150 in the year 2004; 200 in the year 2005; 180 in the year 2006; and 220 in the year 2007. Make a graph to show how the number of students changes over the four-year period. Use your graph to answer the following questions.

- What kind of graph is it?

- What does each dot show?

- How does the number of students change?

- How can circle and line graphs help you to **compare** and **contrast** information?

Lesson 2

An Inland Climate

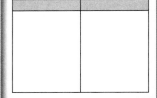

VOCABULARY

lake effect
tornado
blizzard

READING STRATEGY

Copy this chart. Fill in two facts about summer and winter in the Middle West.

Find Out!

What is the climate like in the Middle West?

Lesson Outline

• Far from the Ocean
• Warm Weather
• Winter Wonderland

BUILD BACKGROUND

The climate of the Middle West is affected by its land and location. Unlike some other regions, the Middle West does not have large oceans or high mountains. It is also not very close to the equator. In this lesson, you will learn how these features affect the region's climate and people.

FAR FROM THE OCEAN

In the Introduction, you learned how ocean breezes affect temperatures on nearby land. The Middle West is far inland, away from the Atlantic or Pacific Oceans. There are no ocean breezes to cool the land during the summer or to warm it in the winter. As a result, temperatures can reach extreme highs and lows for much of the summer and winter seasons.

The Lake Effect

In the northeastern part of the region, the Great Lakes affect the land much like the ocean in other parts of the country. This is called the **lake effect**. It gives the area a gentler climate than other parts of the region. Southern Michigan is affected the most. There temperatures stay warm long enough for some farmers to grow berries and other fruit. Every year, festivals celebrate the harvest.

 READING CHECK What is the lake effect?

Chicago (above) is located on Lake Michigan. These workers are serving cherry pie at the National Cherry Festival in Michigan (below).

Courtesy National Cherry Festival

259

A Changing Climate

The climate of the Middle West changes with the seasons. Study the graph and map to answer the questions.

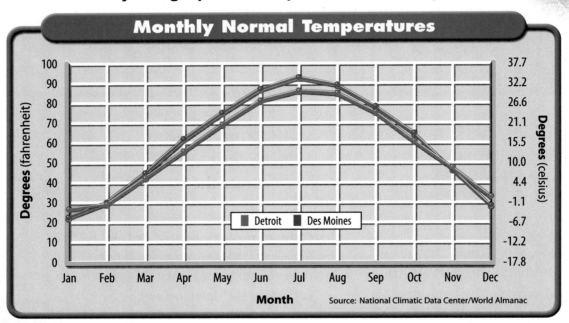

Monthly Normal Temperatures

Degrees (fahrenheit): 100, 90, 80, 70, 60, 50, 40, 30, 20, 10, 0

Degrees (celsius): 37.7, 32.2, 26.6, 21.1, 15.5, 10.0, 4.4, -1.1, -6.7, -12.2, -17.8

Month: Jan, Feb, Mar, Apr, May, Jun, Jul, Aug, Sep, Oct, Nov, Dec

Detroit   Des Moines

Source: National Climatic Data Center/World Almanac

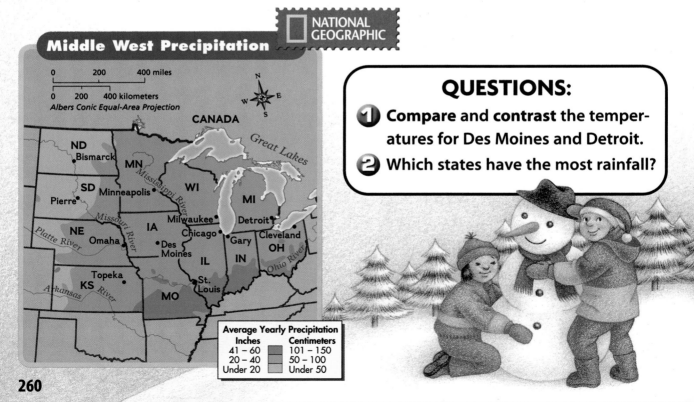

Middle West Precipitation

NATIONAL GEOGRAPHIC

0   200   400 miles
0   200   400 kilometers
Albers Conic Equal-Area Projection

CANADA
Great Lakes
ND   Bismarck
MN
SD   Minneapolis   WI
Pierre•   MI
Mississippi River
Milwaukee•   Detroit•
NE   IA   Chicago•   Gary•   Cleveland•
Omaha•   •Des Moines   OH
Missouri River   IL   IN   Ohio River
Platte River
Topeka   •St. Louis
KS   Arkansas River   MO

Average Yearly Precipitation

Inches	Centimeters
41 – 60	101 – 150
20 – 40	50 – 100
Under 20	Under 50

QUESTIONS:

1 **Compare** and **contrast** the temperatures for Des Moines and Detroit.

2 Which states have the most rainfall?

© Illinois Department of Agriculture

This cow won a ribbon at a state fair.

WARM WEATHER

The growing season of the Middle West is short. Farmers cannot plant crops too early, or spring frosts will kill the young plants. However, they must have enough time to grow and be harvested before the first frost of autumn.

Although the climate is perfect for growing corn and wheat, farmers must also worry about droughts. Most use irrigation to make sure their crops get enough water when there is not much rain. However, long droughts can make irrigation difficult if the water level of rivers, lakes, and wells becomes too low.

Summer Storms

From June to September, people in this region stay on alert for thunderstorms and **tornadoes**. A tornado is a dangerous storm that forms into a fast-moving funnel of wind. Tornadoes, or twisters, can move at speeds up to 200 miles per hour. The force of the winds can destroy everything in its path. Many people in the Middle West have special shelters in their basements where they can stay safe until a tornado passes.

Summer Recreation

Outdoor sports are popular throughout the region. The Great Lakes are perfect for boating. In late summer, many parts of the Middle West host festivals and state fairs to celebrate the harvest.

READING CHECK ✓ What is a tornado?

A **tornado** on the Kansas prairie

WINTER WONDERLAND

Without warm ocean breezes, much of the Middle West stays cold and frozen in the winter. Icy winds travel at high speeds across the plains, chilling everything in their path.

Many winter storms begin in the colder parts of Canada. Temperatures fall below the freezing mark. Sometimes **blizzards** form. Blizzards are winter storms with temperatures below 20°F, strong winds, and a lot of snow. In a blizzard, it can be difficult to see in front of you because of the heavy snow!

Lake-Effect Snow

Cities near the Great Lakes, such as **Chicago, Illinois** and **Green Bay, Wisconsin**, receive heavy snowfall every winter. This lake-effect snow occurs when cold, dry air from Canada meets warmer, damp air over the Great Lakes. Moisture in the air cools and forms snow. Some areas can receive more than 200 inches of lake-effect snow each year.

People of the Middle West find ways to enjoy the winter season. Ice skating, skiing, and snowshoeing are popular winter sports. Many communities also have winter fairs where they build houses out of snow and make sculptures from snow or ice.

READING CHECK Where does lake-effect snow form?

Kids climb a snow sculpture at a winter carnival (above). Heavy snow falls during a Minnesota **blizzard** (far left). Ice skating is a popular winter sport (left).

PUTTING IT TOGETHER

Weather in the Middle West is extreme and can affect the whole country. Farmers count on the hot summers to grow their crops. Unusual weather such as droughts can damage their fields and affect the food supply for our whole country. People working in weather stations inform the public about sudden changes that can produce tornadoes or blizzards.

Making snowballs and sledding are part of winter in the Middle West.

Review and Assess

1. Write one sentence for each of the vocabulary words:

   blizzard   **tornado**
   lake effect

2. Why do temperatures reach extreme highs and lows in the Middle West?

3. Describe the climate of the Middle West region.

4. What **economic** effect do you think a drought would have on farmers?

5. **Compare** and **contrast** the seasons of the Middle West and Southeast regions.

Activities

Using the map on page 260, identify a Middle West city located near one of the Great Lakes. Research the average monthly temperatures for that city using your school library or the Internet. Create a line graph showing the results.

• •

Suppose you lived in the Middle West. Choose a season and **write** a paragraph describing the types of activities you might do after school and how the weather would affect your plans.

Into the Hills

Lesson Outline
• Mount Rushmore
• Mining for Metal

VOCABULARY

iron
ore
open-pit mining
taconite
reclamation

PEOPLE

Gutzon Borglum
Calvin Coolidge

READING STRATEGY

Copy this word web. Fill in four details about iron mining in the Middle West.

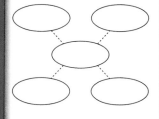

BUILD BACKGROUND

From farmlands to forests, people of the Middle West change the land in a number of ways. Some of the biggest changes can be found in the region's hills. Miners dig deep pits in Minnesota's **Mesabi Range**. In the **Black Hills** of South Dakota, a sculptor has changed the face of a mountain in honor of four presidents. It is called **Mount Rushmore National Memorial**.

The images of Presidents Washington, Jefferson, Roosevelt, and Lincoln

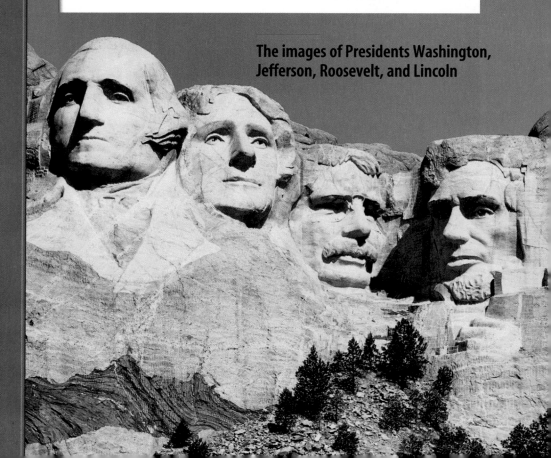

MOUNT RUSHMORE

In 1927, sculptor **Gutzon Borglum** began work on Mount Rushmore. The heads of four United States Presidents were carved into a mountain. It shows Presidents George Washington, Thomas Jefferson, Theodore Roosevelt, and Abraham Lincoln. The faces are from 50 to 70 feet tall!

At a special ceremony, President **Calvin Coolidge** presented Borglum with tools to start the project. Read the following excerpt from the President's speech at the site.

The Crazy Horse Memorial (above) was designed by sculptor Korczak Ziolkowski. The finished monument will look like this model (right).

Primary Source:

excerpt from **Mount Rushmore Dedication Ceremony**
— *August 10, 1927*

*This memorial will crown the height of land between the Rocky Mountains and the Atlantic **seaboard**, where coming generations may view it for all time. . . .*

Why will "coming generations" be able to view the memorial?

seaboard: seashore

President Calvin Coolidge

Crazy Horse Memorial

In the literature selection at the start of this unit, you read about Crazy Horse, who led the Lakota group. About 17 miles from Mount Rushmore, a memorial is being created in his honor. It is also being carved out of a mountain in the Black Hills. The face of Crazy Horse was completed in 1998.

When the entire project is finished it will stand almost 600 feet tall.

READING CHECK
Why do you think Borglum chose those four presidents?

265

MINING FOR METAL

Steel is an important product made in the Middle West. It is used for making buildings, tools, and many other things. Steel is made from a metal called **iron**.

During the 1840s, deposits of iron **ore** were discovered in the Middle West. Ore is a rock that contains a metal, such as iron. The largest amounts were later found in the Mesabi Range in northeastern Minnesota. Find it on the map on the next page.

From there, the ore could easily be shipped in huge boats on the Great Lakes. **Duluth,** Minnesota, became a major port for shipping iron ore. The iron ore was then delivered to large cities, such as **Detroit,** Michigan.

Open-Pit Mining

You have already read about the tunnels used to mine coal in the

Southeast. Much of the iron ore in the Mesabi, however, was close to the surface. So miners used **open-pit mining**, sometimes called strip mining. To create an open-pit mine, bulldozers clear all plants and soil from an area. Then miners use explosives and giant power shovels to dig the iron ore out.

Today, most of the Middle West's high-grade iron ore has been mined. Miners now look for other sources of iron, such as **taconite**. This is a flint-like rock that contains smaller iron minerals. Huge reserves of taconite can still be found in the Mesabi Range.

In the past these "stripped" areas were often abandoned when the ore ran out. Today the law requires miners to restore the land. This is called **reclamation**. First the land is returned to its old shape with machinery. Then trees, grass, and other plants are replanted. Reclamation has turned many open-pit mines into farms or parks.

This reclaimed area in Minnesota (above) was once an **open-pit mine**. A truck loads **iron ore** (below). At a Minnesota state park (opposite) visitors can fish in a former mining area.

READING CHECK

Why is reclamation important?

266

PUTTING IT TOGETHER

Many important natural resources are found in the Middle West. One of the most valuable is iron, which is used to make steel. In the next chapter, you will learn more about the steel industry.

Middle West: Iron Ore

0   150   300 miles
0   150 300 kilometers
Albers Conic Equal-Area Projection

■ Iron ore deposit
● Major city

CANADA

Lake Superior
MESABI RANGE
Duluth
Superior
Lake Huron
ND
SD
MN
WI
MI
Lake Erie
Mississippi River
Lake Michigan
Detroit
NE
IA
Chicago
Gary
Cleveland
OH
IL
IN
WV
KS
MO
KY
TN
OK
AR

Map Skill

1. **Which of the Great Lakes is closest to the Mesabi Range?**

2. **Where is iron mined in the Middle West?**

Review and Assess

1. Write one sentence for each of the vocabulary words:

   iron   **reclamation**
   open-pit mining **taconite**
   ore

2. Which presidents are carved into Mount Rushmore National Memorial?

3. Describe how iron is mined in the Middle West.

4. Why is the Mesabi Range in a good location for shipping?

5. **Compare** and **contrast** the Mount Rushmore and Crazy Horse memorials.

Activities

Using the map on this page, list the lakes a boat would cross to get from Duluth, Minnesota to Gary, Indiana.

• •

Using the Internet or school library, research one of the presidents on the face of Mount Rushmore and **write** a one-page report on his life.

VOCABULARY REVIEW

Number a sheet of paper from 1 to 5. Beside each number write the word or term from the list below that matches the description.

blizzard	prairie
livestock	tornado
ore	

1. rock that contains metal
2. fast-moving funnel of wind
3. farm animals
4. flat area with tall grasses and wildflowers
5. winter storm with wind and snow

CHAPTER COMPREHENSION

6. Which two areas make up the Interior Plains in the Middle West?
7. Name the four Great Lakes found in the Middle West.
8. Where is corn mainly grown in the Middle West?
9. Where is wheat mainly grown?
10. How do the Great Lakes affect the region's climate?
11. Describe the winter season in much of the Middle West.
12. Who was Gutzon Borglum?
13. What method is used to mine iron in the Middle West?

SKILL REVIEW

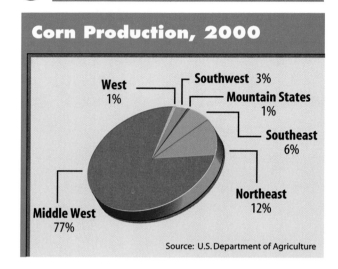

Corn Production, 2000

West 1%
Southwest 3%
Mountain States 1%
Southeast 6%
Northeast 12%
Middle West 77%

Source: U.S. Department of Agriculture

14. **Study Skill** What kind of graph is this?
15. **Study Skill** What does it show?
16. **Study Skill** Which region produced the most corn in 2000?
17. **Study Skill** Was more corn produced in the Southeast or the Southwest?
18. **Study Skill** How can graphs help you **compare** and **contrast** information?

USING A GRAPH

19. What time period does this line graph show?

20. When was the greatest amount of soybeans harvested?

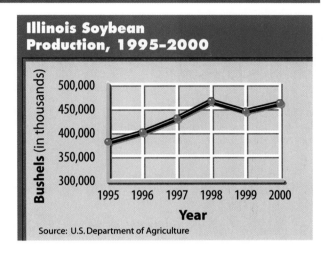

Illinois Soybean Production, 1995–2000

Bushels (in thousands)

500,000
450,000
400,000
350,000
300,000

1995 1996 1997 1998 1999 2000

Year

Source: U.S. Department of Agriculture

Activity

Learning About Agriculture Suppose you were visiting a state fair in the Middle West celebrating the yearly harvest. Use your textbook, the school library, or the Internet to learn more about state fairs. Then **write** a paragraph that describes the kind of activities and animals that you might see.

Foldables

Use your Foldable to review what you have learned about the environment of the Middle West. Review what you have learned by reading your notes under the tabs. Record any questions that you have on the back of your Foldable and discuss them with classmates, or review the chapter to find answers.

THE Big IDEAS ABOUT...

History and Economy of the Middle West

In the late 1700s, pioneers began to move to the Middle West. The Lakota, who were native to the region, struggled to hold on to their land. In the early 1900s, people continued to move into the Middle West as industries grew. Today, agriculture and manufacturing help keep the economy strong.

PIONEERS HEAD WEST

Corcoran Gallery of Art

Settlers traveled to the Middle West to establish new communities.

PEOPLE OF THE PLAINS

Chief Sitting Bull fought to preserve the Lakota way of life.

MOTOR CARS AND DETROIT

The new automobile industry led to the growth of manufacturing in Michigan and other states in the Middle West.

TODAY IN THE MIDDLE WEST

Resources such as iron ore are key parts of the region's economy.

Foldables

Use this Foldable study guide to record what you learn about the "History and Economy of the Middle West."

1. Fold a sheet of paper crosswise into thirds.

2. Open to find three columns. Refold it into thirds lengthwise, then fold this in half, forming six rows.

3. Label the columns "Middle West," "History," and "Economy." Label the next four rows with the lesson numbers and use the bottom row for vocabulary.

Wagon Trains and Pioneer Life

Find Out!

What was life like for pioneers in the Middle West?

Lesson Outline
• On the Frontier
• Traveling West
• Pioneer Life

VOCABULARY

frontier
pioneer
flatboat
Conestoga wagon
sod

PEOPLE

Jean Baptiste
  Point du Sable
Abraham Lincoln
John Deere

READING STRATEGY

Copy the word web. Use it to describe how people in the Middle West were self-sufficient.

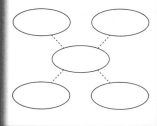

BUILD BACKGROUND

In the 1800s, European American settlers began moving across the Appalachian Mountains. These settlers called this region the **frontier**. A frontier is the area beyond a settlement. The settlers hoped to buy cheap land to farm and to build communities of their own.

Re-enactment of settlers moving west

You Are Here
1790 – 1860

ON THE FRONTIER

Some of the first settlers in this region were French traders. **Jean Baptiste Point du Sable** (JAHN bap TEEST PWAHN dih SAH bluh) was a trader from Haiti, a French colony in the Caribbean. His trading post would become the city of Chicago.

Thousands of American **pioneers** followed these traders. Pioneers are people who settle on land that is new to them. Some pioneers wanted to get away from growing cities. Others wanted to build new communities.

By 1840, more than 4 million settlers had moved west of the Appalachian Mountains. Many settled in the Ohio River valley. Use the map on this page to see how the frontier changed during the 1800s.

Settlers were encouraged to move west by the national government. The government sold land to the settlers for as little as one dollar an acre in some parts of the Middle West.

READING CHECK Why did pioneers move west?

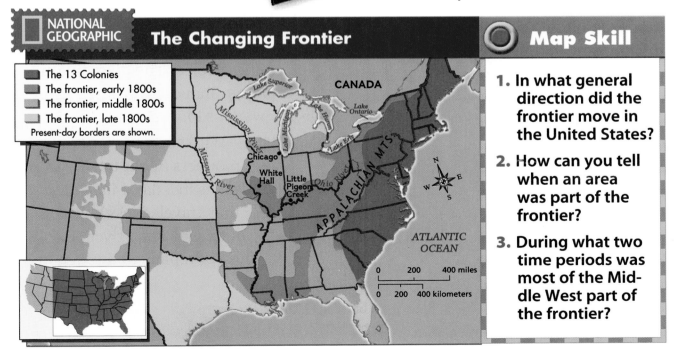

Small trunks held settlers' personal items.

NATIONAL GEOGRAPHIC — The Changing Frontier

Map Skill

Legend:
- The 13 Colonies
- The frontier, early 1800s
- The frontier, middle 1800s
- The frontier, late 1800s

Present-day borders are shown.

CANADA

Lake Superior
Lake Michigan
Lake Huron
Lake Ontario
Lake Erie
Mississippi River
Missouri River
Ohio River
APPALACHIAN MTS.

Chicago
White Hall
Little Pigeon Creek

ATLANTIC OCEAN

0   200   400 miles
0   200   400 kilometers

1. In what general direction did the frontier move in the United States?

2. How can you tell when an area was part of the frontier?

3. During what two time periods was most of the Middle West part of the frontier?

273

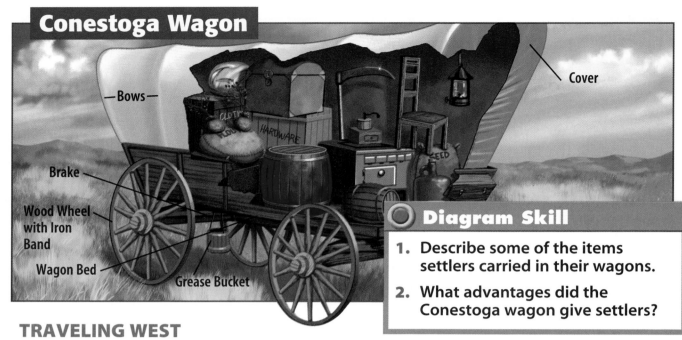

Conestoga Wagon

Bows

Cover

Brake

Wood Wheel with Iron Band

Wagon Bed

Grease Bucket

Diagram Skill

1. Describe some of the items settlers carried in their wagons.

2. What advantages did the Conestoga wagon give settlers?

TRAVELING WEST

Reaching the Middle West region was not easy for pioneers. Most traveled hundreds of miles with everything they needed for their journey and new lives.

There were few clear roads through the frontier. One trail used by many settlers was the Wilderness Road. It ran from the Appalachian Mountains to the Ohio River. Some families made the journey on foot or with horses carrying their belongings.

Another way to head west was by water. Large, flat-bottomed, wood boats, called **flatboats**, were used to travel downriver. Two or three families with their belongings could fit in one flatboat. The trip downriver was faster and easier than traveling over land. After

Plate from German settlers

the trip, the settlers would break up the boats to use or sell the wood.

As trails widened and roads were built, settlers began to use **Conestoga** (kahn us STOH guh) **wagons** pulled by horses, mules, or oxen. These sturdy wagons had a rounded frame on top that was covered in layers of heavy cloth. The covering kept furniture, food, tools, and other goods safe from the weather. It also provided shelter as the settlers traveled. The diagram on this page shows how these wagons looked.

With covered wagons, pioneers might travel 25 miles in a day. Many days they traveled less because of bad weather, river crossings, or repairs to the wagons.

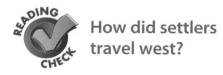

READING CHECK How did settlers travel west?

BIOGRAPHY

Focus On: Honesty

Abraham Lincoln was born in 1809 to pioneer parents in Kentucky. Eight years later, the pioneer family moved to Little Pigeon Creek, Indiana. Lincoln helped his father chop firewood, plow fields, and harvest crops. He also read as many books as he could.

When Lincoln moved away from home to Illinois, he worked as a clerk and continued to educate himself. People often told stories about "Honest Abe." In one story he walked three miles to return money to a customer who was accidentally charged too much.

Whether or not this story is true, Lincoln's reputation made people trust him. He was elected to his state legislature and then to Congress. He became our 16th president and led the nation through the difficult time of the Civil War.

Link to Today

Interview a teacher, friend, or family member about why they think it is important to be honest. Then write about what they have told you.

THE LIFE OF ABRAHAM LINCOLN	1809 Born in a log cabin in Kentucky	1834 Elected to Illinois General Assembly	1846 Elected to House of Representatives	1860 President of the United States

1800   **1825**   **1850**   **1875**   **1900**

LIFE AROUND THE WORLD	1803 United States purchases Louisiana Territory	1815 Napoleon defeated at Waterloo	1834 McCormick invents grain reaper	1861 Civil War begins	1865 Civil War ends

PIONEER LIFE

At the end of the trip west, there were no homes or businesses nearby. Pioneers had to provide for their own needs. When they arrived, they made houses of **sod**, or soil and grass, in the sides of hills. They lived there while they built more permanent homes.

To build a home, settlers began by clearing the land. The trees that were cut down were used to build simple log cabins like the one below. Around the cabin, underbrush had to be cleared and plowed so crops could be planted. Corn, beans, and potatoes would provide most of their food. Pioneers also made their own furniture, clothing, soap, and candles.

In some parts of the region, the soil was too tough for the farmers' wooden plows to cut. One pioneer thought of a better way. **John Deere** made plows from the blade of a saw. His invention

Sod houses required few materials to build.

was so successful other settlers wanted plows like his. Deere quickly had a growing business making farming tools. You can read one girl's memory of pioneer days on the next page.

 **READING CHECK** What was life like for pioneers?

Diagram Skill

1. **What items would settlers use to prepare a meal?**

2. **Which items are similar to things people have in their homes today?**

Pioneer Cabin

Farm Tools

Cupboard

Table

Bed

Fireplace

Spinning Wheel

excerpt from **Little House on the Prairie**
— *by Laura Ingalls Wilder, published in 1935*

Almost every day Laura and Mary . . . stared in surprise at a wagon slowly creaking by on that road. . . . In the West the land was level, and there were no trees. The grass grew thick and high. There the wild animals wandered and fed as though they were in a pasture that stretched much farther than a man could see, and there were no settlers.

Where were the wagons going?

PUTTING IT TOGETHER

Some settlers reached their new homes and found the new life wasn't what they expected. Frontier life was difficult and sometimes dangerous. A few returned to their earlier homes, but most stayed and kept working. Their hard work and self-sufficient nature defined the American spirit for many generations to come.

Review and Assess

1. Write one sentence for each of the vocabulary words:

   Conestoga wagon   **pioneer**
   flatboat   **sod**
   frontier

2. What was John Deere known for?

3. Describe the life of pioneers once they arrived in the Middle West.

4. What **economic** reason did settlers have for moving west?

5. What **generalization** can you make about the life of pioneers in the Middle West?

Compare the map on page 273 to the one on page 253. Then list all of the Middle West states that could be reached by traveling down the Ohio River.

Suppose you were a pioneer in the 1800s. **Write** a journal entry describing a day's work on your new land.

Making Generalizations

Suppose that in your area the heaviest rainfalls occur in March, April, and May. What do these months have in common? They are the months of spring. Knowing this, you might state, *"In my community, spring is the rainiest season."*

The above statement is a **generalization**. It ties together different examples to show how they share a similar idea or feature. A generalization can help you see what different facts, items, or events have in common. It can also help you make sense of new information about a topic.

VOCABULARY

generalization

Pioneer families with covered wagons

LEARN THE SKILL

Follow these steps to make a generalization about pioneers in the 1800s.

1. **Identify the topic.**
   To make a generalization, identify a topic. In this case, the topic is *pioneers*.

2. **Gather examples.**
   Gather examples about your topic. In Lesson 1, you read that pioneers made their own furniture, clothing, soap, and candles.

3. **Identify similarities in the examples.**
   What do these items have in common? They are usually purchased from a store.

4. **Make a statement or generalization.**
   Make a statement showing how the examples share a similar idea or feature. *"Pioneers had to provide for themselves"* is a generalization about the topic. You might be able to make more than one generalization from the same information.

TRY THE SKILL

In the last lesson, you also read about the journey west. Pioneers experienced bad weather. They had to cross wide rivers and tall mountains. Sometimes they were forced to stop and repair their wagons. Use these examples to answer the following questions.

1. What is a generalization?

2. What generalization can you make about the journey west?

3. What steps did you take to make your generalization?

4. Why is it important to have several examples to make a generalization?

EXTEND THE SKILL

Understanding how to make a generalization can also help you to understand history. It helps you see how different facts and events from the past are related. Only a few pioneers traveled to the Middle West at first. Then the government began to sell land to settlers for as little as one dollar an acre. By 1840, more than four million settlers had moved west of the Appalachians. Use these examples to answer the following questions.

• What generalization can you make about settlers in the 1800s?

• How does making a generalization help you understand history?

© Library of Congress

African American pioneers traveling west.

279

The Lakota

How did settlers in the Middle West change the Lakota culture?

VOCABULARY

teepee

PEOPLE
Sitting Bull
George Custer
Crazy Horse

READING STRATEGY

Copy the main idea pyramid. Write the main idea of this lesson at the top. Fill in supporting details as you read.

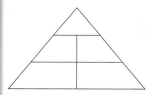

Lesson Outline

- People on the Move
- Following the Buffalo
- Fighting for a Way of Life

BUILD BACKGROUND

Before the settlers arrived, the Middle West was home to more than a dozen Native American groups. The Eastern Woodlands people included the groups near the Great Lakes and Ohio River. Farther west were the Native Americans of the Great Plains. In this lesson, you will learn more about Native American life on the plains.

Native American Plains village

PEOPLE ON THE MOVE

The Lakota lived in what is now Minnesota long before Europeans arrived in North America. They lived near the source of the Mississippi, where there were a lot of natural resources.

The Lakota fished in lakes and rivers, gathered plants, and hunted animals for food. During the 1600s, the Lakota began to migrate west to the prairies near the Missouri River. Look at the map to see how far the Lakota moved.

Transportation was very difficult for people of the Great Plains. Canoes were not useful because there were few rivers in the region. The Lakota could walk, but it was slow and difficult to move goods. To make it easier, they sometimes used dogs to pull sleds loaded with goods.

By the 1500s, Spanish explorers and colonists had arrived in North America. They brought horses with them for their new colonies. Over time, some horses escaped and formed herds that roamed the plains. The Lakota learned to catch these wild horses. They learned to ride them, hunt with them, and use them to carry goods across the plains.

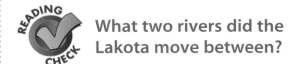

READING CHECK What two rivers did the Lakota move between?

Herd of wild horses on the plains

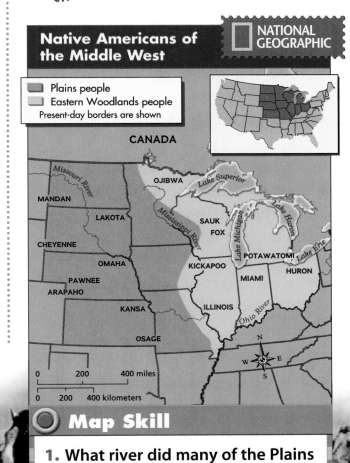

Native Americans of the Middle West

NATIONAL GEOGRAPHIC

Plains people
Eastern Woodlands people
Present-day borders are shown

CANADA

Missouri River

OJIBWA
Lake Superior

MANDAN

LAKOTA

Mississippi River

SAUK
FOX

Lake Michigan

Lake Huron

CHEYENNE

POTAWATOMI

Lake Erie

OMAHA

KICKAPOO

HURON

PAWNEE
ARAPAHO

MIAMI

ILLINOIS

KANSAS

Ohio River

OSAGE

N
W   E
S

0   200   400 miles
0   200   400 kilometers

Map Skill

1. What river did many of the Plains people live near?

2. What Middle West states took their names from Native American groups?

This painting by Edward Borein depicts a buffalo hunt.

FOLLOWING THE BUFFALO

Once the Lakota had horses, their lifestyle changed. They no longer had to stay in one place and began following the herds of buffalo on the plains.

The Lakota even moved the **teepees** they lived in. Teepees were cone-shaped dwellings made of poles and animal hides. They could be put up or taken down quickly and did not weigh very much. Teepees and other belongings were tied to wooden frames that could be pulled by horses to a new location.

When a buffalo herd was located, a group of Lakota formed a hunting party. They rode out on horseback and tried to frighten the animals by forming a circle around them. Then hunters would ride into the herd and shoot the animals with arrows.

The Lakota community depended on the success of its hunters. The buffalo made up almost their entire economy. The meat could be eaten right away or dried in the sun to be eaten later. The dried buffalo meat could last through an entire winter. The buffalo hide, horns, hair, and bones were all used by the Lakota. You can see some examples of how buffalo were used in the diagram on this page.

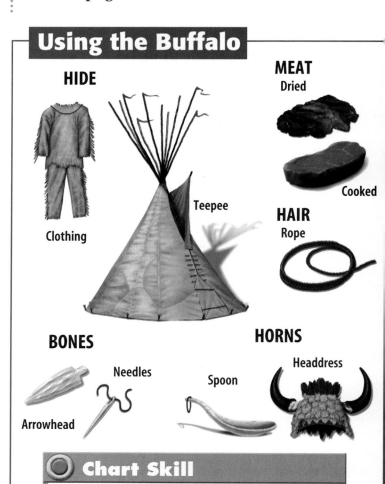

Using the Buffalo

HIDE
Clothing

MEAT
Dried
Cooked

Teepee

HAIR
Rope

BONES
Arrowhead
Needles

HORNS
Spoon
Headdress

Chart Skill

1. How was the buffalo's hide used?
2. What part of the buffalo was used to make spoons?

Thinning Herds

By the 1800s, settlers from the east began pouring over the Appalachian Mountains and moving west. Many of them wanted to move to the plains for the cheap and plentiful land there.

In the 1860s, railroad companies began laying train tracks through the Middle West. Hundreds of men came to work for the railroad companies. These men had to be fed while they worked. Hunters were hired to shoot buffalo to feed them.

With rifles, the hunters were able to kill as many as 150 buffalo in a day. William F. Cody killed so many he became known as "Buffalo Bill." The meat was used to feed the workers, and the hunters sold the hides. Hides were so valuable that some hunters shot the animals for their hides and did not use the rest of the buffalo.

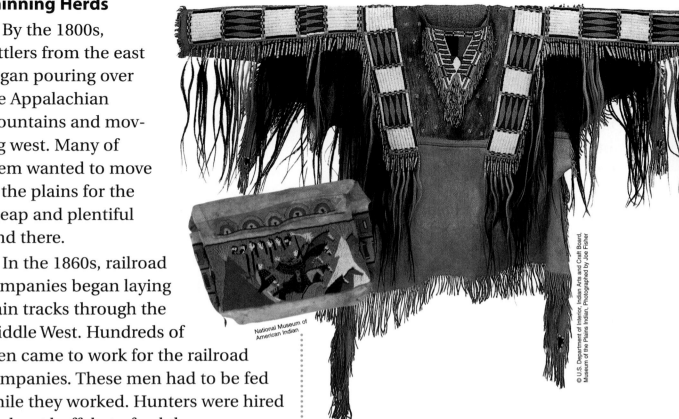

National Museum of American Indian

© U.S. Department of Interior, Indian Arts and Craft Board, Museum of the Plains Indian, Photographed by Joe Fisher

Buffalo hides were used to make Lakota clothing, bags, and boxes.

By the late 1800s, few buffalo were left on the plains of North America. Without the buffalo, the Lakota's way of life was ruined. They needed the buffalo for food, clothing, and shelter. Many Lakota blamed the settlers and some began fighting with them.

READING CHECK

How did the hunters for the railroad and the Native Americans treat the buffalo differently?

283

FIGHTING FOR A WAY OF LIFE

To end the fighting, the national government forced the Lakota to move to a reservation in South Dakota. The Lakota did not like being forced to stay in one place. Instead of hunting buffalo, they had to rely on the government for food. The agents in charge of the reservation did not always give them the food and supplies the government promised.

The Lakota did like one part of the reservation, called the Black Hills. It was the best hunting ground during

George Custer

the hard winters and was mentioned in many Lakota legends.

In 1874, gold was discovered in the Black Hills. Settlers moved there to look for gold. The Lakota fought to defend the land they had been given. The government wanted the Lakota to give up the land. **Sitting Bull**, an important Lakota chief, had seen the changes of the 1800s. He did not want a war with the government, but he refused to give up the land promised to the Lakota.

Battle of Little Bighorn

In June 1876, Lieutenant Colonel **George Custer** led 750 United States soldiers toward the Little Bighorn River in Montana. They were sent to gather information about the area.

Custer's troops found a large camp of Lakota warriors, led by Sitting Bull and the war chief **Crazy Horse**. Custer decided to fight the Native Americans, even though he was greatly outnumbered. Custer and one third of his troops died in the battle. Some call this battle "Custer's Last Stand."

READING CHECK Why did settlers want to move to the Black Hills?

Sitting Bull fought for Lakota lands.

PUTTING IT TOGETHER

The Lakota had won the Battle of Little Bighorn, but this victory would not end the fighting. Many more government soldiers were sent to the Great Plains. The Lakota could not fight them all and split into smaller groups. Soldiers tracked the smaller groups down and forced them to surrender. In May 1877, Crazy Horse led one of the last groups of Lakota to surrender at Fort Robinson, Nebraska.

The Battle of Little Bighorn is remembered with this Lakota painting (above) and bronze statue of Crazy Horse (right).

Review and Assess

1. Write one sentence for the following vocabulary word:

   teepee

2. What were some ways the Lakota used the buffalo they hunted?

Find Out!

3. What **effect** did settlers in the Middle West have on the Lakota?

4. What **effect** did the buffalo hunters have on the **culture** of the Lakota?

5. How else might the national government have **solved problems** between the Lakota and settlers?

Activities

Use the map on page 281 to list the Native American groups of the Middle West and classify them into Plains and Woodlands people. How else could you use geography to classify the groups?

Suppose you were a Lakota living in the 1700s. **Write** a paragraph about how horses changed your way of life. Describe how you might have caught and used the horses.

Lesson 3

Booming Industry

Find out!

How did the automobile industry change the Middle West?

Lesson Outline

- Henry Ford
- Work in Factories
- Changes and Growth

VOCABULARY

migration
mass production
assembly line
robot

PEOPLE

Henry Ford
Amelia Earhart

READING STRATEGY

Copy the flow chart. List events about the automobile industry in the correct sequence.

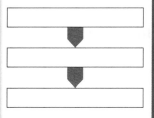

BUILD BACKGROUND

During the early 1900s, many people found themselves looking for work. Why? Changes in technology meant fewer people were needed on farms. New machines did much of the work. Farm workers moved to cities such as Detroit, Michigan, to make their living in manufacturing.

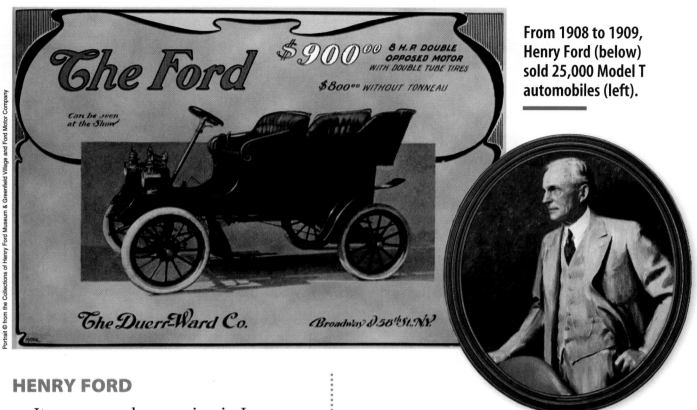

From 1908 to 1909, Henry Ford (below) sold 25,000 Model T automobiles (left).

HENRY FORD

It was an early morning in June 1896. A young engineer named **Henry Ford** and his assistant wheeled an odd-looking vehicle into an alleyway in Detroit. It did not need a horse to drive down the street. The vehicle, an automobile, ran on engine power.

The Model T

Ford's automobile was not the first vehicle powered by gasoline. However, his was the first to reach the heights of success. Within 12 years, his company was selling a car called the Model T. The "Tin Lizzie," as it was nicknamed, became the most popular automobile in the United States.

Ford was not the only carmaker in Detroit. In 1903 alone, 57 automobile manufacturers set up shop in the city! Before long Americans were calling Detroit "Motor City."

READING CHECK Predict how Ford's automobile would change people's lives.

287

WORK IN FACTORIES

The booming automobile industry needed many workers. Thousands of people flooded into Detroit and other Great Lakes cities. Unlike pioneers, these people were looking for jobs, not land.

Car factories welcomed men from all over. Large numbers of immigrants arrived from Poland, Germany, and countries in Scandinavia. Others came from Russia and Great Britain.

The Great Migration

Thousands of African Americans from the Southeast also arrived. Many were farm workers who could no longer make a living. They hoped to find work and equality.

The Phillips Collection

Group movement from one region to another is called **migration**. There were so many African Americans making this journey during the early 1900s, that it came to be known as the Great Migration. Before this time, most African Americans had lived in the Southeast. During the Great Migration, many came to live in the Middle West and Northeast, where most factory jobs were found.

Mass Production

In 1908 a Model T cost $900. That is equal to about $15,000 today. As the years passed,

In 1941, the artist Jacob Lawrence made a series of paintings about the Great Migration (above). Workers put together automobiles on a Ford assembly line (left).

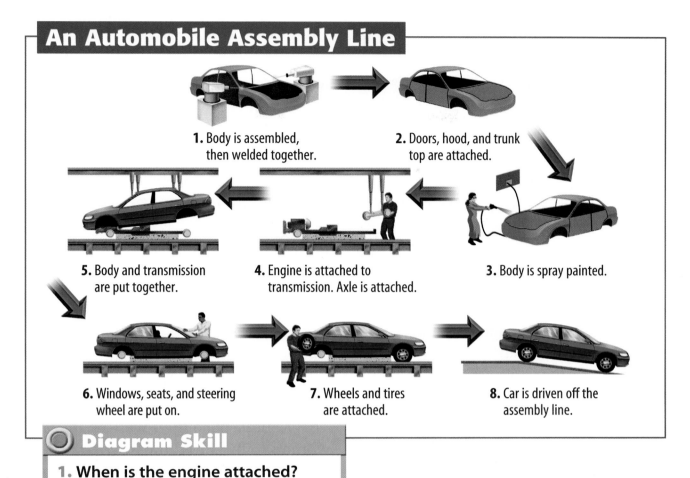

1. Body is assembled, then welded together.

2. Doors, hood, and trunk top are attached.

3. Body is spray painted.

4. Engine is attached to transmission. Axle is attached.

5. Body and transmission are put together.

6. Windows, seats, and steering wheel are put on.

7. Wheels and tires are attached.

8. Car is driven off the assembly line.

◯ Diagram Skill

1. **When is the engine attached?**
2. **Is the car painted before or after the wheels are put on?**

the price kept dropping. By 1927 you could buy a Model T for $290, or $2,500 today.

How could Ford keep lowering the price? One reason was **mass production**. Mass production means manufacturing large numbers of goods using identical parts. With mass production, it cost Ford less to make each Model T than if each one was made separately by hand.

In 1913, Ford set up an **assembly line** in his factory. A moving belt carried the unfinished cars past workers.

Each worker performed a single task. One might attach the engine and another would screw on the steering wheel. This cut the assembly time of a Model T from 12 hours to 93 minutes. By 1927, the company could turn out a new car every 24 seconds!

Ford's mass-production methods quickly spread. Today, cars and many other products are built on assembly lines. Machines also do far more work than in Ford's time. The diagram above shows how an automobile assembly line runs today.

READING CHECK

How did mass production make manufacturing easier?

HISTORY MYSTERY

Amelia Earhart's Final Flight

In 1937, Amelia Earhart set off on another famous flight. She planned to become the first woman to fly around the world. Earhart set off from Miami, Florida in June of that year. On July 2, her plane disappeared near Howland Island in the Pacific Ocean. A search was held, but no trace of Earhart's plane was ever found. Her final flight remains a mystery.

What do you think happened to Amelia Earhart?

During her flights, Earhart used an aviator's cap and goggles like ones shown here.

© International Woman's Air & Space Museum

CHANGES AND GROWTH

During the 1920s, the automobile became a common sight on our country's streets. It made transportation easier between rural areas and cities. The economy was also booming at this time. Millions of Americans enjoyed better living conditions than ever before.

The Roaring Twenties

This period was called the "Roaring Twenties." There were changes to our culture, such as a new invention called the "talking picture." Movies no longer were silent, they now had sound. New celebrities, such as **Amelia Earhart**, also caught the country's attention. This Kansas-born pilot was the first woman to fly across the Atlantic Ocean in 1928. She flew with two other pilots. Earhart later flew solo across the Atlantic in 1932. She made the trip in record time.

Robots and Computers

Since the 1920s, the manufacturing industry has seen great changes. Many tasks are now performed by **robots**—machines controlled by computers. They can do more work in less time. But this also means that there are fewer jobs for people on assembly lines.

New companies, however, now build robots and computer equipment. These factories need workers. Here, as in other parts of our country, the high-tech industry holds promise for workers in the future.

READING CHECK What changes occurred during the 1920s?

Today, robots are used to weld car bodies (far right) on a factory assembly line. In the future, robots will be able to do many things. The one shown here (right) can walk on its own!

PUTTING IT TOGETHER

Automobiles changed transportation in our country. Travel from one city to another became much faster. People in rural areas could get to doctors and schools more easily. The auto industry also helped the Middle West grow as a manufacturing region. Today, cars are one of our country's most important products.

Review and Assess

1. Write one sentence for each of the vocabulary words:

   assembly line   **migration**
   mass production   **robot**

2. Who was Amelia Earhart?

3. Analyze how the automobile industry changed the Middle West.

Find out!

4. What effect has **technology** had on manufacturing?

5. What **generalization** can you make about automobiles and the 1920s?

Activities

Look at the diagram on page 289. What is the first step to building a car? What is the last step?

• •

Suppose you went to work in an auto factory after having lived on a farm. **Write** a paragraph explaining how the two jobs are different.

The Middle West Today

Find Out!

How are industries in the Middle West changing in the modern economy?

VOCABULARY

combine
agribusiness
food processing
specialize

READING STRATEGY

Copy the main idea pyramid below. Write the main idea of the lesson at the top. Add supporting details as you read.

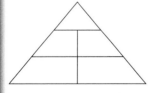

Lesson Outline

• A Changing Business
• Companies of All Kinds
• Growing Up and Out

BUILD BACKGROUND

By the late 1800s, railroads began carrying tons of corn, grain, and other crops from the Middle West across the country. The region became known as America's "breadbasket." The spread of railroads and modern technology also brought new industries to the Middle West. Some, like the steel industry, helped our country to grow faster during the early 1900s.

Hot liquid steel being poured

You Are Here
1880 – Present

A CHANGING BUSINESS

Agriculture in the Middle West is still an important part of our country's food supply. However, the farms today have come a long way from the days of pioneers. Today enormous machines plow the fields and plant the seeds. Another machine, called a **combine**, helps to harvest grains such as wheat. The combine cuts wheat and threshes it, or removes the grain from the stalk.

Farmers also use computers to help them manage the many details of their growing farms. Computers can provide detailed weather forecasts, help them plan budgets and orders, and calculate prices for crops when they are sold.

This technology has allowed many farms to grow very large. For example,

Farmers today use computers to monitor the growth of livestock and irrigation of crops on farms.

one family can work more than 700 acres by using machines, computers, and other technology.

Farm ownership has also changed in the last century. In 1900, most farms were family owned. However, many young people soon left farms to work in urban areas. Other family farms have been taken over by large companies. These companies often own many different kinds of agricultural businesses.

How has technology changed farming?

293

COMPANIES OF ALL KINDS

Whether families or companies run modern farms, most are involved in **agribusiness**. An agribusiness is a farm or ranch which is combined with other businesses, such as **food processing**. Food processing includes any business that uses raw food to create products to be sold. Food processing factories may package grains, can beans, or even make potato chips.

Some food processing plants in Wisconsin package cheddar cheese in the shape of a cow.

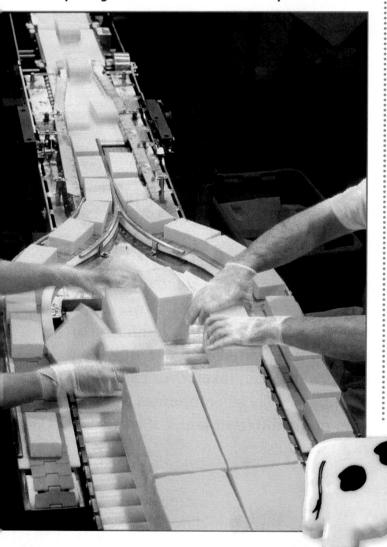

Exploring ECONOMICS

Grain Elevators

Many farmers sell their crops through a grain elevator, another part of agribusiness. A grain elevator is a kind of huge storage bin. People who run them also find buyers for farmers. Wheat is driven by truck from grain elevators to flour mills. Or it is taken to ports where it is shipped to other countries. Grain elevators are also used to store corn and other crops.

Activity

Suppose a grain elevator that could hold up to 1 million bushels of wheat was full. How much would the entire bin be worth, at a cost of 2 dollars per bushel?

Special Businesses

Some agribusinesses are successful because they **specialize** in only one aspect of farming. Specialize means to concentrate on a particular product. A specialized agribusiness might produce cattle feed or fertilizer to sell to other farmers.

Many of these specialized agribusinesses work together to do all of the work that was once done on one farm.

An Industry from Iron

You already read about how iron is mined. Although there have always been many uses for iron, the Middle West built another strong industry around it. This is the steel industry.

One way that steel is produced from iron is by heating the iron in a container called a furnace. When the iron reaches 3000°F it melts. Then a gas called oxygen is mixed with the molten iron. This mixture forms a new material—liquid steel. As the steel is cooled, it becomes solid again.

Steel is made from iron, but steel is stronger, lighter, and lasts longer. It quickly became a popular material for making things such as automobiles, railroad cars, and bridges. It is also used to make smaller items, like forks and spoons.

Because iron mainly came from the Middle West, many steel companies also started in this region. Other companies in the region used middle western steel to build cars, airplanes, and other goods.

READING CHECK Describe the process used to make steel from iron.

Steel is used to make screws and bolts, as well as bridges like the Centennial Bridge in Davenport, Iowa.

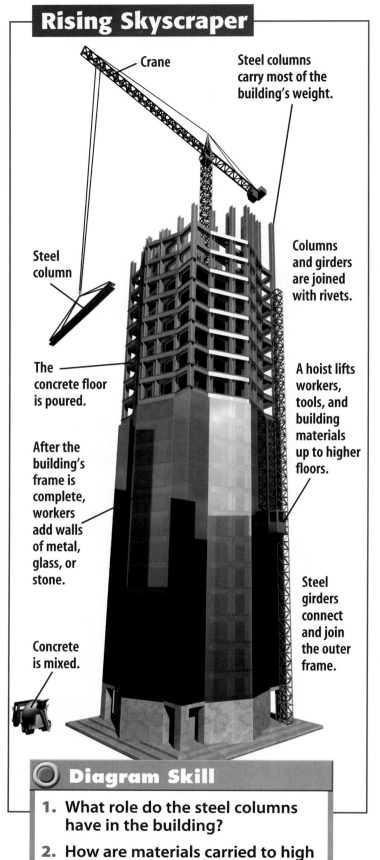

Rising Skyscraper

Crane

Steel columns carry most of the building's weight.

Steel column

Columns and girders are joined with rivets.

The concrete floor is poured.

A hoist lifts workers, tools, and building materials up to higher floors.

After the building's frame is complete, workers add walls of metal, glass, or stone.

Steel girders connect and join the outer frame.

Concrete is mixed.

Diagram Skill

1. What role do the steel columns have in the building?

2. How are materials carried to high floors of the skyscraper?

GROWING UP AND OUT

If you visited any city in the United States in the late 1800s, you might be surprised to see the buildings were not more than six stories high. In 1885, a ten-story building was built in Chicago, Illinois. Instead of using wood or bricks, the builder used a frame of iron and steel to support the building.

Steel-framed buildings soon towered above many cities. Steel was also used to make stronger, safer elevators to be used in the taller buildings. Chicago is still called the "home of the skyscraper." The 110-story Sears Tower, our country's tallest skyscraper, is located there.

Competition From Overseas

Today the steel industry has more competition from other countries. Steel manufacturers in Japan and Europe have been able to build more modern steel factories. These factories produce steel faster and cheaper. By the 1970s, many American factories imported steel from other countries.

Many American steel companies closed because they could not compete with the lower prices. Today, there are fewer steel companies in the region, but they are working hard to stay competitive by developing new ways to produce steel.

PUTTING IT TOGETHER

The resources of the Middle West helped pioneers to establish industries that would last for many years. The region supplies crops such as corn, wheat, and soybeans. These foods may be processed for use in our country or exported to countries such as China, Russia, and Brazil.

Steel is another part of the modern economy of the Middle West. Although this industry faces increased competition, it is working hard to stay an important part of the region's economy.

READING CHECK Where is our country's tallest skyscraper located?

The Sears Tower contains enough steel to build 50,000 automobiles. Tourists can buy a model of it when they visit Chicago.

Review and Assess

1. Write one sentence for each of the vocabulary words:

   agribusiness   **food processing**
   combine   **specialize**

2. What is one example of an agribusiness?

3. *Find Out!* How are industries in the Middle West changing in the modern economy?

4. Describe the effect imported steel had on the industry in the Middle West.

5. **Compare** and **contrast** farming methods on the frontier and today.

 **Activities**

Using your textbook, school library, or the Internet, create a time line of changes in the agriculture industry. Include important inventions and technology that have led to the modern farms of today.

• • • • • • • • • • • • • • • • •

Suppose you lived in Chicago in the 1880s. **Write** a letter to a friend in another city describing the first skyscraper being built.

From Farming to Industry

VOCABULARY

subsistence
 farming

commercial
 farming

industrialization

Find out!

What goals for the future do we share with other countries?

Lesson Outline
• Developing Economies
• The Road to Industry

READING STRATEGY

Copy the chart. Write the main idea of this lesson. Add supporting details as you read.

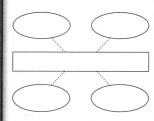

BUILD BACKGROUND

The combination of farming and industry has made our country's economy strong. Other countries in the Western Hemisphere also want to improve their economies. Agriculture trade is one way these countries are working to achieve their goals.

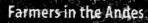

Farmers in the Andes

298

they probably came from South America. When it is winter in the United States, it is summer in countries below the equator. Trade agreements with other countries in the Western Hemisphere mean we can have a variety of fruits and vegetables all year. The agreements also help to encourage commercial farming in other countries.

How are commercial and subsistence farming different?

DEVELOPING ECONOMIES

In the United States, our economy continues to grow stronger because of our free-enterprise system. However, many countries still depend on an economy of **subsistence farming**. This means people grow only enough food to live on, not to sell.

One way governments of some countries are trying to improve their economies is by **commercial farming**. Farmers who run commercial farms raise crops and livestock to sell to people in their country and to export, or sell, to other countries.

Commercial farmers in Brazil supply most of the world's coffee beans. Farmers in Peru export sugar and cotton to other countries in the Western Hemisphere, Europe, and Asia.

Do you enjoy eating grapes or berries in the middle of winter? Well,

Bananas (above) and coffee beans (below) are harvested for export to the United States.

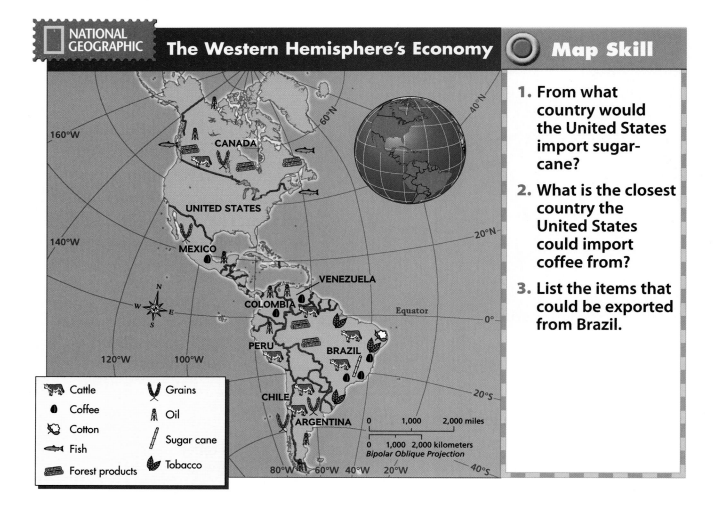

1. From what country would the United States import sugar-cane?

2. What is the closest country the United States could import coffee from?

3. List the items that could be exported from Brazil.

Cattle
Coffee
Cotton
Fish
Forest products
Grains
Oil
Sugar cane
Tobacco

0   1,000   2,000 miles
0   1,000 2,000 kilometers
Bipolar Oblique Projection

THE ROAD TO INDUSTRY

Another way countries are trying to improve their economies is by **industrialization**, or the development of manufacturing industries. Industrialization makes goods less expensive to make and buy, encourages trade, and improves the quality of life for people. The United States became industrialized when factories were built in the 1800s.

Today, the United States works with other countries that are trying to industrialize their economies. Compa-nies in Venezuela and Argentina often hire Americans with manufacturing experience to build and oversee their factories. Each new business helps to develop the economy by providing jobs, income, and goods that people want and need.

Use the map on this page to find out what products are made by busi-nesses in the Western Hemisphere.

READING CHECK   **What is industrialization?**

300

PUTTING IT TOGETHER

When countries agree to work together, there can be many challenges. There are differences in forms of government, economic systems, and kinds of money. Some of these countries are finding ways to work together through trading and sharing knowledge. They try to encourage people to make good economic decisions. This helps the cooperating countries to meet the needs and wants of their people.

Each country's economy includes its own money, some of which is shown here.

Review and Assess

1. Write one sentence for each of the vocabulary words:

   commercial farming
   industrialization
   subsistence farming

2. What types of industries are developing in South America?

3. What might be a common goal that countries of the Western Hemisphere share? *Find Out!*

4. Identify two countries in the Western Hemisphere and their **economic** relationship to the United States.

5. Make a **prediction** about how cooperation will change the future of the Western Hemisphere.

Activities

Using the map on page 300 and your school library or Internet, find out how seasons are different for countries above and below the equator. Write the current season for each country in the Western Hemisphere.

Using an encyclopedia or the Internet, research your state's economy. **Write** a report listing what your state imports and exports.

Being a Good Citizen
Share a Friend

When Michael Kay, age 12, was looking for a community service project, he thought of his younger brother Kyle. Kyle was born with cerebral palsy, a condition that left him with mental and physical disabilities. "Because of my brother's disabilities," said Michael, "I got to know many other people like him. Kyle and the other kids I knew were often left out of activities. I wanted to do something to include them. I thought it would be good for them and good for the community."

Michael started a program called Share a Friend. His idea was to match up kids from his 4-H club with people in group homes in Wilmington and in a nearby community. A group home is a place where disabled people live together with workers who help them. The 20 members of his 4-H Club agreed to join the program. By the time Share a Friend was ready to begin, more than 60 people from the group homes wanted to take part. Michael gave talks to school clubs and youth groups, telling about the program. Over the course of a year, he signed up more than 80 teenagers.

"I thought it would be . . . good for the community.**"**

Michael persuaded civic clubs and local businesses to help pay for his group's outings. Through Share a Friend, the new friends went bowling, played miniature golf, and took part in other activities. On the Fourth of July, all the Share a Friend members had a picnic. "Working on this program," says Michael, "gives me a good feeling. Even if it's in small ways, we can all make a difference in someone's life. I get just as much, if not more, out of the program than the people we work with."

Wilmington, Illinois

Be a Good Citizen

Making Connections

- **What are some activities in your school or city that bring together different groups?**

- **Are there any service programs in your community that were inspired by the personal experiences of one leader?**

Talk About It!

- **Why do you suppose Michael named his program "Share a Friend"?**

- **What experiences inspired Michael to start the "Share a Friend" program?**

Act On It!

In the Classroom

As a class, think of ideas for a new community service project. Write an outline for the project, showing who would benefit from the program.

In the Community

Identify a group that is not active in community events where you live. Write a letter to your city's mayor or town council. In it, describe how you would include this group.

303

VOCABULARY REVIEW

Number a sheet of paper from 1 to 5. Beside each number write the word or term from the list below that matches the description.

agribusiness   migration

assembly line   teepee

frontier

1. the area beyond a settlement
2. cone-shaped dwelling made of poles and animal hides
3. farm combined with another business
4. group movement from one region to another
5. a moving belt that carries unfinished cars past workers

CHAPTER COMPREHENSION

6. How did the government encourage settlers to move west?
7. How did some families cross the Wilderness Road?
8. How did John Deere help farmers?
9. How did horses change Lakota life?
10. Name one reason why people came to the Middle West in the 1860s.
11. Describe the events that happened at Little Bighorn.
12. What is a grain elevator?
13. List two ways in which farming has changed in the Middle West.

SKILL REVIEW

14. **Reading/Thinking Skill** What is a generalization?
15. **Reading/Thinking Skill** Look back at Lesson 1. What generalization can you make about life on the frontier?
16. **Reading/Thinking Skill** What generalization can you make about the effects of the changing frontier on Native Americans and the buffalo?
17. **Reading/Thinking Skill** Why is it important to have several examples in order to make a generalization?
18. **Reading/Thinking Skill** How can generalizations help you understand history?

USING A TIME LINE

1800		1850		1900		1950		2000

1816	1836	1860	1876	1900s	1913		Today
The Lincoln family moves to Indiana	John Deere invents the plow	Railroads come to the Middle West	The Battle of Little Bighorn	The Great Migration	Ford sets up first automobile assembly line		Farmers use modern technology to improve harvests

19. Were railroads built before or after the Battle of Little Bighorn?

20. What year was the first automobile assembly line set up? How did it change the way cars were produced?

Activity

Learning About History Suppose you were a Native American living in the 1800s. How did the discovery of gold in the Black Hills lead to the Battle of Little Bighorn? Use your textbook, the school library, or the Internet to learn more about the battle and the events that led up to it. Then **write** a paragraph that describes the causes of the battle.

Foldables

Use your Foldable table to review what you have learned about the history and economic growth of the Middle West. As you look at the data collected in your Foldable table, select a word or phrase and using complete sentences, explain what it means. Review your "main idea" words in your Foldable to check your understanding of the chapter. Record any questions that you have on the back of your Foldable table and discuss them with classmates, or review the chapter to find answers.

Middle West	History	Economy
L1	• pioneers move to settle in Middle West • travel by flatboats or Conestoga Wagon	• land sold for as little as a dollar per acre • settlers had to grow or make everything they needed
L2	• arrival of horses lets Lakota follow buffalo herds • Lakota fought to keep their land and way of life	• Buffalo is central part of Lakota economy • Hunters for railroads destroy herds of buffalo
L3	• Henry Ford produces the automobile • African Americans migrate to find work and equal rights	• mass production makes goods easier to produce for less cost • assembly lines in factories create more jobs
L4	• technology and computers change the agriculture industry • the steel industry grows as more skyscrapers are built	• agribusinesses grow and specialize • steel industry competes to make steel faster and cheaper
Vocabulary	• frontier • migration • sod • teepee	• agribusiness • mass production • specialize

305

VOCABULARY REVIEW

Number a sheet of paper from 1 to 10. Beside each number write the term that best completes the sentence.

agribusiness	migration
Conestoga wagon	ore
food processing	prairie
frontier	reclamation
lake effect	tornado

1. ___ is the practice of restoring land after it has been mined.

2. The Great Lakes affect temperatures on land. This is called the ___.

3. ___ turns crops and animal products into the foods found in boxes, bags, bottles, and jars in the store.

4. The ___ became a more popular method of travel as trails widened and roads were built.

5. A ___ is a flat area covered with wildflowers and tall grasses.

6. Iron ___ is dug out of the earth.

7. Summer storms can create a dangerous weather condition called a ___.

8. African Americans in the Middle West arrived as a part of the Great ___.

9. An ___ packages the foods grown on farms for sale in grocery stores.

10. During the 1800s, the ___ moved west as people settled new areas.

TECHNOLOGY

For more resources to help you learn about the places you read about, visit **www.mhschool.com** and follow the links for Grade 4 Regions, Unit 4.

◯ SKILL REVIEW

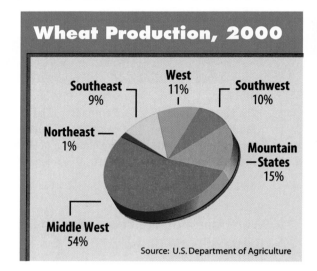

Wheat Production, 2000

West 11%
Southeast 9%
Southwest 10%
Northeast 1%
Mountain States 15%
Middle West 54%

Source: U.S. Department of Agriculture

11. **Study Skill** How can graphs make information easier to understand?

12. **Study Skill** Which region produced more wheat in 2000, the Middle West or the Mountain States?

13. **Study Skill** What type of graph would you use to find how much wheat was produced over a period of time?

14. **Reading/Thinking Skill** What steps do you take to make a generalization?

15. **Reading/Thinking Skill** What generalization can you make about robots and the automobile industry?

1   Without warm ocean breezes, much of the Middle West stays cold and frozen in the winter. Icy winds travel across the plains, chilling everything in their path. Many winter storms begin in the colder parts of Canada. Temperatures fall below the freezing mark. Sometimes blizzards form. Blizzards are winter storms with strong winds and a lot of snow.

2   Cities near the Great Lakes receive heavy snowfall every winter. This lake-effect snow occurs when cold, dry air from Canada meets warmer, damp air over the Great Lakes. Moisture in the air cools and forms snow. Some areas can receive more than 200 inches of lake-effect snow each year.

1   Lake-effect snow is caused when—

   A   warm ocean breezes meet icy winds
   B   temperatures fall below the freezing mark
   C   cold, dry air meets warm, damp air over lakes
   D   air cools to form blizzards over Wisconsin

2   What generalization can you make about winter in the Middle West?

   F   Most people move south during winter in the Middle West.
   G   Blizzards in the Middle West occur only near the Great Lakes.
   H   All areas in the Middle West get 200 inches of snow each year.
   J   Weather in Canada affects winter in the Middle West.

WRITING ACTIVITIES

Writing to Inform **Write** a letter to someone who lives in Europe describing how pioneers lived in the 1800s. Include as many details as you can about their self-sufficient lifestyle.

Writing to Persuade Suppose you were an inventor of a new type of farming equipment. **Write** a letter to a local farmer or an agribusiness to persuade them to use your invention.

Writing to Express Suppose you are visiting Chicago. **Write** a diary entry about a trip to the Sears Tower. Describe the building and the view from the top. You can research the tower in your school library or on the Internet.

LITERATURE

COOLIES

By Yin
Illustrated by Chris Soentpiet

This is the story of Shek and Wong, two brothers who came to America from China. They faced a hard life helping to build a railroad from California into the Mountain States region. In the 1860s, many Chinese workers came to the United States to work on the railroads. They faced prejudice and were called "coolies." The Chinese workers were often given the most dangerous duties. They were also paid less than other workers. Although life was difficult, they were determined to succeed in their new home.

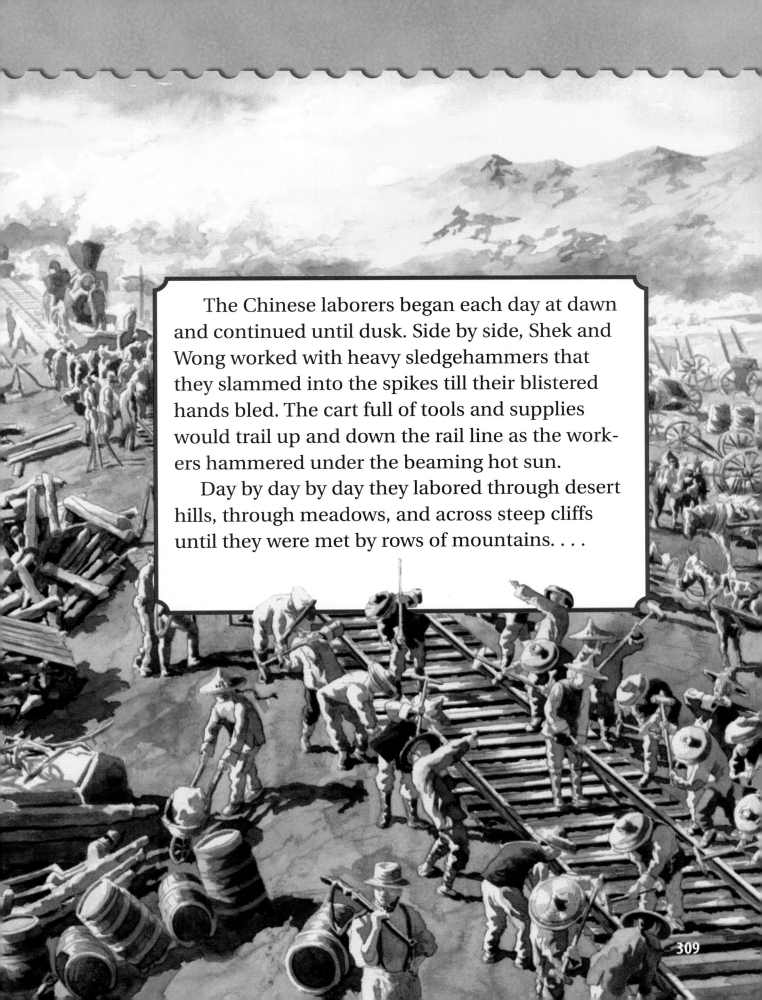

The Chinese laborers began each day at dawn and continued until dusk. Side by side, Shek and Wong worked with heavy sledgehammers that they slammed into the spikes till their blistered hands bled. The cart full of tools and supplies would trail up and down the rail line as the workers hammered under the beaming hot sun.

Day by day by day they labored through desert hills, through meadows, and across steep cliffs until they were met by rows of mountains. . . .

The loud whistle sounded each evening, a signal to the end of a hard workday. When the Chinese laborers returned to their camps, the cooks prepared hot water in tubs so the exhausted workers could bathe.

The brothers also looked forward to mealtime, when the cooks prepared their favorite **Cantonese** dishes—rice with dried fish, mushrooms, bamboo shoots, noodles, and, of course, hot tea.

Cantonese (can tən ēz) of the city or culture of Canton, China

Once a month they wrote to their mother and sent money across the sea to her.

Ma, they wrote. *We hope you are able to buy some crops with this money. Please do not worry about us. Even in this foreign land, someday our family will be rich forever. Your sons, Shek and Wong.*

. . . As seasons passed, the Chinese laborers carried twice their expected workloads at **astonishing** speeds!

One time, as they headed back to their camp . . . Shek turned to admire a **trestle** they had just finished. "Someday our family will see our great accomplishment," he said to his little brother.

---

astonishing (ə ston′ ə shing) surprising
trestle (tres′ əl) frame used to support a railroad bridge

Write About It!

Write a letter for Shek and Wong to their mother. Describe their life in America.

The Mountain States

TAKE A LOOK

How are the Mountain States different?

The Rocky Mountains offer great natural beauty and outdoor activities that attract millions of visitors each year.

Explore more about the Rocky Mountains at our Web site www.mhschool.com

THE **Big** IDEAS ABOUT...

Environment of the Mountain States

Montana, Idaho, Wyoming, Utah, and Colorado are the five states of the Mountain States region. This region is known for the majestic Rocky Mountains, plentiful rivers and forests, and a wealth of mineral resources.

MOUNTAIN MAJESTIES

Tall mountain peaks, thick forests, and hot springs are found in the region's Rocky Mountains.

SNOWY PEAKS

The mountain elevation affects the temperature and amount of precipitation in areas of this region.

MINING IN THE MOUNTAINS

The mining of metals such as copper, gold, and silver led to the region's economic growth.

Foldables

Make this Foldable study guide and use it to record what you learn about the "Environment of the Mountain States."

1. Fold an 8 ½" x 8 ½" square of paper in half on a diagonal.

2. Open and fold in half in the opposite direction. This makes two folds that form an X.

3. Cut up one of the folds stopping at the intersection.

4. Fold and glue one of the cut legs behind the other forming a pyramid.

The Rocky Mountains

Find out!

What are the major natural features of the Mountain States?

Lesson Outline
- The Mountain States
- Nature in the Rockies
- Mesa Verde

VOCABULARY

geyser
Continental Divide

READING STRATEGY

Copy the word web. Use it to fill in the major natural features of the Rocky Mountains.

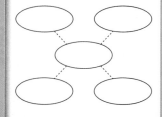

BUILD BACKGROUND

"When I saw the view, I felt great joy. All the wonder of America seemed displayed there, with the sea-like expanse," wrote Katherine Lee Bates. She was writing about being at the top of **Pikes Peak** in the Rocky Mountains. The view also inspired her to write the poem "America the Beautiful." Her words were later set to music.

THE MOUNTAIN STATES

The Mountain States are located west of the Great Plains and east of the states bordering the Pacific Ocean. The region's name comes from the Rocky Mountains, which run through all of its states.

The Rocky Mountains, also known as the "Rockies," begin in Canada and extend all the way to Mexico. They cover a total distance of about 2,000 miles.

The Rockies are actually more than one group of mountains. They are a mountain chain made up of at least 100 different mountain ranges. The highest point is Mount Elbert in Colorado. Its elevation is 14,433 feet.

Golden eagle

The Rockies are known for rugged mountain ranges with deep valleys. These features make it a good home for many different animals and plants.

READING CHECK ✓ What gives the Mountain States region its name?

Pikes Peak

317

NATURE IN THE ROCKIES

Black bears, grizzly bears, mountain lions, and wolverines are just some of the larger animals living in the Rockies. Mountain goats and bighorn sheep are able to live high up on the craggy mountain peaks. Moose live near the northern lakes and streams that cut through the mountains.

Some parts of the mountains have hot springs. These warm pools of water allow birds such as geese, eagles, owls, and turkeys to spend the winter there instead of flying south.

Plant life in the Rocky Mountains changes depending on the elevation. In the valleys, grasses and wildflowers such as columbine, larkspur, and Indian paintbrush grow. Along the lower mountains are trees such as aspen, yellow pine, western red cedar, white spruce, and Douglas fir.

Most of these trees are evergreens and keep their leaves even in the very cold winters. However, trees can't grow near the tops of the mountains. There are only grasses and shrubs, and further up there is nothing but rocks and snow.

Each year 3 million Yellowstone visitors see the **geyser** Old Faithful (above) and wildlife like the bighorn sheep (below).

National Parks

Much of the land in the Rocky Mountains is protected in national parks and wilderness areas. In fact, **Yellowstone National Park** is the oldest national park in the United States. It stretches over 3,468 square miles and includes parts of Wyoming, Montana, and Idaho.

Yellowstone contains fossil forests and over 10,000 hot springs. Some of the hot springs are **geysers**.

318

A geyser is a kind of hot spring that releases jets of steam and water. Old Faithful is the most famous geyser in the park. It erupts regularly every 33 to 120 minutes.

Grand Teton National Park covers 484 square miles in northwestern Wyoming. Its highest peak is Grand Teton, which is 13,766 feet above sea level. Visitors to the park can see buffalo, elk, and antelope living there.

The Continental Divide

The **Continental Divide** is an imaginary line that runs north to south along the peaks of the Rocky Mountains. Find the Continental Divide on the map on this page.

As you can see, the Continental Divide crosses Colorado, Wyoming,

Blue columbine

Idaho, and Montana. It also runs through parts of Canada, the state of New Mexico, Mexico, and Central America.

The Continental Divide is also called the "Great Divide." It separates rivers that flow east from rivers that flow west. Rivers that flow east include the Missouri, Yellowstone, and Arkansas rivers. Others flow west to the Pacific Ocean.

READING CHECK **Where do rivers that flow west end up?**

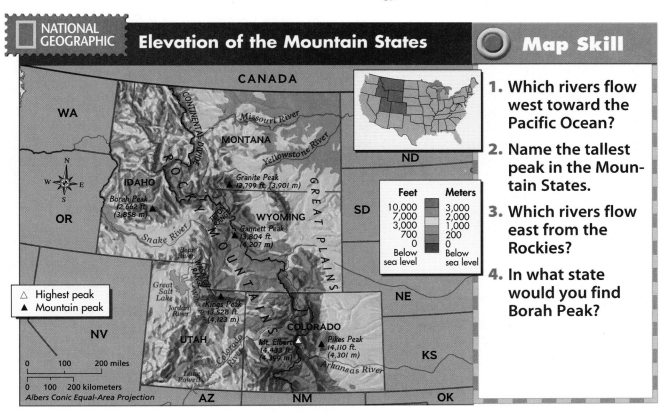

NATIONAL GEOGRAPHIC **Elevation of the Mountain States**

Map Skill

CANADA

WA

MONTANA

Missouri River

Yellowstone River

ND

CONTINENTAL DIVIDE

IDAHO

Granite Peak
12,799 ft. (3,901 m)

ROCKY

Borah Peak
12,662 ft.
(3,858 m)

OR

WYOMING

TETON RANGE

Gannett Peak
13,804 ft.
(4,207 m)

Snake River

SD

GREAT PLAINS

Bear River

MOUNTAINS

WIND RIVER RANGE

Feet	Meters
10,000	3,000
7,000	2,000
3,000	1,000
700	200
0	0
Below sea level	Below sea level

NE

Great Salt Lake

Jordan River

Kings Peak
13,528 ft.
(4,123 m)

△ Highest peak
▲ Mountain peak

NV

UTAH

COLORADO

Mt. Elbert
14,433 ft.
(4,399 m)

Pikes Peak
14,110 ft.
(4,301 m)

KS

Colorado River

0   100   200 miles
0   100   200 kilometers
Albers Conic Equal-Area Projection

Lake Powell

Arkansas River

AZ

NM

OK

1. Which rivers flow west toward the Pacific Ocean?

2. Name the tallest peak in the Mountain States.

3. Which rivers flow east from the Rockies?

4. In what state would you find Borah Peak?

MESA VERDE

Scientists have found evidence of people living in the Mountain States for more than 1,500 years. Ancient people known as the Anasazi lived in **Mesa Verde**, which is in southwestern Colorado. *Mesa Verde* means "green table" in Spanish.

The Anasazi built their homes under the overhanging cliffs of Mesa Verde. Because of this, they are also called the Cliff Dwellers. Their homes were built of sandstone, shaped into blocks. Some of the dwellings had over 200 rooms.

The Anasazi grew corn, beans, and squash in fields high above their homes in the canyons. They were also skilled potters and basket weavers.

Mesa Verde cliff dwellings

HISTORY MYSTERY

What Happened to the Cliff Dwellers?

The Cliff Dwellers lived in Mesa Verde for hundreds of years. But by A.D. 1300 the area was abandoned. No one is entirely sure why.

Some scientists believe that a drought caused the Anasazi people to leave. It is also possible that wars with other Native American groups forced them to move south into New Mexico and Arizona. In 1906, the government set aside the abandoned area as a national park.

Why do you think a drought would make people leave an area?

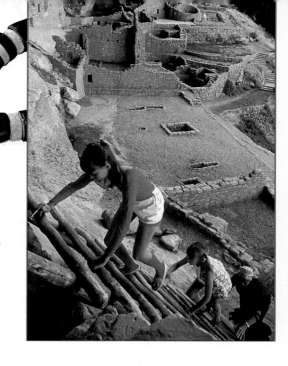

Today people learn about the Anasazi by visiting the cliff dwellings and studying artifacts, such as this Anasazi necklace.

Anasazi Culture

Decorated bowls, ladles, mugs, and other beautifully crafted items have been found throughout the region. Today, people can visit Mesa Verde National Park to see the ancient cliff dwellings. They can climb ladders into rooms. They can also see Anasazi pottery and jewelry. Visits to Mesa Verde help people learn about one of the ancient cultures of our country.

READING CHECK

Why are the Anasazi people also known as the Cliff Dwellers?

PUTTING IT TOGETHER

Today our country's government is faced with many issues affecting the natural features of the Mountain States. Decisions must be made about protecting the region's national parks and wildlife. The goal is to preserve the natural beauty of the region while making the best use of its natural resources.

Review and Assess

1. Write one sentence for each of the vocabulary words:

   Continental Divide   geyser

2. What is the Continental Divide?

3. Describe some natural features of the Mountain States.

   Find out!

4. What do we know about the Anasazi?

5. List some possible **causes** for the disappearance of the Cliff Dwellers.

Look at the map on page 319. Make a three-column chart of the states that fall to the east and west of the Divide. In the third column, list the states that are on both sides of the Divide.

• •

Write a short story describing what it might be like to visit the Rocky Mountains.

Lesson 2

Snowy Peaks

How does elevation affect the Mountain States?

Lesson Outline

• Elevation and Climate
• Mountain Plants and Water

VOCABULARY

timberline

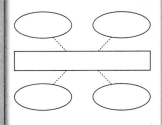

READING STRATEGY

Copy the main idea map you see here. Fill in the main idea. Add supporting details as you read.

BUILD BACKGROUND

Many hikers enjoy the challenge of climbing in the Rockies. The higher into the mountains they climb, the colder it gets. Even during the summer, hikers must be prepared for snow and ice storms. All climbers, even the most skilled, take care to have warm clothes and the right equipment before setting out.

Hiker in the Rocky Mountains

San Luis Valley, Colorado

ELEVATION AND CLIMATE

You have already learned how elevation affects climate. In the Rocky Mountains, precipitation increases with elevation. Low regions of the Rockies tend to be dry. The **San Luis Valley** in Colorado has a desert-like climate that is one of the driest areas in the region.

The mountain peaks receive much more precipitation throughout the year. The amount changes depending on the direction the mountainside faces. Northern slopes receive about three times as much precipitation as the southern slopes. Much of the precipitation in the Rockies falls as snow. Sometimes, however, there are fierce thunderstorms in the summer.

Elevation also affects temperature. Between 7,000 and 10,000 feet, the winters are cold and the summers are cool. Above 10,000 feet the climate is extremely cold all year. The highest mountain peaks in the Rockies are usually covered with snow. Read how one traveler described the climate of the mountains.

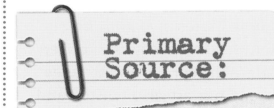

READING CHECK How does elevation affect precipitation in the Rockies?

Primary Source:

excerpt from a letter by
Isabella Bird *describing Longs Peak in Colorado in 1879*

*It is one of the noblest of mountains, but in one's imagination it grows to be much more than a mountain. In its **caverns** . . . one comes to **fancy** that it **generates** . . . the strong winds, to let them loose in its fury. The thunder becomes its voice, and the lightnings do it **homage**.*

Why do you think Isabella Bird called thunder the voice of the mountain?

caverns: caves
fancy: believe
generates: produces
homage: respect, honor

MOUNTAIN PLANTS AND WATER

The Rocky Mountains, like all high mountains, have a **timberline**. The timberline is the point above which it is too cold for trees to grow. The timberline in the central Rockies is around 11,500 feet above sea level.

Elevation also affects plant life in the Rockies. Sagebrush can be found along the valley areas. Forests of fir, pine, and spruce trees are found in higher areas. At about 11,000 feet above sea level, there are krummholz (KRUM holts) forests. *Krummholz* is a German word that means "crooked wood." Here the spruce and fir trees are shorter. They are also twisted and bent. The unusual shapes of these trees help them to survive the lower temperatures and harsh winds.

Above the timberline, there are no trees. Instead there are stretches of grass, and low-growing, plant-like

Unusual Rocky Mountain features include the Great Salt Lake (above) and krummholz (below).

lichens (LI kenz). Lichens require little warmth to survive.

Great Salt Lake

The **Great Salt Lake** is located in northern Utah. It is the largest inland body of salt water in the Western Hemisphere. This lake is fed by the Bear, Weber, and Jordan rivers. Water flows into the lake, but it does not flow out. The mineral salts from the river water are trapped in the lake. Over time, salt buildup made the lake even saltier than the ocean. The Great Salt Lake is considered an important source of minerals.

The size of the Great Salt Lake depends on annual precipitation and the flow of the rivers that feed into it. The area is a popular beach and water-sports attraction, but because of the high salt levels, there is very little

If you climbed a peak in the Rocky Mountains, you would find the temperature falls about 3 degrees Fahrenheit for each thousand feet you climb. Your surroundings would also change as you got higher. Spruce and fir trees would give way to krummholz forests. Then above the timberline, you would find only grass and lichens. Here you could easily see the great effect that elevation has on climate in the Mountain States region.

Heron

wildlife near the lake. Nearby marshes, however, attract birds such as pelicans, herons, and gulls.

Why is the Great Salt Lake saltier than the ocean?

Review and Assess

1. Write one sentence for the following vocabulary word:

   timberline

2. Describe the seasons in the mountains.

3. What effect does high elevation have on the climate of the Mountain States?

4. In what way is the Great Salt Lake a natural resource of the Mountain States?

5. **Compare** and **contrast** the Great Salt Lake with the Pacific Ocean.

Activities

Make a chart with two columns. On one side list three different elevations of the Rocky Mountains. On the other side, list what plant life you would find at each level of elevation.

Suppose you wanted to climb a tall mountain peak in the Rockies. **Write** a paragraph describing the changes you would see as you climbed higher and higher.

Geography Skills

Using Special Purpose Maps: Vegetation Maps

In Chapter 6, you learned about special purpose maps. Distribution maps are one kind of special purpose map. **Vegetation maps** are another. They show the kind of plant life that grows throughout an area. Vegetation maps can include forests, deserts, and even wetlands. Different kinds of vegetation grow in each of those areas. In forests you find trees. In wetlands, you find tall marshy grasses.

VOCABULARY

vegetation map

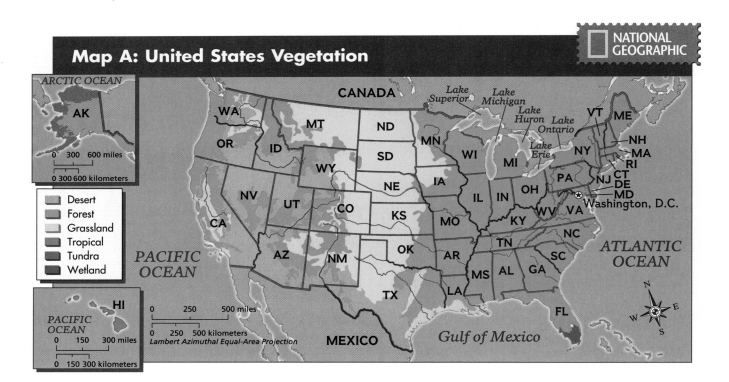

Map A: United States Vegetation

NATIONAL GEOGRAPHIC

LEARN THE SKILL

Study Map A on this page. Then follow the steps below to read vegetation maps.

1. **Locate the title of the map.**
   The title of this map is United States Vegetation. It shows the different kinds of plants that are found throughout our country.

2. **Locate the map key.**
   A vegetation map uses colors to show different kinds of plant areas. A map key can tell you what each color stands for. On Map A, the color blue represents wetlands.

TRY THE SKILL

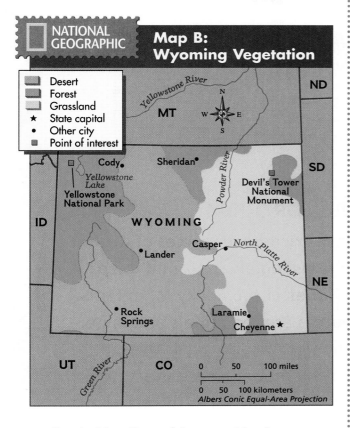

NATIONAL GEOGRAPHIC

Map B: Wyoming Vegetation

- Desert
- Forest
- Grassland
- ★ State capital
- • Other city
- ■ Point of interest

ND
MT
Yellowstone River
N
W E
S
Cody•
Sheridan•
Powder River
SD
■ Yellowstone Lake
Devil's Tower National Monument
Yellowstone National Park
ID
WYOMING
Casper•
North Platte River
•Lander
NE
•Rock Springs
Laramie•
Cheyenne ★
UT
CO
Green River
0   50   100 miles
0   50   100 kilometers
Albers Conic Equal-Area Projection

Study Map B on this page. Use it to answer the following questions.

1. What is the title of the map?

2. Why is this a vegetation map?

3. What does the color yellow stand for?

4. What type of vegetation areas are shown on Map A but not Map B?

EXTEND THE SKILL

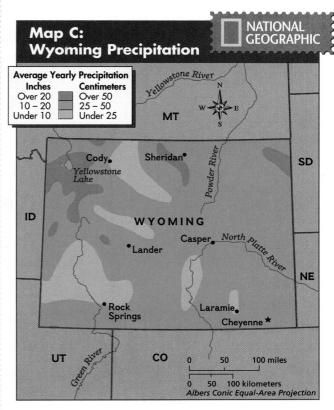

Map C: Wyoming Precipitation

NATIONAL GEOGRAPHIC

Average Yearly Precipitation

Inches	Centimeters
Over 20	Over 50
10 – 20	25 – 50
Under 10	Under 25

Yellowstone River
N
W E
S
MT
Cody•
Sheridan•
Powder River
SD
Yellowstone Lake
ID
WYOMING
Casper•
North Platte River
•Lander
NE
•Rock Springs
Laramie•
Cheyenne ★
UT
CO
Green River
0   50   100 miles
0   50   100 kilometers
Albers Conic Equal-Area Projection

Vegetation maps can help you better understand climate. Different plants grow in different climates. Desert scrub lives on a small amount of water. Trees and grasses need a heavy amount of rain to survive. Compare Map B to Map C, a precipitation map of Wyoming. Then answer the following questions.

- Where are forests mainly found in Wyoming?

- Are the deserts located in the eastern, central, or western part of the state?

- Which area receives the most rain?

- How can reading vegetation maps help you understand plants and climate?

Mining in the Mountains

Find! out!

What are the major natural resources of the Mountain States?

VOCABULARY

smelt

slag

READING STRATEGY

Copy the chart. Fill in the main idea of this lesson. Add supporting details as you read.

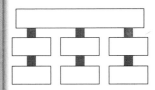

Lesson Outline

• Rocky Mountain Resources

• Copper Mining

BUILD BACKGROUND

Some of the richest resources of the Mountain States region are found deep within the slopes of the Rocky Mountains. These resources are the metals and minerals found in the rock that forms the mountains. They have made mining one of the most important industries in the area since the middle 1800s.

Cut and uncut sapphires

Copper is used to make pennies, electrical wire, and household items such as teapots.

ROCKY MOUNTAIN RESOURCES

The Rocky Mountains supply natural resources to the entire region. Forests provide lumber for the region's mills and timber industry. Mountain rivers and streams supply water to the region's cities.

Metals and Minerals

The region also uses the resources found in the ground in and around the mountains. The most valuable metal found in the Rocky Mountains is copper. It is mined in Montana, Utah, and parts of Canada near the Mountain States region. Copper is used in products like electrical wires, computers, pots, and pans. Natural gas is a resource that is drilled in the Rockies. It is an important source of energy.

The Rockies also contain underground mines for metals such as silver, gold, lead, zinc, and uranium. There are also a few gem mines in the Rockies where dark blue gemstones, known as sapphires, are mined. There is even a rich supply of coal.

The metals, minerals, and gems of the Rockies brought many miners to the Mountain States in the 1860s. The mining towns that sprang up here at the time helped to develop the region's early economy.

What is the most valuable metal found in the Rockies?

329

COPPER MINING

You already know how open-pit mining is used to remove minerals and metals, such as copper, that are close to the surface of Earth. Once the copper ore is removed, it must be processed to separate the metal from the rock. **Smelting** is one method that was used in the 1800s and is still used today. Smelting is the process of using high temperatures to separate pure metals from rock.

The copper ore is placed in a furnace and heated to very high temperatures. Gradually the ore melts into a liquid. Some parts of the ore burn away or change into a gas. Once these gases are gone, only the liquid is left.

In the smelted liquid, the heavy copper sinks to the bottom. The top layer of the liquid is filled with waste materials. These waste materials are called **slag**. The slag is skimmed off the top of the liquid. The remaining pure copper can be used to make many kinds of goods.

Bingham Canyon Mine

The Bingham Canyon Mine near **Salt Lake City**, Utah is the largest mine in the world. It is two and a half miles wide and nearly a mile deep. It is about the size of 120 football fields. The Bingham Canyon Mine is one of the few man-made things on Earth that can be seen from space.

People began open-pit mining in the Bingham Canyon Mine in 1906. The main products of the mine are copper, gold, and silver. However, the mine also produces 20 different kinds of minerals.

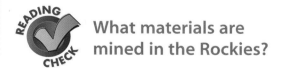

READING CHECK What materials are mined in the Rockies?

Liquid copper ore (left) is hardened into bars (above) that can be stored or used.

PUTTING IT TOGETHER

The Bingham Canyon Mine has decided to end open-pit mining by the year 2012. Soon miners will dig tunnels in from the side so they can start mining under the pit. New methods of mining are important in order to conserve the natural resources in this region. Without these resources, the cities of the Mountain States would not have fresh water, lumber for building, or metals and minerals used to manufacture goods.

Visitors to the Bingham Canyon Mine can look down into the open pit where copper is removed to make the items shown here.

© Courtesy of Kennecott Utah Copper Corporation

Review and Assess

1. Write a sentence for each of the vocabulary words:

   slag   smelt

2. How large is the Bingham Canyon Mine?

3. Name three natural resources of the Mountain States region.

4. What effect did mining have on the early **economy** of the Mountain States?

5. What can you **infer** about the future of the Bingham Canyon Mine?

Activities

Make a flowchart showing the sequence of events that happen when copper is removed from the ground and prepared for use.

• • • • • • • • • • • • • • • • • • •

What else would you like to know about the largest mine in the world? **Write** a letter to the Bingham Canyon Mine asking for more information about the mine.

331

Chapter 9 REVIEW

VOCABULARY REVIEW

Number a sheet of paper from 1 to 5. Beside each number write the word or term from the list below that matches the description.

Continental Divide	smelt
geyser	timberline
slag	

1. waste materials produced during the process of removing pure metal from ore
2. a method of separating metal from rocks and other minerals in ore
3. a kind of hot spring that releases jets of water and steam
4. the line on high mountains above which it is too cold for trees to grow
5. an imaginary line that runs north to south along the peaks of the Rockies.

CHAPTER COMPREHENSION

6. Name at least three animals that make their home in the Rockies.
7. What is the oldest national park in the United States?
8. How would you know that you have reached the timberline of the Rockies?
9. Describe some climate changes that are caused by mountain elevations.
10. Where is the Great Salt Lake located?
11. What metals are mined in the Rocky Mountains?
12. What is the largest open pit mine in the world and where is it located?
13. Describe how copper is processed after it is removed from the ground.

SKILL REVIEW

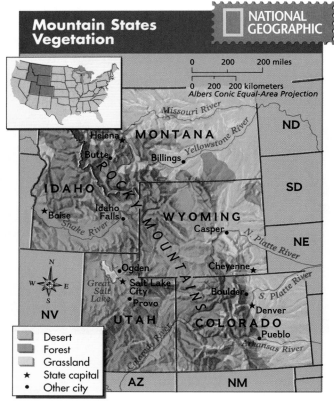

Mountain States Vegetation

NATIONAL GEOGRAPHIC

0   200   200 miles
0   200   200 kilometers
Albers Conic Equal-Area Projection

- Desert
- Forest
- Grassland
- ★ State capital
- • Other city

14. **Geography Skill** What information can you get from a vegetation map?
15. **Geography Skill** Name the states where grassland is found in the region.
16. **Geography Skill** What type of vegetation surrounds Great Salt Lake?
17. **Geography Skill** What are some reasons why you would want to use a vegetation map?
18. **Geography Skill** How does the climate of the Rockies affect the region's vegetation?

USING A CHART

19. During what month does Denver receive the smallest amount of rainfall?

20. Which of the four seasons brings the greatest amount of rainfall to Denver?

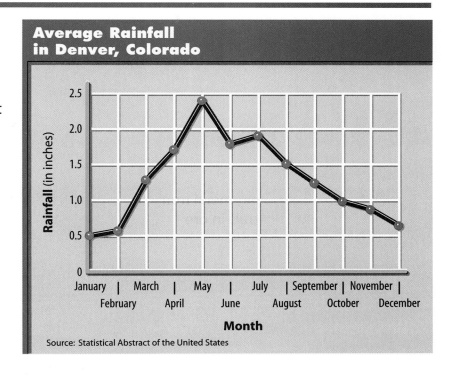

Average Rainfall in Denver, Colorado

Rainfall (in inches)

Month

Source: Statistical Abstract of the United States

Activity

Writing about Local Environment Using your school library or the Internet, research some of the issues facing our national parks. Choose one issue and summarize the problems and solutions being considered. Add supporting details to explain which solution you think would work best.

Foldables

Use your Foldable to review what you have learned about the environment of the Mountain States. Arrange the classroom Foldables to form a mountain range. As you look at the mountains, discuss as a class what you learned about the five mountain states—Idaho, Wyoming, Colorado, Utah, and Montana. Review your notes on the inside of your Foldables to check your memory and responses.

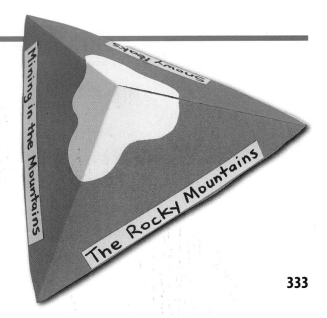

Chapter 10

THE Big IDEAS ABOUT...

History and Economy of the Mountain States

Shoshone Native Americans have lived on the eastern and western edges of the Rocky Mountains for hundreds of years. In the middle 1800s, they were joined by thousands of settlers in search of gold. Today the Mountain States is a region of open land and growing cities.

THE SHOSHONE

© American Heritage Center, University of Wyoming

The way of life of the Shoshone people changed with the arrival of settlers.

EXPLORATION AND BOOM TOWNS

The discovery of gold brought thousands of people into the Rockies.

THE FIGHT FOR WOMEN'S RIGHTS

The earliest victories in women's fight for the right to vote occurred in the Mountain States.

THE MOUNTAIN STATES TODAY

Outdoor activities make the Mountain States region a popular destination for tourists.

Foldables

Make this Foldable study guide and use it to record what you learn about the "History and Economy of the Mountain States."

1. Fold a sheet of 8 ½" x 11" paper in half like a hamburger, but leave one side of the paper 1" longer than the other.

2. Make one cut on the short side to form two tabs of equal size.

3. Label the tabs "History" and "Economy." Cut the two tabs to look like mountains. Take notes under the tabs.

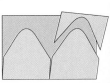

1

The Shoshone

Who are the Native Americans of the Mountain States region?

Lesson Outline

- People of the Mountains
- Different Ways of Life
- The Shoshone Today

VOCABULARY

treaty

PEOPLE

Chief Washakie

READING STRATEGY

Copy the main idea pyramid. Fill in the main idea and the supporting details as you read the lesson.

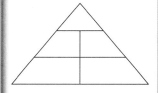

BUILD BACKGROUND

In 1868, **Chief Washakie** of the Shoshone Native Americans explained his relationship with the region's white settlers: "I fought to keep our land, our water and our hunting grounds. . . ." Today many Shoshone people live on their ancestors' land because of Chief Washakie's efforts.

Snake River in Wyoming

PEOPLE OF THE MOUNTAINS

In the past, the Shoshone lived east and west of the Rockies. This included western Wyoming and Montana, central and southern Idaho, and parts of Utah, Nevada, and Oregon. Find them and other Native American groups of the region on the map below.

The Snake Nation

The Shoshone and their neighbors, the Bannock, are also known as the Snake Nation. When the first white explorers arrived in the region, the Shoshone identified themselves by moving their hands in a swimming motion. This meant that they lived near the river with many fish. To explorers the motion looked like that of a snake. The Snake River is named for the Snake Nation.

© Courtesy, National Museum of the American Indian, Smithsonian Institution

Moccasins, late 1800s

READING CHECK

What groups make up the Snake Nation?

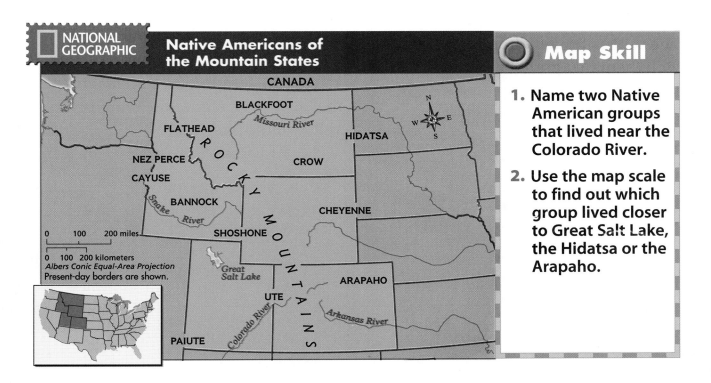

NATIONAL GEOGRAPHIC

Native Americans of the Mountain States

CANADA

BLACKFOOT

FLATHEAD

Missouri River

NEZ PERCE

CAYUSE

HIDATSA

ROCKY

CROW

BANNOCK

Snake River

CHEYENNE

SHOSHONE

MOUNTAINS

0   100   200 miles

0   100   200 kilometers
Albers Conic Equal-Area Projection
Present-day borders are shown.

Great Salt Lake

UTE

ARAPAHO

Colorado River

Arkansas River

PAIUTE

Map Skill

1. **Name two Native American groups that lived near the Colorado River.**

2. **Use the map scale to find out which group lived closer to Great Salt Lake, the Hidatsa or the Arapaho.**

DIFFERENT WAYS OF LIFE

The Shoshone were made up of different groups. In the west, they lived in roofless grass huts and hunted fish, birds, and rabbits. In the north and east, the Shoshone lived in teepees, rode horses, and hunted buffalo.

Northern Shoshone, such as the Lemhi, once lived on the plains in Montana, but rival Blackfeet, Hidatsa, and other groups drove them to the mountains. The Northern Shoshone moved from place to place for food. In between buffalo hunts, they ate roots, berries, salmon, and small animals.

Settlers Arrive

The first white settlers to come in contact with the Shoshone were fur traders in the early 1800s. By the 1860s, many more settlers began arriving in Montana and Idaho in search of gold. The settlers brought horses and cattle with them that grazed on Shoshone land. The settlers also hunted in Shoshone territory. As the grassland and buffalo began to disappear, many Shoshone grew concerned about protecting their land.

© American Heritage Center, University of Wyoming

Chief Washakie

Chief Washakie

Chief Washakie, a noted warrior among the Shoshone, did not believe in warfare with the white settlers. He thought instead that both groups should help each other. He assisted the United States Army against warring Native Americans, such as the Sioux and Cheyenne.

In return, Chief Washakie asked for schools, churches, and hospitals to be built for the Shoshone. He also asked for a reservation in the **Wind River Valley**, which was originally given to the Crow. The United States government decided that the Crow had not kept to the terms of an earlier agreement. In 1868, it gave the Wind River Valley to the Shoshone.

Buffalo near the Grand Teton Mountains

Fort Bridger Treaty

On July 3, 1868, Chief Washakie signed the Fort Bridger Treaty. A **treaty** is an agreement in writing between two or more groups. The Fort Bridger Treaty was one of the last treaties signed between the United States government and a Native American community.

The Fort Bridger Treaty established the Wind River and **Fort Hall Reservations** for the Shoshone Indians. The Shoshone did not have to move from their land, as other Native Americans had been forced to do. Yet the Shoshone's original 44 million acres of land were reduced to less than 3 million acres. In addition, by signing the treaty, Chief Washakie gave permission to the Union Pacific Railroad to build a rail line that went through Shoshone land in western Wyoming.

Read the following excerpt that describes how the Shoshone would live once the treaty was signed.

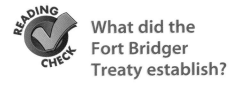

What did the Fort Bridger Treaty establish?

Primary Source:

excerpt from Article 4 of the Fort Bridger Treaty
— *written on July 3, 1868*

*"The Indians herein named agree . . . they will make said reservations their permanent home, and they will make no permanent settlement elsewhere; but they shall have the right to hunt on the unoccupied lands of the United States so long as **game** may be found **thereon**, and so long as peace [exists] among the whites and Indians on the borders of the hunting districts."*

Under what conditions would Indians be allowed to hunt on unoccupied lands of the United States?

game: wild animals
thereon: on it

This painting by Albert Bierstadt shows a Native American settlement in the Wind River Mountains.

© Larry Sanders/Milwaukee Art Museum, Layton Art Collection

THE SHOSHONE TODAY

Today, many Shoshone live on reservations in Idaho, Wyoming, and Nevada. The Shoshone and the Arapaho Indians share the Wind River Reservation in Fremont County, Wyoming. In 1876, the Arapaho were forced to give up their land and move to the Shoshone Reservation. The two groups did not always get along, which made life difficult. However, today both groups equally rule the Wind River Reservation with two separate governments.

The Fort Hall Reservation is located along the Snake River in southeastern Idaho. Members of the Shoshone live there with the Bannock tribe. The reservation's name comes from a trading post that was built on the Shoshone's winter grounds near the Snake River in the early 1800s.

On the Reservation

Many Shoshone live and work on the Fort Hall and Wind River Reservations. They work on farms, in stores, and run a number of different businesses on the reservations. These include galleries of Native American arts and crafts, and historical and cultural centers.

There are also several Native American reservations in the Four Corners region. In Unit 1, you read that the "Four Corners" is located where the borders of Colorado, Utah, Arizona, and New Mexico meet. The Ute, for example, live in Colorado and Utah.

Festivals

Today the Shoshone participate in festivals that honor their culture and history. On the Wind River Reservation, powwows are held in the spring and summer. People dance, sing, and talk together. The Shoshone-Bannock Indian Festival is one of the most popular Native American celebrations in North America. It is held in August every year at the Fort Hall Reservation.

What happens at a powwow?

These two Shoshone women are standing before a row of teepees on a Wyoming reservation.

PUTTING IT TOGETHER

The Wind River Reservation is the only reservation in the United States where Native Americans could choose where they wanted to live. This was because of the treaty Chief Washakie signed. When he died in 1900, he was buried in Fort Washakie. This is the only military fort in the United States to be named after a Native American chief.

This dancer performs at a Fort Hall Reservation powwow (above). A Shoshone artist designed these gloves (right).

Review and Assess

1. Write a sentence using the following vocabulary word:

   treaty

2. Where do most Shoshone live today?

3. Identify the Native Americans of the Mountain States region.

4. How do Shoshone celebrate their **cultural** heritage today?

5. What **inference** can you make about Chief Washakie and the Shoshone?

Activities

Compare the map on page 337 to the one on page 319. Make a chart that lists the Native American groups found in each state.

• •

Using the school library or the Internet, research *powwows*. **Write** a one-page report describing the activities held during a powwow.

Exploration and Boom Towns

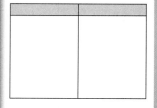

What led to the settlement of the Mountain States region?

Lesson Outline
- Lewis and Clark
- Boom Towns
- Building Railroads

VOCABULARY

Louisiana Purchase
expedition
ghost town
transcontinental

PEOPLE

Meriwether Lewis
William Clark
York
Sacagawea

READING STRATEGY

Copy the two-column chart. Fill in facts about exploration and settlement in the region.

BUILD BACKGROUND

For many years only Native Americans were familiar with the lands west of the Mississippi River. In 1804, President Jefferson asked **Meriwether Lewis** and **William Clark** to explore this territory. In a letter, Jefferson told them to, "take observations . . . at all remarkable points. . . ."

Courtesy of the Montana Historical Society

LEWIS AND CLARK

In 1803, the United States purchased the Louisiana Territory from France. This was known as the **Louisiana Purchase**. The Louisiana Territory stretched from the Mississippi to the Rocky Mountains. With this purchase, the United States doubled in size.

President Thomas Jefferson organized an **expedition** to explore this vast, unknown territory. An expedition is a journey taken for a specific purpose. Captain Meriwether Lewis and Lieutenant William Clark led the expedition. They brought with them about 40 people, including **York**, Clark's African American servant. **Sacagawea**, a Shoshone, served as the expedition's guide and translator.

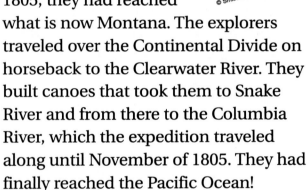
© Smithsonian Institution

Across the Rockies

Lewis and Clark's expedition started on the Missouri River in 1804. By the spring of 1805, they had reached what is now Montana. The explorers traveled over the Continental Divide on horseback to the Clearwater River. They built canoes that took them to Snake River and from there to the Columbia River, which the expedition traveled along until November of 1805. They had finally reached the Pacific Ocean!

Lewis and Clark brought back journals that told of their adventures across the West. In addition, they mapped over 3,000 miles of land. The entire journey took them 18 months. Today, the trip would only take about 5 hours by plane.

READING CHECK Why did President Jefferson send Lewis and Clark on an expedition?

Clark's compass (above). This painting (left) shows Lewis and Clark with Sacagawea in the center, possibly York on the left, and other members of the **expedition**.

343

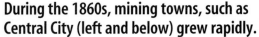
Colorado Historical Society

During the 1860s, mining towns, such as Central City (left and below) grew rapidly.

Pikes Peak

In 1859 gold nuggets were discovered in a stream near Pikes Peak, in Colorado. Thousands of people rushed into the Rockies to seek their fortune. Many covered wagons were painted with the words "Pikes Peak or Bust" on the side.

The miners who first came to the region made a temporary home in a settlement called Cherry Creek. By 1860, this bustling settlement had been given a new name—**Denver**. It became a supply center for miners all over the region.

BOOM TOWNS

For many years, trappers were the only settlers who came to the Mountain States region. In the 1840s, Mormons arrived seeking freedom to practice their religion. Then, in 1859, a discovery was made that brought overwhelming numbers of people to the Mountain States region. It also encouraged the economic growth of the region.

From Boom Towns to Ghost Towns

Many towns grew rapidly during the days of "gold fever." In just two months, the population of **Central City,** Colorado grew to 10,000 people once gold was discovered nearby. Churches, schools, and even an opera

house were quickly built for the growing community.

By 1900, many of the miners in the region were gone. The gold had run out and there was no longer a reason to stay in the mining towns. Without customers, the storekeepers closed up shop. So did the people who ran the hotels, stables, and other businesses. Almost overnight, a community could turn into a **ghost town**—an empty town without people.

Today there are still ghost towns scattered around the Mountain States. They have deserted streets and crumbling buildings. Visitors can come to these towns to see what the region was like over 100 years ago.

Why did some mining towns become ghost towns?

Visitors explore St. Elmo in Colorado (above), an empty **ghost town**. Miners used pans and picks to search for gold (below).

BUILDING RAILROADS

In the 1860s, work on the first **transcontinental** railroad began. Transcontinental means "across the continent." This railroad would connect the Pacific and Atlantic coasts. Using axes, picks, shovels, and dynamite, crews laid tracks through the deserts and mountains.

© Stanford University Museum of Art

The tracks started from two places, one in the Middle West, and one in the West. On May 10, 1869, the two lines met at **Promontory Point** in Utah. With the railroad complete, people could now travel to the west cheaply and quickly. Goods could also be shipped more easily.

Hard Work

Chinese immigrants did much of the building of the transcontinental railroad. The workers were paid very little and the work was dangerous. They were lowered by ropes from the tops of cliffs in baskets. There, they chipped away at the rock and planted explosives that were used to blast tunnels. Many Chinese workers died from the dangerous conditions and harsh winters.

The transcontinental railroad forever changed the way of life for Native Americans in the Mountain States.

The buffalo population was almost entirely killed off during the building of the railroads. Native Americans could no longer rely on the animals for their survival.

READING CHECK Describe working conditions for Chinese immigrants on the railroads.

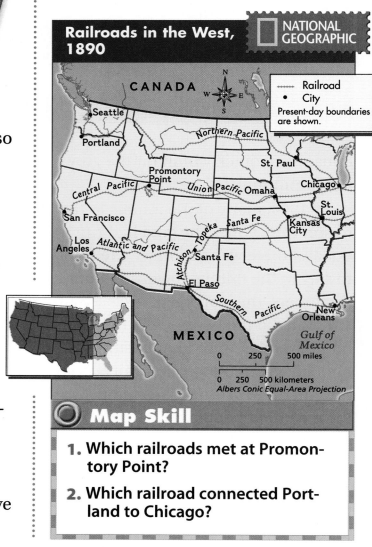

Railroads in the West, 1890

NATIONAL GEOGRAPHIC

Railroad
• City
Present-day boundaries are shown.

CANADA

Seattle
Portland
Northern Pacific
St. Paul
Promontory Point
Central Pacific
Union Pacific Omaha
Chicago
San Francisco
St. Louis
Los Angeles
Atlantic and Pacific
Atchison
Topeka
Santa Fe
Kansas City
Santa Fe
El Paso
Southern Pacific
New Orleans
MEXICO
Gulf of Mexico

0   250   500 miles
0   250   500 kilometers
Albers Conic Equal-Area Projection

Map Skill

1. Which railroads met at Promontory Point?

2. Which railroad connected Portland to Chicago?

Exploring TECHNOLOGY

Transcontinental Telegraph

In 1861, the Western Union Telegraph Company built the first transcontinental telegraph. The telegraph transmitted messages using Morse code. Before that, the Pony Express was the fastest way to send messages across our country. One team worked on the telegraph line from the west. Another team worked from the east. The line was completed on October 24 in Salt Lake City. That night, the first message was sent to President Abraham Lincoln.

Write a message that someone might have sent the day the telegraph line was completed.

PUTTING IT TOGETHER

Lewis and Clark's expedition opened up the western United States to exploration and settlement. Discoveries of gold soon brought thousands of people to the Mountain States in the middle 1800s. The building of the transcontinental railroad made it even easier for people to settle in the region. But for Native Americans, the railroads marked the end of their traditional way of life.

Review and Assess

1. Write one sentence using each of the following vocabulary words:

   **expedition   Louisiana Purchase
   ghost town   transcontinental**

2. Who was Sacagawea?

3. Explain the **causes** behind the settlement of the Mountain States region.

4. How did new **technology** improve communications in the United States?

5. What **generalizations** can you make about boom towns in the 1800s?

Using the information in this lesson, create a time line listing events between 1800 and 1900.

. . . .

Suppose you moved to Central City, Colorado in the year 1861. **Write** a journal entry describing what you might have seen.

Drawing Conclusions

Suppose you knew the following facts. Your school's softball team lost all the games it played in April. Rosa, a new pitcher, joined the team in May. The team went on to win the rest of the season. Based on these facts, you conclude that Rosa led the softball team to a winning streak.

VOCABULARY

conclusion

Sometimes meanings or connections are not always clear. Drawing inferences is one way to better understand what you read. Drawing **conclusions** can also help.

A conclusion is a statement based on several pieces of information. It tries to explain what the information means. A conclusion does not repeat facts. Instead, it adds them up and tells you how they are connected.

LEARN THE SKILL

Follow these steps to draw a conclusion.

1. **Identify a topic.**
   First, you must identify a topic. For example, suppose people in your area are concerned about an increase in traffic.

2. **Gather facts.**
   Next, gather facts about the topic. After reading about the traffic problem in your local newspaper, you learn the following:

   - The population in your area has increased over the last five years.

   - The roads are always crowded with traffic.

   - The city council has started construction on a new highway.

3. **Make a conclusion or a statement.**
   After looking at the facts, you make the following statement. *"The city council is building a highway to deal with the growing number of people in the community."* This conclusion connects all three facts. It finds a common idea behind them and says it in one sentence.

TRY THE SKILL

While reading an article on Central City, Colorado, you learn the following facts:

- Central City became a boom town when settlers arrived in search of gold.

- Homes, schools, and even an opera house were built for the growing community.

- Today, Central City is one of the last examples of an old mining town.

- Tourists can visit restored buildings, historic gold mines, and the Central City Opera House.

Draw a conclusion about tourists and the history of Central City. Then answer the following questions.

1. What is your conclusion?

2. How did you reach it?

3. Is the statement *"Tourists can visit historic buildings in Central City"* a conclusion about the topic? Why or why not?

4. How can drawing conclusions help you better understand what you read?

EXTEND THE SKILL

In the last lesson, you learned about the Lewis and Clark expedition. Read the following passage and draw a conclusion. Use your conclusion to answer the questions below.

Sacagawea served as a translator and guide on the expedition. She helped the group get food, horses, and supplies. Sacagawea also established ties between the explorers and the region's Native American groups.

- What conclusion can you make about Sacagawea's role on the expedition?

- Name some occasions when drawing conclusions can help you study.

Women Fight for Their Rights

How did American women win the right to vote?

Lesson Outline
- The Right to Vote
- A Growing Movement
- The Nineteenth Amendment

VOCABULARY

suffrage

PEOPLE

Elizabeth Cady Stanton

Lucretia Mott

Susan B. Anthony

Esther Morris

Jeannette Rankin

Nellie Tayloe Ross

READING STRATEGY

Copy this chart. Fill in the major events from the right to vote movement in the correct sequence.

BUILD BACKGROUND

Wyoming's official nickname is "The Equality State." In this lesson you will learn how Wyoming —and other Mountain States—became known for equal rights. It took many years for women to earn the right to vote in our country. As you will read, the first great victories were in the Mountain States region.

Women protesting in 1910

© National Museum of American History

350

1800	1850	1900	1950	2000

You Are Here
1848 – 1920

THE RIGHT TO VOTE

Every citizen has the right to vote. This right is called **suffrage** (SUF rihj). Yet for much of our country's history, many Americans were not allowed to vote. For many years African Americans could not elect our leaders. Neither could Native Americans or women of any ethnic group.

The fight for women's suffrage began in 1848. In that year, a meeting was held at Seneca Falls, New York. Led by **Elizabeth Cady Stanton** and **Lucretia Mott**, the women argued for equality between men and women. They summed up their ideas in a document called the Declaration of Rights and Sentiments. In this statement they demanded "all the rights and privileges which belong to [women] as citizens of the United States."

Susan B. Anthony

In 1851 **Susan B. Anthony** met Elizabeth Cady Stanton at Seneca Falls, New York. They discussed how women could win a wide variety of rights, such as voting, holding public office, and serving on juries. For the next 50 years, they led the fight for women's suffrage. In 1872, Susan B. Anthony was arrested for trying to vote in the presidential election. Read part of a speech she gave the following year.

READING CHECK What is suffrage?

excerpt from **a speech by Susan B. Anthony**
— *1873*

*It was we, the people; not we . . . the male citizens; but we the whole people, who formed the Union. And we formed it, not to give the blessings of liberty, but to **secure** them; not to the half of ourselves . . . but to the whole people—women as well as men. And it is a downright **mockery** to talk to women of their enjoyment of the blessings of liberty while they are denied . . . the ballot.*

What do you think "securing" liberty means?

secure: to fix or fasten
mockery: joke

351

BIOGRAPHY

Focus On: Responsibility

Elizabeth Cady Stanton spent a lot of time in her father's law office as a young girl. She saw that her father could not always help the women who came to him because the law did not treat women equally. It often kept them from claiming property or controlling their family's money. Women also could not vote to change the laws.

Years later, Stanton held a meeting on women's rights and called for women to gain the right to vote. She also created the National Woman Suffrage Association with activist Susan B. Anthony. They worked for legal, economic, and political changes to improve all women's rights.

Stanton died before women got the right to vote. However, she is still remembered for her work and dedication to improving the rights of women.

Link to Today

Using your school library or the Internet, research women's rights issues since 1920. Describe some women's rights issues today and what might be done about them.

THE LIFE OF ELIZABETH CADY STANTON	1815 Born in Johnstown, New York	1848 Holds meeting in Seneca Falls	1868 Founds suffrage association	1881 Publishes a history of women's rights	1902 Dies eighteen years before women can vote
	1800	1825	1850	1875	1900
LIFE AROUND THE WORLD	1846 Mexican American war is fought	1861 American Civil War begins	1863 Emancipation Proclamation	1875 Alexander Graham Bell invents the telephone	1901 President McKinley is assassinated

This engraving (above) shows women voting in Cheyenne, Wyoming during the 1888 presidential election.

Courtesy of the Sophia Smith Collection/Smith College

A GROWING MOVEMENT

During the 1860s and 1870s, Stanton and Anthony traveled throughout the Mountain States to speak about their cause. Gradually the suffrage movement gained support in the region.

The women who moved west worked alongside men in jobs women did not usually have. They also wanted to take a role in citizenship. Many men there agreed. These men had started new lives and were open to new ideas. Women's suffrage was one of them.

Women Win the Right

In 1869 only about 1,000 women lived in the entire state of Wyoming. One of those women, **Esther Morris**, of **South Pass City**, had just arrived from Illinois.

Morris was a strong speaker who supported women's suffrage. She helped convince Wyoming's lawmakers to create a bill giving women the right to vote. In December 1869 the legislature passed a law declaring that "every woman of the age of twenty-one years residing in this territory may at every election . . . cast her vote."

Some of the lawmakers who voted for the bill thought it would encourage women to live in Wyoming. A delighted Susan B. Anthony urged her followers to move there. One year later the women of the Utah Territory won the same right.

Esther Morris

READING CHECK Which state first gave women the right to vote?

THE NINETEENTH AMENDMENT

In Wyoming women could vote, but not in many other states. In some states women could vote for president, but not in other elections.

To grant women throughout our country the right to vote, Congress would have to pass an amendment to the Constitution. But who would fight for such an amendment?

The answer came in 1916. In that year Montana voters elected **Jeannette Rankin** to the United States House of Representatives. She was the first woman to serve in Congress.

In 1919 Congress passed the Nineteenth Amendment to the Constitution. The state legislatures approved it the next year. Women's right to vote became the law across the United States at last.

A Governor for Wyoming

The struggle for equal rights did not end with the Nineteenth Amendment. Women continued to work for equality.

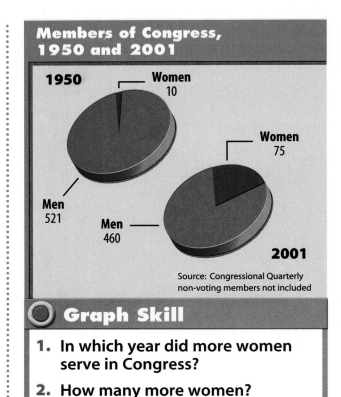

Members of Congress, 1950 and 2001

1950
Women 10
Men 521

Women 75
Men 460
2001

Source: Congressional Quarterly
non-voting members not included

Graph Skill

1. **In which year did more women serve in Congress?**

2. **How many more women?**

Several years later another victory took place in Wyoming. In 1924 Wyoming voters elected **Nellie Tayloe Ross** as their governor. She was the first woman to serve as a governor in our country's history. More than 50 years later, on her 100th birthday, Ross was quoted as saying that her career marked "a milestone in the battle for women's equality."

When did state legislatures approve the Nineteenth Amendment?

Representative Jeannette Rankin speaks on the floor of the United States Congress in 1917.

PUTTING IT TOGETHER

The struggle for women's suffrage began in the East. Yet its earliest victories occurred in the Mountain States region. Why? The people who moved west left behind many of the customs of their old homes. This might have made them open to new ideas. The suffrage movement took many years of effort. The women you just read about, struggled long and hard to win the rights we all enjoy today.

Women suffragists used posters and buttons to help fight for their cause.

Courtesy of the Sophia Smith Collection/Smith College

Review and Assess

1. Write a sentence using the following vocabulary word:

   suffrage

2. How did Susan B. Anthony help women win suffrage?

3. How did American women fight to win the vote?

4. Why is it important for every citizen to have the right to vote?

5. What **conclusion** can you draw about the women's suffrage movement in the Mountain States region?

Activities

Look at the graph on page 354. How many members of Congress, men and women, served in 2001 compared to 1950?

. . . .

Suppose you are on a speaking tour with Susan B. Anthony. **Write** a short speech that you will deliver in support of women's suffrage.

Reference Sources

Suppose you wanted to learn more about a topic from this textbook. You could do research using **reference sources**. These are books and other sources that contain facts about many different subjects. They can be found in a special part of the library called the reference section.

LEARN THE SKILL

The steps below show ways to use reference sources.

1. **Use a dictionary.**
   You might want to know the exact meaning of the word *souvenir*. To find out, you would look in a **dictionary**. A dictionary gives the meanings of words. It shows how to pronounce and spell each word.

2. **Use guide words.**
   The words in a dictionary are arranged in alphabetical order. To find your word quickly, you can refer to **guide words**. These appear at the top of each page of the dictionary. They tell you the first and last words defined on that page.

3. **Use an encyclopedia or a CD-ROM.**
   Another useful reference tool is an **encyclopedia**. This book or set of books gives information about people, places, things, and events. Like a dictionary, topics in an encyclopedia are arranged in

alphabetical order. Suppose you want to learn more about suffrage. You would look in the encyclopedia volume, or book, with the letter *S* on the spine.

A newer kind of reference source is the **CD-ROM**. A CD-ROM is a compact disc that you "read" with the aid of a computer. Like an encyclopedia, a CD-ROM contains facts about many subjects. It may also include sounds, music, and even short movies! The **Internet** is another new kind of reference source. It is a computer network. If you use a computer that has an Internet connection, you can "visit" sources of information such as schools or government offices.

TRY THE SKILL

Look at the sample dictionary page below. Use it to answer the following questions.

1. What is the last word to be defined on the page?

2. Would the word *star* appear on the page? How about the word *spaceship*?

3. Which volume of the encyclopedia would you use to learn more about Susan B. Anthony?

4. Some encyclopedias have guide words instead of letters. Suppose you had a volume covering everything from *Election* to *Government*. Would it contain an article about the *governor*? What about *equality*?

EXTEND THE SKILL

Use reference sources in your school or local library to write a paragraph on Nellie Tayloe Ross. Include the meaning of the word *governor*. Use your paragraph to answer the following questions.

- Which reference source did you use to find the meaning of the word *governor*?

- Which reference source did you use to research the life of Nellie Tayloe Ross?

- When are reference sources useful to students?

S **southwards ➤ space shuttle**

ward slope of the mountain. Adjective.
south·ward (south′wərd) *adverb; adjective.*
southwards Another spelling of the adverb southward: *They drove southwards.* **south·wards** (south′wərdz) *adverb.*
southwest 1. The direction halfway between south and west. 2. The point of the compass showing this direction. 3. A region or place in this direction. 4. **the Southwest.** The region in the south and west of the United States. *Noun.*
  ○ 1. Toward or in the southwest: *the southwest corner of the street.* 2. Coming from the southwest: *a southwest wind. Adjective.*
  ○ Toward the southwest: *The ship sailed southwest. Adverb.*
south·west (south′west′) *noun; adjective; adverb.*
souvenir Something kept because it reminds one of a person, place, or event: *I bought a pennant as a souvenir of the baseball game.* **sou·ve·nir** (sü′və nir′ *or* sü′və nir′) *noun, plural* **souvenirs.**
sovereign A king or queen. *Noun.*
  ○ 1. Having the greatest power or highest rank or authority: *The king and queen were the sovereign rulers of the country.* 2. Not controlled by others; independent: *Mexico is a sovereign nation. Adjective.*
sov·er·eign (sov′ər ən *or* sov′rən) *noun, plural* **sovereigns;** *adjective.*
Soviet Union Formerly, a large country in eastern Europe and northern Asia. It was composed of 15 republics and was also called the U.S.S.R. The

largest and most important of the 15 republics was Russia.
sow¹ 1. To scatter seeds over the ground; plant: *The farmer will sow corn in this field.* 2. To spread or scatter: *The clown sowed happiness among the children.*
  Other words that sound like this are **sew** and **so.**
sow (sō) *verb,* **sowed, sown** *or* **sowed, sowing.**
sow² An adult female pig. **sow** (sou) *noun, plural* **sows.**
soybean A seed rich in oil and protein and used as food. Soybeans grow in pods on bushy plants.
soy·bean (soi′bēn′) *noun, plural* **soybeans.**
space 1. The area in which the whole universe exists. It has no limits. The planet earth is in space. 2. The region beyond the earth's atmosphere; outer space: *The rocket was launched into space.* 3. A distance or area between things: *There is not much space between our house and theirs.* 4. An area reserved or available for some purpose: *a parking space.* 5. A period of time: *Both jets landed in the space of ten minutes. Noun.*
  ○ To put space in between: *The architect spaced the houses far apart. Verb.*
space (spās) *noun, plural* **spaces;** *verb,* **spaced, spacing.**
spacecraft A vehicle used for flight in outer space. This is also called a spaceship.
space·craft (spās′kraft′) *noun, plural* **spacecraft.**
space shuttle A spacecraft that carries a crew into space and returns to land on earth. The same

Lesson 4

The Mountain States Today

What are the main attractions of the Mountain States region?

Lesson Outline

• Few People
• Public Lands
• Rocky Mountain Industry

READING STRATEGY

Copy the diagram. Use it to list similarities and differences of life in the Middle West and Mountain States regions today.

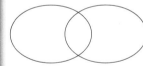

BUILD BACKGROUND

The Mountain States region has more open land, but fewer people than other regions. Montana is the fourth largest state, but less than 1 million people live there. Most of the region's people live in cities at the base of mountains or in river valleys. The rest is mostly empty. It is possible to drive for hours through the region's rural areas without seeing a single person!

Aspen, Colorado

358

Denver (above) is the region's largest city. The Olympic flag (below) flew when Salt Lake City hosted the 2002 winter games.

FEW PEOPLE

Although the population of the Mountain States continues to grow, the numbers are still quite low. In 2000, there were a little more than 9 million people living in the entire region. That is only a million more than the number of people who live in New York City.

Scattered Cities

Few cities in the Mountain States have populations greater than 50,000. Denver and Salt Lake City are the region's largest cities.

Denver is known as the "mile-high city." It was built on high plains near the Rocky Mountains and is the region's business center.

Salt Lake City was founded in 1847 by the Mormon community. Beginning in the 1860s, hundreds of copper, silver, gold, and lead mines were opened in nearby canyons. This brought many more settlers to the region. Today, the city's industries range from mining to high technology.

The 2002 Winter Olympics were held in Salt Lake City. Some of the many sports featured were ice skating, hockey, and skiing. They drew thousands of tourists to the region.

 READING CHECK **What are the region's largest cities?**

The Gunnison River (above) winds through Black Canyon. The Mountain States are home to a variety of butterflies, including the Western Black Swallowtail (below) and the Sulphur Buckwheat (right).

PUBLIC LANDS

A large portion of the region's land is public land. This is land owned by the federal government. Public lands are used as sources of energy and lumber, and also for grazing, irrigation, wildlife protection and wilderness areas. Many of the region's famous parks, such as Yellowstone, are public land areas.

The Bureau of Land Management is an organization set up by the United States government. It manages 262 million of the 700 million acres of America's public lands. This land is part of our national heritage. We must protect it for future generations.

Gunnison Gorge

The Gunnison Gorge National Conservation Area in Colorado consists of nearly 58,000 acres of public lands. The Bureau of Land Management manages this area to preserve and protect it.

For millions of years, the Gunnison River flowed through the **gorge**. A gorge is a narrow passage through land, such as a canyon. The river created Gunnison Gorge's unique black granite walls. These walls are layered with red sandstone. The wilderness area that surrounds the gorge is home to bighorn sheep, elk, deer, bald eagles, and water birds. Popular activities in the area include trout fishing, whitewater rafting, hiking, and mountain biking.

READING CHECK **What are public lands?**

Fighting Wildfires

In the summer of 2000, wildfires burned in every state west of the Continental Divide. It was the worst fire season in 50 years. Today agencies like the Bureau of Land Management work to keep the blazes under control. Study the graph and map on this page, then answer the questions.

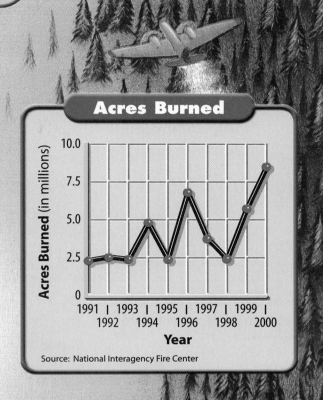

Acres Burned

Source: National Interagency Fire Center

Wildfires, 2000

0   250   500 miles
0   250   500 kilometers
Lambert Azimuthal Equal-area Projection

▲ Wildfire

QUESTIONS:

1. What state had more wildfires, Idaho or Colorado?

2. In which year did the greatest number of acres burn?

3. How many total acres burned in 2000? In 1991?

To learn more, visit our Web site:
www.mhschool.com

Skiing and rafting are popular sports in the Mountain States.

ROCKY MOUNTAIN INDUSTRY

Because of the Rocky Mountains' rugged terrain, very little farming or manufacturing takes place in the region. Instead, the region relies on its valuable natural resources for its economic growth. This makes mining and tourism the most important industries of the Mountain States.

Tourism

The Mountain States region has long been a popular destination for tourists. Outdoor recreation, such as skiing, mountain climbing, and rafting, also brings thousands of tourists a year.

Sun Valley, Idaho is a famous year-round recreation area for winter sports. The area's mountains and snowfall make it an excellent place to ski.

Vail, Colorado is the largest ski resort in North America. Fifteen square miles around Vail Mountain are open for skiing and other winter sports.

The city of **Aspen,** Colorado, was a silver-mining boom town in the late 1800s. Then in the 1930s, it became a very popular resort area.

The Sundance Film Festival is held every January in **Park City,** Utah. Filmmakers from around the world come to Park City each year to celebrate the art of making movies.

READING CHECK

What recreational activities does the region offer?

United States Mint

The United States has four official mints in Denver, Philadelphia, San Francisco, and West Point, New York. A mint is a place where coins are made. The Denver mint was set up in 1859 for miners to bring gold dust and nuggets. There the gold was melted into bars. In 1906, the Denver mint began to manufacture gold and silver coins. Today it makes over 50 million coins a day. Tourists from across the country visit to see the coin-making process in person.

Activity

Draw a design for a new coin that celebrates the Mountain States region.

Courtesy of The U.S. Mint

Courtesy of The U.S. Mint

PUTTING IT TOGETHER

Although the number of people who live in the Mountain States is low, the number of tourists who visit the region is high. The abundance of national parks, forests, rivers, and mountains attracts people to the region all year. Cities such as Salt Lake City, Denver, and their surrounding suburbs are also among the fastest-growing areas in our country.

Review and Assess

1. Write one sentence for the following vocabulary word:

   gorge

2. What does the Bureau of Land Management protect?

3. Describe some of the attractions that draw tourists to the Mountain States.

   Find Out!

4. How does the **environment** of the Mountain States affect the region's recreational activities?

5. What **conclusion** can you draw about the population of the Mountain States?

Activities

Create a two-column chart. In the first column, describe activities that draw tourists to the Mountain States. In the second column, describe activities popular in the Southeast. You can look back to Unit 2 for help.

Write a travel brochure that advertises some of the attractions of the Mountain States region.

5
The World Around Us

Find out! How have land-forms affected the country of Switzerland?

Lesson Outline
• A High Country
• Working In the Alps

Swiss Alps

VOCABULARY

landlocked
canton

READING STRATEGY

Copy the diagram below. Fill in different effects caused by Switzerland's geography.

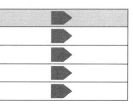

BUILD BACKGROUND

Switzerland is a tiny country located in central Europe. According to businessman Nicolas Hayek, the Swiss have always been "a mountain people." Switzerland is surrounded on all sides by land, or **landlocked**. Many of its borders are along two mountain ranges, the **Jura Mountains** and the **Alps**.

A HIGH COUNTRY

You can see from the map that mountains separate the Swiss from their neighbors. As a result, the Swiss have become very independent.

The Alpine peaks are not an easy place to live. Most people live between the Alps and the Jura Mountains.

When Switzerland was founded in 1291, it had three **cantons**, or states. Gradually 20 more cantons were added to form regions that are very different from one another. Even their languages are different.

Musketeer fountain in Bern, Switzerland

In western Switzerland most people speak French. They call their country Suisse (SWEES). To the north, most people speak German and call the country Schweiz (SHVIGHTZ). In the southeast, Italian-speaking Swiss call it Svizzera (SVEET tsay rah). You might hear all these languages in Bern, Switzerland's capital.

READING CHECK What are the mountain ranges of Switzerland?

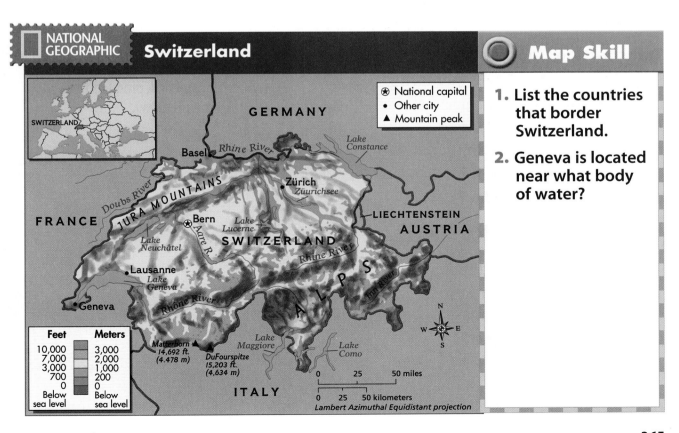

NATIONAL GEOGRAPHIC — Switzerland

- ⊛ National capital
- • Other city
- ▲ Mountain peak

GERMANY

Rhine River
Lake Constance
Basel
Doubs River
JURA MOUNTAINS
Zürich
Züurichsee
FRANCE
Bern
Lake Lucerne
LIECHTENSTEIN
AUSTRIA
Lake Neuchâtel
Aare R.
SWITZERLAND
Rhine River
Lausanne
Lake Geneva
A L P S
Rhône River
Geneva
Matterhorn ▲ 14,692 ft. (4,478 m)
DuFourspitze 15,203 ft. (4,634 m)
Lake Maggiore
Lake Como
ITALY

Feet	Meters
10,000	3,000
7,000	2,000
3,000	1,000
700	200
0	0
Below sea level	Below sea level

0   25   50 miles
0   25   50 kilometers
Lambert Azimuthal Equidistant projection

Map Skill

1. **List the countries that border Switzerland.**

2. **Geneva is located near what body of water?**

WORKING IN THE ALPS

Not much of Switzerland's land can be used for crops. Instead, farmers in the Jura Mountains herd cattle. They are famous for their dairy products. In fact, the Swiss gave their name to a type of cheese!

The most important part of the economy is manufacturing. Switzerland has long been famous for handmade clocks, tools, and furniture. During the Industrial Revolution, they also began to use the mountain rivers to power machinery. Textile mills were built throughout the country along with other factories. Most of Switzerland's electricity is still hydroelectric power.

Transporting Goods

Switzerland has few minerals or other natural resources. Because they must import many resources, the Swiss use them carefully. They skillfully turn them into excellent finished products. Then they export the goods to other countries.

Swiss manufacturing means "high quality" all around the world. Their most famous goods are Swiss time pieces.

Medicines, dyes, and textiles are other important exports.

You may have noticed that these goods are all small. This is because most early transportation used roads that wound through steep mountain passes. Large goods were difficult to transport on these roads.

Today transportation is easier. In 1872, engineers began digging the first tunnel through the Alps. Goods could be shipped through the mountains instead of over them. In 1992, the citizens voted to build two new tunnels for railroads. These tunnels, which will be completed by 2006, will cut down on air pollution from cars.

READING CHECK What goods do the Swiss export to other countries?

Swiss industries include watches (above) and milk products from dairy cows (below).

PUTTING IT TOGETHER

Tourism is another part of the country's industries. Some of the world's best skiers go to Switzerland to try the slopes. In warm weather, people from all over Europe come to hike and climb. Around 7 million people visit each year. That's equal to the number of people who live there!

Mountains shaped the Swiss economy by limiting resources and the products manufactured there. However, their rivers also provide hydroelectric power for factories. The mountains have also affected the culture by creating very different regions.

Swiss mountains provide beautiful and challenging slopes for skiers.

Review and Assess

1. Write one sentence for each of the vocabulary words:

   canton   landlocked

2. Why has Switzerland been isolated from other countries?

3. What **effect** have landforms had on Switzerland?

Find! Out!

4. What three languages are spoken in different parts of Switzerland?

5. What **effect** will new railroad tunnels have on transportation in Switzerland?

Activities

Using the maps of the Mountain States and Switzerland on pages 319 and 365, make a chart that compares the two regions. Include such features as highest elevation, important rivers, lakes, mountains, and other landforms.

. . . .

Write a paragraph to explain why you would or would not like to live in Switzerland. Include things that would be different or similar to your hometown.

Points of View
How should natural gas be developed?

Interest in drilling for natural gas, a major energy resource in the Mountain States, is growing. Many different groups decide how and where drilling takes place. Read and think about three different points of view, then answer the questions that follow.

TOM FITZSIMMONS
Operations Manager, Pennaco Energy
Denver, Colorado
Excerpt from an interview, 2001

66 Natural gas is the cleanest-burning fuel. Many natural gas resources are on federal lands. Some people worry that the roads put on these lands will damage the plants and animals. After we drill, the federal government requires us to return these areas to the way they looked before we drilled. 99

GWEN LACHELT
Executive Director, Oil and Gas Accountability Project, Durango, Colorado
Excerpt from an interview, 2001

66 We must make sure the energy companies find ways of getting to these natural resources that do as little damage as possible to the environment. We don't want gas wells in wilderness areas or very close to people's homes. We don't want drilling to affect water quality. 99

WES MARTEL

Wind River Reservation, Member of the Business Council of the Eastern Shoshone
Fort Washakie, Wyoming
Excerpt from an interview, 2001

"Our reservation has 2.5 million acres of land. For over 30 years we have allowed companies to drill for natural gas on some of this land. Drilling for gas has made a big difference to our economy. We don't allow any drilling in our mountains. We want to protect the mountains for religious and cultural reasons, but also because of the trees and animals living there."

Thinking About the Points of View

1. Tom Fitzsimmons works for an energy company. How might this influence his point of view?

2. Gwen Lachelt belongs to a group that represents people who live near areas where natural gas is drilled. How might this affect her opinion?

3. Wes Martel is an Eastern Shoshone Native American who lives on the Wind River Reservation. How might this affect his opinion?

4. What other points of view might people have on this issue?

Building Citizenship

Responsibility

Many people think the decisions about using natural gas should show responsibility for the environment. List some ways companies could do this based on the points of view you read.

Write About It!

Use your school library or the Internet to research places in Wyoming, Montana, or Colorado where drilling for natural gas has taken place recently. Then write a letter to a government leader there giving your opinion about drilling for natural gas.

VOCABULARY REVIEW

Number a sheet of paper from 1 to 5. Beside each number write the word or term from the list below that matches the description.

expedition   **transcontinental**

ghost town   **treaty**

suffrage

1. a deserted town
2. an agreement in writing between two or more groups
3. the right to vote
4. across the continent
5. a journey taken for a specific purpose

CHAPTER COMPREHENSION

6. How was Chief Washakie able to protect the land for the Shoshone?
7. What caused the rise of boom towns in the Mountain States in the 1860s?
8. Why was the transcontinental railroad important?
9. Which state was the first to give women the right to vote?
10. **Write** a paragraph that summarizes the women's suffrage movement.
11. Where do most people in the Mountain States region live today?
12. Why did tourism become a major industry in the Mountain States?

 ## SKILL REVIEW

13. **Reading/Thinking Skill** What is a conclusion?
14. **Reading/Thinking Skill** What steps do you take to draw a conclusion?
15. **Reading/Thinking Skill** Look back at Lesson 3. What conclusion can you draw about how women suffragists felt about gaining the right to vote?
16. **Study Skill** Which reference source would you use to find the meaning of *wildfire*?
17. **Study Skill** What are guide words?

USING A TIME LINE

1800	1850		1900		1950		2000

1805
Lewis and Clark expedition

1859
Gold discovered at Pikes Peak

1868
Fort Bridger Treaty signed

1869
Transcontinental railroad completed; Women earn the right to vote in Wyoming

1919
Nineteenth Amendment passed

1946
Bureau of Land Management created

1990s
Denver becomes one of the fastest-growing cities in the United States

18. Was the railroad completed before or after Lewis and Clark's expedition?

19. When was the Fort Bridger Treaty signed?

20. How many years before the Nineteenth Amendment was passed did women in Wyoming have the right to vote?

Activity

Learning About Exploration Suppose you were a member of Lewis and Clark's expedition. Write a letter home describing your trip. Explain what you might have seen along the way.

Foldables

Use your Foldable to review what you have learned about the Mountain States that makes them special. As you look at the front of your Foldable, mentally recall what you know and what you learned about the history and economics of the region. Review your notes under the tabs of your Foldable to check your memory and responses. Record any questions that you have on the back of your Foldable and discuss them with classmates, or review the chapter to find answers.

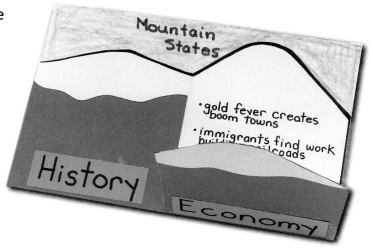

VOCABULARY REVIEW

Number a sheet of paper from 1 to 5. Beside each number write the word or term from the list below that best completes the sentence.

geyser   **timberline**

ghost town   **treaty**

smelting

1. The process of using high temperatures to separate metals from rock is called ___.

2. Chief Washakie signed a ___ with the United States government that established the Wind River and Fort Hall Reservations.

3. An abandoned town is a ___.

4. The ___ is the point above which it is too cold for trees to grow.

5. Old Faithful is the most famous ___ in Yellowstone National Park.

TECHNOLOGY

For more resources to help you learn about the people and places you studied in this unit, visit **www.mhschool.com** and follow the links for Grade 4, Unit 5.

SKILL REVIEW

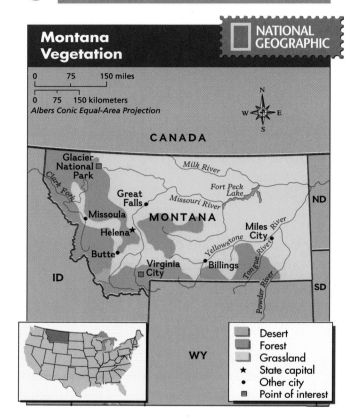

Montana Vegetation

NATIONAL GEOGRAPHIC

0 75 150 miles
0 75 150 kilometers
Albers Conic Equal-Area Projection

Legend:
Desert
Forest
Grassland
★ State capital
• Other city
■ Point of interest

6. **Geography Skill** What do vegetation maps show?

7. **Geography Skill** Where are the forests found in Montana?

8. **Reading/Thinking Skill** How can drawing conclusions help you better understand what you read?

9. **Study Skill** What are reference sources?

10. **Study Skill** When are reference sources useful to students?

1   The Rocky Mountains, like all high mountains, have a timberline. The timberline is the point above which it is too cold for trees to grow. The timberline in the central Rockies is around 11,500 feet above sea level.

2   Elevation also affects plant life in the Rockies. Sagebrush can be found along the valley areas. Forests of fir, pine, and spruce trees are found in higher areas. At about 11,000 feet above sea level, there are krummholz forests. Here the spruce and fir trees are shorter and bent.

3   Above the timberline, there are no trees. Instead there are stretches of grass and lichens. Lichens require little warmth to survive.

1   The purpose of this selection is to—

   A   tell about plants and trees in the Rocky Mountains
   B   give an opinion about saving Rocky Mountain forests
   C   convince readers to visit Rocky Mountain forests
   D   entertain readers with stories about the Rocky Mountains

2   Which conclusion can you draw about the elevations of the Rockies?

   F   The climate is wetter.
   G   The climate is colder.
   H   Krummholz trees grow far below 11,000 feet.
   J   Sagebrush grows at the highest elevations.

WRITING ACTIVITIES

Writing to Persuade Suppose you lived in the late 1800s. **Write** a newspaper article in which you try to persuade the United States government to give women the right to vote.

Writing to Inform Suppose you are a newspaper reporter in Colorado in the 1860s. **Write** an article that describes the discovery of gold at Pikes Peak.

Writing to Express **Write** a poem that describes the natural features of the Mountain States region.

THE LEGEND OF FREEDOM HILL

By Linda Jacobs Altman
Illustrated by
Cornelius Van Wright & Ying-Hwa Hu

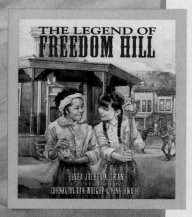

This is the story of Sophie and Rosabel. The two friends lived in California, during the Gold Rush. In the 1850s, California did not allow slavery. But under the Fugitive Slave Act, Rosabel's mother, a runaway slave, is captured and taken away. The girls decide to find a way to buy her freedom, once and for all.

Folks surely did laugh when those little girls went into the hills with their pans and picks and shovels. In two days of trying, Rosabel and Sophie ripped their clothes, bruised their knees, and scraped their knuckles—all for less than half an ounce of gold.

. . . The girls went to see Mr. Thompkins at the **assay** office. He was the man who tested and weighed everybody's gold. Folks said he knew the hills better than any other living soul.

Mr. Thompkins had a fine idea. "You young 'uns oughta be looking in narrow gullies . . . caves and such—places so small grown folks pass 'em by."

The girls thanked him kindly and went off to look for tight little places that grownups might have missed. They found plenty on that hill back of the assay office.

---

assay (ə sā′) to test a metal to determine its quality

375

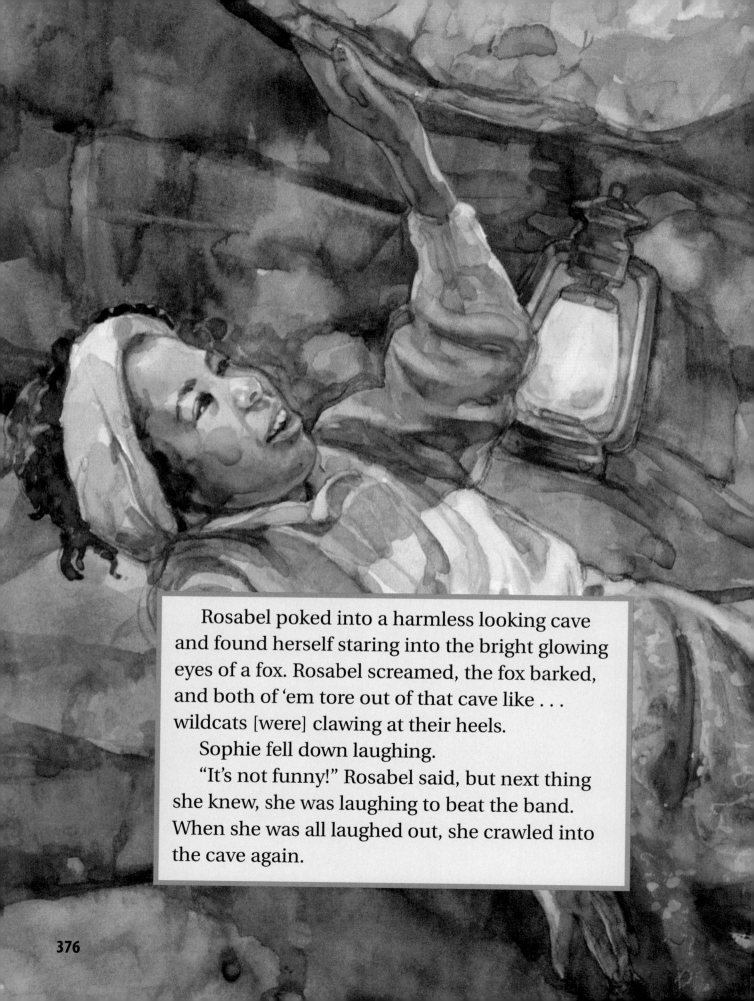

Rosabel poked into a harmless looking cave and found herself staring into the bright glowing eyes of a fox. Rosabel screamed, the fox barked, and both of 'em tore out of that cave like . . . wildcats [were] clawing at their heels.

Sophie fell down laughing.

"It's not funny!" Rosabel said, but next thing she knew, she was laughing to beat the band. When she was all laughed out, she crawled into the cave again.

"Sophie," Rosabel yelled, "I think I've found gold! Come see!"

Sophie scrambled into the cave. "Sure looks like gold to me," she said.

It was gold all right—a great, gleaming chunk of it, and there was more. . . . The girls dug up the nugget that very afternoon and took it to the assay office.

Mr. Thompkins said the nugget was enough to buy Miz Violet's freedom, right by itself.

Write About It!

This is a story about determination. **Write** about a time when you worked very hard and accomplished something that was important to you.

Unit 6

The West

TAKE A LOOK

What is life like in the West today?

San Francisco, site of the Golden Gate Bridge, is one of several western cities with growing industries in new technology.

Explore more about western
industries at our Web site
www.mhschool.com

379

11

THE Big IDEAS ABOUT...

Environment of the West

Alaska, California, Hawaii, Nevada, Oregon, and Washington, are the six states of the western region. The West is known for long coastlines, lush forests, hot deserts, and coastal mountains.

WESTERN PEAKS

Rugged coastal mountain ranges rise along the Pacific Coast.

DESERTS AND RAIN FORESTS

From the dry deserts of California and Nevada, to the rain-soaked forests of Oregon and Washington, the West has a variety of climates.

FORESTS AND VALLEYS

People of the West build dams to irrigate farms, cut down trees for lumber, and fish the region's waters.

Foldables

Make this Foldable study guide and use it to record what you learn about the "Environment of the West."

1. Fold a piece of paper in half like a hot dog, but make one side 1" longer than the other.

2. Make two cuts, equal distance apart, on the short side to form three tabs.

3. Write the chapter title on the 1" tab, and label the three small tabs "Western Peaks," "Deserts and Rain Forests," and "Thick Forests and Wide Valleys."

Western Peaks

What are the natural features of the West?

Lesson Outline
• Western Landforms
• Earthquakes and Volcanoes

VOCABULARY

earthquake
volcano
lava

READING STRATEGY

Copy the diagram below. Fill in the similarities and differences between the landforms of the West and the Mountain States region.

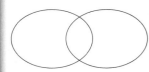

BUILD BACKGROUND

One western state—Alaska—is about one-fifth the size of all the other 49 states put together. Another—California—has more people than any other state. The West is also a region of low valleys and tall mountains. It is home to **Mt. McKinley**, our country's highest peak.

Mount McKinley is more than 20,000 feet above sea level.

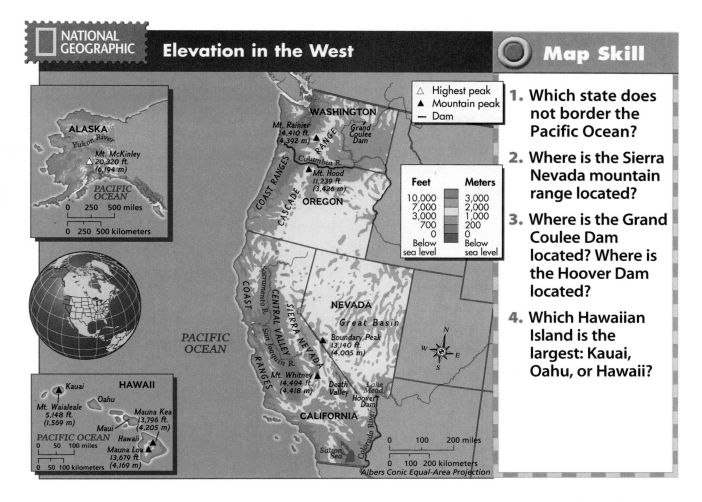

△ Highest peak
▲ Mountain peak
— Dam

ALASKA
Yukon River
Mt. McKinley
△ 20,320 ft.
(6,194 m)
PACIFIC OCEAN
0 250 500 miles
0 250 500 kilometers

WASHINGTON
Mt. Rainier
14,410 ft.
(4,392 m) ▲
Grand Coulee Dam
Columbia R.
Mt. Hood
11,239 ft.
(3,426 m) ▲
OREGON
COAST RANGES
CASCADE RANGE

Feet	Meters
10,000	3,000
7,000	2,000
3,000	1,000
700	200
0	0
Below sea level	Below sea level

COAST RANGES
Sacramento R.
San Joaquin R.
CENTRAL VALLEY
SIERRA NEVADA
NEVADA
Great Basin
Boundary Peak
13,140 ft.
(4,005 m)
Mt. Whitney ▲
14,494 ft.
(4,418 m)
Death Valley
Lake Mead
Hoover Dam
Colorado River
CALIFORNIA
Salton Sea

PACIFIC OCEAN

N W E S

0 100 200 miles
0 100 200 kilometers
Albers Conic Equal-Area Projection

HAWAII
▲ Kauai
Oahu
Mt. Waialeale
5,148 ft.
(1,569 m)
Maui
Mauna Kea
13,796 ft.
(4,205 m)
Hawaii
Mauna Loa
13,679 ft.
(4,169 m)
PACIFIC OCEAN
0 50 100 miles
0 50 100 kilometers

1. Which state does not border the Pacific Ocean?

2. Where is the Sierra Nevada mountain range located?

3. Where is the Grand Coulee Dam located? Where is the Hoover Dam located?

4. Which Hawaiian Island is the largest: Kauai, Oahu, or Hawaii?

WESTERN LANDFORMS

The region lies west of the Rockies. Several mountain ranges are found in the West, including the **Cascade Range**, **Sierra Nevada**, and the **Coast Ranges**. Locate them on the map.

The Great Basin

The **Great Basin** covers most of Nevada, and parts of Utah, Idaho, Oregon, and California. This landform is a low, bowl-shaped area that is almost completely surrounded by higher land. Many of the desert areas of the United States are found in the Great

The Great Basin of Nevada

Basin. Death Valley is located in the southern part of this landform.

READING CHECK **What is the Great Basin?**

383

This street in Santa Cruz, California (above) suffered damage during an **earthquake**.

EARTHQUAKES AND VOLCANOES

Earthquakes often strike along the Pacific Coast. An earthquake is a sudden shaking of the ground. It is caused when rock layers beneath Earth's surface suddenly shift or crack. Each year many small earthquakes occur in the West. Often people do not feel them and they do little or no damage.

Larger ones, however, can cause buildings and bridges to collapse. Giant ocean waves can swell and landslides can occur. This kind of large earthquake does not happen often.

A **volcano** is a break in Earth's surface where hot gases and rock shoot out. Volcanoes may sleep for hundreds or thousands of years. Then suddenly the pressure of hot gas breaks

through, and **lava**, or liquid molten rock, pours out. Over long periods of time, volcanoes can create mountains as the lava cools and builds up. The islands of **Hawaii** were formed by volcanoes in the Pacific Ocean.

Eruptions rarely occur today. However, a blast shot out from **Mount St. Helens** on May 18, 1980. This mountain is located in the Cascade Range in Washington. The eruption killed 57 people and covered a vast area with ash and rock. In the passage below, a survivor describes what she saw that day.

Primary Source:

excerpt from Remembering Mount St. Helens
— **by Shelley Powers, 2000**

"The birds stopped singing. That caught my attention. . . . When I got outside, my Dad pointed to the west . . . I noticed a huge dark gray cloud rolling towards us. This was not an ordinary cloud. This was something new, and thick. . . . The next we knew, we were in an ash storm."

How does she describe the cloud of ash?

Staying Safe

Earthquakes and eruptions cannot be prevented. But the damage they cause can be reduced. Buildings are now designed to stand up to the shaking. Scientists are also studying rock layers below ground and inside volcanoes. They hope to find ways to predict future activity to prevent damage and save lives.

How do volcanoes form?

A scientist (right) studies a seismograph, which measures the force of an **earthquake**.

PUTTING IT TOGETHER

There is great variety in the landforms of the West, including rugged mountains and deep basins. The region sometimes experiences earthquakes and, very rarely, volcanic eruptions. Scientists and government agencies work hard to keep people in the region safe.

Review and Assess

1. Write one sentence for each of the vocabulary words:

   earthquake   lava   volcano

2. What is the tallest mountain in the United States?

3. Describe the natural features of the western region.

4. How can volcanoes affect **geography**?

5. What **causes** an earthquake?

Look at the map on page 383. List all of the mountain ranges found in the region.

• •

Suppose you were on a trip through the western region. **Write** a postcard home describing the natural features you see along your journey.

385

Reading Road Maps

Suppose you and your family wanted to drive to Death Valley National Park in California. How could you figure out how to get there? One way would be to use a **road map** to find your route. Road maps show the roads you can use to get from one place to another.

> **VOCABULARY**
>
> road map
> interstate highway

LEARN THE SKILL

Look at Map A on this page. Use it as you follow the steps below to learn more about reading road maps.

1. **Look for symbols and a map key.**
   Map A shows several different kinds of roads. Look at the map key. As you can see, a heavy green line shows that a road is an **interstate highway**. An interstate highway connects two or more states. Usually these roads have at least two lanes in each direction and have a speed limit of 55 miles per hour or more.

   Look again at the map key. You can see that a red line stands for a United States highway. What kind of road does a gray line stand for?

2. **Identify road numbers.**
   You probably noticed that most roads on the map have numbers inside a special symbol. Those numbers are the "names" of the roads. What is the number of the road that connects Sacramento to Los Angeles? What kind of road is it?

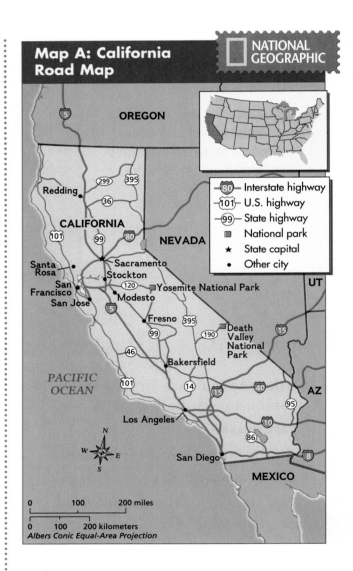

Map A: California Road Map

NATIONAL GEOGRAPHIC

Map key:
- 80 — Interstate highway
- 101 — U.S. highway
- 99 — State highway
- ■ National park
- ★ State capital
- • Other city

0   100   200 miles
0   100   200 kilometers
Albers Conic Equal-Area Projection

386

3. **Identify directions.**
   Most even-numbered roads usually run east and west. Odd-numbered roads usually run north and south. This fact can help lost drivers figure out which way they are going.

4. **Identify destinations.**
   Besides highways and cities, road maps can also show parks, historic sites, and other places of interest. They can help you find routes to popular locations and well-known landmarks.

TRY THE SKILL

Suppose you wanted to plan a trip from San Jose to Yosemite National Park. Along the way you want to pass through Sacramento and Stockton. Which route would you take? What kind of roads are on the route?   Now use Map A to answer the following questions.

1. What does a road map show?

2. According to the map, which interstate highways connect California with Nevada? With Oregon?

3. Why do road maps usually show more than one kind of road?

4. Why is it important to be able to read a road map?

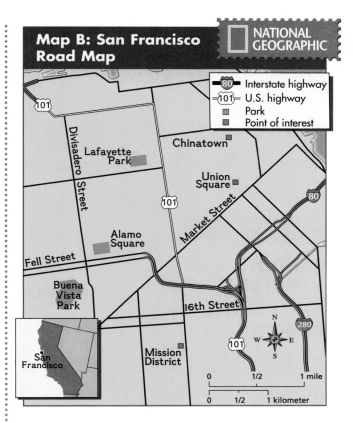

Map B: San Francisco Road Map

EXTEND THE SKILL

Road maps can also help you get around smaller areas. They can not only show highways, but also major streets. Map B on this page shows roads in and around San Francisco. Study it, then answer the following questions:

● What route would you take to get from United States highway 101 to Union Square?

● What types of roads would be included on a map of your city or town?

● Contact your local Chamber of Commerce to find out about major roads and highways in your community. Then create a road map for your area. Include a legend, scale, and compass rose.

Lesson 2

Deserts and Rain Forests

VOCABULARY

rain forest
rain shadow

READING STRATEGY

Copy the chart you see here. Fill in two facts about deserts and rain forests as you read.

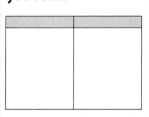

Lesson Outline

- Extreme Climates
- Rain Shadow

BUILD BACKGROUND

The western climate can go from one extreme to another. Our country's driest place is **Death Valley**. It gets less than two inches of rain each year. The wettest place in our country is also found in this region. **Mount Waialeale** (wigh ah lay AH lay) in Hawaii gets nearly 500 inches of rain every year.

Death Valley

EXTREME CLIMATES

Why does the West have so many different climates? One reason is the area is very large. In the north, the state of Alaska lies partly in the Arctic Circle. The climate is cold for much of the year. In the south, the state of Hawaii sits close to the equator. It is the southernmost state in our country. The climate there is warm all year.

Rainfall also varies across the region. Some areas are very wet, while others are quite dry.

Desert Plains

Desert plains are found east of the Sierra Nevada mountain range. On average, the area receives about five inches of rain each year. Temperatures are high during the day because clear desert skies allow Earth's surface to heat up. In the evening, those temperatures can drop quickly.

Death Valley is located in this area along the California-Nevada border. It has been preserved as a National Park. A half-million tourists visit each year.

Warm Rain Forests

West of the mountains, the amount of rain increases. **Rain forests** are found in Oregon, Washington and Hawaii.

A rain forest is a warm, wet forest where many trees and plants grow closely together. The rain forests of the West can receive more than 80 inches of precipitation each year. **Olympic National Park** in Washington has several rain forest areas. Besides a few warm, sunny summer months, the area experiences fog and drizzle almost every day.

READING CHECK What kind of climate is found in Death Valley?

A rattlesnake (above) is one of several animals that can survive in Death Valley's dry climate. Lush trees and plants grow in Olympic National Park (below).

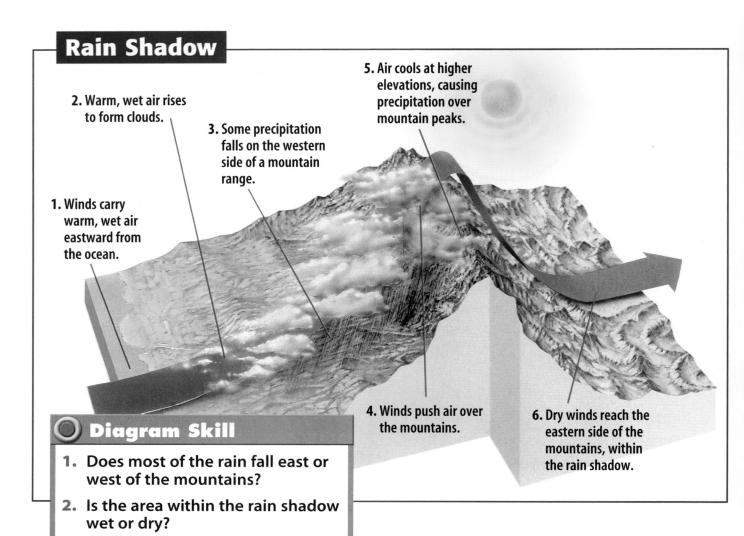

Rain Shadow

2. Warm, wet air rises to form clouds.

3. Some precipitation falls on the western side of a mountain range.

5. Air cools at higher elevations, causing precipitation over mountain peaks.

1. Winds carry warm, wet air eastward from the ocean.

4. Winds push air over the mountains.

6. Dry winds reach the eastern side of the mountains, within the rain shadow.

Diagram Skill

1. Does most of the rain fall east or west of the mountains?

2. Is the area within the rain shadow wet or dry?

RAIN SHADOW

The high elevations of mountains in the West create the region's deserts and rain forests. Winds blowing over the Pacific Ocean bring warm, wet air to this region. This warm air rises to form clouds. When the clouds gain in elevation, the air grows cooler. Since cool air cannot hold as much water as warm air, the water falls back to Earth in the form of rain. If the air is cold, the water will freeze into snow or sleet. Rain-heavy clouds help western rain forests grow.

Cloudbursts In the Mountains

When the clouds reach the mountains of the Cascade Range, they have dropped most of their water. By the time the clouds cross the mountains, little water is left. The eastern side stays much drier because it is in the **rain shadow**. The diagram on this page shows how the rain shadow works. On the next page, a map shows how much precipitation falls across Washington.

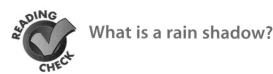

What is a rain shadow?

CANADA

Colville

OLYMPIC
PENINSULA

Seattle
Tacoma
Aberdeen

Spokane

WASHINGTON

ID

PACIFIC OCEAN

CASCADE RANGE

Yakima

Walla
Walla

OR

Average Yearly Precipitation	
Inches	**Centimeters**
Over 100	Over 250
80 – 100	200 – 250
60 – 80	150 – 200
40 – 60	100 – 150
20 – 40	50 – 100
Under 20	Under 50

0   50   100 miles
0   50   100 kilometers
Albers Conic Equal-Area Projection

Map Skill

1. **Which city receives less precipitation, Aberdeen or Yakima? Why?**

2. **How many inches of precipitation fall in Seattle each year?**

PUTTING IT TOGETHER

Other kinds of climates are also found in the West. Along the southern coast of California, the temperatures are mild with dry summers and rainy winters. Eastern Washington and Oregon experience cold winters and hot summers, much like the Middle West. All of these add variety to the region's environment.

Review and Assess

1. Write one sentence for each of the vocabulary words:

   rain forest   rain shadow

2. In which states are rain forests found in the western region?

3. Describe the different climates found in the West.

4. What is the **cause** of the rain shadow?

5. **Compare** and **contrast** the climate of the West with the Mountain States.

Activities

Look at the map on this page. List all the cities in Washington that lie within the rain shadow.

• •

Using the Internet or school library, research the Olympic National Park. **Write** a paragraph that describes some of the plants found there.

Recognizing Point of View

Suppose you and your friends are talking about pets. Steve says German shepherds make the best pets because they are loyal and easy to train. Felicia believes Siamese cats are better because they are playful and easy to care for.

VOCABULARY

point of view
fact
opinion
editorial

Each of your friends has a different **point of view**. A point of view is the way a person looks at something. People often look at the same subject from different points of view. Being able to recognize a person's point of view helps you make up your own mind about a subject.

LEARN THE SKILL

Read the passage below. Then follow the steps to recognize a person's point of view.

Death Valley is the best national park in the country. It is located on the border of California and Nevada. You can find a number of interesting animals there, including coyote, horned toads, and lizards. Plus, the desert scenery is spectacular. I believe it is better than Yosemite or even Yellowstone Park.

1. **Identify the subject.**
   In the passage above, the subject is Death Valley National Park.

2. **Identify statements of fact and opinion.**
   To identify a point of view, you need to know if the person is expressing **facts** or **opinions**. A fact is a statement that can be proven. Facts can be looked up in reference sources, such as dictionaries and encyclopedias. In the passage to the left, *"It is located on the border of California and Nevada"* is a statement of fact.

   An opinion expresses a person's belief. It cannot be proven. *"Death Valley is the best national park in the country"* is an opinion. Opinions are one way a person expresses point of view.

3. **Identify clue words or phrases.**
   Clue words or phrases like *"I feel," "I think,"* and *"I believe"* can tell you how a person feels about a subject.

An example is, *"I believe it is better than Yosemite or even Yellowstone Park."* How a person feels about a subject is also part of his or her point of view.

4. **State the point of view expressed.** Carefully examine the person's opinions and feelings on the subject. Then in your own words, state the person's point of view. *"The writer thinks Death Valley is the best of our country's national parks"* is a statement about the passage.

TRY THE SKILL

Read the following exchange from a debate. Then answer the questions.

Ahmad: Skateboarding is a fun way for kids to get exercise. Doctors report that skateboarding strengthens muscles and improves balance. Most skateboarders behave responsibly. I think we do not need to create laws to keep them safe.

Julia: Skateboarding is a dangerous sport. If kids skateboard in the street, it can back up traffic and cause accidents. Over a thousand skateboards were sold in our community last year. I believe we should create laws to limit their use.

1. What is the subject?

2. What is Ahmad's point of view?

3. What is Julia's point of view?

4. What clue words or phrases did you use?

5. After reading both sides, what is your point of view on the subject?

EXTEND THE SKILL

Newspapers print **editorials**, which give an editor's point of a view on a subject. Unlike a news article, it mainly states an opinion rather than facts. Read the following editorial on a small town election. Then answer the questions below.

The National

WHO'LL MAKE THE BEST MAYOR?

By Sam Ginsberg

I believe Adrienne Kim has been the best mayor we have ever had. She understands the concerns of our citizens better than Mike Powell, the candidate running against her. Mayor Kim has served our city for the past four years. She has built new parks, opened a hospital, and started a clean-up campaign.

Mike Powell has had a lot of success in the business world. However, he has not worked in government before. I think Powell should work for community organizations for a few years to gain experience. Then, he can run for mayor in the next election. For all these reasons, I urge you to re-elect Mayor Adrienne Kim.

- What is the subject?

- What facts are included in the editorial?

- What is the editor's point of view?

- Why is it important to recognize a person's point of view?

Lesson 3

Thick Forests and Wide Valleys

Find Out!

What natural resources of the West do people use?

Lesson Outline
- The Central Valley
- Northwestern Forests
- Conserving Forests

VOCABULARY

Central Valley Project
fertilizer
logging
deforestation

READING STRATEGY

Copy the main idea pyramid. Fill in the main idea and supporting details as you read.

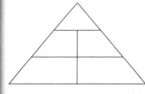

BUILD BACKGROUND

The West has a treasure of natural resources. Rivers teem with fish. Forests grow dense and tall. There is also plenty of fertile soil for farming. Western farmers grow a variety of fruits and vegetables, including grapes in California vineyards. The people of the region use a wide range of resources and share a responsibility to the land.

————

Grapes grow in a California vineyard.

These workers (above) are harvesting grapes in Sonoma Valley. California's Shasta Dam (below right) helps farmers irrigate their fields.

THE CENTRAL VALLEY

One area that is good for farming is California's **Central Valley**. It is located between two mountain ranges. The Sierra Nevadas rise to the east. The Coast Ranges overlook the Pacific Ocean to the west.

The Central Valley is more than 50 miles wide and 450 miles long! The state of Delaware could fit inside this area eight times. Two major rivers flow through the valley, the Sacramento and the San Joaquin.

Farming In the Central Valley

The Central Valley is flat with fertile soil. Summer, however, is the "dry sea-

son." For many years, farmers could grow few crops in the Central Valley because little rain falls there during the summer.

Between 1919 and 1955, an irrigation system was built. It became known as the **Central Valley Project**. A series of dams and canals brings water from the rivers to different parts of the valley. Some canals stretch more than 150 miles.

Today, the Central Valley is one of the most important agricultural areas in our country. It is also an important center of agricultural technology. Scientists work to develop new **fertilizers**. Fertilizers are items added to soil to make it better for growing crops.

READING CHECK What mountain ranges enclose the Central Valley?

NORTHWESTERN FORESTS

The forests of the West provide one of the region's most valuable resources. Wood from the region is used to make everything from houses and furniture to pencils and musical instruments. Trees are used to make other products, too. A kind of cloth called *rayon* comes from wood. So does camera film and chemicals such as turpentine.

Western forests include an amazing variety of trees. Pine, cedar, and hemlock are among the most common. There are trees, like the Sitka spruce, that grow nowhere else except along the Pacific Coast. There are bristlecone pines, which may live to be more than 4,500 years old!

The West is also home to the tallest trees in the world—redwoods. These trees grow in the valley of California's Coast Ranges. Many redwoods are 300 feet tall.

Logging

The process by which trees are cut down and transported out of the forest is called **logging**. About 20 years ago, most logging in the West was done by clear-cutting. Clear-cutting means that all of the trees in an area are cut down. Today, however, many people are concerned about **deforestation**—the loss of whole forests. Many modern loggers cut only certain kinds of trees or damaged trees, leaving the others standing.

Once the trees have been cut down, they are hauled to sawmills, where they are sawed into lumber.

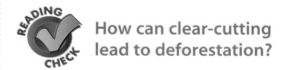

READING CHECK How can clear-cutting lead to deforestation?

Giant redwoods (left) grow in Sequoia National Park. This logger is preparing to haul lumber from an Oregon forest (below).

DATAGRAPHIC

Western Logging

The West and Mountain States regions are known for their logging industry. Use the diagram and map to answer the questions.

How Trees Are Harvested

1. Foresters decide which trees can be cut.

2. Fallers, who cut down trees, use power saws or tree shears, which are like giant scissors.

3. Logs are transported to sawmills by cables, trucks, boats, balloons, or helicopters.

5. A band saw slices logs into boards for lumber.

4. Bark is removed and a circular saw cuts logs into sections.

NATIONAL GEOGRAPHIC

Western Forests

CANADA

WA
MT
ND
OR
ID
SD
WY
NE
NV
UT
CO
KS
CA
OK
AZ
NM
TX

N
W E
S

PACIFIC OCEAN

| 0 | 200 | 400 miles |

| 0 | 200 | 400 kilometers |

Albers Conic Equal-Area Projection

Mountain evergreen forest
Pacific coastal forest

QUESTIONS:

1. In which states are Pacific coastal forests found?
2. What is the first step to harvest a tree?
3. How are logs transported to sawmills?

To learn more, visit our Web site:
www.mhschool.com

397

CONSERVING FORESTS

Forests are a renewable resource, because new trees can be planted. However, logging still affects the environment. Loggers, for example, prefer to cut the oldest trees in the forest. These trees are bigger and more valuable. A single tree in Washington might be worth $50,000!

Conservationists worry that our country's forests will disappear. Therefore, logging companies now plant new trees to replace what they cut. They also plant fast-growing trees, such as pine.

Logging may also threaten some forest animals. Animals that live in the forest lose their homes and food when trees are cut down. These animals that have adapted to the forest environment are in danger of not surviving. We all must work to preserve forests and protect the environment while finding and using valuable lumber.

READING CHECK What are some ways logging companies work to protect forests?

A lumber worker (left) plants young trees to replace those that have been cut down. Students gaze up at an old-growth tree in a redwood forest (above).

PUTTING IT TOGETHER

The West is rich in both fertile farmland and forest resources. Fertilizers and irrigation have transformed the Central Valley into one of the most productive farming areas in the world. Loggers to the north harvest trees for lumber that is shipped across our country. By working with the environment, people are getting the most from the land. We must also protect it to ensure that western resources are available for future generations.

Spotted owls make their home in forests of the West.

Review and Assess

1. Write a sentence for each of the vocabulary words:

   Central Valley Project   **fertilizer**
   deforestation   **logging**

2. Where is the Central Valley located?

3. Describe the natural resources of the western region.

4. What **effect** does logging have on the **environment** of the West?

5. Make a **prediction** about conservation of forest resources.

 Activities

Look at the map on page 397. Find the state that has no forests. Write a paragraph that explains why this is the case. You may look back at Lesson 2 for help.

Using the Internet or school library, research the lumber industry. **Write** a diary entry describing a typical day of a lumber worker in a forest.

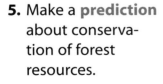

399

VOCABULARY REVIEW

Number a sheet of paper from 1 to 5. Beside each number write the word or term from the list below that matches the description.

editorial **logging**

fertilizer **rain forest**

lava

1. liquid rock that pours from a volcano
2. warm, wet forest where trees grow close together
3. an article that gives an editor's point of view on a subject
4. items added to soil to make it better for growing crops
5. the process of cutting down trees and transporting them out of a forest

CHAPTER COMPREHENSION

6. What is the Great Basin?
7. How can volcanoes form mountains?
8. What is the rain shadow?
9. Where are rain forests found in the western region?
10. Where is the Central Valley located?
11. What is deforestation?
12. How can logging companies help protect the forests?

SKILL REVIEW

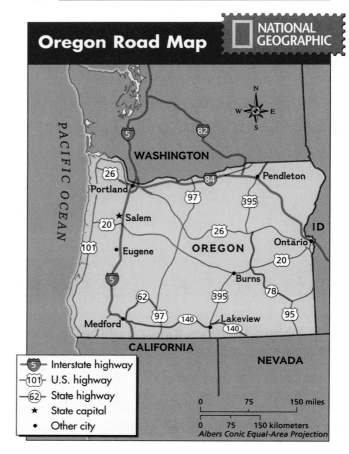

Oregon Road Map

NATIONAL GEOGRAPHIC

Legend:
- Interstate highway (5)
- U.S. highway (101)
- State highway (62)
- ★ State capital
- • Other city

0 75 150 miles
0 75 150 kilometers
Albers Conic Equal-Area Projection

13. **Geography Skill** What does a road map show?
14. **Geography Skill** What is an interstate highway? How do you know?
15. **Geography Skill** Which roads run from Oregon to Washington?
16. **Geography Skill** Which route would you take to get from Salem to Burns?
17. **Reading/Thinking Skill** What is the difference between a fact and an opinion?
18. **Reading/Thinking Skill** Why is it important to recognize point of view?

USING A CHART

19. Which city receives the most precipitation each year?

20. Based on the chart, which city do you think lies in the rain shadow?

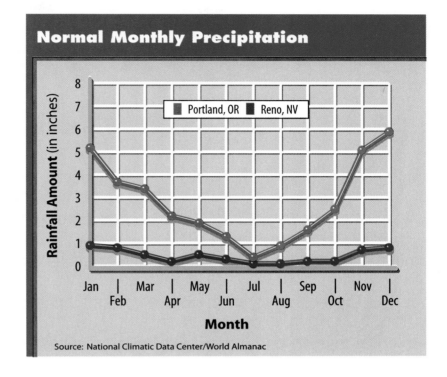

Normal Monthly Precipitation

■ Portland, OR   ■ Reno, NV

Rainfall Amount (in inches) — Month (Jan through Dec)

Source: National Climatic Data Center/World Almanac

Activity

Writing About Conservation Using your school library or the Internet, research some of the issues about forests and conservation. Choose one issue and summarize the problems and solutions being considered. Add supporting details to explain which solution you think would work best.

Foldables

Use your Foldable to review what you have learned about the West, as part of the United States and North America. As you look at the three tabs of your Foldable, mentally review what you learned. Explain why the environment of the West is so varied and explain its effect on life in the region. Look at your notes under the tabs to check your memory and responses.

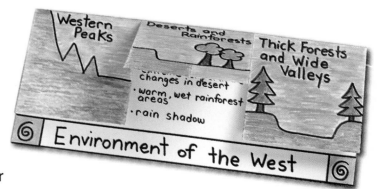

Chapter

12

THE Big IDEAS ABOUT...

History and Economy of the West

People came to the West from many different places. Settlers in Hawaii came from islands off the coast of Asia. European settlers came to hunt for gold. Many Chinese and Mexican immigrants moved to the region to work for railroads, farms, and mining towns. Each group's history and culture have helped shape the region.

THE HAWAIIANS

Once a kingdom of its own, the islands of Hawaii became this country's 50th state.

THE GOLD RUSH

Courtesy of Bancroft Library, University of California.

Thousands of people moved to California where they hoped to find gold.

IMMIGRANTS IN THE WEST

Courtesy of the Arizona Historical Society/Tucson

New groups of immigrants continued to come to the West and bring their own cultures and histories.

THE WEST TODAY

Movies and high technology are just two of the industries that have kept this region growing.

Foldables

Make this Foldable study guide and use it to record what you learn about the "History and Economy of the West."

1. Fold a large sheet of paper into a shutter fold.
2. Fold the shutter fold in half like a hamburger.
3. Form four tabs by cutting along the fold lines in the middle of the two long tabs.

4. Label the four tabs "The Hawaiians," "Gold Rush," "Immigrants," and "The West Today."

The Hawaiians

What events have affected Hawaii's people and culture?

Find out!

Lesson Outline
- Early People of the West
- Changes in Hawaii

BUILD BACKGROUND

Hawaii is more than 2,000 miles away from the West Coast of our country. The state is made up of 132 islands, although most Hawaiians live on only seven of the islands. Hawaii is also near a larger group of islands in the Pacific Ocean called Polynesia. In this lesson, you will learn about the people of Hawaii and how this group of islands came to join our country.

Double-hulled canoe

EARLY PEOPLE OF THE WEST

The first Hawaiians were people from the Polynesian Islands near Asia. They arrived in Hawaii more than 1,000 years ago. Research shows they probably traveled to the islands in large canoes with two hulls, or frames. They brought plants and animals, including dogs, with them to the island.

Early Hawaiians raised pigs for meat and harvested crops such as bananas, coconuts, and **taro**. Taro is a tropical plant that has a starchy root like a potato. The roots and leaves of the taro plant can be eaten.

The Inuit (IHN oo iht) are another group of early settlers in the West. Sometimes called Eskimos, the Inuit are Native Americans who settled in what is now the state of Alaska.

In other parts of the West, early Native American groups also included the Yakama, Klamath, and Chumash. Use the map on this page to locate these and other Native American groups of the West.

 **READING CHECK** How did the first Hawaiians arrive on the islands?

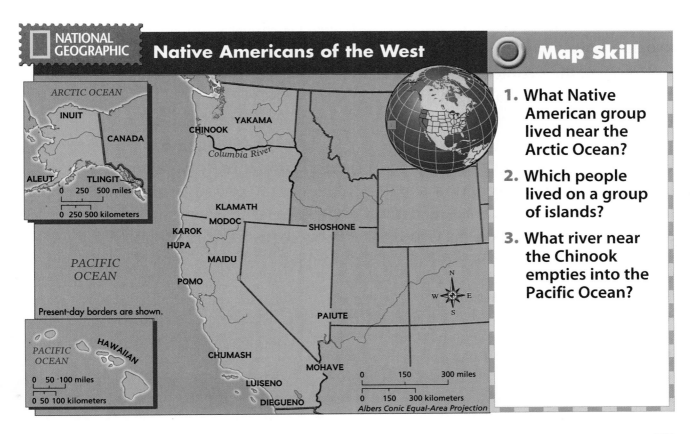

NATIONAL GEOGRAPHIC   **Native Americans of the West**   **Map Skill**

ARCTIC OCEAN
INUIT
CANADA
ALEUT   TLINGIT
0   250   500 miles
0   250   500 kilometers

YAKAMA
CHINOOK
Columbia River
KLAMATH
MODOC
KAROK
HUPA
MAIDU
POMO
SHOSHONE

PACIFIC OCEAN

Present-day borders are shown.

PACIFIC OCEAN
HAWAIIAN
0   50   100 miles
0   50   100 kilometers

CHUMASH
LUISENO
DIEGUENO
MOHAVE
PAIUTE

N   W   E   S

0   150   300 miles
0   150   300 kilometers
Albers Conic Equal-Area Projection

1. **What Native American group lived near the Arctic Ocean?**

2. **Which people lived on a group of islands?**

3. **What river near the Chinook empties into the Pacific Ocean?**

CHANGES IN HAWAII

The Polynesian settlers spread out over eight separate islands of Hawaii. The groups shared a common language and culture. However, each group was ruled by a different chief. Over time, the groups began to fight with one another.

In 1782, one chief, **Kamehameha** (kuh MAY hah MAY hah), set out to rule over all eight of the islands. His armies fought against the other chiefs. Slowly, the individual islands became part of the Kingdom of Hawaii. Kamehameha promised the people of Hawaii they would live in peace.

However, the people of Hawaii were already facing new challenges from traders arriving on the islands. Four years before Kamehameha's war, British Captain **James Cook** became the first European to reach the islands in 1778. Although Cook was killed in a fight while on the islands, his visit encouraged more traders to come from Europe and the United States.

James Cook (top)
King Kamehameha (above)

Some traders used the islands as bases for whaling voyages. Others wanted to sell the natural resources of the island, by cutting down sandalwood forests for lumber. In the 1800s, many Europeans and Americans bought land in Hawaii for plantations. In less than a hundred years, people from other countries owned all of Hawaii's sugarcane plantations.

From Kingdom to Statehood

Like other plantations you have read about, many workers were needed to grow sugarcane and pineapples in Hawaii. Immigrant workers came from China, the

A traditional Hawaiian necklace of flowers, called a lei (LAY).

A ceremony at Iolani Palace (above) and local newspapers (below) celebrated Hawaii's statehood.

Philippines, Japan, and Europe. By 1886, fewer than half the people in Hawaii were related to the Polynesians.

As the plantations grew larger and more profitable, the owners wanted more influence over the government of Hawaii. When Queen **Lydia Liliuokalani** (lee LEE oo woh kah LAH nee) came to power in 1891, she tried to keep the plantation owners from making decisions for her kingdom. However, powerful business leaders who wanted Hawaii to join the United States overthrew Liliuokalani in 1893. You can read more about the last queen of Hawaii on the next page.

In 1898 Hawaii became part of the United States. It took more than sixty years for the islands to become the nation's 50th state. In 1959, thousands of people attended the ceremonies held in Honolulu, Hawaii's capital.

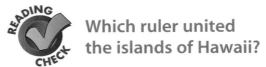 **Which ruler united the islands of Hawaii?**

BIOGRAPHY

Focus On: Respect

Lydia Paki Liliuokalani was born in 1838, when sugar plantations were already common in Hawaii. Liliuokalani's brother became king in 1874. He gave American plantation owners the power to change Hawaii's constitution. They gave foreign business owners the right to vote, but kept most native Hawaiians from voting. This gave plantation owners more power.

When Liliuokalani became queen in 1891, she fought for rights and respect for her people. She tried to take power away from the plantation owners. They revolted and asked the United States to take over Hawaii. Queen Liliuokalani was placed under house arrest for eight months before she agreed to give up her throne.

Link to Today List ways you would show your teacher, parent, other adult, or community leader respect.

Bishop Museum Archives

THE LIFE OF QUEEN LILIUOKALANI	1838 Born in Honolulu, Hawaii	1891 Becomes queen of Hawaii	1893 Revolt of American plantation owners	1895 Placed under arrest by leaders in favor of joining United States	1898 Hawaii becomes part of the United States	1917 Dies due to a stroke

1825	1850	1875	1900	1925

LIFE AROUND THE WORLD	1829 Colony founded in Western Australia	1861 American Civil War begins	1865 American Civil War ends	1901 Queen Victoria of England dies	1907 Construction of Panama Canal begins	1918 World War I ends

PUTTING IT TOGETHER

Today the islands of Hawaii have also become a popular place for tourists. The warm island climate, lush vegetation, active volcanoes, and beautiful waterfalls are just some of the islands' attractions.

Visitors can still see much of the Hawaiian culture that was passed down from the original Polynesian settlers. It is also possible to tour Iolani Palace, where Queen Liliuokalani lived before her rule was ended.

Orchid flowers are a colorful part of traditional Hawaiian dress.

Review and Assess

1. Write one sentence for the following vocabulary word:

   taro

2. List two of the first groups of people to live in the western region of the United States.

3. Name two events that caused changes for the Hawaiian people.

4. What **economic** change took power away from the native Hawaiians?

5. Describe the **sequence of events** that led to Hawaii's becoming a state.

Activities

Using the map on page R4, find a route that British Captain James Cook could have taken to Hawaii. Write a set of directions to describe the route.

. . . .

Suppose you lived in Hawaii in the 1800s. **Write** a paragraph describing the changes happening on the islands. Include two different points of view that people on the islands might have about these changes.

The Gold Rush

 **Find Out!**

How did the discovery of gold change the West?

Lesson Outline
• Heading West
• The Gold Rush Begins
• Empty Towns

VOCABULARY

gold rush
Forty-Niner
mother lode

PEOPLE

James Marshall
Jim Beckwourth

READING STRATEGY

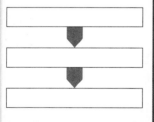

Copy the chart. Fill in information about the gold rush in the correct sequence of events.

BUILD BACKGROUND

During the early 1800s, the West was a quiet region with small villages and open spaces. By the 1850s, it was bustling with people and activity. What happened? A California carpenter named **James Marshall** made a surprising discovery that changed the face of the region.

Courtesy of The National Cowboy and Western Heritage Museum

HEADING WEST

Throughout the 1800s, the United States grew in size. You have already read about the purchase of the Louisiana Territory in 1803. The Southwest also became part of our country during the early 1800s. Soon the United States stretched from the Atlantic Ocean to the Pacific Ocean.

Gold!

In 1848, a businessman named John Sutter decided to build a saw-mill. He hoped to sell cut lumber to new settlers in the region. Sutter chose a spot along the **American River**, near today's Sacramento. He hired a carpenter named James Marshall to build it. One day while working on the mill, Marshall made an amazing discovery. He found pieces of gold.

At first Sutter tried to keep this discovery a secret. However, the word got out. By May 29 a newspaper called *The Californian* reported that "the whole country . . . resounds [echoes] to the . . . cry of gold! gold! GOLD!" Read what Marshall later wrote about it.

Where was gold first discovered in the West?

Primary Source:

excerpt by
James Marshall— 1848

My eye was caught by something shining in the bottom of the ditch. I reached my hand down and picked it up; it made my heart thump, for I was certain it was gold. The piece was about half the size and shape of a pea. Then I saw another. . . .

How would you have reacted to the discovery if you were Marshall?

The painting (left) shows miners searching for gold. This drawing shows Sutter's Mill in California.

Posters announced increased transportation to the West Coast.

THE GOLD RUSH BEGINS

The discovery at Sutter's Mill marked the beginning of the **Gold Rush** of 1848. A gold rush is a sudden movement of people to an area where gold has been found.

At first it was mainly people in the west who hurried to the gold area. By the fall of 1848, however, newspapers in the east told of the fortunes to be made. One paper reported that gold nuggets could be "collected at random and without any trouble."

Of course, finding gold was not that easy. Getting to the western region was also a difficult task. Miners had to cross the Rocky and the Sierra Nevada Mountains. There were few roads or trails. Yet the idea of riches tempted many people in the east to join the rush.

Forty-Niners

San Francisco, California, had 800 people in 1848. By 1849, that figure had risen to 25,000! So many people came to California in 1849 that they were known as **Forty-Niners**.

Some traveled by wagon. In 1850, an explorer named **Jim Beckwourth** found a pass through the Sierra Nevadas. The Beckwourth Pass made the journey by land easier. Other people sailed all the way around South America. The journey could take up to six months. Forty-Niners left jobs and families behind for the dream of finding gold.

Jim Beckwourth

Panning for Gold

The miners headed for the **mother lode**. This gold-rich area near the Sierra Nevada Mountains is shown in the map on the next page.

Most miners worked in streams. They scooped up soil in pans and swirled it around with water. The heavy, gold nuggets stayed in the pan, while pebbles and sand washed out. This process was known as "panning" for gold. Others used a pick and shovel to dig.

Gold Country Towns

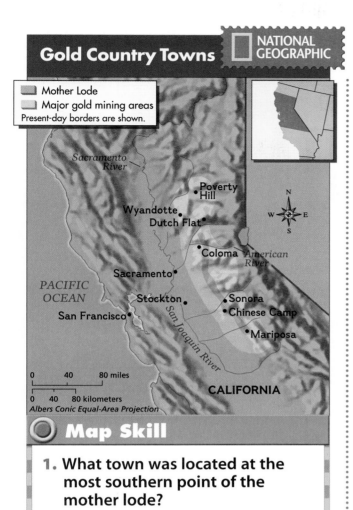

Mother Lode
Major gold mining areas
Present-day borders are shown.

Sacramento River
Poverty Hill
Wyandotte
Dutch Flat
Coloma
American River
PACIFIC OCEAN
Sacramento
Stockton
San Francisco
San Joaquin River
Sonora
Chinese Camp
Mariposa

0   40   80 miles
0   40   80 kilometers
Albers Conic Equal-Area Projection

CALIFORNIA

Map Skill

1. **What town was located at the most southern point of the mother lode?**

2. **Which rivers could be used to transport gold from Coloma to the Pacific Ocean?**

Gold Fever

By 1852, more than 250,000 people lived in California. That was enough for California to become a state with its own state government.

Other gold rushes took place throughout the country. You have already read about the discovery at Pikes Peak in Colorado. In 1860, people also rushed to Nevada. The last great gold rush took place in 1899, when gold was discovered near **Nome,** Alaska.

The 1848 gold rush also influenced the culture of the region. Stories and songs, such as the one on page 414, were written about the rush.

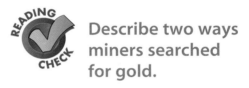

READING CHECK

Describe two ways miners searched for gold.

The miners camped along the streams where they panned. Some camps had colorful names, such as Humbug Hill, Fiddletown, or Sixbit Gulch.

In 1850, miners found more than 40 million dollars worth of gold! However, few struck it rich. Most found nothing and left empty-handed and broke.

Gold nuggets (above) were brought by miners to banks to be weighed and stored.

413

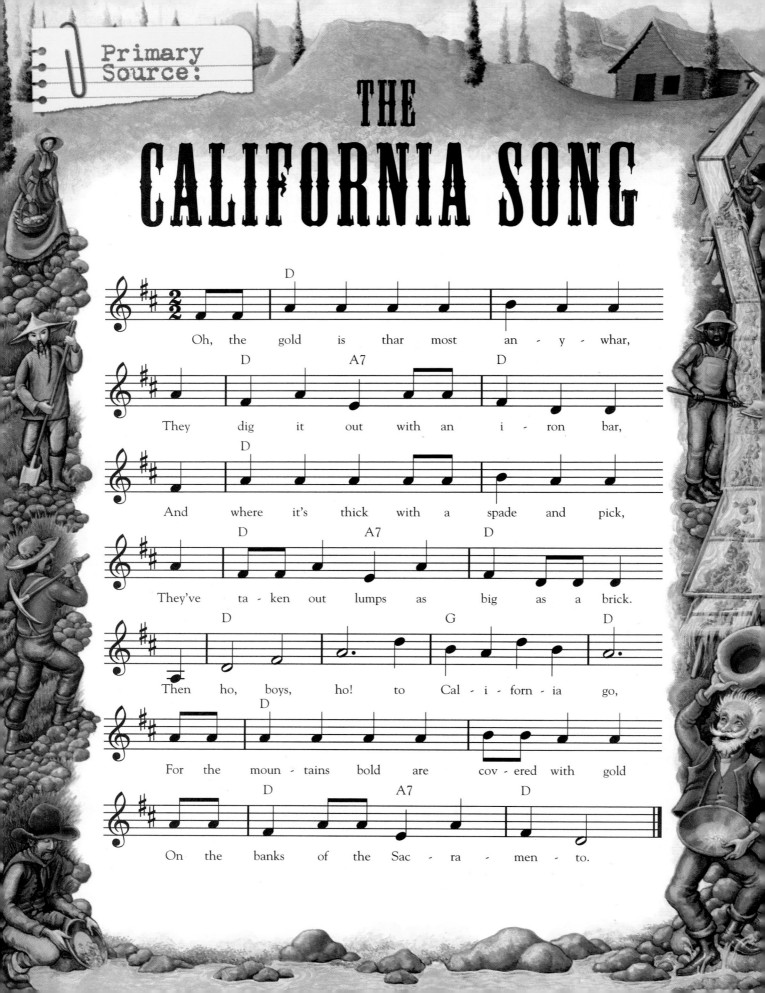

EMPTY TOWNS

Similar to the Mountain States region, cities and towns in the West grew rapidly during the days of "gold fever." In many cases, however, the miners left as soon as the gold ran out. The towns emptied after the miners moved on. Almost overnight a community could turn into a ghost town. Today there are still ghost towns scattered around the West.

What happened to many towns after the gold rush ended?

This miner's gold scale could be used to determine the value of a gold nugget.

PUTTING IT TOGETHER

Before the California gold rush, the west was a land of ranches, small towns, and Native American villages. News of the gold discovery brought thousands to the region. The west changed almost overnight into a land with bustling cities and booming populations.

Review and Assess

1. Write one sentence for each of the vocabulary words:

Forty-Niner   mother lode gold rush

2. Why was the journey west difficult for Forty-Niners?

3. In what ways did the gold rush change the West?

4. How was gold first discovered in California?

5. What **effect** did Jim Beckwourth's exploration have on the gold rush?

Activities

Look at the map on page 413. Make a two-column chart listing all of the towns in the mother lode area and all the towns in the major mining area.

. . . .

Suppose you were one of the Forty-Niners who arrived in California. **Write** a letter back home telling your family about your plans.

Using Primary and Secondary Sources

We get information from two different kinds of sources. One is a **primary source**. A primary source is information produced by someone who saw or took part in what they are describing. A primary source might be a diary, a letter, or an autobiography.

Most of the information in this textbook, however, is from a **secondary source**. Secondary sources are written by people who were not present at the events described. History textbooks and encyclopedias are examples of secondary sources.

LEARN THE SKILL

Read the excerpt below. Then follow the steps to learn more about primary and secondary sources.

I moved to San Diego with my family last summer. We used to live in the Northeast. I prefer life in the West. The climate here is warm and sunny most of the year. I hope to stay in this area a long time.

1. **Look for words like "I," "we," "my," or "our."**
   In primary sources, a writer will often mention himself or herself. Writers of secondary sources do not refer to themselves. In the passage, the writer includes the word "I" several times.

2. **Identify facts and opinions.**
   Primary sources often include a writer's thoughts or feelings. Secondary sources contain more facts than opinions. The passage includes several opinions such as "I prefer life in the West."

3. Identify source as primary or secondary.

Put all the clues together to identify if the source is primary or secondary. In this case, the passage is a primary source.

It is important to read and study both kinds of sources. A primary source can make us feel as though "we were there." A secondary source may help us see a broader view or summary of events.

TRY THE SKILL

Study the excerpt below. Use it to answer the following questions.

In the 1940s, millions of Americans began moving to an area known as the Sun Belt. The Southeast, Southwest, and parts of the West are all in the Sun Belt. The area got its name from its warm and sunny climate throughout the year. Popular Sun Belt cities include Los Angeles and San Diego in California; Dallas, Texas; and Atlanta, Georgia.

1. Does the writer mention himself or herself in the passage?

2. Does the passage include more facts or more opinions?

3. Is the passage a primary source or a secondary source?

4. What is the difference between primary and secondary sources?

EXTEND THE SKILL

Write a paragraph describing how you spent last weekend. Exchange your paragraph with a classmate's. Use your classmate's paragraph to answer the following questions.

- Is the paragraph a primary source or a secondary source?

- How can you tell?

- Is a biography a primary source or a secondary source? What about an autobiography?

- How do both primary and secondary sources help us understand history?

Immigrants in the West

Find! out!

What was life like for immigrants in the West?

Lesson Outline
- City of Immigrants
- Working the Fields
- Hard Times

VOCABULARY

strike
discrimination

PEOPLE

César Chávez
Dolores Huerta

READING STRATEGY

Copy the main idea pyramid. Fill it in as you read the lesson.

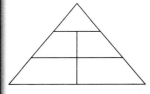

BUILD BACKGROUND

The gold rush brought people from Mexico, Peru, Chile, and Hawaii to the West. As you read in Chapter 10, Chinese immigrants helped build the transcontinental railroads. Many of them also settled in the West when the work was complete. All of these immigrants helped build the region and greatly influenced its history and culture.

CITY OF IMMIGRANTS

One city that didn't turn into a ghost town after the gold rush ended was San Francisco. As you have already read, the population jumped after the discovery of gold.

By 1850, many of San Francisco's muddy streets had been covered with wooden planks. Ten years later, streetcars carried San Franciscans from one end of the city to the other. As San Francisco grew, it attracted newcomers from Mexico, Italy, Germany, France, Japan, and Russia. The largest group of immigrants came from China.

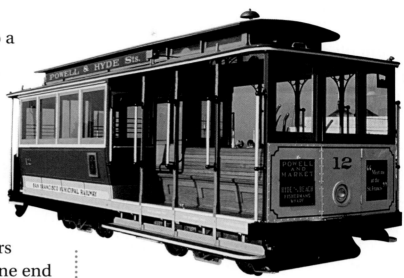

A trolley car is a common sight on the streets of San Francisco.

Chinatown

At first most Chinese people came to work in the gold mines. They called California *Gum San*—"Golden Mountain." Around 10,000 Chinese immigrants arrived in 1852 alone. Chinese laborers also worked on the railroads in the Mountain States.

Most of the Chinese settled in San Francisco. Thousands lived in an area around Sacramento Street. Eventually this neighborhood became known as Chinatown.

Today Asian Americans live all over California and other parts of the West. Many Chinese immigrants started their own businesses. They opened restaurants, laundries, and shops.

San Francisco's Chinatown continues to be a thriving community where many Chinese Americans live. Chinatowns can also be found in other western cities, including Los Angeles, and **Seattle**, Washington.

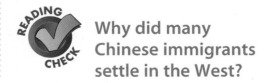

READING CHECK Why did many Chinese immigrants settle in the West?

419

WORKING THE FIELDS

Many immigrants came from Mexico to work on farms. Whole families—children as well as parents—often worked in the fields as migrant workers. That meant they moved from place to place to harvest crops as they ripened.

Life was hard for migrant workers. They often worked 14 hours a day, planting, weeding, and picking produce. Many workers lived in shacks or tents. Clean, running water was rare. Children often got sick from drinking dirty water.

Farmworkers Organize

César Chávez had worked on farms in California since he was a child. When he grew up, he became a leader in the fight to improve conditions for migrant workers. In 1962, Chávez and Dolores Huerta formed a labor union. They traveled to farms urging workers to join. The union became known as the United Farm Workers, or the UFW.

The UFW helps farmworkers using boycotts and strikes. A strike is when workers stop working until business owners meet their demands.

Boycott

In 1968, the UFW called for a boycott of grapes grown in California. Grape pickers wanted higher wages and better conditions. Many people across the

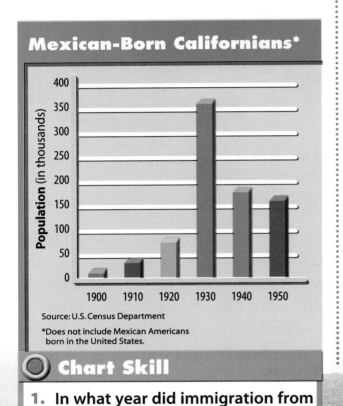

Mexican-Born Californians*

Population (in thousands)

Source: U.S. Census Department

*Does not include Mexican Americans born in the United States.

Chart Skill

1. In what year did immigration from Mexico increase the most?

2. When did the fewest number of immigrants arrive from Mexico?

country supported the farmworkers and did not buy California grapes.

In 1970, 26 grape growers signed an agreement with the UFW to end the boycott. The agreement gave the workers better pay, time off for vacation, and improved conditions.

César Chávez died in 1993. Today, the UFW continues the work he began. The union fights to help workers in many agricultural industries.

 READING CHECK How did a boycott help migrant workers in 1970?

Dolores Huerta (below left) and César Chávez (below right) speak out for migrant workers.

Exploring
ECONOMICS

Striking for Fair Wages

Wages were low for all farm workers. Mexican workers, however, were paid 50 cents to one dollar less than others. Mexican and other workers began to organize strikes to demand better treatment. Strikes often force owners to shut down factories or stop harvesting crops. They can cost owners a great deal of money. Owners often agree to workers' demands to stop or avoid a strike.

Activity

If a lettuce farm earns $2,000 a day, how much would the owner lose during a 15-day strike?

Buy only UFWOC AFL-CIO lettuce

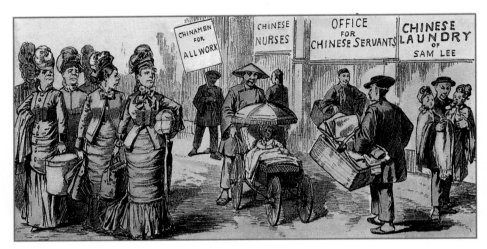

HARD TIMES

In the late 1800s, many of the new immigrants faced **discrimination** (dih skrihm uh NAY shun). Discrimination is an unfair difference in the way people are treated.

Many Americans wanted to stop Chinese people from entering the country. They feared Chinese workers would take away their jobs. In 1882, the United States Congress passed a law that excluded, or kept out, Chinese immigrants. Japanese people and other Asian immigrants also faced discrimination.

Many Mexican new-comers experienced discrimination as well. Some people tried to make them go back to Mexico. The immigrants were in danger of being deported, or forced to leave the country. Between 1931 and 1933, as many as 100,000 Mexicans were sent across the border from California back to Mexico.

Chinese and Mexican immigrants fought against the discrimination they faced. They were determined to make a life in their new country. Although they faced hard times, immigrants from China, Mexico, and other countries built strong communities. They also helped make the region a better place.

What is discrimination?

The political cartoon (above) shows the **discrimination** Chinese workers faced in the 1800s. In 1938, Josefina Fierro de Bright (right) led the Congress of Spanish Speaking People, a group that protects immigrants' rights.

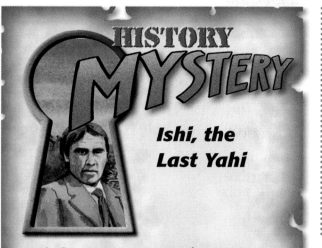

HISTORY MYSTERY

Ishi, the Last Yahi

In August 1911, a mysterious man wandered out of the foothills near California's Mount Lassen. His name was Ishi, and he was a Yahi Native American. The Yahi were driven into the mountains by miners during the gold rush years. Many were killed during attacks. Ishi had been in hiding for forty years and was the last surviving member of his group. He was taken to an anthropology museum in San Francisco. Ishi lived there, teaching visitors about the traditions of Yahi, until his death in 1916.

Why do you think museumgoers wanted to learn about Ishi's life?

PUTTING IT TOGETHER

In the late 1800s and early 1900s, many Chinese and Mexican immigrants came to the West looking for work and new opportunities. They faced hard times, but managed to make a way in their new home. Today thriving Asian and Hispanic communities can be found throughout the region and our country.

Review and Assess

1. Write one sentence for each of the vocabulary words:

   discrimination   strike

2. Who was César Chávez?

3. Describe life for some immigrants in the West.

4. Name one way a long strike might affect the **economy** of a community.

5. What **generalization** can you make about discrimination?

Look at the chart on page 420. How did the number of immigrants change over the 50–year period?

• •

Suppose you were a Chinese or Mexican immigrant in the early 1900s. **Write** a poem that describes your experiences in your new country.

Recognizing Frame of Reference

VOCABULARY

frame of reference

In the last chapter, you learned how to recognize a person's point of view. A person's point of view is shaped by his or her **frame of reference**. Your frame of reference is your background. It includes all the things you have learned and experienced. It helps shape your thoughts, feelings, and opinions.

LEARN THE SKILL

Read the passage below. It is the point of view of Susan, a professional musician. Then follow the steps to recognize frame of reference.

> Every child should learn to play an instrument. Children who study music do better in math and work well with others. I have played instruments since I was in elementary school. I started on piano, then learned bass and guitar. Music helped improve my grades. It also helped me make new friends from playing in the school orchestra. I now work as a bass player in a ragtime band.

1. **Identify the subject.**
   In the passage, the subject is music education for all children.

2. **Identify the person's point of view.**
   Susan's point of view is that all children should learn to play an instrument.

3. **Examine the person's background.**
   Susan's music education has helped her a great deal. She made better grades, gained friends, and now is a musician.

4. **Explain how the person's point of view is shaped by his or her frame of reference.**
   Susan's positive experiences with music education have shaped her point of view. It is the frame of reference that forms her opinion on the subject. She wants others to find the same success in school and life that she has.

   If you recognize a person's frame of reference, you can understand why they reached their point of view. Recognizing frame of reference can also help you understand your own points of view.

TRY THE SKILL

Two fourth-graders, Claire and Miguel, each prepared a review of a concert they both attended. A country band and a *mariachi* band performed. *Mariachi* (mah ree AH chee) is a style of Mexican music. Claire is a fan of country music. Miguel enjoys listening to *mariachi*. Read their reviews, then answer the questions.

Claire's Review:

The concert was a lot of fun. There were two bands, one played country music and the other played mariachi. I feel the country band put on the best show. They sang several of my favorite songs, including "On the Road Again." Their performance was truly special.

Miguel's Review:

I enjoyed the concert very much. The country band did a good job, but I believe the mariachi band stole the show. Several people in the crowd danced along with the music. I would love to see them perform again.

1. What is Claire's point of view?

2. How is it shaped by her frame of reference?

3. What is Miguel's point of view?

4. How is it shaped by his frame of reference?

5. If you had attended the concert, what would your point of view have been?

6. How is your opinion of the bands shaped by your frame of reference?

EXTEND THE SKILL

An artist's frame of reference can shape the kind of art they create. Gary Soto is a Mexican American writer. In his stories and poems, he describes life growing up in a barrio, a Mexican neighborhood. Read the passage then answer the questions.

> Even though I write a lot about life in the barrio, I am really writing about the feelings and experiences of most American kids: having a pet, going to the park for a family cook-out, running through a sprinkler on a hot day, and getting a bee sting! You may discover that you have had many of the same experiences and feelings as the characters in my stories and poems.

- What is Gary Soto's point of view?

- How is it shaped by his frame of reference?

- Why is it important to recognize a person's frame of reference?

The West Today

How is the West growing and changing today?

Lesson Outline
• Population Changes
• Leading Industries
• Effects of Change

VOCABULARY

silicon
software
urban sprawl

READING STRATEGY

Copy the main idea pyramid. Write the main idea of this lesson at the top. Add supporting details as you read.

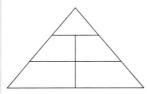

BUILD BACKGROUND

Explorers, gold miners, and immigrants have all been a part of the growth of the West. Agriculture, from Washington apples to California oranges, also became an important part of the region's economy. Over time, new industries also developed in the region. Today these industries have made the West one of the fastest-growing parts of our country.

Golden Gate Bridge

POPULATION CHANGES

According to the 2000 Census, a study of our country, the West is still a growing region. Many people move to the West from other parts of our country. Many more are immigrants from other countries, such as Mexico, China, and Japan.

Most of the western states grew by about one-fifth of their population between 1990 and 2000. Nevada was our country's fastest-growing state during this time period. Its population grew by 66 percent.

Like many parts of our country, cities in the West continue to grow. Suburbs outside of cities also keep growing and pushing the boundaries of cities closer together. In some parts of the West, like southern California, the cities may one day be as close together as they are in the Northeast region.

Some people move to the West to enjoy the region's many beaches, mountains, and forests. Others want to work in the region's unique industries.

 According to the 2000 Census, which state's population increased the fastest?

Suburbs are rapidly growing around Reno, Nevada (above). Hikers are drawn to the region's natural features (right).

LEADING INDUSTRIES

In the late 1800s, the first silent films were created. By the 1930s, movies were being shown in theaters across the country. Once sound and color were added to the films they became even more popular.

The first companies to make movies were located in the Northeast, but filming required a lot of space and good weather. As more films were made, movie producers found they had a hard time getting these things in the Northeast. They solved this prob-

lem by moving to California. Many of the film companies settled in a suburb of Los Angeles called **Hollywood**.

Los Angeles and Hollywood are now at the center of the movie and television industry. Other related companies also thrive in Southern California. They provide equipment, music, and special effects for many of the movies seen in this country.

Thousands of people move to California each year hoping to find work in the movies. The region is also the largest exporter of movies. People in countries all over the world see movies made in the West.

The Digital West Coast

In the 1980s, parts of Northern California and Washington became known for their engineering and science colleges. Students often stayed in the region after graduating to work or start their own businesses. Many of these businesses built computers that

Computer animation (above and right) is often used in films today. The Hollywood sign is a famous landmark.

Some built programs to make computers easier to use. Other companies created software to let people write, calculate, and play games on computers. So many of these computer companies moved to one part of central California that it became known as **Silicon Valley**.

 What element is found in many electronics products?

Today, palm-sized computers can do more work than earlier, larger computers.

used **silicon** chips. Silicon is an element found in Earth's crust and used in electronics.

Later the companies began creating **software**, or the programs that run on computers. Software companies sprang up in cities such as **Cupertino**, California and **Redmond**, Washington.

Exploring TECHNOLOGY

Computers

Early computers were so large and expensive that only universities and the government owned them. In fact, one of the first computers weighed more than 30 tons! Technology companies in the West knew smaller and more powerful computers were needed. After years of experiments, they made computers small enough to sit on a desk. Today, computers can fit in a briefcase or even your pocket.

Activity

There are 2,000 pounds in a ton. How many of today's five-pound computers would it take to equal 30 tons?

EFFECTS OF CHANGE

The West has grown faster than many other parts of our country. However, rapid growth also brings many challenges. One issue is the use of the land as businesses and homes expand. As more land is used for buildings, the region's forests and wildlife can be threatened.

Many towns and counties in the West are also trying to limit **urban sprawl**. This is the uncontrolled spread of buildings around a city. In the West, sprawl leads to increased traffic because people must drive everywhere. Pollution from the traffic damages the environment.

To solve this problem, parts of the West have passed laws limiting how much pollution cars produce. City planners are also encouraging new building patterns and trying to make public transportation more available.

Another problem faced in the West is the need to supply energy to all of the homes and businesses. In the summer of 2001, states like California had trouble generating enough electricity to meet consumer demands. When the demand for electricity exceeded the amount being produced, the power went out leaving many parts of the state in the dark.

Government officials are looking for new ways to get the energy the region needs. They are also encouraging people to reduce the amount of energy they use at home and at work.

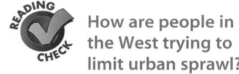

How are people in the West trying to limit urban sprawl?

In high traffic areas, cars are tested to make sure they do not cause too much pollution.

PUTTING IT TOGETHER

The entertainment and high technology industries continue to draw people to the West. This migration has made the region one of the fastest growing parts of our country. As more people live and work in the West, the cities and suburbs are also growing. This growth can cause problems, such as urban sprawl that western states are working to solve.

Los Angeles

Review and Assess

1. Write one sentence for each of the vocabulary words:

   silicon   **urban sprawl**
   software

2. Why did the film industry move to California?

3. What changes in the West were observed in the 2000 Census?

4. How has the **technology** industry in the West changed the way we use computers?

5. What are some **causes** of urban sprawl?

Activities

Create a sequence of events that shows how the computer industry in the West has grown and changed.

• •

Write a paragraph that summarizes the major differences between life in the West in the years 1900 and 2000.

431

VOCABULARY

Pacific Rim
electronics
hybrid car
robotics

READING STRATEGY

Draw a main idea pyramid like the one here. Fill in the main idea and supporting details as you read.

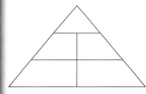

New Technology in Japan

Which industries make up a major part of the economy of Japan?

Find out!

Lesson Outline
• An Island Nation
• Export Economy

BUILD BACKGROUND

The United States exports and imports a variety of products to and from other countries. Which countries do we trade with? Many of our trading partners are located along the **Pacific Rim**. This term describes the countries that border the Pacific Ocean. One of these countries is **Japan**. Its economy is second only to the United States. New technology industries have helped Japan grow.

Tokyo, Japan

AN ISLAND NATION

Japan is an island nation located off the eastern coast of Asia. It has four main islands and hundreds of smaller ones. Steep mountains cover about three-quarters of the country. Most people live in large cities on the coast.

Japan's capital city, **Tokyo**, forms part of the largest megalopolis in the world. Other cities included are **Yokohama**, **Nagoya**, **Osaka**, and **Kobe**. Over 30 million people live in this area. This huge population makes housing very expensive. Many people who work in Tokyo have chosen to live outside the city. Some commute as much as two hours to and from work.

READING CHECK Where do most people live in Japan?

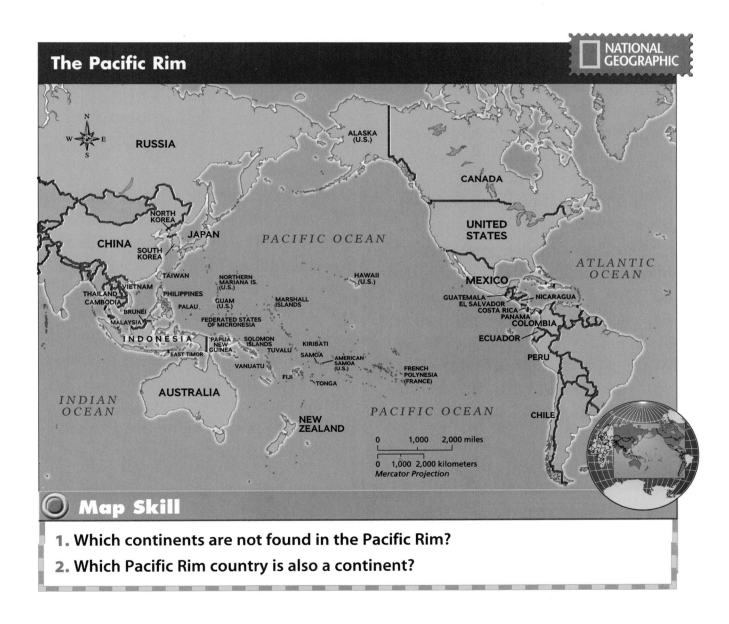

The Pacific Rim

NATIONAL GEOGRAPHIC

Map Skill

1. **Which continents are not found in the Pacific Rim?**

2. **Which Pacific Rim country is also a continent?**

EXPORT ECONOMY

Japan has few natural resources. Therefore, it imports raw materials, manufactures goods from them, and exports these new products around the world. Japan is a leader in the **electronics** industry. This industry creates high-tech products such as televisions, computers, compact disc players, and cellular phones. Every year millions of Americans buy electronic products from Japan.

Automobiles

Currently, Japanese inventors are working on a new advance in automobiles called the **hybrid car**. This kind of automobile combines a battery-powered motor with a gas engine.

Hybrid cars are designed to cut down on pollution and use less gasoline. They are also made with lighter materials and smaller engines, all of which help conserve energy. The first hybrid car available for sale in North America was exported from Japan in 1999.

An inventor plays a duet with his robotic creation, Wabot-2 (above). A **hybrid car** (below) has two sources of energy—electricity and gasoline.

Robotics

Another scientific advance produced in Japan are **robotics**. This technology deals with the design, construction, and operation of robots. Robots can handle repetitive work more quickly and cheaply than people. They can also perform dangerous or unpleasant tasks, such as loading heavy machinery. More than half of the world's robots are manufactured in Japan. Study the map of Japan and its major cities on the next page.

READING CHECK Name three electronic products made in Japan.

PUTTING IT TOGETHER

Japan is a leader in new technology industries, including electronics and robotics. Interdependence and international trade have also helped the country grow. In 2000, Japan exported over $450 billion in goods. Its imports totaled more than $350 billion. In this way, it has become a giant in the global economy.

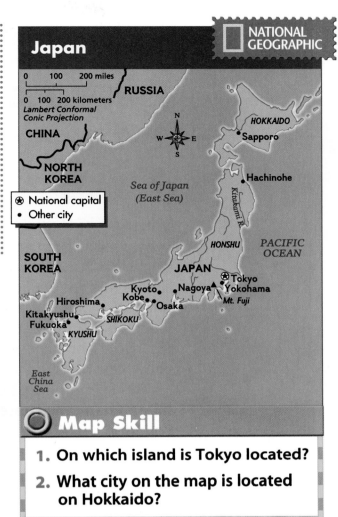

Compact disc players manufactured in Japan.

Map Skill

1. **On which island is Tokyo located?**

2. **What city on the map is located on Hokkaido?**

Review and Assess

1. Write one sentence for each of the vocabulary words:

   electronics   **Pacific Rim**
   hybrid car   **robotics**

2. Which cities make up the megalopolis in Japan?

3. Describe the industries that make up Japan's economy.

4. How are Japanese inventors working to conserve energy and protect the **environment**?

5. What are some **effects** of Tokyo's large population?

Activities

Look at the map on page 433. List all the countries in North America located on the Pacific Rim.

• •

Using an encyclopedia or the Internet, research how one kind of robot is used. Then **write** a paragraph about it.

Being a Good Citizen
The Salmon Corps

When Anne Hudson joined the Salmon Corps, she didn't know much about salmon or any other fish. "Growing up on the Yakama Indian reservation," says Anne, "we have always had special celebrations that honor the salmon, but until I joined the Salmon Corps, I never really thought much about them. I didn't know the salmon were in trouble." Now Anne knows a lot about salmon. She is one of about one hundred young people in the Salmon Corps.

The Salmon Corps is working to restore, or bring back, salmon habitats. These are the places where salmon live. Pollution, water use practices, and other conditions have greatly reduced the salmon population. Most Salmon Corps projects are along the Columbia River or one of the rivers and streams that flow into it. Many young people in the Salmon Corps belong to the Umatilla, Warm Springs, Nez Perce, Shoshone-Bannock, or Yakama Native American groups.

"(The salmon) need us and we need them. "

436

The Salmon Corps works at different places along the rivers. Anne's group works near Toppenish, Washington. They build fences to keep cows out of the water where salmon lay their eggs. They plant trees along river banks to provide shade over the water. "If the water gets too hot, the salmon cannot survive," explains Anne. She hopes that one day the rivers of the Pacific Northwest will again be full of salmon. "I think we can make a difference. We have to. They need us and we need them."

Toppenish, Washington

Be a Good Citizen

Making Connections

- **What are some important plants or animals in your community?**

- **What are some ways in which people work to protect these plants and animals?**

Talk About It!

- **Describe two ways the Salmon Corps is working to save salmon habitats.**

- **What does Anne Hudson mean when she says, "They need us and we need them?"**

Act On It!

In the Classroom

In small groups, research an endangered animal in your region. Paste a picture of the animal on poster board and write a short description of it. Explain why the animal is in danger and why it should be saved.

In the Community

Using the information you learned from doing the project above, write a letter to the editor of your local newspaper. In your letter, explain how people might help restore the endangered animal you chose.

VOCABULARY REVIEW

Number a sheet of paper from 1 to 5. Beside each number write the word or term from the list below that matches the description.

Forty-Niner	**silicon**
gold rush	**taro**
primary source	

1. information that comes from someone who was present at what he or she is describing

2. a tropical plant eaten as a food

3. a person who went to California in 1849, usually to seek gold

4. an element found in Earth's crust and used in electronics

5. a sudden movement of people to a place where gold has been found

CHAPTER COMPREHENSION

6. What is Kamehameha remembered for in Hawaii?

7. What led to the overthrow of Queen Liliuokalani in Hawaii?

8. Where was gold first discovered in the state of California?

9. Describe how miners searched for gold in California.

10. What brought many immigrants to the West in the middle 1800s?

11. How has the population of the West changed according to the 2000 Census?

12. What are two growing industries in the West today?

SKILL REVIEW

October, 1849

I've been panning for gold for the last few months. It is hard, back-breaking work. First, you scoop some dirt into a shallow pan. Next, you fill the pan with water. Then, you swish the pan around, spilling out water and dirt. You have to do this slowly and carefully. If there's any gold, it stays in the pan because gold is very heavy. You have to do this over and over. By day's end, my muscles ache and my fingers are red and raw. It will all be worth it, though, if I make a lucky strike.

13. **Study Skill** What is the difference between a primary and secondary source?

14. **Study Skill** Read the diary entry above and decide whether it is a primary or secondary source. How do you know?

15. **Study Skill** What clues and words in the entry helped you to decide?

16. **Reading/Thinking Skill** What is your frame of reference?

17. **Reading/Thinking Skill** Why is it important to recognize a person's frame of reference?

USING A TIME LINE

1800	1850	1900	1950	2000

1810
Kamehameha forms the Kingdom of Hawaii

1848
Gold is discovered at Sutter's Mill

1869
Transcontinental railroad is completed

1913
Movies begin being produced in Hollywood

1959
Hawaii becomes a state

2000
Census shows Nevada is fastest-growing state

18. When was the Kingdom of Hawaii formed?

19. How many years has Hawaii been a part of the United States?

20. How many years after gold was discovered was the railroad completed?

Learning About Immigration Suppose you were going to move to the West. Choose an industry you would like to work in. Use your textbook, school library, or the Internet to write about the role this industry plays in the West. Include information about the type of work you might do at your job.

Foldables

Use your Foldable to review what you have learned about the West as part of the United States, the North American Continent, and the world. As you look at the four tabs of your Foldable, test yourself to see what you remember about each of the four topics. Look at your notes under the tabs to check your memory and responses.

Unit 6 REVIEW

VOCABULARY REVIEW

Number a sheet of paper from 1 to 5. Beside each number write the word or term from the list below that best completes the sentence.

fertilizer   **silicon**

lava   **taro**

rain forest

1. Hawaiians grew ___ and used its roots and leaves for food.
2. The element ___ is used in electronics that are in computers.
3. ___ from a volcano burns plants, animals, and homes.
4. Farmers use ___ to improve the condition of the soil for crops.
5. Olympic National Park in Washington has several ___ areas.

TECHNOLOGY

For more resources to help you learn about the people and places you studied in this unit, visit **www.mhschool.com** and follow the links for Grade 4, Unit 6.

○ SKILL REVIEW

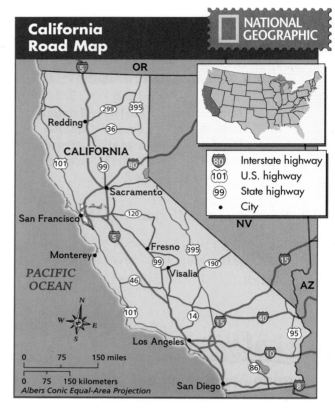

California Road Map

6. **Geography Skill** When might you need to use a road map?
7. **Geography Skill** What route could you take to travel along the coast from San Francisco to Los Angeles?
8. **Reading/Thinking Skill** What clues might tell you that a statement is an opinion?
9. **Reading/Thinking Skill** How might knowing a person's frame of reference help you understand his or her point of view?
10. **Study Skill** Give one example of both a primary and a secondary source.

Test Power

1   Forests are a renewable resource, because new trees can be planted. However, logging still affects the environment. Loggers, for example, prefer to cut the oldest trees in the forest. These trees are bigger and more valuable.

2   Conservationists worry that our country's oldest forests will disappear. Therefore, logging companies now plant new trees to replace what they cut. They also plant fast-growing trees, such as pine.

3   Logging may also threaten some forest animals. Animals that live in the forest lose their homes and food when trees are cut down. We all must work to preserve forests and protect the environment while find-

ing and using valuable lumber.

1 Which sentence, if added, would make sense in the selection above?

   A The West is rich in farmland and forests.

   B Logging companies know they must help protect forests.

   C Logging companies like to do public service work.

   D Logs are transported to sawmills after they are cut.

2 Which of the following is an opinion, not a fact?

   F Forests are a renewable resource.

   G Pines are fast-growing trees.

   H Animals that live in forests can lose their homes.

   J We all must work to preserve trees.

TEST PREP

WRITING ACTIVITIES

Writing to Persuade *Write* a letter to persuade people who live on the East Coast to move to California to search for gold. Include information about what is happening in the state and what it is like to live there in the 1800s.

Writing to Inform Suppose you are traveling down the West Coast of the United States. *Write* a letter to a friend describing the landforms you observe on your trip.

Writing to Express Suppose you lived in Hawaii before it became a state. *Write* a paragraph explaining how you would feel about the plantation owners who were trying to gain control of the islands.

441

Reference Section

The Reference Section has many parts, each with a different type of information. Use this section to look up people, places, and events as you study.

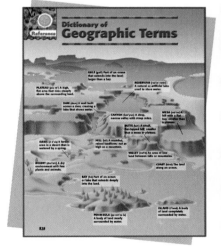

Susan B. Anthony

160°W   120°W   80

80°N
ARCTIC
OCEAN

GREENLA
(DENMA

ALASKA
(U.S.)
Arctic Circle
60°N

CANADA

NORTH
AMERICA

40°N

ATLAN
OCEA

UNITED STATES

BERMUDA
(U.K.)

MIDWAY ISLANDS
(U.S.)

Tropic of Cancer

HAWAII
(U.S.)
20°N

MEXICO

See inset below

Caribbean Sea

VENEZUELA

GUYANA
SURINAME
FRENCH GUIA
(FRANCE)

COLOMBIA

PACIFIC OCEAN

Equator

GALÁPAGOS ISLANDS
(ECUADOR)

0°

ECUADOR

SOUTH
AMERICA

PERU

BRAZIL

SAMOA

AMERICAN SAMOA
(U.S.)

BOLIVIA

TONGA

FRENCH POLYNESIA
(FRANCE)

PARAGUAY

20°S
Tropic of Capricorn

URUGUAY

ARGENTINA

CHILE

40°S

FALKLAND
(U.K.)

60°S

Antarctic Circle

80°S

ANTARCTICA

160°W   120°W   8

Central America and West Indies

90°W

FLORIDA
(U.S.)

70°W

Gulf of Mexico

Tropic of Cancer

BAHAMAS

ATLANTIC
OCEAN

60°W

20°N

CUBA

TURKS AND
CAICOS IS. (U.K.)

VIRGIN ISLANDS
(U.K.)

ST. KITTS
AND NEVIS

20°N

CAYMAN IS.
(U.K.)

MEXICO

HAITI

DOMINICAN
REPUBLIC

ANTIGUA AND
BARBUDA

BELIZE

JAMAICA

PUERTO RICO
(U.S.)

VIRGIN
ISLANDS
(U.S.)

GUADELOUPE
(FRANCE)

GUATEMALA

DOMINICA

HONDURAS

Caribbean Sea

MARTINIQUE (FRANCE)

ST.
LUCIA

EL SALVADOR

N

W   E

S

NETHERLANDS
ANTILLES
(NETHERLANDS)

ST. VINCENT AND
THE GRENADINES

BARBADOS

NICARAGUA

ARUBA
(NETHERLANDS)

GRENADA

PACIFIC
OCEAN

10°N

COSTA
RICA

TRINIDAD AND
TOBAGO

10°N

0   250   500 miles

0   250   500 kilometers

PANAMA

VENEZUELA

COLOMBIA

GUYANA

90°W   80°W   70°W

R4

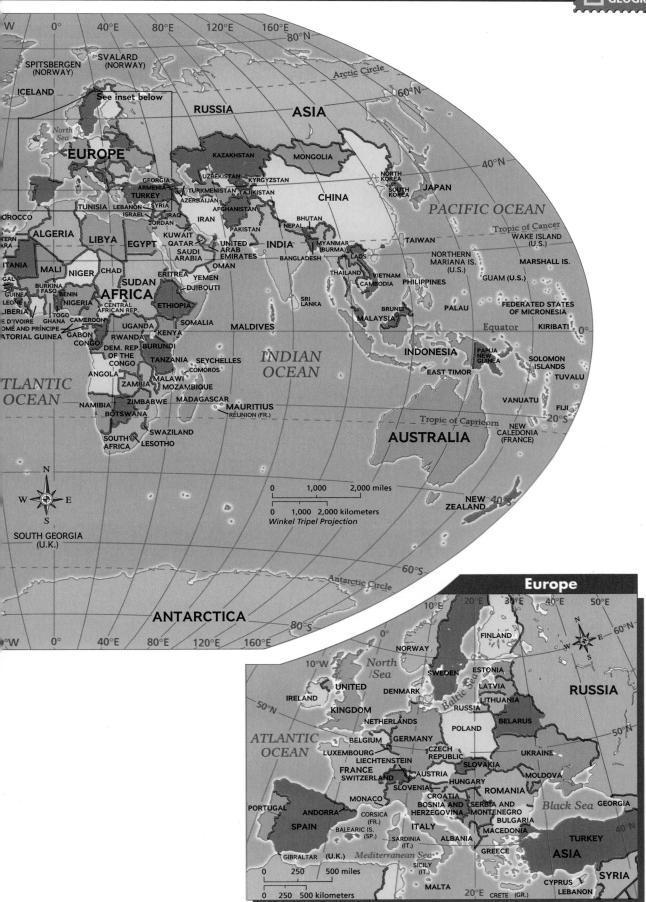

NATIONAL GEOGRAPHIC

W 0° 40°E 80°E 120°E 160°E 80°N

SPITSBERGEN (NORWAY)
SVALARD (NORWAY)
ICELAND
Arctic Circle
60°N
See inset below
North Sea
RUSSIA
ASIA
EUROPE
40°N
KAZAKHSTAN
MONGOLIA
GEORGIA
ARMENIA
UZBEKISTAN KYRGYZSTAN
NORTH KOREA
TURKMENISTAN TAJIKISTAN
TURKEY
JAPAN
AZERBAIJAN
SOUTH KOREA
TUNISIA LEBANON SYRIA
AFGHANISTAN
CHINA
PACIFIC OCEAN
ISRAEL IRAQ
JORDAN
PAKISTAN
IRAN
TAIWAN
Tropic of Cancer
WAKE ISLAND (U.S.)
OROCCO
BHUTAN
ALGERIA
LIBYA
EGYPT
KUWAIT
QATAR
NEPAL
INDIA
MYANMAR (BURMA)
NORTHERN MARIANA IS. (U.S.)
MARSHALL IS.
ITANIA
SAUDI ARABIA
UNITED ARAB EMIRATES
BANGLADESH
LAOS
GUAM (U.S.)
MALI NIGER CHAD
OMAN
THAILAND
VIETNAM
PHILIPPINES
GAL
BURKINA FASO
SUDAN
ERITREA YEMEN
CAMBODIA
PALAU
FEDERATED STATES OF MICRONESIA
GUINEA
BENIN
DJIBOUTI
SRI LANKA
LEONE NIGERIA
AFRICA
CENTRAL AFRICAN REP.
ETHIOPIA
IBERIA
TOGO GHANA
SOMALIA
MALDIVES
BRUNEI
KIRIBATI
E D'IVOIRE
CAMEROON
UGANDA
KENYA
MALAYSIA
Equator 0°
OMÉ AND PRÍNCIPE
GABON
RWANDA
INDIAN OCEAN
INDONESIA
PAPUA NEW GUINEA
ATORIAL GUINEA
CONGO
BURUNDI
SOLOMON ISLANDS
DEM. REP. OF THE CONGO
TANZANIA
SEYCHELLES
EAST TIMOR
TLANTIC OCEAN
ANGOLA
COMOROS
TUVALU
ZAMBIA
MALAWI
MOZAMBIQUE
NAMIBIA ZIMBABWE
MADAGASCAR
MAURITIUS
VANUATU
FIJI
BOTSWANA
RÉUNION (FR.)
Tropic of Capricorn
NEW CALEDONIA (FRANCE)
20°S
SWAZILAND
SOUTH AFRICA LESOTHO
AUSTRALIA

N
W E
S

SOUTH GEORGIA (U.K.)

0 1,000 2,000 miles
0 1,000 2,000 kilometers
Winkel Tripel Projection

NEW ZEALAND 40°S

Antarctic Circle
60°S
ANTARCTICA
80°S
W 0° 40°E 80°E 120°E 160°E

Europe

10°E 20°E 30°E 40°E 50°E
60°N
10°W
NORWAY
FINLAND
North Sea
SWEDEN
ESTONIA
RUSSIA
IRELAND
UNITED KINGDOM
DENMARK
Baltic Sea
LATVIA
LITHUANIA
50°N
ATLANTIC OCEAN
NETHERLANDS
RUSSIA
BELARUS
50°N
BELGIUM
GERMANY
POLAND
LUXEMBOURG
CZECH REPUBLIC
UKRAINE
LIECHTENSTEIN
FRANCE
SLOVAKIA
SWITZERLAND
AUSTRIA
MOLDOVA
SLOVENIA
HUNGARY
ROMANIA
MONACO
CROATIA
PORTUGAL
ANDORRA
BOSNIA AND HERZEGOVINA
SERBIA AND MONTENEGRO
Black Sea
GEORGIA
CORSICA (FR.)
BULGARIA
SPAIN
ITALY
MACEDONIA
BALEARIC IS. (SP.)
ALBANIA
TURKEY
SARDINIA (IT.)
GREECE
ASIA
GIBRALTAR (U.K.)
Mediterranean Sea
SICILY (IT.)
SYRIA
MALTA
CYPRUS
LEBANON
20°E
CRETE (GR.)
40°N

0 250 500 miles
0 250 500 kilometers

R5

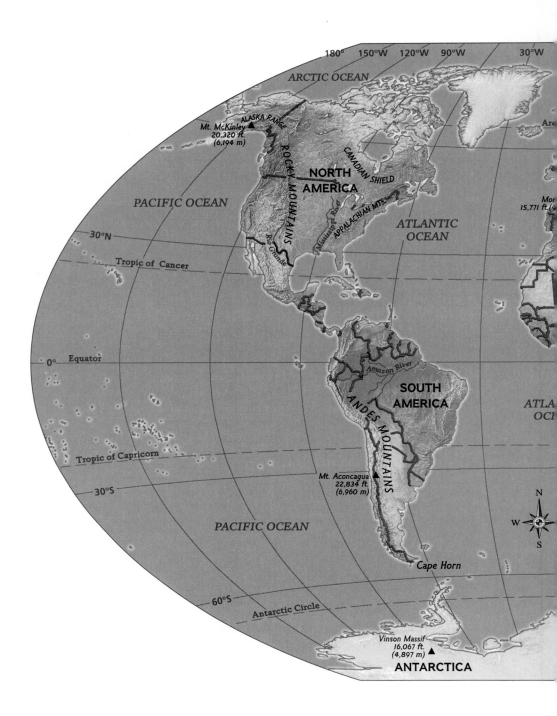

180°   150°W   120°W   90°W   30°W

ARCTIC OCEAN

ALASKA RANGE
Mt. McKinley
20,320 ft.
(6,194 m)

CANADIAN SHIELD

ROCKY MOUNTAINS

NORTH
AMERICA

PACIFIC OCEAN

Mississippi River

APPALACHIAN MTS.

ATLANTIC
OCEAN

Mor
15,771 ft.(4

30°N

Tropic of Cancer

Rio Grande

0°   Equator

Amazon River

SOUTH
AMERICA

ATLA
OC

Tropic of Capricorn

ANDES MOUNTAINS

Mt. Aconcagua
22,834 ft.
(6,960 m)

30°S

PACIFIC OCEAN

N
W   E
S

Cape Horn

60°S

Antarctic Circle

Vinson Massif
16,067 ft.
(4,897 m) ▲

ANTARCTICA

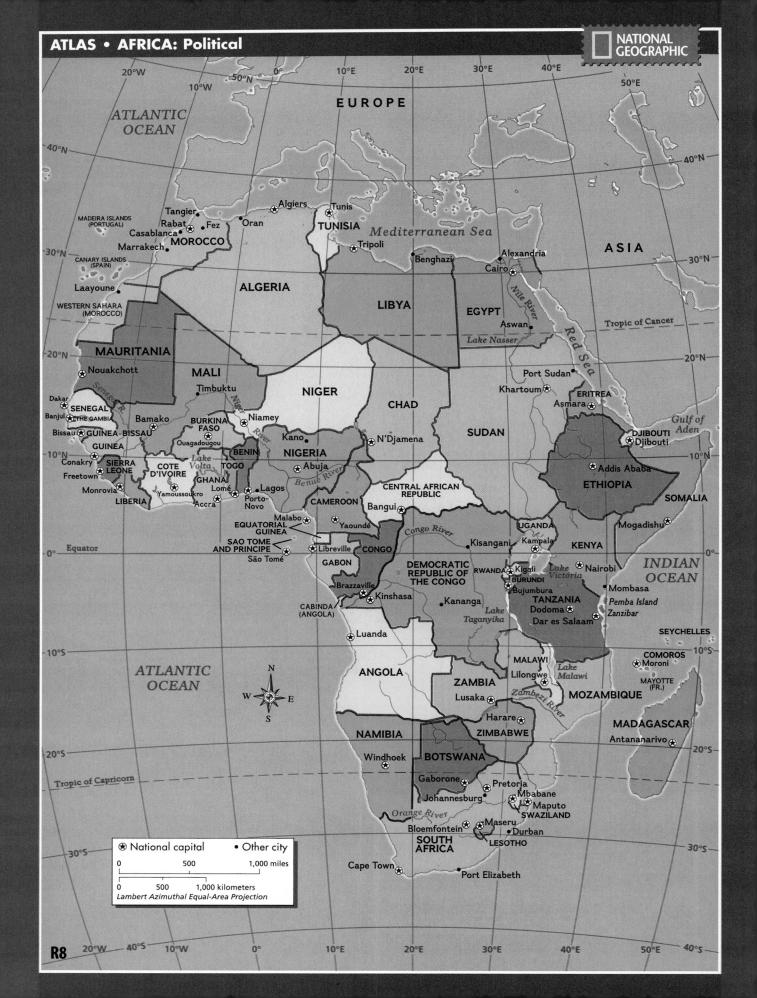

EUROPE

ATLANTIC OCEAN

ASIA

Mediterranean Sea

40°N

30°N

20°N

10°N

0° Equator

10°S

20°S

30°S

20°W · 10°W · 0° · 10°E · 20°E · 30°E · 40°E · 50°E

MADEIRA ISLANDS (PORTUGAL)

Tangier
Rabat
Casablanca
Marrakech
MOROCCO
Fez
Oran
Algiers
Tunis
TUNISIA
Tripoli
Benghazi

CANARY ISLANDS (SPAIN)

Laayoune
WESTERN SAHARA (MOROCCO)

ALGERIA
LIBYA
EGYPT
Alexandria
Cairo
Aswan
Lake Nasser

Nile River
Red Sea
Tropic of Cancer

MAURITANIA
Nouakchott
MALI
Timbuktu
NIGER
CHAD
SUDAN
Port Sudan
Khartoum
ERITREA
Asmara

Dakar
SENEGAL
Banjul
THE GAMBIA
Bissau
GUINEA-BISSAU
GUINEA
Conakry
SIERRA LEONE
Freetown
Monrovia
LIBERIA

Bamako
BURKINA FASO
Ouagadougou
Niamey
Kano
N'Djamena
Gulf of Aden
DJIBOUTI
Djibouti

Senegal R.
Niger River
Lake Volta
BENIN
TOGO
GHANA
COTE D'IVOIRE
Yamoussoukro
Accra
Lomé
Porto-Novo
Lagos
NIGERIA
Abuja
Benue River
CAMEROON
CENTRAL AFRICAN REPUBLIC
Bangui
Addis Ababa
ETHIOPIA
SOMALIA
Mogadishu

Malabo
EQUATORIAL GUINEA
Yaoundé
SAO TOME AND PRINCIPE
São Tomé
Libreville
CONGO
GABON
Congo River
DEMOCRATIC REPUBLIC OF THE CONGO
Kisangani
UGANDA
Kampala
RWANDA
Kigali
BURUNDI
Bujumbura
Lake Victoria
KENYA
Nairobi
INDIAN OCEAN
Mombasa
Pemba Island
Zanzibar

Brazzaville
CABINDA (ANGOLA)
Kinshasa
Kananga
Lake Tanganyika
TANZANIA
Dodoma
Dar es Salaam
SEYCHELLES

Luanda
ANGOLA
ZAMBIA
Lusaka
MALAWI
Lilongwe
Lake Malawi
Zambezi River
MOZAMBIQUE
COMOROS
Moroni
MAYOTTE (FR.)

ATLANTIC OCEAN

NAMIBIA
Windhoek
BOTSWANA
Gaborone
Harare
ZIMBABWE
MADAGASCAR
Antananarivo

Tropic of Capricorn

Johannesburg
Pretoria
Mbabane
Maputo
SWAZILAND
Orange River
Bloemfontein
Maseru
LESOTHO
Durban
SOUTH AFRICA
Cape Town
Port Elizabeth

N
W E
S

⊛ National capital   • Other city

0   500   1,000 miles
0   500   1,000 kilometers
Lambert Azimuthal Equal-Area Projection

20°W · 40°S · 10°W · 0° · 10°E · 20°E · 30°E · 40°E · 50°E · 40°S

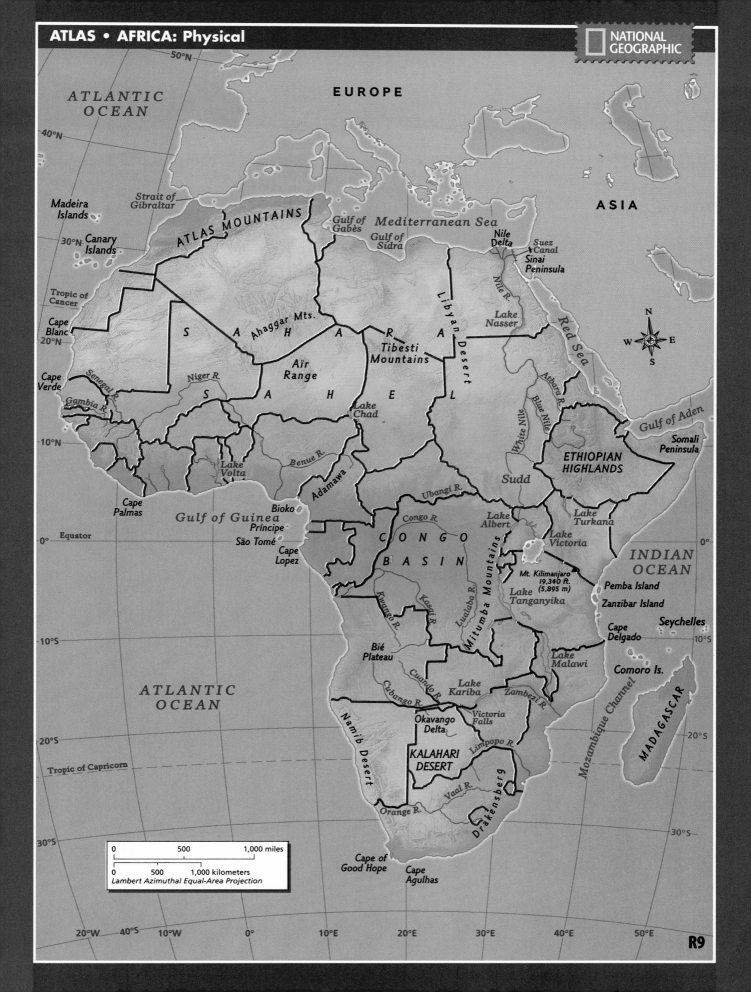

NATIONAL GEOGRAPHIC

EUROPE

ASIA

ATLANTIC OCEAN

Madeira Islands

Canary Islands

Strait of Gibraltar

ATLAS MOUNTAINS

Gulf of Gabès

Mediterranean Sea

Gulf of Sidra

Nile Delta

Suez Canal

Sinai Peninsula

Tropic of Cancer

Cape Blanc

S   A   H   A   R   A

Ahaggar Mts.

Tibesti Mountains

Libyan Desert

Nile R.

Lake Nasser

Red Sea

Cape Verde

Senegal R.

Niger R.

Aïr Range

S   A   H   E   L

Atbara R.

Gambia R.

Lake Chad

White Nile

Blue Nile

Gulf of Aden

Somali Peninsula

Cape Palmas

Lake Volta

Benue R.

Adamawa

ETHIOPIAN HIGHLANDS

Gulf of Guinea

Bioko

Príncipe

São Tomé

Cape Lopez

Ubangi R.

Congo R.

C O N G O   B A S I N

Lake Albert

Sudd

Lake Turkana

Lake Victoria

Equator

INDIAN OCEAN

Mt. Kilimanjaro 19,340 ft. (5,895 m)

Mitumba Mountains

Lake Tanganyika

Pemba Island

Zanzibar Island

Seychelles

Kwango R.

Kasai R.

Lualaba R.

Cape Delgado

Bié Plateau

Comoro Is.

Lake Malawi

Cuando R.

Lake Kariba

Zambezi R.

MADAGASCAR

Cubango R.

Victoria Falls

Namib Desert

Okavango Delta

Mozambique Channel

ATLANTIC OCEAN

Limpopo R.

Tropic of Capricorn

KALAHARI DESERT

Vaal R.

Drakensberg

Orange R.

Cape of Good Hope

Cape Agulhas

0   500   1,000 miles
0   500   1,000 kilometers
Lambert Azimuthal Equal-Area Projection

20°W   10°W   0°   10°E   20°E   30°E   40°E   50°E

40°S   30°S

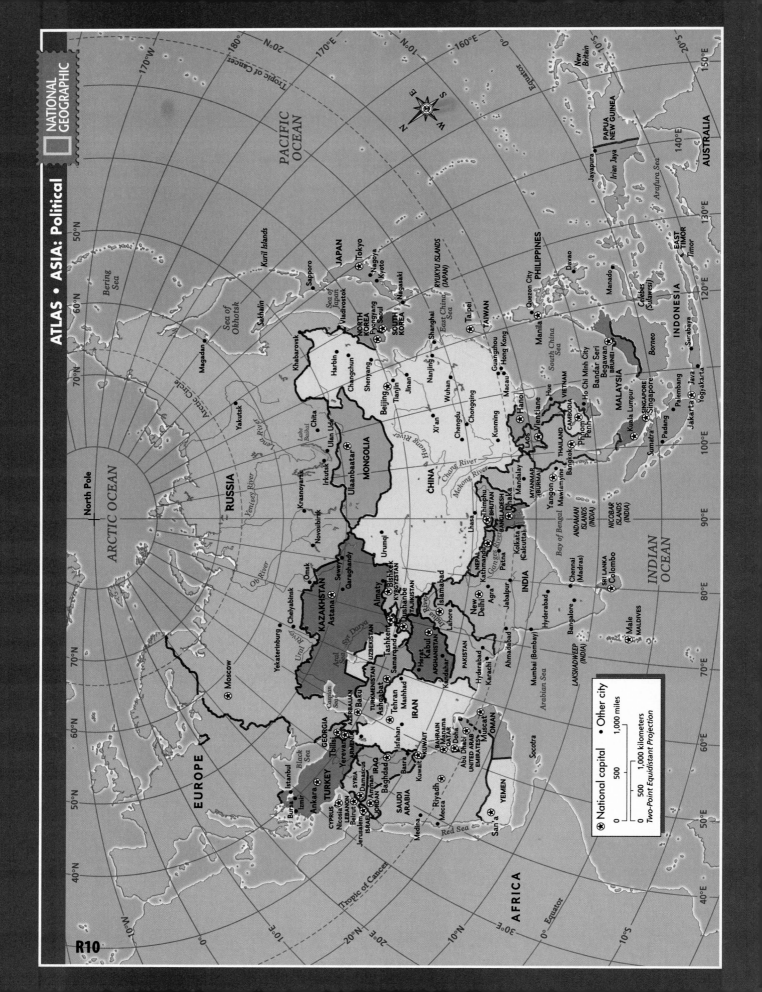

NATIONAL GEOGRAPHIC

PACIFIC OCEAN

North Pole

ARCTIC OCEAN

RUSSIA

EUROPE

Moscow

Yekaterinburg
Chelyabinsk
Omsk
Novosibirsk
Krasnoyarsk
Irkutsk
Ulan Ude
Chita
Yakutsk
Magadan
Khabarovsk
Vladivostok

Sea of Okhotsk
Bering Sea
Kuril Islands
Sakhalin

JAPAN
Sapporo
Tokyo
Nagoya
Kyoto
Nagasaki

Sea of Japan

NORTH KOREA
Pyongyang
SOUTH KOREA
Seoul

Harbin
Changchun
Shenyang
Beijing
Tianjin
Jinan
Shanghai
Nanjing
Wuhan
Xi'an
Chengdu
Chongqing
Kunming
Guangzhou
Hong Kong
Macau

CHINA

MONGOLIA
Ulaanbaatar

Lake Baikal
Lena River
Yenisey River
Ob River
Ural River

East China Sea
RYUKYU ISLANDS (JAPAN)
TAIWAN
Taipei
South China Sea

PHILIPPINES
Manila
Quezon City
Davao

PAPUA NEW GUINEA
New Britain
Jayapura
Irian Jaya

AUSTRALIA

Arafura Sea

EAST TIMOR
Timor

INDONESIA
Manado
Celebes (Sulawesi)
Borneo
Surabaya
Java
Yogyakarta
Jakarta
Padang
Palembang
Sumatra

MALAYSIA
Kuala Lumpur
SINGAPORE
Singapore

BRUNEI
Bandar Seri Begawan

VIETNAM
Hanoi
Hue
Ho Chi Minh City

LAOS
Vientiane

CAMBODIA
Phnom Penh

THAILAND
Bangkok

MYANMAR (BURMA)
Yangon
Mandalay
Mawlamyine

Chang River
Huang River
Mekong River

KAZAKHSTAN
Astana
Sewey
Qaraghandy
Almaty

Aral Sea
Caspian Sea

KYRGYZSTAN
Bishkek
UZBEKISTAN
Tashkent
Samarqand
TAJIKISTAN
Dushanbe
TURKMENISTAN
Ashgabat

Syr Darya

Urumqi

NEPAL
Kathmandu
BHUTAN
Thimphu
BANGLADESH
Dhaka

Lhasa

INDIA
New Delhi
Agra
Jabalpur
Jaipur
Patna
Kolkata (Calcutta)
Hyderabad
Bangalore
Chennai (Madras)
Mumbai (Bombay)
Ahmadabad
Ganges River
Indus River

PAKISTAN
Islamabad
Lahore
Hyderabad
Karachi

AFGHANISTAN
Kabul
Herat
Kandahar

Bay of Bengal
ANDAMAN ISLANDS (INDIA)
NICOBAR ISLANDS (INDIA)

SRI LANKA
Colombo

INDIAN OCEAN

LAKSHADWEEP (INDIA)

Male
MALDIVES

IRAN
Tehran
Isfahan
Mashhad

GEORGIA
Tbilisi
ARMENIA
Yerevan
AZERBAIJAN
Baku

TURKEY
Ankara
Istanbul
Izmir
Bursa

CYPRUS
Nicosia
LEBANON
Beirut
SYRIA
Damascus
ISRAEL
Jerusalem
JORDAN
Amman

IRAQ
Baghdad
Basra

KUWAIT
Kuwait

BAHRAIN
Manama
QATAR
Doha
UNITED ARAB EMIRATES
Abu Dhabi

OMAN
Muscat

YEMEN
San'a

SAUDI ARABIA
Riyadh
Mecca
Medina

Red Sea
Socotra

Arabian Sea

AFRICA

Black Sea

Tropic of Cancer
Equator

Arctic Circle

National capital
Other city

1,000 miles
1,000 kilometers
Two-Point Equidistant Projection

R10

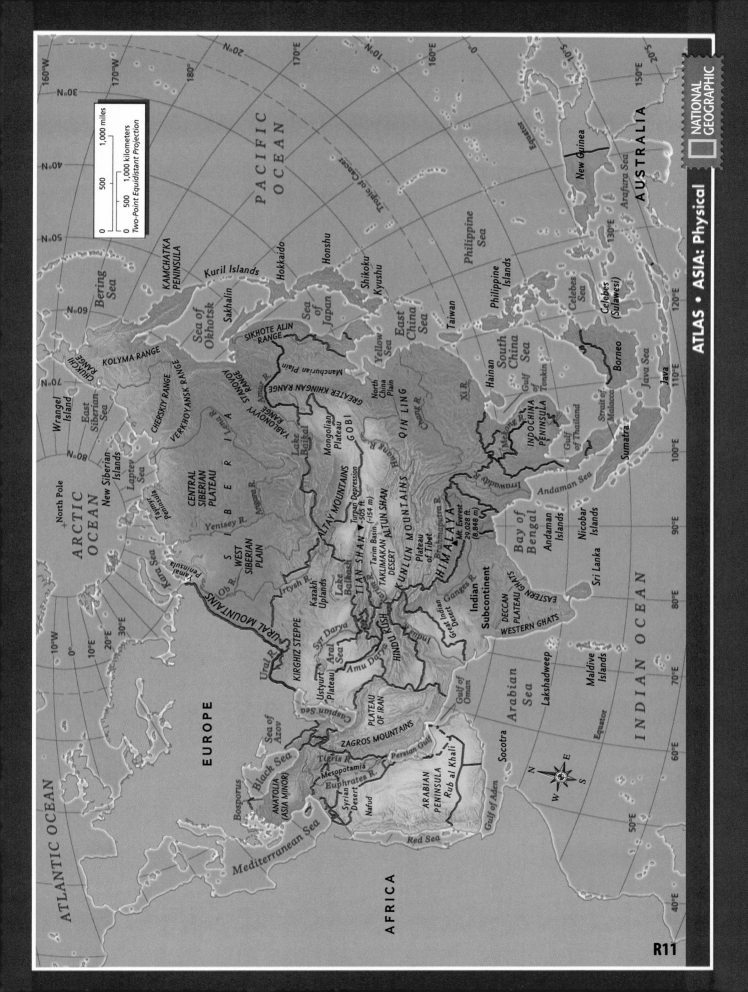

1,000 miles
500
0

1,000 kilometers
500
0
Two-Point Equidistant Projection

ATLANTIC OCEAN

ARCTIC OCEAN

North Pole

PACIFIC OCEAN

EUROPE

AFRICA

AUSTRALIA

New Guinea

INDIAN OCEAN

Equator

Tropic of Cancer

Mediterranean Sea

Black Sea

Sea of Azov

Bosporus

ANATOLIA (ASIA MINOR)

Caspian Sea

Tigris R.

Euphrates R.

Mesopotamia

Syrian Desert

Nafud

Red Sea

Gulf of Aden

ARABIAN PENINSULA

Rub al Khali

Persian Gulf

Gulf of Oman

ZAGROS MOUNTAINS

PLATEAU OF IRAN

Socotra

Arabian Sea

Lakshadweep

Maldive Islands

Ustyurt Plateau

Aral Sea

Amu Darya

Syr Darya

KIRGHIZ STEPPE

Kazakh Uplands

Lake Balkhash

HINDU KUSH

Kabul

Indus R.

Great Indian Desert

Indian Subcontinent

Ganges R.

Brahmaputra R.

DECCAN PLATEAU

WESTERN GHATS

EASTERN GHATS

Sri Lanka

Bay of Bengal

Andaman Islands

Nicobar Islands

Andaman Sea

URAL MOUNTAINS

Ural R.

Ob R.

WEST SIBERIAN PLAIN

Irtysh R.

Yenisey R.

CENTRAL SIBERIAN PLATEAU

Angara R.

Lena R.

Taymyr Peninsula

Yamal Peninsula

Kara Sea

New Siberian Islands

Laptev Sea

East Siberian Sea

Wrangel Island

CHUKCHI RANGE

KOLYMA RANGE

CHERSKIY RANGE

VERKHOYANSK RANGE

YABLONOVYY RANGE

STANOVOY RANGE

Lake Baikal

Amur R.

GREATER KHINGAN RANGE

Mongolian Plateau

GOBI

ALTAY MOUNTAINS

Turpan Depression −505 ft (−154 m)

Tarim Basin

TAKLIMAKAN DESERT

TIAN SHAN

ALTUN SHAN

KUNLUN MOUNTAINS

Plateau of Tibet

HIMALAYA

▲Mt. Everest 29,028 ft (8,848 m)

QIN LING

Huang R.

North China Plain

Chang R.

Xi R.

Yellow Sea

East China Sea

Manchurian Plain

SIKHOTE ALIN RANGE

Sea of Japan

Sakhalin

Kuril Islands

KAMCHATKA PENINSULA

Bering Sea

Sea of Okhotsk

Hokkaido

Honshu

Shikoku

Kyushu

Taiwan

Hainan

South China Sea

Gulf of Tonkin

INDOCHINA PENINSULA

Mekong R.

Gulf of Thailand

Irrawaddy R.

Strait of Malacca

Sumatra

Borneo

Java

Java Sea

Celebes (Sulawesi)

Celebes Sea

Philippine Islands

Philippine Sea

Arafura Sea

S I B E R I A

N S

W E

R11

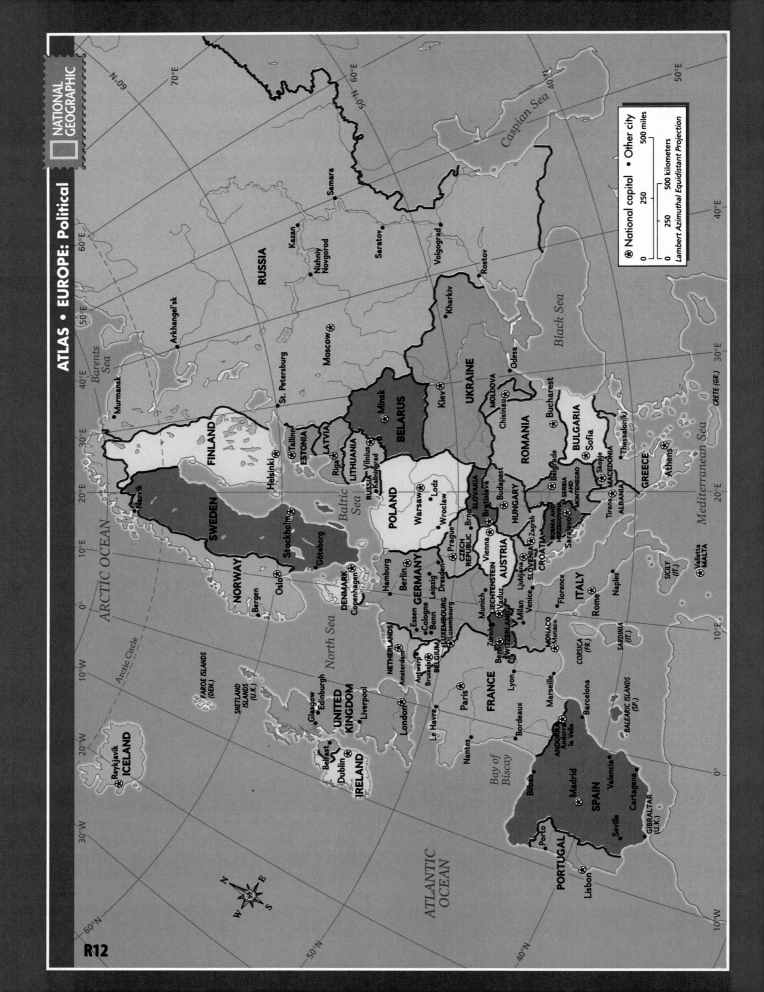

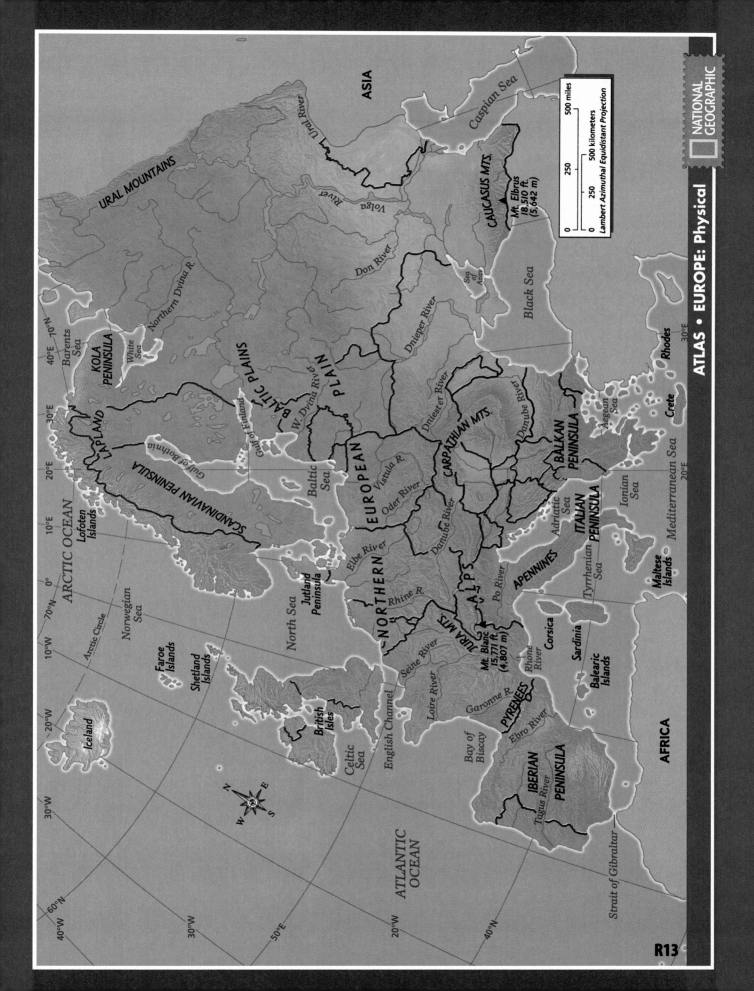

NATIONAL GEOGRAPHIC

ASIA

URAL MOUNTAINS

Ural River

Caspian Sea

Volga River

CAUCASUS MTS.

Mt. Elbrus
18,510 ft.
(5,642 m)

Don River

Sea of Azov

Black Sea

500 miles
250
0
500 kilometers
250
0
250
0
500
Lambert Azimuthal Equidistant Projection

BALTIC PLAINS

Northern Dvina R.

Dnieper River

Barents Sea

40°N 70°N

KOLA PENINSULA

White Sea

30°E

LAPLAND

W. Dvina River

PLAIN

Dniester River

CARPATHIAN MTS.

Danube River

Rhodes

30°E

40°E

20°E

SCANDINAVIAN PENINSULA

Gulf of Bothnia

EUROPEAN

Vistula R.

Oder River

BALKAN PENINSULA

Aegean Sea

Crete

Mediterranean Sea

20°E

Lofoten Islands

ARCTIC OCEAN

Baltic Sea

NORTHERN

Danube River

Adriatic Sea

ITALIAN PENINSULA

Ionian Sea

10°E

Elbe River

ALPS

APENNINES

Tyrrhenian Sea

Maltese Islands

0°

Jutland Peninsula

Rhine R.

Po River

Corsica

Sardinia

Balearic Islands

70°N

Faroe Islands

Shetland Islands

North Sea

JURA MTS.

Mt. Blanc
15,771 ft.
(4,807 m)

Rhône River

AFRICA

Arctic Circle

Norwegian Sea

Seine River

Loire River

PYRENEES

Ebro River

10°W

Iceland

British Isles

English Channel

Celtic Sea

Bay of Biscay

Garonne R.

IBERIAN PENINSULA

Tagus River

20°W

30°W

N
W E
S

30°W

20°W

40°N

Strait of Gibraltar

60°N

40°N

ATLANTIC OCEAN

50°E

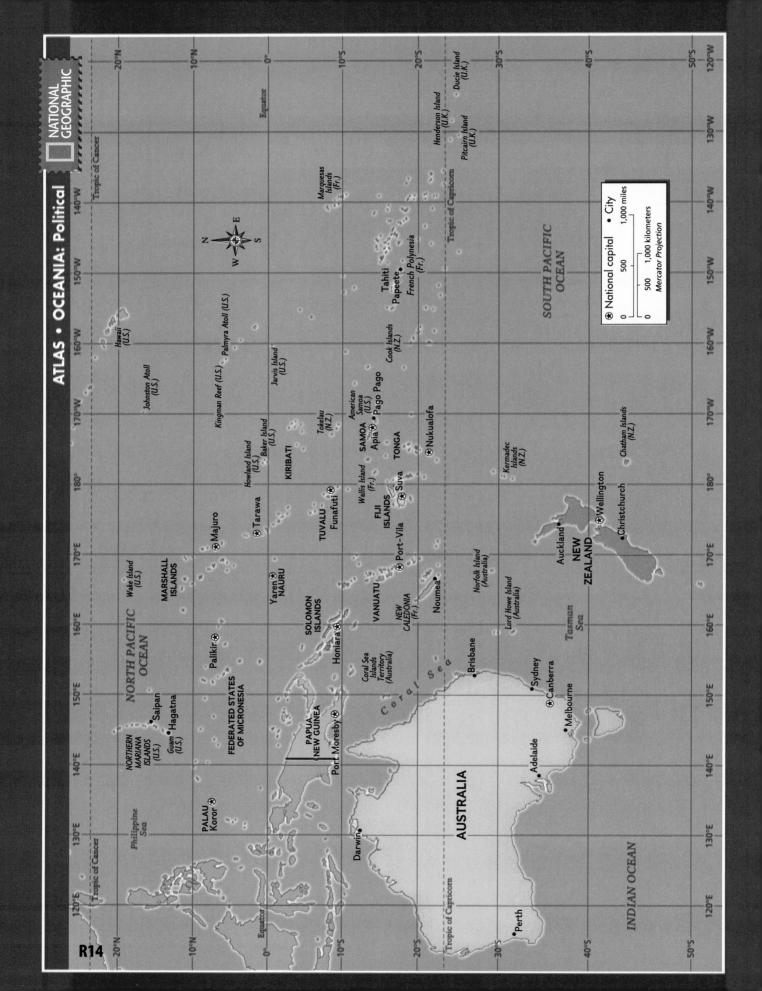

NATIONAL GEOGRAPHIC

National capital   • **City**

0   500   1,000 miles

0   500   1,000 kilometers

Mercator Projection

SOUTH PACIFIC OCEAN

NORTH PACIFIC OCEAN

Tropic of Cancer

Equator

Tropic of Capricorn

Philippine Sea

PALAU
Koror

NORTHERN MARIANA ISLANDS (U.S.)
Saipan
Guam (U.S.)
Hagatna

FEDERATED STATES OF MICRONESIA
Palikir

PAPUA NEW GUINEA
Port Moresby

Darwin

AUSTRALIA

Perth

Adelaide

Melbourne
Canberra
Sydney

Brisbane

Coral Sea

Coral Sea Islands Territory (Australia)

SOLOMON ISLANDS
Honiara

MARSHALL ISLANDS
Majuro

Wake Island (U.S.)

NAURU
Yaren

KIRIBATI
Tarawa

Howland Island (U.S.)
Baker Island (U.S.)

Johnston Atoll (U.S.)

Hawaii (U.S.)

Kingman Reef (U.S.)
Palmyra Atoll (U.S.)

Jarvis Island (U.S.)

TUVALU
Funafuti

FIJI ISLANDS
Suva

VANUATU
Port-Vila

NEW CALEDONIA (Fr.)
Noumea

Norfolk Island (Australia)

Lord Howe Island (Australia)

Tasman Sea

Wallis Island (Fr.)

SAMOA
Apia

American Samoa (U.S.)
Pago Pago

Tokelau (N.Z.)

TONGA
Nukualofa

Cook Islands (N.Z.)

French Polynesia (Fr.)
Tahiti
Papeete

Marquesas Islands (Fr.)

Kermadec Islands (N.Z.)

NEW ZEALAND
Auckland
Wellington
Christchurch

Chatham Islands (N.Z.)

Pitcairn Island (U.K.)
Henderson Island (U.K.)
Ducie Island (U.K.)

INDIAN OCEAN

N E S W

NATIONAL GEOGRAPHIC

120°W 20°N 130°W 10°N 0° Equator 10°S 20°S 30°S 40°S 50°S 120°W 130°W

Tropic of Cancer

Ducie Island

Henderson Island

Pitcairn Island

Tropic of Cancer

Marquesas Islands

Tuamotu Archipelago

French Polynesia

Hawaiian Islands

N E W S

Society Islands

Austral Islands

Tropic of Capricorn

SOUTH PACIFIC OCEAN

Johnston Atoll

Kingman Reef   Palmyra Atoll

Line Islands

P O L Y N E S I A

Jarvis Island

Cook Islands

Howland Island   Baker Island

Phoenix Islands

Tokelau

Samoa Islands

Tonga Islands

Fiji Islands

Tuvalu

Wake Island

Bikini   Marshall Atoll   Islands

Ratak Chain

Gilbert Islands

Ralik Chain

Nauru

Santa Cruz Island

Vanuatu

New Caledonia

Norfolk Island

Kermadec Islands

Chatham Islands

North Island

NEW ZEALAND

South Island

Stewart Island

Mt. Cook 12,349 ft. (3,764 m)

Lord Howe Island

Tasman Sea

Mt. Kosciuszko 7,310 ft. (2,228 m)

GREAT DIVIDING RANGE

NORTH PACIFIC OCEAN

M I C R O N E S I A

M E L A N E S I A

Caroline Islands

Solomon Islands

Coral Sea

Northern Mariana Islands

Guam

Yap Islands

Palau

New Guinea

Torres Strait

Gulf of Carpentaria

Arafura Sea

Darling River

Murray River

AUSTRALIA

Macdonnell Ranges

Kimberley Plateau

GREAT VICTORIA DESERT

Tasmania

Philippine Sea

Philippine Islands

South China Sea

Borneo

Sulawesi (Celebes)

East Timor

Timor

INDIAN OCEAN

1,000 miles
500
1,000 kilometers
500   1,000
Mercator Projection

130°E 140°E 150°E 160°E 170°E 180° 170°W 160°W 150°W 140°W 130°W

Tropic of Cancer 20°N 10°N Equator 10°S 20°S 30°S 40°S

R15

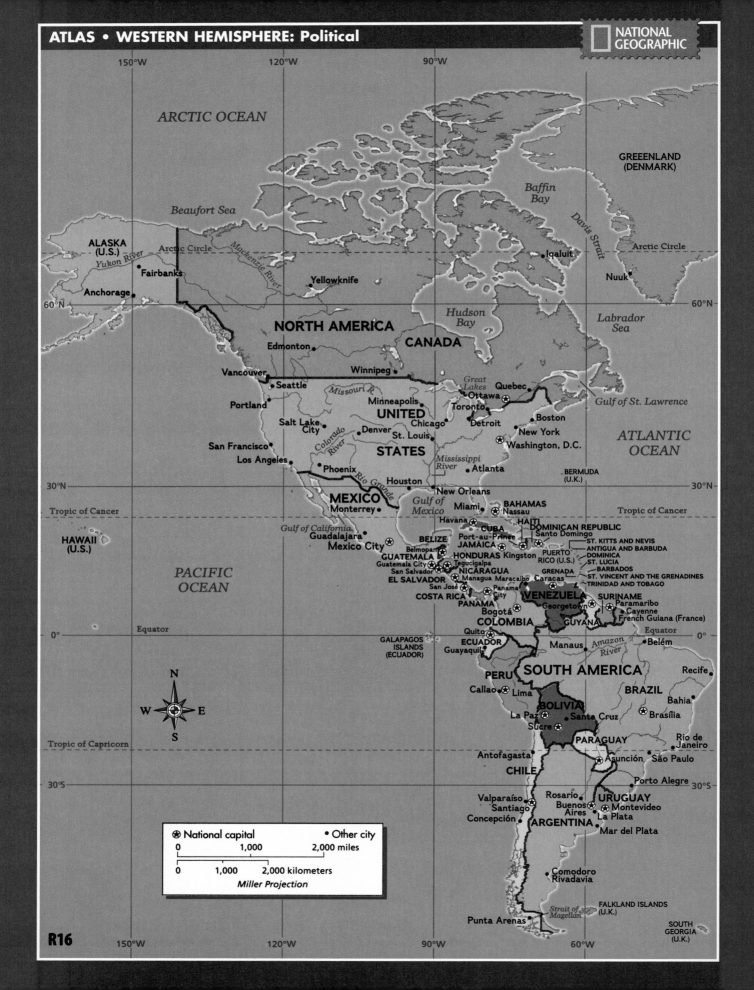

NATIONAL GEOGRAPHIC

ARCTIC OCEAN

GREEENLAND
(DENMARK)

Baffin
Bay

Beaufort Sea

ALASKA
(U.S.)

Arctic Circle

Davis Strait

Arctic Circle

Yukon River

Mackenzie River

Fairbanks

Iqaluit

Nuuk

Anchorage

60°N

60°N

NORTH AMERICA

Hudson
Bay

Labrador
Sea

CANADA

Edmonton

Yellowknife

Winnipeg

Great
Lakes

Quebec

Vancouver

Ottawa

Gulf of St. Lawrence

Seattle

Missouri R.

Toronto

Portland

Minneapolis

Chicago

Detroit

Boston

UNITED

Salt Lake
City

Denver

St. Louis

New York

Washington, D.C.

ATLANTIC
OCEAN

San Francisco

Colorado River

STATES

Mississippi River

Los Angeles

Phoenix

Atlanta

Rio Grande

Houston

BERMUDA
(U.K.)

30°N

30°N

New Orleans

MEXICO

Gulf of
Mexico

Miami

BAHAMAS

Tropic of Cancer

Monterrey

Havana

Nassau

Tropic of Cancer

HAWAII
(U.S.)

Gulf of California

Guadalajara

CUBA

HAITI

DOMINICAN REPUBLIC

Santo Domingo

BELIZE

Port-au-Prince

ST. KITTS AND NEVIS

Mexico City

Belmopan

JAMAICA

ANTIGUA AND BARBUDA

PACIFIC
OCEAN

GUATEMALA

HONDURAS

Kingston

PUERTO
RICO (U.S.)

DOMINICA

Guatemala City

Tegucigalpa

ST. LUCIA

San Salvador

NICARAGUA

BARBADOS

EL SALVADOR

Managua

Maracaibo

GRENADA

ST. VINCENT AND THE GRENADINES

Caracas

TRINIDAD AND TOBAGO

San José

Panama
City

VENEZUELA

SURINAME

COSTA RICA

Georgetown

Paramaribo

PANAMA

Cayenne

Bogotá

GUYANA

French Guiana (France)

COLOMBIA

0°

Quito

Equator

0°

GALAPAGOS
ISLANDS
(ECUADOR)

ECUADOR

Manaus

Amazon
River

Belém

Guayaquil

PERU

SOUTH AMERICA

Recife

Callao

Lima

BRAZIL

Bahia

BOLIVIA

La Paz

Santa Cruz

Brasília

Sucre

Rio de
Janeiro

PARAGUAY

Tropic of Capricorn

Antofagasta

Asunción

São Paulo

CHILE

Porto Alegre

30°S

30°S

Valparaíso

Rosario

URUGUAY

Santiago

Buenos
Aires

Montevideo

Concepción

La Plata

ARGENTINA

Mar del Plata

⊛ National capital   • Other city

0   1,000   2,000 miles

0   1,000   2,000 kilometers

Comodoro
Rivadavia

Miller Projection

FALKLAND ISLANDS
(U.K.)

Strait of
Magellan

Punta Arenas

SOUTH
GEORGIA
(U.K.)

R16

150°W

120°W

90°W

60°W

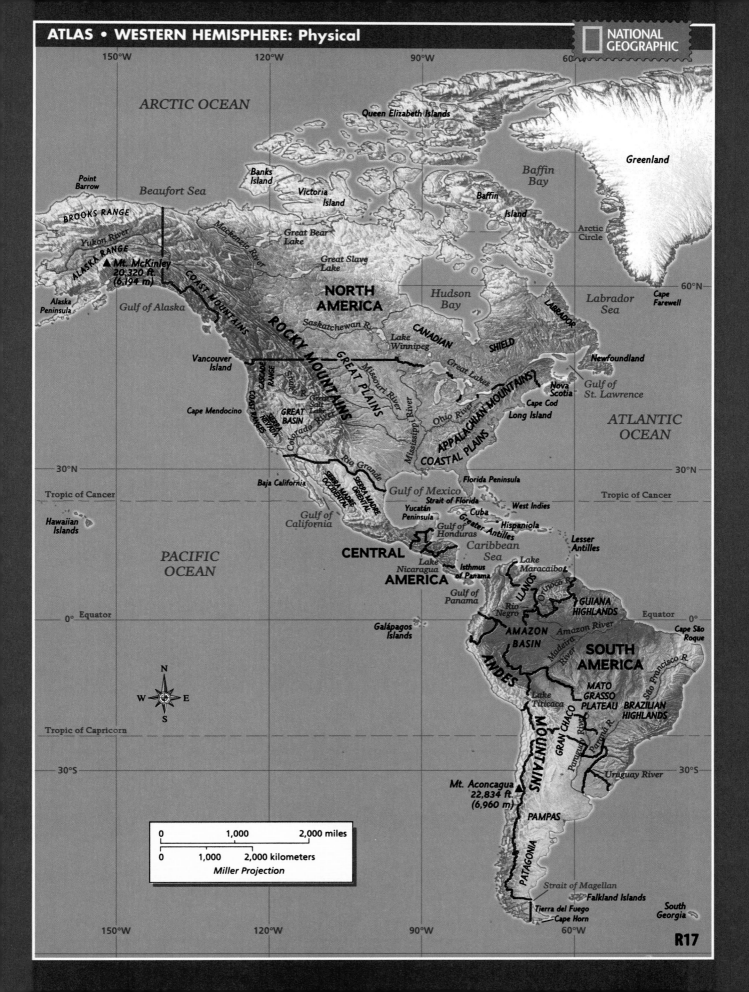

NATIONAL GEOGRAPHIC

ARCTIC OCEAN

Queen Elizabeth Islands

Greenland

Banks Island

Victoria Island

Baffin Bay

Baffin Island

Point Barrow

Beaufort Sea

BROOKS RANGE

Yukon River

ALASKA RANGE

▲ Mt. McKinley 20,320 ft (6,194 m)

Alaska Peninsula

Gulf of Alaska

COAST MOUNTAINS

Mackenzie River

Great Bear Lake

Great Slave Lake

NORTH AMERICA

Hudson Bay

Arctic Circle

60°N

Labrador Sea

Cape Farewell

Saskatchewan R.

Lake Winnipeg

CANADIAN

SHIELD

LABRADOR

Great Lakes

Newfoundland

Vancouver Island

ROCKY MOUNTAINS

CASCADE RANGE

COAST RANGES

SIERRA NEVADA

GREAT PLAINS

Missouri River

Mississippi River

Ohio River

APPALACHIAN MOUNTAINS

Nova Scotia

Gulf of St. Lawrence

Cape Cod

Long Island

ATLANTIC OCEAN

Cape Mendocino

GREAT BASIN

Great Salt Lake

Snake R.

Colorado R.

COASTAL PLAINS

30°N

Tropic of Cancer

30°N

Tropic of Cancer

Baja California

Rio Grande

SIERRA MADRE OCCIDENTAL

SIERRA MADRE ORIENTAL

Gulf of Mexico

Florida Peninsula

Strait of Florida

Hawaiian Islands

Gulf of California

Yucatán Peninsula

West Indies

Cuba

Greater Antilles

Hispaniola

Lesser Antilles

PACIFIC OCEAN

CENTRAL

Gulf of Honduras

Caribbean Sea

Lake Maracaibo

Lake Nicaragua

Isthmus of Panama

AMERICA

Gulf of Panama

ILLANOS

Orinoco R.

GUIANA HIGHLANDS

0° Equator

Galápagos Islands

Rio Negro

AMAZON BASIN

Amazon River

Madeira River

SOUTH AMERICA

São Francisco R.

Equator 0°

Cape São Roque

N W E S

ANDES

Lake Titicaca

MATO GRASSO PLATEAU

BRAZILIAN HIGHLANDS

Tropic of Capricorn

GRAN CHACO

Paraguay River

Paraná R.

30°S

Mt. Aconcagua 22,834 ft (6,960 m)

MOUNTAINS

Uruguay River

30°S

PAMPAS

0 1,000 2,000 miles
0 1,000 2,000 kilometers
Miller Projection

PATAGONIA

Strait of Magellan

Falkland Islands

Tierra del Fuego

Cape Horn

South Georgia

150°W   120°W   90°W   60°W

R17

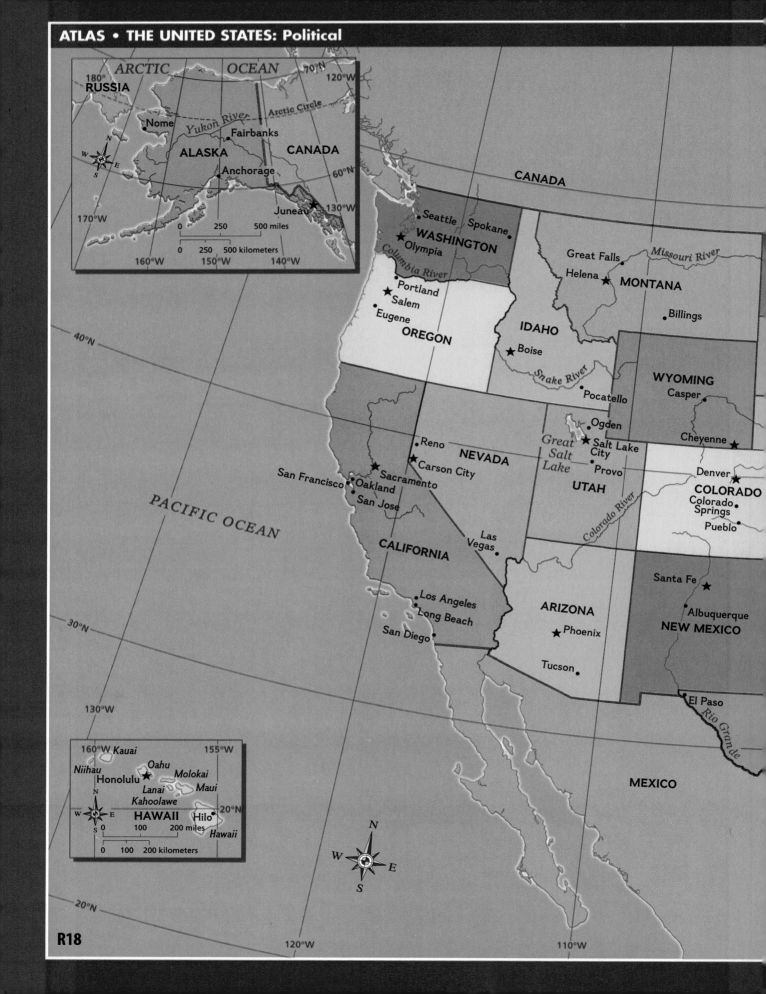

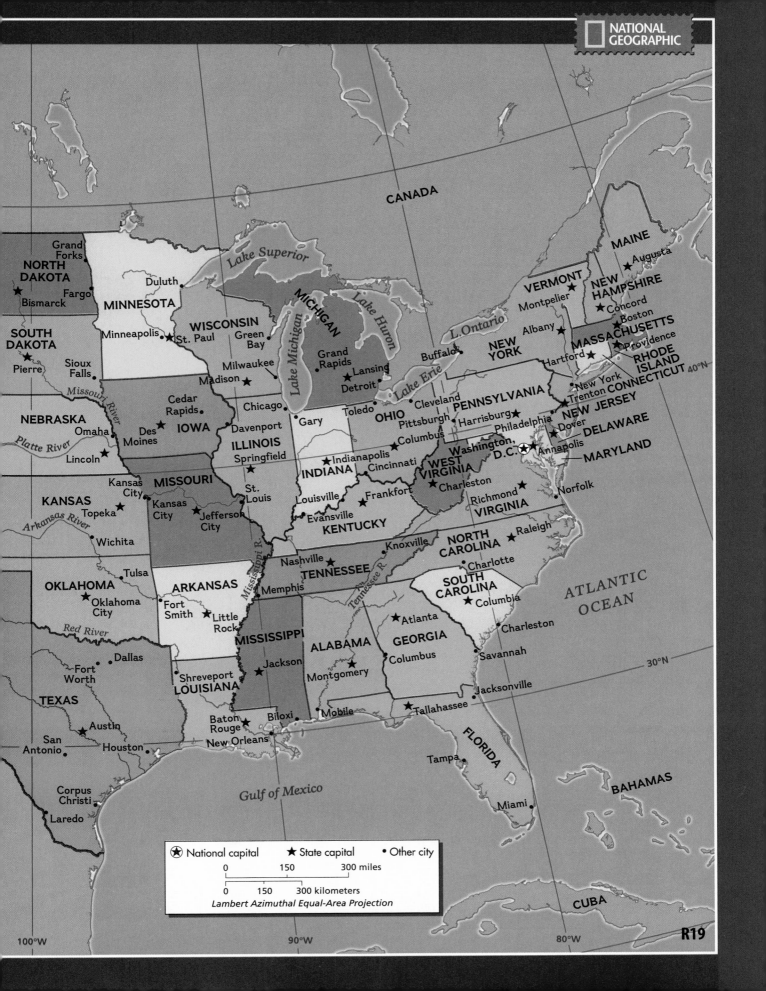

NATIONAL GEOGRAPHIC

CANADA

Lake Superior

NORTH DAKOTA
Grand Forks
Fargo
Bismarck

MINNESOTA
Duluth

SOUTH DAKOTA
Pierre
Sioux Falls

Missouri River

NEBRASKA
Omaha
Lincoln

WISCONSIN
Green Bay
Milwaukee
Madison
Minneapolis
St. Paul

Cedar Rapids
Des Moines
IOWA

Platte River

KANSAS
Topeka
Wichita

Arkansas River

OKLAHOMA
Oklahoma City
Tulsa

Kansas City
Kansas City
MISSOURI
Jefferson City
St. Louis

ILLINOIS
Springfield
Chicago
Davenport
Gary

MICHIGAN
Lake Michigan
Grand Rapids
Lansing
Detroit

Lake Huron

OHIO
Toledo
Cleveland
Columbus
Cincinnati

INDIANA
Indianapolis

KENTUCKY
Louisville
Frankfort
Evansville

Lake Erie

Buffalo

L. Ontario

NEW YORK
Albany

PENNSYLVANIA
Pittsburgh
Harrisburg
Philadelphia

VERMONT
Montpelier

NEW HAMPSHIRE
Concord

MAINE
Augusta

Boston
MASSACHUSETTS
Providence
RHODE ISLAND
Hartford
CONNECTICUT
New York
Trenton
NEW JERSEY
Dover
DELAWARE
MARYLAND
Annapolis
Washington, D.C.

40°N

WEST VIRGINIA
Charleston
Richmond
VIRGINIA
Norfolk

Mississippi R.

ARKANSAS
Fort Smith
Little Rock
Memphis

Red River

Nashville
TENNESSEE
Knoxville

Tennessee R.

NORTH CAROLINA
Raleigh
Charlotte

SOUTH CAROLINA
Columbia
Charleston

ATLANTIC OCEAN

TEXAS
Dallas
Fort Worth
Austin
San Antonio
Houston
Corpus Christi
Laredo

Shreveport
LOUISIANA
MISSISSIPPI
Jackson

ALABAMA
Montgomery

Columbus
GEORGIA
Atlanta
Savannah

Jacksonville

30°N

Baton Rouge
Biloxi
Mobile
New Orleans

Tallahassee
FLORIDA
Tampa
Miami

BAHAMAS

Gulf of Mexico

National capital   ★ **State capital**   • Other city

0   150   300 miles

0   150   300 kilometers
Lambert Azimuthal Equal-Area Projection

CUBA

100°W   90°W   80°W

R19

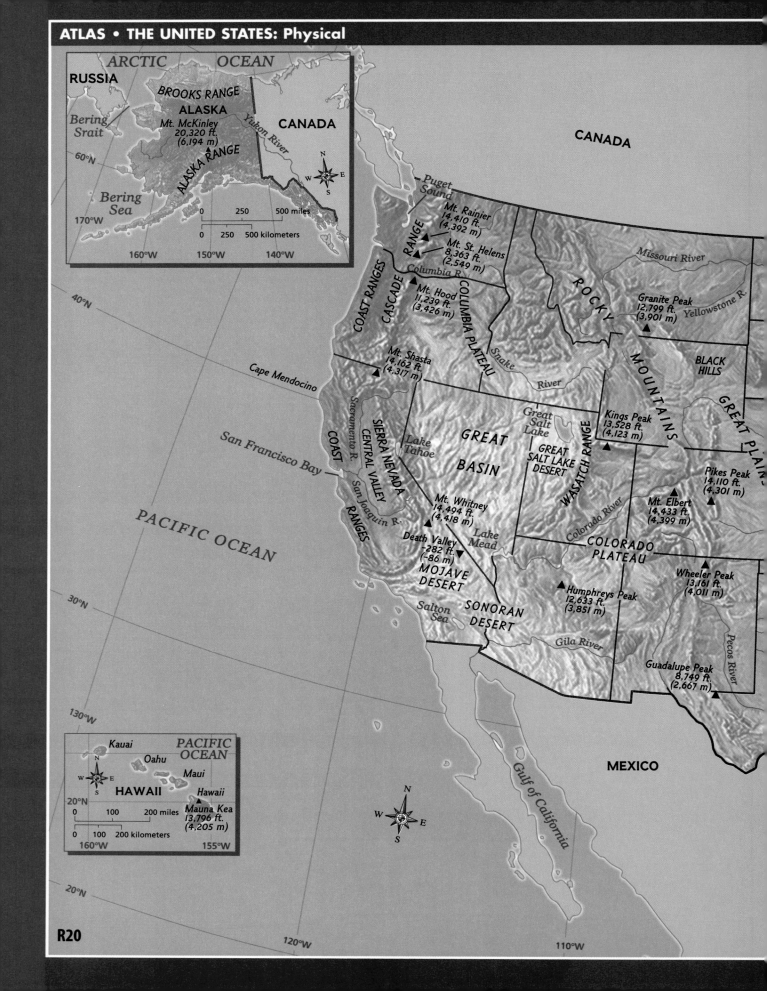

ARCTIC OCEAN

RUSSIA

BROOKS RANGE

ALASKA

Mt. McKinley
20,320 ft.
(6,194 m)

CANADA

Bering
Srait

Yukon River

ALASKA RANGE

60°N

N
W E
S

Bering
Sea

170°W

0   250   500 miles
0   250   500 kilometers

160°W   150°W   140°W

CANADA

CANADA

Puget
Sound

Mt. Rainier
14,410 ft.
(4,392 m)

Missouri River

COAST RANGES

CASCADE RANGE

Mt. St. Helens
8,363 ft.
(2,549 m)

Columbia R.

ROCKY

Granite Peak
12,799 ft.
(3,901 m)

Yellowstone R.

40°N

Mt. Hood
11,239 ft.
(3,426 m)

COLUMBIA PLATEAU

Snake

MOUNTAINS

BLACK
HILLS

GREAT PLAIN

Mt. Shasta
14,162 ft.
(4,317 m)

River

Cape Mendocino

Sacramento R.

Great
Salt
Lake

Kings Peak
13,528 ft.
(4,123 m)

SIERRA NEVADA

CENTRAL VALLEY

Lake
Tahoe

GREAT

GREAT
SALT LAKE
DESERT

WASATCH RANGE

Pikes Peak
14,110 ft.
(4,301 m)

San Francisco Bay

COAST

BASIN

Mt. Elbert
14,433 ft.
(4,399 m)

San Joaquin R.

Mt. Whitney
14,494 ft.
(4,418 m)

Colorado River

RANGES

Death Valley
-282 ft.
(-86 m)

Lake
Mead

COLORADO
PLATEAU

Wheeler Peak
13,161 ft.
(4,011 m)

PACIFIC OCEAN

MOJAVE
DESERT

30°N

Salton
Sea

SONORAN
DESERT

Humphreys Peak
12,633 ft.
(3,851 m)

Pecos River

Gila River

Guadalupe Peak
8,749 ft.
(2,667 m)

130°W

Kauai

PACIFIC
OCEAN

N
W E
S

Oahu

Maui

HAWAII

Hawaii

20°N

Mauna Kea
13,796 ft.
(4,205 m)

0   100   200 miles
0   100   200 kilometers

160°W   155°W

MEXICO

Gulf of California

N
W E
S

20°N

R20

120°W   110°W

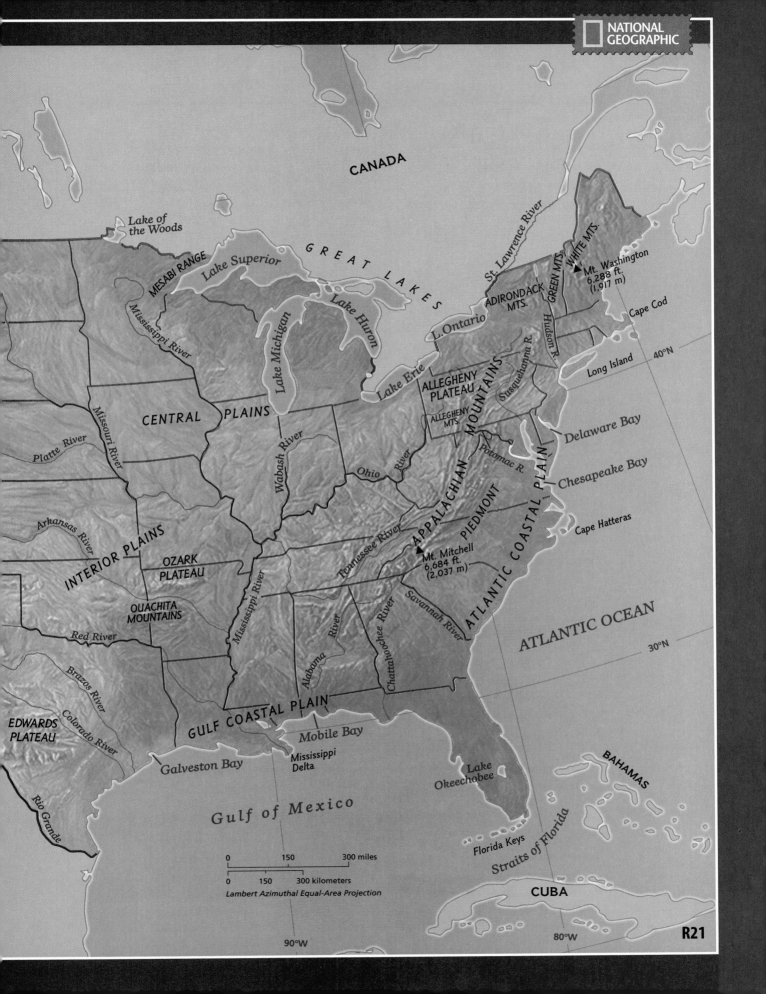

CANADA

Lake of
the Woods

MESABI RANGE

Lake Superior

G R E A T   L A K E S

St. Lawrence River

GREEN MTS.

WHITE MTS.

Mt. Washington
6,288 ft.
(1,917 m)

ADIRONDACK
MTS.

Cape Cod

Mississippi River

Lake Michigan

Lake Huron

L. Ontario

Hudson R.

Susquehanna R.

40°N

Long Island

Lake Erie

ALLEGHENY
PLATEAU

APPALACHIAN   MOUNTAINS

Delaware Bay

CENTRAL   PLAINS

ALLEGHENY
MTS.

Chesapeake Bay

Missouri River

Platte River

Wabash River

Ohio   River

Potomac R.

Cape Hatteras

Arkansas River

INTERIOR   PLAINS

OZARK
PLATEAU

Tennessee River

Mt. Mitchell
6,684 ft.
(2,037 m)

PIEDMONT

ATLANTIC   COASTAL   PLAIN

ATLANTIC OCEAN

OUACHITA
MOUNTAINS

Mississippi River

Red River

Alabama   River

Chattahoochee River

Savannah River

30°N

Brazos River

Colorado River

EDWARDS
PLATEAU

GULF COASTAL PLAIN

Mobile Bay

BAHAMAS

Galveston Bay

Mississippi
Delta

Lake
Okeechobee

Rio Grande

Gulf of Mexico

0   150   300 miles

0   150   300 kilometers

Lambert Azimuthal Equal-Area Projection

Florida Keys

Straits of Florida

CUBA

90°W

80°W

R21

Our Fifty States

ALABAMA
★ Montgomery

Date of Statehood 1819

Nickname **Heart of Dixie**

Population **4,447,100**

Area **52,423 sq mi; 135,776 sq km**

Region **Southeast**

Date of Statehood 1788

Nickname **Constitution State**

Population **3,405,565**

Area **5,544 sq mi; 14,359 sq km**

Region **Northeast**

★ Hartford
CONNECTICUT

ALASKA
Juneau ★

Date of Statehood 1959

Nickname **The Last Frontier**

Population **626,932**

Area **656,424 sq mi; 1,700,138 sq km**

Region **West**

Date of Statehood 1787

Nickname **First State**

Population **783,600**

Area **2,489 sq mi; 6,447 sq km**

Region **Northeast**

★ Dover
DELAWARE

ARIZONA
★ Phoenix

Date of Statehood 1912

Nickname **Grand Canyon State**

Population **5,130,632**

Area **114,006 sq mi; 295,276 sq km**

Region **Southwest**

Date of Statehood 1845

Nickname **Sunshine State**

Population **15,982,378**

Area **58,664 sq mi; 151,939 sq km**

Region **Southeast**

★ Tallahassee
FLORIDA

ARKANSAS
★ Little Rock

Date of Statehood 1836

Nickname **The Natural State**

Population **2,673,400**

Area **53,182 sq mi; 137,741 sq km**

Region **Southeast**

Date of Statehood 1788

Nickname **Peach State**

Population **8,186,453**

Area **58,910 sq mi; 152,576 sq km**

Region **Southeast**

★ Atlanta
GEORGIA

CALIFORNIA
★ Sacramento

Date of Statehood 1850

Nickname **Golden State**

Population **33,871,648**

Area **163,707 sq mi; 424,001 sq km**

Region **West**

Date of Statehood 1959

Nickname **The Aloha State**

Population **1,211,537**

Area **10,932 sq mi; 28,314 sq km**

Region **West**

HAWAII
★ Honolulu

Denver ★
COLORADO

Date of Statehood 1876

Nickname **Centennial State**

Population **4,301,261**

Area **104,100 sq mi; 269,619 sq km**

Region **Mountain States**

Date of Statehood 1890

Nickname **Gem State**

Population **1,293,953**

Area **83,574 sq mi; 216,457 sq km**

Region **Mountain States**

IDAHO
★ Boise

Reference

ILLINOIS
★
Springfield

Date of Statehood **1818**

Nickname **The Prairie State**

Population **12,419,293**

Area **57,918 sq mi; 150,008 sq km**

Region **Middle West**

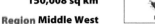

MAINE
Augusta
★

Date of Statehood **1820**

Nickname **Pine Tree State**

Population **1,274,923**

Area **35,387 sq mi; 91,652 sq km**

Region **Northeast**

INDIANA
★
Indianapolis

Date of Statehood **1816**

Nickname **Hoosier State**

Population **6,080,485**

Area **36,420 sq mi; 94,328 sq km**

Region **Middle West**

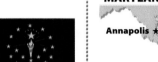

MARYLAND
Annapolis ★

Date of Statehood **1788**

Nickname **Free State**

Population **5,296,486**

Area **12,407 sq mi; 32,134 sq km**

Region **Northeast**

IOWA
★
Des Moines

Date of Statehood **1846**

Nickname **Hawkeye State**

Population **2,926,324**

Area **56,276 sq mi; 145,755 sq km**

Region **Middle West**

Boston ★
MASSACHUSETTS

Date of Statehood **1788**

Nickname **Bay State**

Population **6,349,097**

Area **10,555 sq mi; 27,337 sq km**

Region **Northeast**

Topeka ★
KANSAS

Date of Statehood **1861**

Nickname **Sunflower State**

Population **2,688,418**

Area **82,282 sq mi; 213,110 sq km**

Region **Middle West**

MICHIGAN
★
Lansing

Date of Statehood **1837**

Nickname **Wolverine State**

Population **9,938,444**

Area **96,810 sq mi; 250,738 sq km**

Region **Middle West**

KENTUCKY
★
Frankfort

Date of Statehood **1792**

Nickname **Bluegrass State**

Population **4,041,769**

Area **40,411 sq mi; 104,664 sq km**

Region **Southeast**

MINNESOTA
St. Paul ★

Date of Statehood **1858**

Nickname **North Star State**

Population **4,919,479**

Area **86,943 sq mi; 225,182 sq km**

Region **Middle West**

LOUISIANA
Baton Rouge ★

Date of Statehood **1812**

Nickname **Pelican State**

Population **4,468,976**

Area **51,843 sq mi; 134,273 sq km**

Region **Southeast**

MISSISSIPPI
★
Jackson

Date of Statehood **1817**

Nickname **Magnolia State**

Population **2,844,658**

Area **48,434 sq mi; 125,444 sq km**

Region **Southeast**

Our Fifty States
Missouri • Oregon

MISSOURI
★
Jefferson City

Date of Statehood **1821**

Nickname **Show Me State**

Population **5,595,211**

Area **69,709 sq mi; 180,546 sq km**

Region **Middle West**

NEW YORK
Albany ★

Date of Statehood **1788**

Nickname **Empire State**

Population **18,976,457**

Area **54,475 sq mi; 141,090 sq km**

Region **Northeast**

MONTANA
★
Helena

Date of Statehood **1889**

Nickname **Treasure State**

Population **902,195**

Area **147,046 sq mi; 380,849 sq km**

Region **Mountain States**

NORTH CAROLINA
Raleigh ★

Date of Statehood **1789**

Nickname **Tar Heel State**

Population **8,049,313**

Area **53,821 sq mi; 139,396 sq km**

Region **Southeast**

NEBRASKA
Lincoln ★

Date of Statehood **1867**

Nickname **Cornhusker State**

Population **1,711,263**

Area **77,358 sq mi; 200,357 sq km**

Region **Middle West**

NORTH DAKOTA
Bismarck
★

Date of Statehood **1889**

Nickname **Peace Garden State**

Population **642,200**

Area **70,704 sq mi; 183,123 sq km**

Region **Middle West**

NEVADA
★ Carson City

Date of Statehood **1864**

Nickname **Silver State**

Population **1,998,257**

Area **110,567 sq mi; 286,369 sq km**

Region **West**

OHIO
★
Columbus

Date of Statehood **1803**

Nickname **Buckeye State**

Population **11,353,140**

Area **44,828 sq mi; 116,105 sq km**

Region **Middle West**

NEW HAMPSHIRE
Concord
★

Date of Statehood **1788**

Nickname **Granite State**

Population **1,235,786**

Area **9,351 sq mi; 24,219 sq km**

Region **Northeast**

OKLAHOMA
★
Oklahoma City

Date of Statehood **1907**

Nickname **Sooner State**

Population **3,450,654**

Area **69,903 sq mi; 181,049 sq km**

Region **Southwest**

NEW JERSEY
★
Trenton

Date of Statehood **1787**

Nickname **Garden State**

Population **8,414,350**

Area **8,722 sq mi; 22,590 sq km**

Region **Northeast**

NEW MEXICO
★
Santa Fe

Date of Statehood **1912**

Nickname **Land of Enchantment**

Population **1,819,046**

Area **121,598 sq mi; 314,939 sq km**

Region **Southwest**

★ Salem

OREGON

Date of Statehood **1859**

Nickname **Beaver State**

Population **3,421,399**

Area **98,386 sq mi; 254,820 sq km**

Region **West**

PENNSYLVANIA

Harrisburg ★

Date of Statehood **1787**

Nickname **Keystone State**

Population **12,281,054**

Area **46,058 sq mi; 119,290 sq km**

Region **Northeast**

VERMONT

★ Montpelier

Date of Statehood **1791**

Nickname **Green Mountain State**

Population **608,827**

Area **9,615 sq mi; 24,903 sq km**

Region **Northeast**

RHODE ISLAND

Providence ★

Date of Statehood **1790**

Nickname **Ocean State**

Population **1,048,319**

Area **1,545 sq mi; 4,002 sq km**

Region **Northeast**

VIRGINIA

Richmond ★

Date of Statehood **1788**

Nickname **Old Dominion**

Population **7,078,515**

Area **42,769 sq mi; 110,772 sq km**

Region **Southeast**

SOUTH CAROLINA

★

Columbia

Date of Statehood **1788**

Nickname **Palmetto State**

Population **4,012,012**

Area **32,007 sq mi; 82,898 sq km**

Region **Southeast**

★ Olympia

WASHINGTON

Date of Statehood **1889**

Nickname **Evergreen State**

Population **5,894,121**

Area **71,303 sq mi; 184,675 sq km**

Region **West**

Pierre ★

SOUTH DAKOTA

Date of Statehood **1889**

Nickname **Mount Rushmore State**

Population **754,844**

Area **77,121 sq mi; 199,743 sq km**

Region **Middle West**

WEST VIRGINIA

★ Charleston

Date of Statehood **1863**

Nickname **Mountain State**

Population **1,808,344**

Area **24,231 sq mi; 62,758 sq km**

Region **Southeast**

TENNESSEE

★ Nashville

Date of Statehood **1796**

Nickname **Volunteer State**

Population **5,689,283**

Area **42,146 sq mi; 109,158 sq km**

Region **Southeast**

WISCONSIN

Madison ★

Date of Statehood **1848**

Nickname **Badger State**

Population **5,363,675**

Area **65,503 sq mi; 169,653 sq km**

Region **Middle West**

TEXAS

Austin ★

Date of Statehood **1845**

Nickname **Lone Star State**

Population **20,851,820**

Area **268,601sq mi; 695,677 sq km**

Region **Southwest**

★

Salt Lake City

UTAH

Date of Statehood **1896**

Nickname **Beehive State**

Population **2,233,169**

Area **84,904 sq mi; 219,901 sq km**

Region **Mountain States**

WYOMING

Cheyenne ★

Date of Statehood **1890**

Nickname **Equality State**

Population **493,782**

Area **97,818 sq mi; 253,349 sq km**

Region **Mountain States**

Sources: Population — U.S. Bureau of Census, 2000; Area — U.S. Bureau of Census, 2000.

R25

Dictionary of Geographic Terms

GULF (gulf) Part of an ocean that extends into the land; larger than a bay.

RESERVOIR (rez'ər vwär) A natural or artificial lake used to store water.

PLATEAU (pla tō') A high, flat area that rises steeply above the surrounding land.

DAM (dam) A wall built across a river, creating a lake that stores water.

MESA (mā'sə) A hill with a flat top; smaller than a plateau.

CANYON (kan'yən) A deep, narrow valley with steep sides.

BUTTE (būt) A small, flat-topped hill; smaller than a mesa or plateau.

OASIS (ō ā'sis) A fertile area in a desert that is watered by a spring.

HILL (hil) A rounded, raised landform; not as high as a mountain.

VALLEY (val'ē) An area of low land between hills or mountains.

DESERT (dez'ərt) A dry environment with few plants and animals.

COAST (kōst) The land along an ocean.

BAY (bā) Part of an ocean or lake that extends deeply into the land.

ISLAND (ī'lənd) A body of land completely surrounded by water.

PENINSULA (pə nin'sə lə) A body of land nearly surrounded by water.

VOLCANO (vol kā'nō) An opening in Earth's surface through which hot rock and ash are forced out.

MOUNTAIN (moun'tən) A high landform with steep sides; higher than a hill.

HARBOR (här'bər) A sheltered place along a coast where boats dock safely.

PEAK (pēk) The top of a mountain.

GLACIER (glā'shər) A huge sheet of ice that moves slowly across the land.

CANAL (kə nal') A channel built to carry water for irrigation or transportation.

LAKE (lāk) Body of water completely surrounded by land.

TRIBUTARY (trib'yə ter ē) A smaller river that flows into a larger river.

PORT (pôrt) A place where ships load and unload their goods.

SOURCE (sôrs) The starting point of a river.

TIMBERLINE (tim'bər līn) A line above which trees do not grow.

WATERFALL (wô'tər fôl) A flow of water falling vertically.

PLAIN (plān) A large area of nearly flat land.

RIVER BASIN (riv'ər bā'sin) All the land that is drained by a river and its tributaries.

MOUNTAIN RANGE (moun'tən rānj) A row or chain of mountains.

RIVER (riv'ər) A stream of water that flows across the land and empties into another body of water.

BASIN (bā'sin) A bowl-shaped landform surrounded by higher land.

DELTA (del'tə) Land made of soil left behind as a river drains into a larger body of water.

MOUNTAIN PASS (moun'tən pas) A narrow gap through a mountain range.

MOUTH (mouth) The place where a river empties into a larger body of water.

OCEAN (ō'shən) A large body of salt water; oceans cover much of Earth's surface.

Gazetteer

This Gazetteer is a geographical dictionary that will help you to pronounce and locate the places discussed in this book. Latitude and longitude are given for cities and some other places. The page numbers tell you where each place first appears on a map or in the text.

A

Abilene (ab'ə lēn) A city in central Kansas; in the 1860s, Abilene was the northern end of the Chisholm Trail; 39°N, 98°W. (t. 94)

Africa (af'ri kə) A continent located in the Eastern and Southern hemispheres. (m. H12, t. H11)

Alabama (al ə bam'ə) A state of the Southeast region. (m. 8–9)

Alamo, The (al' ə mō) Also known as the San Antonio de Valero mission. In 1836, it was the site of the most famous battle in Texas history; 26°N, 98°W. (t. 88)

Alaska (ə las'kə) One of the Pacific states of the West region. (m. t. 382)

Alps (alps) The highest mountains in Europe. They curve between the Mediterranean coast and the Balkans. (m. 365, t. 365)

Amazon Rain Forest (amə' zôn rān fôr' ist) A forest in Brazil that is home to a variety of plants and animals. (t. 5)

American River (ə mer'i kən riv'ər) A river in Northern California near Sacramento. (t. 411)

Andes Mountains (an´dēz moun´tənz) A mountain range along the west coast of South America, the world's longest chain of mountains. (m. R17, t. 5)

Antarctica (ant ärk'ti kə) A continent located in the Southern Hemisphere. (m. H12)

Appalachian Mountains (ap ə lā'chē ən moun'tənz) A chain of mountains with rounded peaks that run through the eastern United States. (m. 8–9, 188)

Appalachian Trail (ap ə lā'chē ən trāl) A marked hiking path that runs through the Appalachian Mountains. (m. 187, t. 189)

Arctic Ocean (ärk'tik ō'shən) An ocean that surrounds the North Pole. (m. H12)

Arizona (ar ə zō'nə) A state of the Southwest region. (m. 8–9, t. 104)

Arkansas (är'kən sô) A state of the Southeast region. (m. 8–9)

Asia (ā'zhə) The largest continent, located in the Eastern and Northern hemispheres. (m. H12, t. H11)

Aspen (as' pen) A silver-mining boom town in Colorado that became a popular recreation area; 39°N, 107°W. (t. 362)

Atlanta (at lan'tə) Capital of the state of Georgia and a regional center of the Southeast; 33°N, 84°W. (m. H16, t. 166)

Atlantic Ocean (at lan'tik ō'shən) Ocean that borders North and South America and western Europe and Africa. (m. H11, t. H11)

Australia (ôs trāl'yə) A continent and country located in the Eastern and Southern hemispheres. (m. H12)

pronunciation key

a	at	ī	ice	u	up	th	thin
ā	ape	îr	pierce	ū	use	th	this
ä	far	o	hot	ü	rule	zh	measure
âr	care	ō	old	ů	pull	ə	about, taken,
e	end	ô	fork	ûr	turn		pencil, lemon,
ē	me	oi	oil	hw	white		circus
i	it	ou	out	ng	song		

B

Baltimore (bôl′tə môr) The largest city in Maryland and a port on Chesapeake Bay; 39°N, 77°W. (m. 234, t. 198)

Beaumont (bō′mänt) City in southeastern Texas, site of early oil boom; 30°N, 94°W. (t. 68)

Birmingham (bûr′ ming ham) The largest town in Alabama; 33°N, 86°W. (t. 170)

Black Hills (blak hilz) Mountains in southwestern South Dakota and northeastern Wyoming. (m. 8–9, t. 253)

Boswash (bôs′wôsh) A name for the group of Northeastern cities from Boston, Massachusetts, to Washington, D.C. (m. 234, t. 234)

Buffalo (buf′ə lō) A city and port on Lake Erie in western New York; endpoint of the Erie Canal; 43°N, 79° W. (m. 199, t. 199)

C

California (kal ə fôr′nyə) One of the Pacific states of the West region. (m. 8–9)

Canada (kan′ə də) A country in North America, north of the United States. (m. H16, t. 4)

Cape Town (kāp toun) Seaport city in South Africa, settled by the Dutch in the late 1600s; 34°S, 18°E. (m. 153, t. 153)

Cascade Range (kas kād′ rānj) Mountain range in Washington, Oregon, and California in the West. (m. 8–9, t. 383)

Central City (sen′trəl sit′ē) Town in Colorado that grew rapidly during the gold rush of the 1860s; 39°N, 105°W. (t. 344)

Central Plains (sen′trəl plānz) Eastern part of the Interior Plains. They are lower in elevation and have more rainfall than the Great Plains. (m. 253, t. 253)

Central Valley (sen′trəl val′ē) A flat valley in California between the Sierra Nevada and the Coast Ranges. (m. 8–9, t. 395)

Chesapeake Bay (ches′ə pēk bā) Bay of the Atlantic Ocean shared by Maryland and Virginia. (t. 147)

Chicago (shi kä′gō) Largest city in Illinois and a major transportation hub; 42°N, 88°W. (m. 267, t. 262)

Chisholm Trail (chiz′əm trāl) Cattle drive route in the 1880s from San Antonio, Texas, to Abilene, Kansas. (t. 94)

Coast Ranges (kōst rān′jəz) Mountain range in western California, Oregon, and Washington, on the Pacific Coast. (m. 8–9, t. 383)

Coastal Plain (kōs′təl plān) Low plain along the Atlantic Coast from Massachusetts to Texas; sometimes separated into Gulf and Atlantic Coastal plains. (m. 51, t. 7)

Colorado (kol ə rad′ ō) One of the Mountain States. (m. 8–9, t. 314)

Colorado Plateau (kol′ə rad′ō pla tō) The major plateau found in the Southwest. (m. 51, t. 52)

Colorado River (kol ə rad′ō riv′ər) A river that flows from the Rocky Mountains to the Pacific Ocean. (m. 51, t. 52)

Columbia Plateau (kə lum′ bē ə plə tō) A high, flat landform located in Washington, Idaho, and Oregon. (m. 8–9, t. 7)

Concord (kong′ kərd) A town in eastern Massachusetts, site of one of the first battles of the American Revolution; 42°N, 71°W. (m. 216, t. 216)

Connecticut (kə net′i kət) One of the New England states of the Northeast region. (m. 8–9)

Continental Divide (kon tə nen′təl di vīd′) An imaginary line running along the peaks of the Rocky Mountains that divides rivers that flow east from rivers that flow west. (m. 319, t. 319)

Cupertino (kū′ pər tē nō) A town in Santa Clara county in California where many computer software companies are located; 37°N, 122°W. (t. 429)

D

Delaware (del′ə wâr) One of the Middle Atlantic states of the Northeast region. (m. 8–9)

Denver (den′ vər) Capital of Colorado and a former mining settlement; 40°N, 105°W. (m. H16, t. 344)

Detroit (di troit′) Largest city in Michigan and an important manufacturing center; 42°N, 83°W. (m. 267, t. 266)

Duluth (də lüth′) A port in northeastern Minnesota; 46°N, 91°W. (m. 267, t. 266)

Gazetteer
Eastern Hemisphere • Jura Mountains

Eastern Hemisphere (ēs'tərn hem'i sfir) The half of earth east of the prime meridian. (m. H12)

Echota (ə chä'tə) Cherokee capital in the 1700s, near what is now the North Carolina-Tennessee border; 36°N, 84°W. (m. 141, t. 141)

Ellis Island (el'is ī'lənd) A small island in New York Harbor; from 1892–1954, site of a United States immigration center. Its restored buildings are now part of the Statue of Liberty National Monument; 40°N, 74°W. (t. 224)

Europe (yûr'əp) A continent located in the Eastern and Northern hemispheres. (m. H12)

Everglades (ev'ər glādz) An area of low, swampy ground with dense grasses and many slow-moving streams and small rivers. (m. 8–9, t. 6)

Florida (flôr'i də) A state of the Southeast region. (m. 8–9)

Fort Hall Reservation (fôrt häl rez ər vā' shən) Shoshone reservation in Idaho established under the Fort Bridger Treaty in 1868; 43°N, 112°W. (t. 339)

Georgia (jôr'jə) A state of the Southeast region. (m. 8–9)

Gobi Desert (gō'bē dez'ərt) A large desert in east central Asia. (m. 81, t. 80)

Grand Canyon (grand kan'yən) Canyon on the Colorado River in northwestern Arizona. (m. 8–9, t. 52)

Great Basin (grāt bā sen) A low, bowl shaped landform surrounded by higher land in Nevada, Utah, Idaho, Oregon, and California. (m. 383, t. 383)

Great Lakes (grāt lāks) A chain of five large freshwater lakes between the northern United States and Canada. They are: Lakes Superior, Michigan, Huron, Erie, and Ontario. (m. 8–9, t. 199)

Great Plains (grāt plānz) High, fairly dry plain, the western part of the Interior Plains. (m. 51, t. 253)

Great Salt Lake (grāt sawlt lāk) Located in northern Utah, it is the largest inland body of salt water in the Western Hemisphere. (m. 319, t. 324)

Green Bay (grēn bā) City in northeastern Wisconsin near Lake Michigan. (m. R18, t. 262)

Gulf of Mexico (gulf əv mek'si kō) A gulf of the Atlantic Ocean bordering Mexico and five states of the United States. (m. H16, t. 51)

Hawaii (hə wī'ē) One of the Pacific states of the West region, made up of many islands in the Pacific Ocean. (m. 8–9, t. 384)

Hollywood (hol'ē wŭd) An area within the city of Los Angeles, California, that is a major center of the film industry; 34°N, 118°W. (t. 428)

Honolulu (hon ə lü'lü) Capital of Hawaii, on the southeastern coast of the island Oahu; 21°N, 158°E. (m. H16)

Idaho (ī'də hō) One of the Mountain States. (m. 8–9, t. 314)

Illinois (il ə noi') One of the Great Lakes states of the Middle West region. (m. 8–9)

India (in'dē ə) A country in southern Asia. (m. 227, t. 226)

Indian Ocean (in'dē ən ō'shən) An ocean between Africa, southern Asia, and Australia. (m. H12)

Indiana (in dē an'ə) One of the Great Lakes states of the Middle West region. (m. 8–9)

Interior Plains (in tîr'ē ər plānz) The mostly flat land between the Appalachian and Rocky mountains. (m. 8–9, t. 7)

Iowa (ī'ə wə) One of the Plains states of the Middle West region. (m. 8–9, t. 254)

Japan (jə pan') A country of eastern Asia made up of many islands in the Pacific Ocean. (m. 433, t. 432)

Jura Mountains (jûr'ə moun'tənz) A mountain range that lies in eastern France and western Switzerland. (m. 365, t. 365)

K

Kansas (kan'zəs) One of the Plains states of the Middle West region. (m. 8–9, t. 94)

Kentucky (kən tuk'ē) A state of the Southeast region. (m. 8–9)

Kitt Peak (kit pēk) Mountain near Tucson, Arizona, where the Kitt Peak National Observatory is located; 32°N, 111°W. (t. 102)

Kobe (kō' bē) City and port in Japan; 34°N, 135°E. (m. 435, t. 433)

L

Lake Erie (lāk ir'ē) The most southern of the five Great Lakes; it is located on the border between the United States and Canada. (m. 8–9)

Lake Huron (lāk hyúr'ən) The second-largest of the five Great Lakes; it is located on the border between the United States and Canada. (m. 8–9)

Lake Michigan (lāk mish'i gən) The third-largest of the five Great Lakes; it lies between the states of Michigan and Wisconsin. (m. 8–9)

Lake Ontario (lāk on târ'ē ō) The smallest of the five Great Lakes; it is located on the border between the United States and Canada. (m. 8–9)

Lake Superior (lāk sú pîr'ē ər) The largest of the five Great Lakes; it is located on the border between the United States and Canada. (m. 8–9)

Lexington (lek'sing tən) A town in eastern Massachusetts, site of one of the first battles of the American Revolution; 42°N, 71°W. (m. 216, t. 216)

Louisiana (lü ē'zē an ə) A state of the Southeast region. (m. 8–9)

M

Maine (mān) One of the New England states of the Northeast region. (m. 8–9)

Maryland (mer'ə lənd) One of the Middle Atlantic states of the Northeast region. (m. 8–9)

Massachusetts (mas ə chü'sits) One of the New England states of the Northeast region. (m. 8–9)

Mesa Verde (mā'sə vərd'ē) The name given an Anasazi village built around A.D. 900 into the side of a steep cliff, located in present-day Colorado; 57°N, 108°W. (t. 320)

Mesabi Range (mə sä'bē rānj) A group of hills in Minnesota that is the source of most iron ore in the United States. (m. 253, t. 264)

Mexico (mek'si kō) Country bordering the United States to the south. (m. H16, t. 4)

Michigan (mish'i gən) One of the Great Lakes states of the Middle West region. (m. 8–9, t. 259)

Middle West (mid'əl west) A region of the United States made up of the Great Lakes states of Illinois, Indiana, Michigan, Minnesota, Ohio, and Wisconsin, and the Plains states of Iowa, Kansas, Missouri, Nebraska, North Dakota, and South Dakota. (m. 34, t. 36)

Minnesota (min ə sō'tə) One of the Great Lakes states of the Middle West region. (m. 8–9, t. 266)

Mississippi (mis ə sip'ē) A state of the Southeast region. (m. 8–9)

Mississippi River (mis ə sip'ē riv'ər) One of the longest rivers in North America. It flows south from northern Minnesota into the Gulf of Mexico. (m. 8–9, t. 121)

Missouri (mi zúr'ē) One of the Plains states of the Middle West region. (m. 8–9)

Montana (mon tan'ə) One of the Mountain States. (m. 8–9, t. 314)

Montgomery (mont gum'ə rē) Capital of the state of Alabama; 32°N, 86°W. (m. H16, t. 166)

Montréal (mon trē ôl) A city and port in southern Quebec; Canada's largest city; 46°N, 74° W. (m. 199, t.199)

Mount McKinley (mount mə kin'lē) The highest mountain in North America at 20,030 feet (6,194 m), located in the Alaska Range; 64°N, 153°W. (m. 8-9, t. 382)

Gazetteer

Mount Rushmore National Memorial (mount rush' môr) Carving on a granite cliff in the Black Hills. It shows the faces of George Washington, Thomas Jefferson, Theodore Roosevelt, and Abraham Lincoln; 44°N, 103°W. (m. 253, t. 264)

Mount St. Helens (mount sānt hel' enz) Volcanic peak located in the Cascade Range in Washington; 47°N, 122°W. (t. 384)

Mount Waialeale (mount wī ä lā ä'lā) A mountain in Hawaii that receives nearly 500 inches of rain in most years; 22°N, 159°W. (m. 383, t. 388)

Mountain States (mount ən) A region of the United States made up of Colorado, Idaho, Montana, Utah, and Wyoming. (m. 34, t. 36)

Mumbai (mūm bī') A city and major port in the Arabian sea in India, formerly known as Bombay; 19°N, 73°E. (m. 227, t. 226)

Nagoya (na goy' yə) City in southern Japan; 35°N, 137°E. (m. 435, t. 433)

Nebraska (nə bras'kə) One of the Plains states of the Middle West region. (m. 8–9)

Nevada (nə vad'ə) A state of the West region. (m. 8–9)

New Hampshire (nü hamp'shər) One of the New England states of the Northeast region. (m. 8–9)

New Jersey (nü jûr'zē) One of the Middle Atlantic states of the Northeast region. (m. 8–9)

New Mexico (nü mek'si kō) A state of the Southwest region. (m. 8–9, t. 88)

New York (nü yôrk) One of the Middle Atlantic states of the Northeast region. (m. 8–9)

Nome (nōm) A city in western Alaska, site of the last great gold rush in 1899; 64°N, 165°W. (t. 413)

North America (nôrth ə mer'i kə) A continent in the Northern and Western hemispheres. (m. H11)

North Carolina (nôrth kar ə lī'nə) A state of the Southeast region. (m. 8–9)

North Dakota (nôrth də kō'tə) One of the Plains states of the Middle West region. (m. 8–9, t. 254)

North Pole (nôrth pōl) The most northern place on Earth; 90°N. (m. H11)

Northeast (nôrth ēst') A region of the United States made up of the New England states of Connecticut, Maine, Massachusetts, New Hampshire, Rhode Island, and Vermont, and the Middle Atlantic states of Delaware, Maryland, New Jersey, New York, and Pennsylvania. (m. 34, t. 35)

Northern Hemisphere (nôr'thərn hem'i sfîr) The half of Earth north of the equator. (m. H12)

Ohio (ō hī'ō) One of the Great Lakes states of the Middle West region. (m. 8–9)

Okefenokee Swamp (ō kə fə nō'kē swomp) A large wetland in Georgia and Florida that covers 660 square miles. (t. 124)

Oklahoma (ō klə hō'mə) A state of the Southwest region. (m. 8–9)

Old Oraibi (ōld ôr ī' bē) A Hopi village in northeastern Arizona. It is one of the oldest villages in the United States; 35°N, 110°W. (p. 78)

Olympic National Park (ō lim'pik nash'ə nəl pärk) A national park in northwestern Washington that includes rain forest areas. (t. 389)

Onondaga (än ən dä'gə) A town in New York that is the capital of the Iroquois Confederacy; 43°N, 76°W. (m. 207, t. 209)

Oregon (ôr'i gən) One of the Pacific states of the West region. (m. 8–9)

Osaka (ō sä kə') City and port in southern Japan; 34°N, 135°E. (m. 435, t. 433)

P

Pacific Ocean (pə sif'ik ō'shən) Ocean that borders western North and South America and eastern Asia. (m. H11, t. H11)

Painted Desert (pān'ted dez'ert) Desert in northern Arizona named for its colorful rocks. (m. 51, t. 56)

Park City (park sit' ē) City in Utah where the Sundance Film Festival is held every January; 40°N, 111°W. (t. 362)

Pennsylvania (pen səl vān'yə) A Middle Atlantic state of the Northeast region. (m. 8–9)

Phoenix (fē′niks) The capital and largest city of Arizona, in the south-central part of the state; 33°N, 112°W. (m. H16, t. 104)

Pikes Peak (pīks pēk) A mountain of the Rocky Mountains, in central Colorado, site of a gold rush in 1859; 39°N, 105°W. (t. 316)

Promontory Point (präm′ən tōrē point) The place in northwestern Utah where railroads met in 1869, completing the first transcontinental railroad in the United States; 41°N, 112°W. (m. 346, t. 346)

 R

Redmond (red′ mənd) A town in Washington where many computer software companies are located; 47°N, 122°W. (t. 429)

Rhode Island (rōd ī′lənd) One of the New England states of the Northeast region. (m. 8–9)

Rio Grande (rē′ō grand) A river that starts in Colorado and flows between Texas and Mexico into the Gulf of Mexico. (m. 8–9, t. 51)

Rocky Mountains (rok′ē moun′tənz) A high mountain range that stretches from Canada through the western United States into Mexico. (m. 8–9, t. 4)

 S

Salt Lake City (sawlt lāk sit′ ē) Capital of Utah; 41°N, 112°W. (t. 330)

San Antonio (san an tō′nē ō) A city in south-central Texas; 29°N, 99°W. (m. R18, t. 94)

San Francisco (san frən sis′kō) A port city in central California, on the Pacific Ocean; 38°N, 122°W. (m. 412, t. 413)

San Xavier del Bac (san hä vi yer del bak) Mission near Tucson, Arizona, which was founded by Eusebio Francisco Kino in 1700; 32°N, 111°W. (t. 87)

Santa Fe (san′tə fā) The capital of New Mexico, in the north-central part of the state; 36°N, 106°W. (t. 88)

Seattle (sē at′ əl) A city in northwestern Washington, the largest in the state and a major port; 48°N, 122°W. (m. 391, t. 419)

Sierra Nevada (sē er′ə nə vad′ə) A mountain range in eastern California. (m. 8–9, t. 383)

Silicon Valley (sil′ i kon val′ ē) Area in Central California with a large concentration of computer companies (t.149)

Sonoran Desert (sə nôr′ən dez′ərt) A desert in southern Arizona, southeastern California, and northern Mexico. (m. 51, t. 57)

South Africa (south af′ ri kə) Southern most country in Africa. (m. 153, t. 153)

South America (south ə mer′i kə) A continent in the Southern and Western hemispheres. (m. H11)

South Carolina (south kar ə lī′nə) A state of the Southeast region. (m. 8–9)

South Dakota (south də kō′tə) One of the Plains states of the Middle West region. (m. 8–9, t. 264)

South Pass City (south pas sit′ē) City in Wyoming, former capital of Wyoming Territory; 42°N, 109°W. (t. 353)

South Pole (south pōl) The most southern place on Earth; 90°S. (m. H11)

Southeast (south ēst′) A region of the United States made up of Alabama, Arkansas, Florida, Georgia, Kentucky, Louisiana, Mississippi, North Carolina, South Carolina, Tennessee, Virginia, and West Virginia. (m. 34, t. 35)

Southern Hemisphere (suth′ərn hem′i sfîr) The half of Earth south of the equator. (m. H12)

Southwest (south west′) A region of the United States made up of Arizona, New Mexico, Oklahoma, and Texas. (m. 34, t. 35)

Sun Valley (sun val′ ē) Year-round recreation area in Idaho. (t. 362)

Switzerland (swit′sər lənd) A landlocked, mountainous country in central Europe. (m. 365, t. 364)

T

Tahlequah (tä´lə kwä) A town in Oklahoma that was founded by Cherokee forced to leave the Southeast; 36°N, 95°W. (t. 144)

Tennessee (ten ə sē´) A state of the Southeast region. (m. 8–9)

Texas (tek´səs) A state of the Southwest region. (m. 8–9, t. 94)

Tokyo (tō´ kē ō) The capital and largest city of Japan, on the island of Honshu; 36°N, 140°E. (m. 435, t. 433)

Tucson (tü´sän) City in southeast Arizona; 32°N, 111°W. (m. R18, t. 87)

U

Ulaanbaatar (ü län bä tôr) Capital city of Mongolia; 48°N, 107°E. (m. 81, t. 83)

Utah (ū´tô) One of the Mountain States. (m. 8–9, t. 314)

V

Vail (vayl) The largest ski resort in North America, located in Colorado; 39°N, 106°W. (t. 362)

Vermont (vər mont´) One of the New England states of the Northeast region. (m. 8–9)

Virginia (vər jin´yə) A state of the Southeast region. (m. 8–9)

W

Washington (wô´shing tən) One of the Pacific states of the West region. (m. 8–9)

Washington, D.C. (wô´shing tən dē sē) Capital of the United States; 39°N, 77°W. (m. 8–9, t. 28)

West (west) A region of the United States made up of Alaska, California, Hawaii, Nevada, Oregon, and Washington. (m. 34, t. 36)

West Virginia (west vər jin´yə) A state of the Southeast region. (m. 8–9)

Western Hemisphere (wes´tərn hem´i sfîr) The half of Earth west of the prime meridian. (m. H12, t. 4)

Williamsburg (wil´yəmz bûrg) The capital of the Virginia colony in the 1700s; 37°N, 77°W. (t. 146)

Wind River Reservation (wind riv´ ər rez ər vā´ shən) Shoshone reservation established in 1868 under the Fort Bridger Treaty; 43°N, 109°W. (t. 339)

Wisconsin (wis kon´sən) One of the Great Lakes states of the Middle West region. (m. 8–9)

Wyoming (wī ō´ming) One of the Mountain States. (m. 8–9, t. 314)

Y

Yellowstone National Park (yel ə stōn) The oldest national park in the United States. It stretches over 3,468 square miles and includes parts of Wyoming, Montana, and Idaho. (t. 318)

Yokohama (yō kō ha´ mə) City and port in southeast Japan; 35°N, 139°E. (m. 435, t. 433)

Biographical Dictionary

The Biographical Dictionary tells you about the people you have learned about in this book. The Pronunciation Key tells you how to say their names. The page numbers tell you where each person first appears in the text.

A

Adams, John (ad'əmz), 1735–1826 Second President of the United States from 1797 to 1801. He was a member of the Continental Congress and the Constitutional Convention. (p. 214)

Anthony, Susan B. (an'thə nē), 1820–1906 Early leader of the fight for women's suffrage. (p. 351)

Attucks, Crispus (at'əks, kris'pəs), 1723–1770 Patriot and former slave who was killed by British soldiers in the Boston Massacre. (p. 214)

B

Beckwourth, Jim (bek'wərth), 1798–1867? African American who was born in slavery and became a famous "mountain man." He discovered a pass through the Sierra Nevada mountains. (p. 412)

Borglum, Gutzon (bòr' gləm, gət' sən) 1867–1941 American sculptor who carved out the heads of four American Presidents on Mount Rushmore. (p. 265)

Bush, George W. (bùsh), 1946– The 43rd President of the United States, who took office in 2001. (p. 236)

C

Chávez, César (chä'ves, se'sär) 1927–1993 A founder of the United Farm Workers labor union. (p. 420)

Columbus, Christopher (kə lum'bəs), 1451?–1506 Italian explorer who sailed from Spain across the Atlantic and reached the Bahamas in 1492. (p. 84)

Cook, James (kùk) 1728–1779 First European to reach the Hawaiian Islands in 1778. (p. 406)

Coolidge, Calvin (kü lij, kal' vin) 1872–1933 The 30th President of the United States from 1923 to 1929. (p. 265)

Coronado, Francisco (kôr ə nä'dō, fran sēs'kō), 1510–1554 Spanish explorer and conquistador who led an army from Mexico into the Southwest and Kansas. (p. 85)

Crazy Horse (krā'zē hôrs), 1849?–1877 Chief who led the Lakota forces at the Battle of Little Bighorn in 1876. (p. 284)

Crockett, David (krok'it), 1786–1836 United States Representative and frontier scout who died defending The Alamo. (p. 88)

Custer, George (kus'tər), 1839–1876 Army officer defeated by Lakota forces in the Battle of Little Bighorn in 1876. (p. 284)

D

Davis, Jefferson (dā'vis), 1808–1889 President of the Confederate States of America, 1861–1865. (p. 162)

Dawes, William (dôz'), 1745–1799 Patriot who rode with Paul Revere on April 18, 1775 to warn colonists that British troops were coming. (p. 216)

De Klerk, Frederik W. (də klerk') 1936– South African president from 1989 to 1994. He worked for a peaceful transition from the policy of apartheid to majority rule in South Africa. (p. 154)

Deere, John (dîr), 1804–1886 Blacksmith who invented a steel plow and became a manufacturer of farm machinery. (p. 276)

Deganawida (dā gän ə wē'də), 1500s Huron-born leader of the Iroquois who helped organize the Iroquois Confederacy. (p. 207)

Douglass, Frederick (dug'ləs), 1817–1895 Abolitionist writer and speaker. (p. 159)

---

pronunciation key

a	at	ī	ice	u	up	th	thin
ā	ape	îr	pierce	ū	use	th	this
ä	far	o	hot	ü	rule	zh	measure
âr	care	ō	old	ù	pull	ə	about, taken,
e	end	ô	fork	ûr	turn		pencil, lemon,
ē	me	oi	oil	hw	white		circus
i	it	ou	out	ng	song		

du Sable, Jean-Baptiste Point (dü sä′ blə, zhän′ bap tēst′ pwän′) 1750?–1818 A trader from Haiti who was the first person to settle in Chicago. (p. 273)

E

Earhart, Amelia (ar′härt), 1898–1937 The first woman airplane pilot to fly across the Atlantic in 1928. (p. 290)

F

Ford, Henry (fôrd), 1863–1947 Engineer who first used assembly lines to manufacture automobiles in 1913. (p. 287)

G

Grant, Ulysses S. (grant, ū lis′ēz), 1822–1885 Leader of the Union Army during the Civil War. He became the eighteenth President of the United States, 1869–1877. (p. 163)

H

Hiawatha (hī ə wä′thə), 1500s Mohawk leader who, with Deganawida, helped organize the Iroquois Confederacy. (p. 207)

Huerta, Dolores (wer′tä) 1929– A founder of the United Farm Workers labor union. (p. 420)

J

Jefferson, Thomas (jef′ər sən), 1743–1826 Member of Virginia House of Burgesses who drafted the Declaration of Independence. He became the third President of the United States, 1801–1809. (p. 148)

K

Kamehameha I (kə mā′ə mā′ə), 1753?–1819 Founder of the kingdom of Hawaii, 1810–1819. (p. 406)

King, Martin Luther, Jr. (king), 1929–1968 Civil rights leader who worked to gain equal rights for African Americans and others in the 1950s and 1960s. (p. 167)

Kino, Eusebio Francisco (kē′nō, e ü se′bē ō fran sēs′kō), 1645–1711 Spanish priest and missionary who introduced ranching in Arizona. (p. 87)

L

Lee, Robert E. (lē), 1807–1870 General who led the Confederate Army in the Civil War. (p. 162)

Liliuokalani, Lydia Paki (lē lē′ü ō kä lä′nē), 1838–1917 Queen of Hawaii, 1891–1893, who was overthrown when a group of planters established the Republic of Hawaii. (p. 407)

Lincoln, Abraham (ling′kən), 1809–1865 Congressman from Illinois who became the sixteenth President of the United States, 1861–1865. He led the Union during the Civil War. (p. 161)

Love, Nat (luv), 1854–1921 American cowboy and writer who had been enslaved. (p. 93)

Mandela, Nelson (man del′ə), 1918– South African civil rights leader who became president of South Africa in 1994. (p. 152)

Marshall, James (mär′shəl), 1810–1885 California settler who discovered gold while building Sutter's Mill in 1848. This discovery launched the California gold rush. (p. 410)

Morris, Esther (môr′əs), 1814–1902 Suffragist leader in Wyoming Territory. (p. 353)

Morse, Samuel (môrs), 1791–1872 Inventor of the telegraph. His invention enabled people to communicate quickly over long distances. (p. 222)

Mott, Lucretia (mot), 1793–1880 Abolitionist and women's rights leader who, with Elizabeth Cady Stanton, helped organize the Seneca Falls Convention in 1848. (p. 351)

Parks, Rosa McCauley (pärks), 1913– Civil rights activist whose arrest led to the Montgomery, Alabama bus boycott. (p. 167)

R

Rankin, Jeannette (rang′kən), 1880–1973 Montana suffragist who became the first woman member of the House of Representatives, 1916–1918. (p. 354)

Revere, Paul (rə vir′), 1735–1818 Boston silversmith who, in 1775, warned colonists of the advance of British soldiers at the start of the American Revolution. (p. 216)

Rice, Condoleezza (rīs), 1954– National Security Advisor to President George W. Bush. (p. 170)

Ross, Nellie Tayloe (rôs), 1876–1977 First woman to serve as a governor of a state, Wyoming, 1925–1927. (p. 392)

S

Sacagawea (sak ə jə wä′ə) 1787?–1812 Shoshone guide and translator for the Lewis and Clark expedition from 1805 to 1806. (p. 343)

Sequoyah (si kwoi′ə), 1760s–1844 Cherokee who invented a writing system for the Cherokee language. (p. 142)

Sitting Bull (sit′ing búl), 1831?–1890 Lakota chief who led the Lakota in conflicts with the United States government in the 1870s. (p. 284)

Slater, Hannah Wilkinson (slā′tər), 1774–1812 Invented cotton sewing thread during the Industrial Revolution. (p. 221)

Slater, Samuel (slā′tər), 1768–1835 English engineer who built the first water-powered spinning mill in the United States in 1789. (p. 221)

Stanton, Elizabeth Cady (stant′ən), 1815–1902 Abolitionist and women's rights leader who helped write the "Declaration of Rights and Sentiments" at the Seneca Falls Convention in 1848. (p. 351)

Tubman, Harriet (tub′mən), 1820?–1913 "Conductor" on the Underground Railroad who escaped slavery and made 19 trips to slave states to free others. (p. 160)

Washakie, Chief (wəsh ə kē) 1804?–1900 Shoshone chief who promoted peace with white settlers. Signed the Fort Bridger Treaty in 1868. (p. 339)

Washington, George (wô′shing tən), 1732–1799 Commander of the colonial army in the American Revolution and first President of the United States, 1789–1797. (p. 216)

Williams, Lizzie Johnson (wil′yəmz), 1843–1924 Magazine writer and rancher known as the "Cattle Queen of Texas." (p. 94)

York (yôrk), 1770–1832? A member of the Lewis and Clark expedition from 1804–1806. (p. 343)

---

pronunciation key

a **at**; ā **ape**; ä **far**; âr **care**; e **end**; ē **me**; i **it**; ī **ice**; îr **pierce**; o **hot**; ō **old**; ô **fork**; oi **oil**; ou **out**; u **up**; ū **use**; ü **rule**; u̇ **pull**; ûr **turn**; hw **white**; ng **song**; th **thin**; th **this**; zh measure; ə **about, taken, pencil, lemon, circus**

Glossary

This Glossary will help you to pronounce and understand the meanings of the vocabulary in this book. The page number at the end of the definition tells where the word first appears.

A

abolition (ab ə lish′ən) Ending completely; often used in reference to slavery. (p. 161)

adapt (ad əpt) To make changes over time in order to survive in an environment. (p. 58)

adobe (ə dō′bē) Sun-baked bricks used as a building material, most commonly in the Southwest. (p. 76)

agribusiness (ag′rə biz nis) A farm or ranch which is combined with other businesses, such as food processing. (p. 294)

agriculture (ag′ri kul chər) The business of growing crops and raising animals. (p. 129)

American Revolution (ə mer′i kən rev ə lü′shən) The war fought by the American colonies to end British rule, 1775–1783. (p. 216)

ancestor (an′ses tər) A person in your family, starting with your parents, who was born long before you. (p. 22)

apartheid (ə pär′tīd) The government policy of strict and unequal segregation of races as practiced in South Africa from 1948 to the early 1990s. (p. 153)

aqueduct (ak′wi dukt′) A pipe which carries water to cities and farms. (p. 67)

aquifer (ak′wə fər) A layer of rock or gravel that traps water underground. (p. 67)

assembly line (ə sem′blē līn) A line of workers and machines along which a product is moved as it is made. (p. 289)

astronomer (ə stron′ə mər) A scientist who studies other planets and the stars. (p. 102)

B

barbed wire (bärbd wīr) Wire with sharp points that is used to fence off areas of land. (p. 96)

bay (bā) A part of an ocean or lake that cuts deeply into the land. (p. 187)

blizzard (bliz′ərd) A heavy snowstorm with very strong winds. (p. 262)

Boston Massacre (bôs′tən mas′ə kər) A protest in 1770 against British rule in which five American Patriots were killed. (p. 214)

boycott (boi′kot) The act of joining with other people in refusing to buy or use a company's product or service. (p. 168)

broadleaf (brōd′lēf) Having broad leaves; said of hardwood trees whose leaves change color in the autumn. See **needleleaf**. (p. 190)

C

canal (kə nal′) An inland waterway built for transportation or irrigation. (p. 199)

canton (kan′ton) A governmental division of Switzerland. (p. 365)

canyon (can′yən) A deep, narrow valley with steep sides. (p. 52)

cardinal direction (kär′də nəl di rek′shən) One of the main directions of the globe; north, south, east, and west. (p. H13)

cash crop (kash krop) A crop that is grown to be sold for money rather than to be used on the farm where it is grown. (p. 130)

cashmere (kash mēr) Wool from goats. (p. 81)

cattle drive (cat′əl drīv) A journey in which cowboys herded cattle north to railroad depots in the late 1800s. (p. 94)

pronunciation key

a	at	ī	ice	u	up	th	**th**in
ā	ape	îr	p**ie**rce	ū	use	<u>th</u>	**th**is
ä	far	o	hot	ü	rule	zh	mea**s**ure
âr	care	ō	old	ù	pull	ə	**a**bout, tak**e**n,
e	end	ô	fork	ûr	turn		penc**i**l, lem**o**n,
ē	me	oi	oil	hw	white		circ**u**s
i	it	ou	out	ng	song		

cause (kôz) An event that makes something else happen. (p. 196)

CD-ROM (sē dē rom') A reference source used with a computer that may include writing, pictures, sounds, or short movies. (p. 356)

Central Valley Project (sen'trəl val'ē proj'ekt) The system of dams and canals that irrigates fields in the Central Valley of California. (p. 395)

checks and balances (cheks and bal'ən sez) System by which each branch of government makes sure that no other branch gains too much power. (p. 29)

circle graph (sûr'kəl graf) A graph in the shape of a circle that shows the sizes of different parts of a whole; also called a pie graph. (p. 256)

citizen (sit'ə zən) A person who is born in a country or who has earned the right to become a member of that country by law. (p. 26)

civil rights (siv'əl rīts) The rights of people to be treated equally under the law. (p. 167)

Civil War (siv'əl wôr) The war in the United States between the Union states of the north and the Confederate states of the south, 1861–1865. (p. 162)

climate (klī'mit) The pattern of weather of a certain place over many years. (p. 12)

coal (kōl) A mineral found under Earth's surface that is burned as a fuel. (p. 133)

combine (kom'bīn) A large machine used to harvest crops. (p. 293)

commercial farming (ka mûr' shəl fär' mēng) To raise crops and livestock for sale. (p. 299)

commute (kə mūt') To travel a distance each day from one's home to one's workplace. (p. 200)

compass rose (kum'pəs rōz) A small drawing on a map that shows directions. (p. H13)

Conestoga wagon (kon ə stō'gə wag'ən) A sturdy wooden vehicle covered with cloth and drawn by horses; used in the 1800s. (p. 274)

Confederacy (kən fed'ər ə sē) The government formed by 11 Southern states that seceded from the United States, 1860–1865. See **Civil War**. (p. 162)

Congress (kong'ris) The legislative branch of the United States government, which makes national laws. (p. 28)

conquistador (kōn kēs tä dôr') The Spanish word for the soldiers who conquered the Americas in the 1500s. (p. 83)

conservation (kon sər vā'shən) The careful use of a natural resource. (p. 16)

Constitution (kon sti tü'shən) The plan of government for the United States that explains the parts of the government and outlines the most important laws. (p. 26)

consumer (kon sü'mər) A person who buys products or uses services. (p. 33)

continent (kon'tə nənt) One of Earth's seven large bodies of land—Africa, Antarctica, Asia, Australia, Europe, North America, and South America. (p. H11)

council (koun'səl) A group of people who meet to talk and make decisions. (p. 141)

crude oil (krüd oil) Petroleum as it comes out of the ground. (p. 68)

decision (di sizh'ən) A choice that helps you reach a goal. (p. 156)

deforestation (dē fôr ist ā'shən) The loss of a forest by cutting down all of its trees. (p. 396)

degree (di grē') A unit for measuring distance on Earth's surface; also a unit for measuring temperature. Represented by the symbol °. (p. 62)

delta (del'tə) Land formed by the soil that a river deposits as it flows into a larger body of water. (p. 124)

democratic republic (dem ə krat'ik ri pub'lik) A government in which citizens elect representatives to make decisions for them. (p. 26)

desert (dez'ərt) A dry area that gets less than 10 inches of precipitation each year. (p. 57)

dictionary (dik'shə ner ē) A book that explains the meanings of words and shows how to pronounce and spell them. (p. 356)

discrimination (di skrim' ə nā shən) An unfair difference in the treatment of people. (p. 422)

drought (drout) A period in which very little rain falls. (p. 59)

dry farming (drī fär'ming) Methods of growing crops in arid areas using only rain water. (p. 67)

earthquake (ûrth' kwāk) A sudden shaking of the ground caused when rock layers beneath Earth's surface suddenly shift or crack. (p. 384)

economy (i kon'ə mē) The way a country uses or produces natural resources, goods, and services. (p. 32)

editorial (ed i tôr'ē əl) A newspaper article that gives opinions, rather than facts. (p. 392)

Glossary

effect • House of Burgesses

effect (i fekt′) An event that happens as a result of another event. (p. 196)

electronics (i lek tron′iks) The industry that creates high-technology products such as televisions, computers, and compact disc players. (p. 434)

elevation (el ə vā′shən) The height of land above sea level. (p. 10)

Emancipation Proclamation (i man sə pā′shən prok lə mā′shən) The announcement by President Lincoln in 1863 that all enslaved people living in Confederate states were free. (p. 162)

encyclopedia (en sî klə pē′dē ə) A book or set of books that gives facts about people, places, things, and events. (p. 356)

entrepreneur (än trə prə nûr′) A person who starts and runs his or her own business. (p. 32)

environment (en vī′rən mənt) The surroundings in which people, plants, or animals live. (p. 16)

equator (i kwā′tər) An imaginary line that lies halfway between the North Pole and the South Pole, at 0° latitude. (p. H12)

erosion (i rō′zhən) The action of water, wind, or ice in wearing away soil and rock. (p.53)

expedition (ek spi dish′ən) A journey made for a special purpose. (p. 343)

export (ek′spôrt) To sell goods to another country. See **import**. (p. 213)

fact (fakt) A statement that can be checked and proved to be true. (p. 392)

fall line (fôl līn) The line at which the Piedmont plateau and the Coastal Plain meet, and waterfalls form at rivers. (p. 189)

fertilizer (fûr′tə lī zər) Item added to soil to make it better for growing crops. (p. 395)

flatboat (flat′bōt) A large, flat-bottomed boat used to travel on rivers in the 1800s. (p. 274)

foliage (fō lē ij) A cluster of leaves, flowers, and branches on plants or trees. (p. 193)

food processing (füd pros′es ing) The industry that turns crops and livestock into food products. (p. 294)

Forty-Niner (fôr tē nī′nər) A person who went to California in 1849, usually to seek gold. (p. 412)

frame of reference (frām əv ref′rents) All the things learned or experienced that help shape thoughts, feelings, and opinions. (p. 424)

free-enterprise system (frē en′tər prīz sis′təm) The economic system that allows people to own and run their own businesses. (p. 32)

frontier (frun tîr′) The edge of a settled area. (p. 272)

fuel (fū′əl) A substance used to produce energy. (p. 16)

generalization (jen ər ə lə zā′shən) A statement that applies to several different examples of something. It shows how the examples are all alike in one or more ways. (p. 278)

geography (jē og′rə fē) The study of Earth and the way people, plants, and animals live on and use it. (p. 4)

geyser (gī zər) A hot, underground spring from which steam and hot water shoot into the air. (p. 318)

ghost town (gōst toun) A town without people; used for deserted mining settlements in the West. (p. 345)

glacier (glā′shər) A huge sheet of ice that slowly moves across the land. (p. 188)

global grid (glō′bəl grid) The crisscrossing lines of latitude and longitude on a map or globe. (p. 64)

gold rush (gōld rush) A sudden movement of people to a place where gold has been found; especially the gold rush to California in 1849. (p. 412)

gorge (gôrj) A narrow passage through land, such as a canyon. (p. 360)

government (guv′ərn mənt) The laws and people that run a country, state, county, city, or town. (p. 26)

granite (gran′it) A hard kind of rock used to build monuments and buildings. (p. 194)

graph (graf) A diagram that shows information in a picture. See **circle graph**; **line graph**. (p. 256)

Great Law of Peace (grāt law əv pēs) Document outlining the government of the Iroquois Confederacy. (p. 209)

growing season (grō′ing sē′zən) The time of the year when the weather is warm enough for crops to grow in a certain place. (p. 129)

guide words (gīd wûrdz) Words at the top of each page of a reference book that show the first and last entries on that page. (p. 356)

harbor (här′bər) A sheltered place along a coast where boats can be docked. (p. 186)

hemisphere (hem′i sfîr) Half a sphere; one of the four hemispheres of Earth—Northern, Southern, Eastern, and Western hemispheres. (p. H12)

high technology (hī tek nol′ə jē) The use of advanced scientific ideas and special tools to meet people's needs. (p. 102)

House of Burgesses (hous uv bûr′jis əz) An elected group of citizens who made laws for the Virginia colony beginning in 1619. (p. 148)

hybrid car (hī brid cär) A kind of automobile that combines a battery-powered motor with a gas engine. (p. 434)

immigrant (im'i grənt) A person who comes to a new country to live. (p. 22)

import (im'pôrt) To buy goods from another country. See **export**. (p. 213)

industrialization (in dus'trē əl izā'shun) The development of manufacturing industries. (p. 300)

industry (in'də strē) All the businesses that make one kind of good or provide one kind of service. (p. 101)

inference (in'fə rənts) Something figured out based on clues and information. (p. 218)

interdependent (in tər di pen'dənt) Relying on one another to meet needs and wants. (p. 37)

intermediate direction (in tər mē'dē it di rek'shən) Any direction in between two cardinal directions—northeast, southeast, southwest, northwest. (p. H13)

Internet (in'tər net) A network of computers that connects people around the world. (p. 356)

interstate highway (in'tər stāt hī'wā) A road that connects cities in two or more states with at least two lanes of traffic in each direction. (p. 386)

invention (in ven'shən) Something that is made or thought of for the first time. (p. 221)

investor (in ves'tər) Someone who puts money into a business and expects a share of the profit. (p. 33)

iron (ī'ərn) A hard metal mainly used to make steel. (p. 266)

irrigation (ir i gā'shən) The use of ditches or pipes to bring water to fields. (p. 130)

labor union (lā'bər ūn'yən) A group of workers organized to get better working conditions. (p. 134)

lake effect (lāk i fekt') The effect of the Great Lakes on the climate of parts of the Middle West, similar to the effect of oceans on lands near them. (p. 259)

landform (land'fôrm) Any of the shapes that make up Earth's surface. (p. 4)

landform map (land'fôrm map) A map that shows the landforms of an area. (p. H17)

landlocked (land'lokt) Completely surrounded by land. (p. 365)

latitude (lat'i tüd) A measure of distance on Earth north or south of the equator. See **parallel**. (p. 62)

lava (la' və) Liquid, molten rock that comes out of an erupting volcano. (p. 384)

line graph (līn graf) A graph that shows how a piece of information changes over time. (p. 256)

livestock (līv'stok) Animals kept on a farm, such as cattle, hogs, and chickens. (p. 254)

locator (lō'kāt ər) A small map or globe set onto another map that shows where the main map is located. (p. G8)

lock (lok) A kind of water elevator that moves boats within a canal to higher or lower levels. (p. 199)

logging (lo'ging) The process by which trees are cut down and transported out of the forest. (p. 396)

longhouse (long'hous) A long wooden building in an Iroquois village that housed many families. (p. 208)

longitude (lon'ji tüd) A measure of distance on Earth east or west of the prime meridian. See **meridian**. (p. 63)

Louisiana Purchase (lü ē zē an'ə pûr'chəs) The territory purchased by the United States from France in 1803, reaching from the Mississippi River to the Rocky Mountains and from the Gulf of Mexico to Canada. (p. 343)

map key (map kē) An explanation of what the symbols on a map represent. (p. H14)

map scale (map skāl) A line divided into units of measurement, such as inches, used to represent a real distance on Earth on a map. (p. 126)

map symbol (map sim'bəl) Anything that stands for something else on a map. (p. H14)

mass production (mas prə duk'shən) The manufacture of large numbers of goods using identical parts and assembly-line methods. (p. 289)

meridian (mə rid'ē ən) A line of longitude. (p. 63)

mesa (mā'sä) A flat landform that rises steeply above the surrounding land; smaller than a plateau. (p. 52)

metropolitan area (met rə pol'i tən âr'ē ə) A city and its suburbs together. (p. 200)

migrate (mī'grāt) To move from one place to another. (p. 227)

migration (mī grā'shən) The movement of a group of people from one region to another. (p. 288)

---

pronunciation key

a **at**; ā **ape**; ä **far**; âr **care**; e **end**; ē **me**; i **it**; ī **ice**; îr **pierce**; o **hot**; ō **old**; ô **fork**; oi **oil**; ou **out**; u **up**; ū **use**; ü **rule**;
ù **pull**; ûr **turn**; hw **white**; ng **song**; th **thin**; <u>th</u> **this**; zh **measure**; ə **about, taken, pencil, lemon, circus**

Glossary

mineral (min′ər əl) A nonrenewable natural resource that is found in the earth. (p. 16)

Minutemen (min′it men) Volunteer colonial soldiers who served against the British in the American Revolution; they were said to be ready to fight at a minute's notice. (p. 214)

mission (mish′ən) A Spanish settlement in the Americas where priests taught Native Americans the Christian religion. (p. 86)

mother lode (muth′ər lōd) A gold-rich area in the central Sierra Nevada foothills. (p. 412)

mouth (mouth) The place where a river empties into an ocean, a lake, or a larger river. (p. 121)

NAFTA (naf′tə) North American Free Trade Agreement, which has made trade easier between the United States, Mexico, and Canada. (p. 102)

natural resource (nach′ər əl rē′sôrs) Something found in the environment that people can use. (p. 16)

needleleaf (nē′dəl lēf) Having thin, needle-like leaves; said of softwood trees whose leaves do not change color in autumn. See **broadleaf**. (p. 190)

nomadic (nō ma′dik) Moving from place to place. (p. 81)

nonrenewable resource (non ri nü′ə bel rē sôr′sez) A resource that is limited in supply and cannot be replaced, such as a fuel or mineral. (p. 16)

O

ocean (ō′shən) One of Earth's four largest bodies of water—the Atlantic, Arctic, Indian, and Pacific oceans. (p. H11)

open-pit mining (ō′ pən pit mī′ ning) A method of removing ore deposits close to the surface of the ground using power shovels. (p. 266)

opinion (ə pin′yən) A personal feeling or belief. (p. 392)

ore (ôr) A rock that contains a metal. (p. 266)

outline (out′līn) A plan for organizing written information about a subject. (p. 30)

P

Pacific Rim (pə sif′ik rim) The lands and countries that border the Pacific Ocean. (p. 432)

parallel (par′ə lel) A line of latitude. (p. 62)

Patriot (pā′trē ət) A colonist who was opposed to British rule; any person who loves his or her country. (p. 213)

petrochemical (pet rō kem′i kəl) Any substance made from petroleum, including paint, plastics, cloth, insulation, fertilizers, and pesticides. (p. 68)

petroleum (pə trō′lē əm) A fuel, commonly called oil, that formed underground from dead plants. (p. 60)

physical map (fiz′i kəl map) A map that shows natural features of Earth. (p. H17)

pioneer (pī ə nîr′) A person who leads the way. (p. 273)

plain (plān) A large area of nearly flat land. (p. 4)

plantation (plan tā′shən) A large farm where cash crops were grown. (p. 158)

point of view (point əv vyü) The way a person looks at something. (p. 392)

political map (pə lit′i kəl map) A map that shows information such as cities, capitals, states, and countries. (p. H16)

pollution (pə lü′shən) Any substance, such as a chemical, that makes air, water, or soil dirty. (p. 16)

population (pop yə lā′shən) The number of people who live in a place or area. (p. 22)

port (pôrt) A place where ships load and unload their goods. (p. 124)

prairie (prâr′ē) Flat or gently rolling land thickly covered with grasses and wildflowers. (p. 254)

precipitation (pri sip i tā′shən) The moisture that falls to the ground as rain, snow, sleet, or hail. (p. 12)

President (prez′i dənt) The person who is head of the executive branch of the United States government. (p. 28)

primary source (prī′mer ē sôrs) Information that comes from someone who was present at what he or she is describing. See **secondary source**. (p. 416)

prime meridian (prīm mə rid′ē ən) The line of longitude, marked 0°, from which other meridians are numbered. (p. 63)

profit (prof′it) The money a business earns after it pays for tools, salaries, and other costs. (p. 32)

pueblo (pweb′lō) "Village" in Spanish; any of several Native American groups that live in adobe and stone houses. (p. 75)

Q

quarry (kwôr′ē) A place where stone is cut or blasted out. (p. 194)

R

rain forest (rān fôr′ist) A warm, wet forest where many trees and other plants grow close together. (p. 389)

rain shadow (rān shad′ō) The side of a mountain that is usually dry because precipitation falls on the other side. (p. 390)

rancho (ran′chō) Large farms where animals such as sheep or cattle are raised. (p. 86)

reclamation (rek lə mā'shən) Restoring land to its previous state after it has been mined, particularly by open-pit methods. (p. 266)

reference source (ref'ər əns sôrs) A book or any form of information that contains facts about many different subjects. (p. 356)

refinery (ri fī'nə rē) A factory where crude oil is cleaned, separated into parts, and treated to make petroleum products. (p. 68)

region (rē'jən) An area with common features that set it apart from other areas. (p. 34)

relative location (re' lə tiv lō kā'shən) Location of one place in relation to another. (p. H13)

renewable resource (ri nü'ə bəl rē'sôrs) A natural resource that can be replaced for later use, such as a forest. (p. 16)

reservation (rez ər vā'shən) Land set aside by the United States government for Native Americans to live on. (p. 76)

river basin (riv'ər bā'sin) All the land that is drained by a river and its tributaries. (p. 121)

road map (rōd map) A map that shows roads. (p. 386)

robot (rō'bot) A machine controlled by computers. (p. 290)

robotics (rō bo' tiks) Technology that deals with the design, construction, and operation of robots. (p. 434)

sachem (sā'chəm) A council member of the Iroquois Confederacy. (p. 209)

scale (skāl) The relationship between the distance shown on a map and the real distance on Earth. (p. H15)

secondary source (sek'ən der ē sôrs) Information that comes from someone who was not present at the events he or she is describing. See **primary source**. (p. 416)

segregation (seg ri gā'shən) The practice of setting one group apart from another by law. (p. 167)

service (sûr'vis) A job people do to help others, rather than to make things. (p. 32)

silicon (sil i' kon) An element found in Earth's crust and used in electronics. (p. 429)

slag (slag) Waste that forms on the surface of liquid metal. (p. 330)

slavery (slā'və rē) The practice of making one person the property of another. (p. 22)

smelt (smelt) The process of using high temperatures to separate pure metals from rock. (p. 330)

software (sôft' wâr) Programs that run on computers. (p. 429)

source (sôrs) The place where a river begins. (p. 121)

specialize (spesh'ə līz) To spend most of one's time doing one kind of job. (p. 294)

spring (spring) A place where underground water comes to the surface. (p. 67)

steppe (step) A dry, grassy, treeless plain found in Asia and eastern Europe. (p. 81)

strike (strīk) A refusal of all the workers in a business to work until the owners meet their demands. (p. 420)

subsistence farming (səb sis' təns fär' məng) To grow only enough food to live. (p. 299)

suburb (sub'ûrb) A community outside of but near a larger city. (p. 200)

suffrage (suf'rij) The right to vote. (p. 351)

summary (sum'ə rē) A brief account that contains the main points of something. (p. 164)

Supreme Court (sə prēm' kôrt) The highest court of the United States. (p. 29)

sweatshop (swet'shop) A factory where workers are employed at poor wages and in unhealthy conditions. (p. 225)

syllabary (si'lə ber ē) A system of writing in which each syllable of a word is represented by a symbol. (p. 142)

taconite (tak' ən īt) A flint-like rock that contains smaller iron minerals. (p. 266)

taro (tär'ō) A tropical plant eaten as a food. (p. 405)

tax (taks) Money people pay to the government so that it can perform public services. (p. 26)

teepee (tē'pē) A cone-shaped dwelling traditionally made of animal skins and poles used by Native Americans on the Plains. (p. 282)

telegraph (tel'i graf') A system or equipment used for sending messages by wire over a long distance. The message is sent in Morse code over wires by means of electricity. (p. 222)

temperature (tem'per ə chər) A measurement of how hot or cold something is, often the air. (p. 12)

---

pronunciation key

a **a**t; ā **a**pe; ä f**a**r; âr **ca**re; e **e**nd; ē m**e**; i **i**t; ī **i**ce; îr p**ie**rce; o h**o**t; ō **o**ld; ô f**o**rk; oi **oi**l; ou **ou**t; u **u**p; ū **u**se; ü r**u**le; ù p**u**ll; ûr t**u**rn; hw **wh**ite; ng so**ng**; th **th**in; <u>th</u> **th**is; zh mea**s**ure; ə **a**bout, tak**e**n, penc**i**l, lem**o**n, circ**u**s

Glossary

tenement (ten′ə mənt) A crowded, poorly maintained apartment building. (p. 224)

terrorism (ter′ə riz əm) The use of fear and violence to gain a political goal. (p. 236)

timberline (tim′bər līn) The line on high mountains or in polar regions beyond which it is too cold for trees to grow. (p. 324)

time line (tīm līn) A diagram that shows a series of events in the order in which they happened. (p. 90)

tornado (tôr nā′dō) A destructive funnel of wind that moves over the ground at high speeds. (p. 261)

tourist (tur′ist) A person traveling on vacation. (p. 130)

township (toun′ship) A segregated area where blacks in South Africa were forced to live under apartheid. (p. 153)

Trail of Tears (trāl uv tîrz) The forced movement of Cherokee and some other Native Americans to what is now Oklahoma in 1838. (p. 144)

transcontinental (trans kon tə nen′təl) Crossing an entire continent. (p. 346)

transportation (trans pər tā′shən) The moving of goods or people from one place to another. (p. 37)

transportation map (trans pər tā′shən map) A map that shows how to travel from one place to another. (p. H17)

tributary (trib′yə ter ē) Any river that flows into another, larger river. (p. 121)

tundra (tun′drə) A huge plain that is frozen for most of the year. (p. 4)

Underground Railroad (un′dər ground rāl′rōd) A group of people who helped slaves escape to freedom along secret routes before and during the Civil War. (p. 160)

Union (ūn′yən) The states that remained in the United States after the Confederacy formed. See **Civil War**. (p. 160)

urban (ûr′bən) Of a city. (p. 200)

urban sprawl (ûr′ bən sprawl) The uncontrolled spread of buildings around a city. (p. 430)

vaquero (vä ke′rō) A Spanish word for "cowboy," used to describe workers on cattle ranches. (p. 92)

vegetation map (ve jə tā′shən map) A map that shows different kinds of plant areas. (p. 326)

volcano (vol kä′nō) An opening in Earth's surface from which hot liquid rock and ash may pour out. (p. 384)

wetland (wet′land) An area such as a swamp or marsh where water is at or close to the surface of the ground. (p. 6)

Index

Credits

Maps: National Geographic Society

Chapter Opener Map Illustrations: Joe Lemonnier

Illustrations: Daniel Del Valle: 41t., 197, 231; Julie Downing: 178-181; John Edens: 85, 90-91, 149, 214, 288, 290, 320; George Fryer: 52, 133, 189; Carmen Lomas Garza: 42-45; Patrick Gnan: 15t., 96, 296; Cheryl Harness: 112-115; Doug Horne: 9t., 15b., 20b.r., 21b., 29, 123, 222; Tim Lee: 39; Anthony Lewis: 41b., 111, 177, 243, 307, 373, 441; Ann Losa: 95; Jeff Mangiat: 223, 276, 282, 397; Elsa Myotte: 260; S. D. Nelson: 244-247; John Patrick: 8-9 bkgd., 14-15 bkgd., 20-21 bkgd., 103, 361; Leah Palmer Priess: 414; Michael Saunders: 390; Robert Schuster: 289; Chris Soentpiet: 308-311; Walter Stuart: 274; Bleu Tirrell: 87; Robert Van Nutt: 86; Phil Wilson: 67; Cornelius Van Wright & Ying-Hwa Hu: 374-377.

Photography Credits: All photographs are by Macmillan/McGraw-Hill except as noted below.

Cover/A17: t. Terry Donnelly/Stone; b. Corbis; A1: t.l. ©Michael Krasowitz/FPG International; t.m. ©Jerry Tobias/Corbis; t.r. ©Simon Wilkinson/The Image Bank; m.l.1 ©LWA-Dann Tardif/Corbis Stock Market; m.r.1 ©Elyse Lewin Studio Inc./The Image Bank; m.l.2 ©Vicky Kasala/The Image Bank; m. ©Elyse Lewin Studio Inc./The Image Bank; m.r.2 ©LWA-Dann Tardif/Corbis Stock Market; m.r.3 ©Ghislain & Marie David de Lossy/The Image Bank; b.l. ©Vicky Kasala/The Image Bank; b.m. ©Ross Whitaker/The Image Bank; b.r. ©AJA Productions/The Image Bank. Border: PhotoLink/Photo Disc. A2: t.r. ©Joseph Sohm/Corbis; b.r. ©The Granger Collection. A3: t.r. ©Joseph Sohm, Visions of America/Corbis; b.l. ©National Archives. A4: b.l. ©Ken Karp/McGraw-Hill; t.r. ©Dennis Degnan/Corbis; b.r. ©Joseph Sohm/Corbis. A5: b. ©Ken Karp/McGraw-Hill; t.r. ©Joseph Sohm, Visions of America/Corbis. A6: b. ©Ken Karp/McGraw-Hill; t.r. ©National Archives. A7: bkgd. ©Jim Cummins/FPG; b.r. ©Ken Karp/McGraw-Hill. A8: b.r. ©The Granger Collection; bkgd. ©The Granger Collection. A9: bkgd. ©Hulton Archive/Getty Images; b.r. Bob Schultz/Associated Press, AP. A10: b.r. Cary Wolinsky/Stock Boston; b.l. ©Ron Watts/Corbis. A10–A11: t.c. Bill Banaszewski/Visuals Unlimited. A11: b.l. ©Fritz Polking/Peter Arnold, Inc.; t.r. ©Dick Keen/Visuals Unlimited; m.r. ©Joe Sohm/Photo Researchers, Inc. A12: m.t.r. ©Greenberg/Folio, Inc.; bkgd. Wendell Metzen/Bruce Coleman Inc.; b.r. Jeff Greenberg/Peter Arnold, Inc.; m.b.r. ©Denny Eilers/Grant Heilman Photography, Inc.; t.r. Owen Franken/Stock Boston; l.m. Inga Spence/Visuals Unlimited. A13: b.r. Jeff T. Green/Associated Press, AP; bkgd. Mark E. Gibson/Visuals Unlimited. A14: m.r. Jonathan Novrok/PhotoEdit; t.r. ©Bob Daemmrich/Stock Boston; bkgd. ©Thomas E. Franklin/The Record (Bergen County, NJ)/Corbis SABA. A15: ©Hulton Archive. A16: t.l. ©Tom Bean/Corbis; t.r. ©Larry Lefever/Grant Heilman Photography, Inc.; b.l. ©Grant Heilman Photography; bkgd. ©Arthur C. Smith III/Grant Heilman Photography, Inc.; m.l. ©Corbis; m.r. Jeff Greenberg/Visuals Unlimited. H4: b.r. Stone/Getty Images. H6: t. Colonial Williamsburg. H9–H10: National Geographic Society. 2-3: ©Liz Hymans/Panoramic Images. 4: t.r. ©David T. Roberts/Photo Researchers, Inc. 4-5: bkgd. ©Carr Clifton; b. ©Robert Winslow/ Viesti Associates, Inc. 6: b.l. ©Arthur C. Smith III/Grant Heilman Photography, Inc. 6-7: bkgd. ©Jim Steinberg/Photo Researchers, Inc.; t. ©Jake Rais/Tony Stone Images/Getty; 7: b. ©Charles Pefley/Stock Boston. 8-9: bkgd. ©Dennis Flaherty/Photo Researchers, Inc. 10: ©John Henley/The Stock Market. 12: t.r. ©Getty Images. 12-13: bkgd. ©John Mead/Science Photo Library/Photo Researchers, Inc.; b. ©Ed Bock/Corbis, The Stock Market. 13: t. ©Jeff Schultz/Alaska Stock. 14-15: bkgd. ©Breck P. Kent/Earth Scenes. 16: t.r. Lester Leflowitz/Corbis, The Stock Market; b.r. ©Richard Hutchings/Photoedit. 16-17: bkgd. ©Carr Clifton. 17: b.l. ©Getty Images. 18: t. ©Richard Durnan. 18-19: bkgd. ©Index Stock Imagery, Inc.; b. ©Natalie Fobes. 19: t. ©David Parker/Science Photo Library/Photo Researchers, Inc. 20-21: bkgd. ©John Post/Panoramic Images. 22: t.r. ©Lawrence Migdale; c.r. ©Sherman Hines/Masterfile; b.r. ©Richard Hutchings/PhotoEdit. 22-23: bkgd. ©88 John Gillmoure/Corbis, The Stock Market. 23: t.l. ©97 Jose Pelaez/Corbis, The Stock Market; c.l. ©John Running. 24: b. ©Lawrence Migdale; t.r. ©Ted Spiegel/Corbis. 25: t. ©David M. Grossman/Photo Researchers, Inc.; b.r. ©Haviv/Corbis Saba. 26: b.r. ©Richard Hutchings/Photoedit. 26-27: bkgd. ©Getty Images. 27: t. ©Joseph Sohm; ChromoSohm Inc./Corbis; b. ©Ed Bock/Corbis, The Stock Market. 28: t.r. ©Bassignac-BUU/Gamma Press; b. ©David Burnett/Contact Press Images. 28-29: bkgd. ©Jim Pickerell/Stock Connection/PictureQuest. 29: b.l. ©Supreme Court Historical Society. 30: ©Walter Bibikow/Folio, Inc. 31: t.r. ©Maxwell Mackenzie/Panoramic Images; b.l. ©The Supreme Court of the United States, Office of the Curator. 32-33: Courtesy of Food from the Hood. 34: t.r. ©Grant Heilman/Grant Heilman Photography. 34-35: bkgd. ©Bill Hoyt/Panoramic Images. 35: t. ©Lawrence Migdale; b.l. ©Ann Purcell/Carl Purcell/Words & Pictures/PictureQuest. 36: t.r. ©92 David Pollack/Corbis, The Stock Market; b. ©Getty Images. 36-37: bkgd. ©Carr Clifton. 37: b. ©Greg Ryan and Sally Beyer. 38: t.r. ©Bill Ross/Corbis; b. ©92 Charles Krebs/Corbis, The Stock Market; bkgd. ©Getty Images. 46-47: ©Joe Cornish/ Panoramic Images. 48: ©David Muench. 49: t. ©David Muench; b.l. ©Jeremy Woodhouse/DRK Photo. 50-51: ©Richard Sisk/Panoramic Images. 53: ©Caryl Benson/Masterfile. 54: ©C.C. Lockwood. 55: t. ©Kathleen Norris Cook; c.l. ©Gloria H. Chomica/Masterfile. 56: ©Kathleen Norris Cook. 58: c.r. Courtesy of Carrier Corporation; b.l. ©Superstock. 59: ©Bettmann/Corbis. 60: ©Bill Ross/Corbis. 61: ©John Boykin/Index Stock Imagery. 66: ©Getty Images. 68: t.l. ©Spindletop-Gladys City Boomtown Museum; b. ©Michael T. Sedam/Corbis. 73: t.l. Courtesy of Panhandle Plains Historical Museum, Canyon, TX; t.r. ©Superstock; b.l. Carolyn Brown/Getty Images/The Image Bank. 74: Jerry Jacka Photography; 75: ©John Running. 76-77 t. ©David Muench; b. ©Index Stock Imagery, Inc. 78: t. Jerry Jacka Photography; b. ©Stephen Trimble. 79: t. ©John Running; c.r. ©Stephen Trimble. 80-81: ©Wolfgang Kaehler. 82: t. ©David Samuel Robbins/Corbis; c. ©Dean Conger/Corbis; b. ©Dean Conger/Corbis. 83 t.l. ©Wolfgang Kaehler; c. Courtesy of the Division of Anthropology, American Museum of Natural History. 84: ©Don & Pat Valenti/DRK Photo. 85: Courtesy of Panhandle Plains Historical Museum, Canyon, TX. 86: Sam C. Pierson. 88: t. ©Superstock; t.c. ©Bettmann/Corbis, b. ©Robert Frerck/Odyssey/Chicago. 89: ©Christine Peters/Foodpix. 92: The Thomas Gilcrease Institute of American History and Art, Tulsa. 93: Library of Congress. 94: t. The Institute of Texan Cultures, San Antonio, Texas, Courtesy: Emmett Shelton; b.l. Henry Nelson ©Wichita Art Museum. 96: b.l. Zigy Caluzny; b.r. ©William Manns. 97: Jerry Jacka Photography. 98: ©Michelle Bridwell/PhotoEdit/PictureQuest. 99: t.l. ©Lawrence Migdale/Stock Boston; b.r. ©Archive Photos/PictureQuest. 100: ©Jim McNee/Index Stock Imagery. 101: t.r. Bill Ross/Westlight; b.r. ©Inga Spence/2001 Index Stock Imagery. 102: c.r. ©Roger Ressmeyer/Corbis; b. ©Erwin C. Nielson/Visuals Unlimited. 104: t.l. ©Lawrence Migdale/Stock Boston Inc./PictureQuest; b. ©Renee Lynn/Photo Researchers, Inc. 105: ©Joseph Sohm; ChromoSohm Inc./Corbis. 106: t.l. Courtesy of Diann Shearer; b.r. Courtesy of Jim Baca. 107: Courtesy of Ken Kramer. 116-117: ©Tim Fitzharris/Minden Pictures. 118: ©Getty Images. 119: t. ©Getty Images; b.l. Brown Brothers. 120: ©Philip Gould/Corbis. 122: t.r. ©David R. Frazier/Photo Researchers, Inc.; b.l. ©C.C. Lockwood. 124: t.r. ©CC Lockwood/DDB Stock Photo; b. ©Philip Gould/Corbis. 125: Visuals Unlimited. 128: Thomas Schneider/AGStockUSA. 129: ©Tim Turner/Foodpix. 130: c.r. David R. Frazier/Photo Researchers, Inc.; b. Steve Starr/Stock Boston. 131: ©Getty Images. 132: ©Kentucky Historical Society. 133: Alice M. Prescott/Unicorn Stock Photos. 134: ©Getty Images. 135: Courtesy of Kentucky Coal Mining Museum, Benham, Kentucky. 138: b.l. Lawrence Migdale; b.r. Colonial Williamsburg Foundation. 139: t. The Granger Collection; b.l. ©Getty Images. 140: Courtesy of Cherokee Historical Association. 141: ©Courtesy National Museum of the American Indian, Smithsonian Institution. Photo by Katherine Fogden. 142: t.l. Fred W. Marvel; c. North Wind Pictures. 143: t.r. The Granger Collection; b.l. Bob Annesley, AICA. 144: ©The Granger Collection. 145: t.r. Lawrence Migdale; c. Courtesy Frank H. McClung Museum, The University of Tennessee. W. Miles Wright, Photographer. 146: ©Bryan Hemphill/Index Stock Imagery. 147: t.r. Colonial Williamsburg. 148: b.r. ©Monticello; b.l. Unitversity Art Collection, Iowa State University. 149: Virginia Historical Society. 150: t.l. Walter P. Calahan/Folio, Inc.; b.r. Corbis. 151: t.r. Richard T. Nowitz/Folio, Inc.; l. Larry Fisher/Masterfile. 152: Denis Farrel/AP. 153: c.r. ©Corbis Images/PictureQuest; c. ©A. Ramey/Woodfin Camp & Associates. 154: Tl Mike Hutchings/AP; c. ©Zen Icknow/Corbis; br. Adil Bradlow/AP. 155: ©Roy Franco/Panos. 157: ©Don Rutledge/ Black Star Publishing/PictureQuest. 158: ©Brown Brothers. 159: ©Bettmann/Corbis. 160: ©Corbis. 161: t.r. ©The Corcoran Gallery of Art/Corbis; b.l. The Granger Collection; b.c. The Granger Collection. 162: National Portrait Gallery, Smithsonian Institution/Art Resource, NY. 163: t.r. ©Don Troiani; c. ©Don Troiani. 164: Hulton Deutsch/Woodfin Camp. 165: ©Bill Aron/Photoedit/Picturequest. 166: ©Bettmann/Corbis. 167: t.l. ©Elliot Erwin E/Magnum Photos; b.r. JM/Associated Press, AP. 168: ©Hulton-Duetsch Collection/Corbis. 169: ©Bettmann/Corbis. 170: t. National Conference of Black Mayors, Inc; b.l. Stephen J. Boitano, Stringer/Associated Press, AP. 171: l. Numismatic Collection at the Smithsonian; r. Courtesy of National Conference of Black Mayors, Inc. 172: Courtesy of Susan Snyder. 174: Bettmann Archives/Corbis. 182-183: ©Darrell Gulin/Imagebank. 184: ©Bill Hoyt/Panoramic. 185: t. ©Nancy Rotenberg/Animals Animals; b.l. ©Breck P. Kent/Earth Scenes. 186: ©S. Dunwell. 187: Index Stock Imagery, Inc. 188: t.r. ©William Taufic/Corbis, The Stock Market; c.l. William Johnson/Stock Boston; b. ©Michael P. Gadomski/Photo Researchers, Inc. 189: t.r. ©Steve C. Healey. 190: t. ©John Anderson/Earth Scenes; c.r. The Granger Collection; b.l. ©Micheal P, Gadomski/Photo Researchers. 191: ©D. John McCarthy/Panoramic. 192: ©Gary Crabbe/Earth Scenes. 193: t.r. Superstock; b.r. ©By Warner Bros./Photofest. 194: John W. Warden/Superstock. 195: t.l. ©Kevin Fleming/Corbis; c.r. ©Bill Heinsohn/Getty Images. 198: ©Kevin Fleming/Corbis. 199: ©Breck P. Kent/Earth Scenes. 200: Superstock. 201: ©Dan Cook/Cape Gazette. 202: ©James Randklev/Corbis. 204: t.r. ©Marilyn "Angel" Wynn/Nativestock.com; b. ©Superstock. 205: t. ©Joseph Sohm. ChromoSohm Inc./Corbis; b.l. ©Rafael Macia/Photo Researchers, Inc. 206: ©Jim Amos/Panoramic Images. 207: ©The Granger Collection. 208: t. ©New York State Museum; c.r. ©Marilyn "Angel" Wynn/Nativestock.com. 209: t.c. ©The National Museum of Denmark, Department of Ethnography, Copenhagen, photographed by Jesper Weng, copyright British Museum, London; c.r. ©Buffalo and Erie County Historical Society, copyright British Museum, London; b. ©Rochester Museum. 210: ©Lawrence Migdale. 211: t.l. ©Kit Breen; c.r. ©Courtesy National Museum of the American Indian, Smithsonian Institute. Photo by Carmelo Guadagno; 212: ©Courtesy of the Plimoth Plantation. 213: The Granger Collection. 214: Photri. 215: ©Bettmann/Corbis. 217: ©The Bridgeman Art Library. 219: t.l. ©The Granger Collection; b.r. ©The Granger Collection. 220: ©Paul Rocheleau. 221: t.c. ©Archive Photos/ colorized by Walter Stuart; b.r. ©David H. Wells/Corbis. 222: c.r. ©Charles Harrington, Cornell University Photo; b. ©Smithsonian Institute. 223: t.r. ©Collection of The New-York Historical Society. 224: c.r. ©The Granger Collection; b. ©Brown Brothers. 225: ©Steve Brosnaham/Lower East Side Tenement Museum. 226: ©Wolfgang Kaehler. 227: ©David Wells/Mira. 228: t.l. ©Niteen Kasle/Dinodia Picture Agency; b.r. ©Catherine Karnow/Woodfin Camp & Associates. 229: t. ©John Dominis/Indexstock; c.r. ©Dan Gair Photographic/Index Stock Photography. 232: ©Bill Ross/Corbis. 233: ©Martha Cooper. 234: ©AP Photo/Julia Malakie. 235: ©AP Photo/Chris Pfuhl. 236: t.l. ©Reuters NewMedia Inc./Corbis; b.r. ©Andrea Booher/Timepix. 237: ©Joseph Sohm, Chromo Sohm Inc./Corbis. 238: t.l. Courtesy of Mary Johnson; b.r. Courtesy of Valerie Burnette Edgar. 239: Courtsey of Lynn Wilkins. 248-249: ©Jim Blakeway/Panaromic Images. 250: ©Arthur C. Smith III/Grant Heilman Photography, Inc. 251: t. Annie Griffiths Belt; b.l. ©Grant Heilman, Grant Heilman Photography. 252-253: b. ©John Post/Panoramic Images. 253: t. Courtesy of Racing Champions Ertl Inc. 254: b.c. ©Arthur C. Smith III/Grant Heilman; b. ©Super Stock. 255: t.l. ©B.W. Hoffman/AGstockUSA; t.r. Pauline Madden/Corbis, The Stock Market; b. ©Getty Images. 256: ©BSIP/Chassenet/Science Source/Photo Researchers, Inc. 257: ©Arthur C, Smith III/Grant Heilman Photography. 258: ©Bob Winsett/Index Stock Imagery/PictureQuest. 259: t.

©New Moon Productions, Panoramic Images; c.r. ©PhotoDisc; b.r. Courtesy National Cherry Festival. 261: t.l. ©James Strawser/Grant Heilman Photography; c. ©Illinois Department of Agriculture; b.r. ©Edward R. Degginger/Bruce Coleman, Inc./PictureQuest. 262: t.r. ©David Ryan/Photo 20-20/PictureQuest; l.c. ©Cliff Riedinger/Alaska Stock; b. ©Nancy Sheehan/PhotoEdit. 263: t.r. ©Myrleen Ferguson Cate/PhotoEdit/PictureQuest; c. ©Siede Pries/Getty Images. 264: ©87 Kunio Owaki/Corbis, The Stock Market. 265: c.r. ©Michele Burgess/Corbis, Stock Market; t.r. ©Crazy Horse Memorial; b.r. ©Archive Photo/PictureQuest. 266: t.r. ©Richard Hamilton Smith; b.l. ©Richard Hamilton Smith. 267: ©Minnesota Department of Natural Resources. 270: Corcoran Gallery of Art. 271: t.l. ©The Bridgeman Art Library; t.r. ©Index Stock Imagery; b.l. ©Superstock. 272: ©Jan Butchofsky-Houser/Corbis. 273: Oakland Museum of California. 274: ©Star of the Republic Museum, TX/Lynn A. Hermann. 275: The Granger Collection. 276: ©The Granger Collection. 277: ©Bettmann/Corbis. 278: Denver Historical Society. 279: ©Library of Congress. 280: ©Walter McClintock/Southwest Museum. 281: ©Jeff Vanuga/PhotoEdit. 282: ©Superstock. 283: t.r. ©U.S. Department of Interior, Indian Arts and Craft Board, Museum of the Plains Indian, Photographed by Joe Fisher; t.c. National Museum of American Indian; b.l. Denver Museum. 284: t. ©Little Bighorn Battlefield National Monument, Montana; b.l. ©Corbis. 285: t.l. ©Southwest Museum; c.r. Ernest Berke. 286: ©Bettmann/Corbis. 287: t.l. ©Bettmann/Corbis/Colorized by Walter Stuart; c.r. From the Collections of Henry Ford Museum & Greenfield Village and Ford Motor Company. 288: t.r. The Phillips Collection; b.l. ©National Archives/Corbis. 290: b.l. ©Bettmann/Corbis; b.c. ©International Women's Air & Space Museum. 291: r. ©George Haling/Photo Researchers, Inc.; c. ASIMO photo courtesy of American Honda Motor Co., Inc. 292: ©Superstock. 293: t. ©Charles McDowell/ Grant Heilman Photography, Inc.; c.r. Ed Lallo/Picturequest. 294: t.r. ©Philip Gould/Corbis; b.l. Lester Lefkowitz/Corbis, The Stock Market. 295: c.r. ©Archives/The Image Works; b. ©James Schwabel/Panoramic Images. 297: t. ©Barry Durand/Odyssey/Chicago. 298: Martin Rogers/Stock Boston. 299: t.l. Ed Drew/Photo Researchers, Inc.; b.r. ©Walter Bibikow/FPG. 301: t.l. ©Painet, Inc.; t.r. ©Andy Caulfield/The Image Bank; t.c. Stuart Cohen/The Image Works. 302: Courtesy of Michael Kay. 304: ©Superstock. 312-313: ©Carr Clifton. 314: ©Panoramic Images. 315: t. ©Jack Krawczyk/Panoramic Images; b.l. ©Lenoard L.T. Rhodes/Animals Animals. 316-317: ©Mark Heifner/Panoramic Images. 317: t.r. ©Tom Brakefield/Corbis. 318: b. ©Inga Spence/Visuals Unlimited; t.r. ©William J. Weber/Visuals Unlimited. 319: ©Annie Griffiths Belt/Corbis. 320: ©Superstock. 321: t. ©David Hiser/Photographers Aspen; c.r. ©Jerry Jacka Photography. 322: ©Daniel H. Bailey MR/Index Stock Imagery. 323: t. ©Mark Heifner Panoramic Images; b. ©A. & J. Verkaik/Corbis Stock Market. 324: b.l. ©Patt Murray/Animals Animals/Earth Scenes. 324-325: t.r. ©Richard Elliot Sisk/Panoramic Images. 325: c.r. ©Robin Prange/Corbis Stock Market. 328: ©Vaughan Feleming/Science Photo Libary/Photo Researchers, Inc. 329: c.l. ©Peter Dreyer/The Picture Cube; t.l. ©Paul Lau/Gamma-Liason International; c.r. ©Richard Treplow/Photo Researchers, Inc. 330: t. ©James Foote/Photo Researchers, Inc.; b.l. ©Index Stock Imagery, Inc. 331: t.l. Joel Sartore/©Kennecott Utah Copper Corporation. 334: ©American Heritage Center, University of Wyoming. 335: t.l. ©Denver Public Libary, Colorado Historical Society, and Denver Museum; t.r. ©The Granger Collection New York; b.l. ©Superstock. 336: ©Eastcott/Momatiuk/Animals Animals/Earth Scenes. 337: ©Courtesy National Museum of the American Indian, Smithsonian Institution. 338: t.r. ©American Heritage Center, University of Wyoming. b. ©S. Michael Bisceglie/Animals Animals. 339: b.r. ©Larry Sanders/Milwaukee Art Museum, Layton Art Collection. 340: ©Don Pitcher/Stock Boston, Inc./Picturequest. 341: c.r. ©Marily "Angel" Wynn/Nativestock.com; t.l. ©Marilyn "Angel" Wynn/Nativestock.com. 342-343: Courtesy of the Montana Historical Society, Photographed by Den Beatty. 343: t.r. ©Smithsonian. 344: t.l. Colorado Historical Society; b. ©The Granger Collection, New York. 345: c. ©Jack Olson; c.r. ©Sherman Hines/Masterfile; b.r. ©Don Klumpp/The Image Bank. 346: ©Stanford University Museum of Art. 347: ©Bettmann/Corbis. 348: Bob Daemmrich/Stock Boston. 349: t.l. ©Dave G. Houser; b.r. ©Pat Hertz/North Dakota Tourism. 350: ©National Museum of American History. 351: ©The Granger Collection. 352: ©Corbis. 353: t.l. ©The Granger Collection; c.l. Courtesy of Sophia Smith Collection/Smith College; b.r. ©Culver Pictures. 354: ©Corbis. 355: t.r. ©David J. and Janice L. Frent Collection/CORBIS; c. Courtesy of the Sophia Smith Collection/Smith College. 356: Inset ©2000-2002, Access Idaho. All rights reserved. State of Idaho. 358: ©Mark Segal/Panoramic Images. 359: t.l. ©Bill Ross/Corbis; b.r. ©Karl Weatherly/Corbis; b.c. ©Salt Lake City Corporation, Designed by Cal Nez, Diné. 360: t.l. ©David Muench; c.r. Bertram G. Murray, Jr./Animals Animals; b. R.J. Erwin/Photo Researchers, Inc. 362: t.l. ©SuperStock; b. ©David Stoecklein/Corbis Stock Market. 363: Courtesy of the US Mint. 364: ©Ric Ergenbright/Corbis. 365: ©Wolfgang Kaehler. 366: t.l. Courtesy of Swatch Company; b.r. ©Richard T. Nowitz/Corbis. 367: ©Jess Stock/Stone/Getty. 368: t.l. Courtesy of Tom Fitzsimmons; b.r. Courtesy of Gwen Lachelt. 369: Courtesy of Wes Martel. 370: ©Bettmann/Corbis. 378-379: ©Brenda Tharp/Photo Researchers, Inc. 380: ©Superstock. 381: t. ©Lee Foster/Bruce Coleman, Inc.; b.l. ©John Giustina/Bruce Coleman, Inc. 382: ©Allen Prier/Panoramic Images. 383: ©David Mandison/Bruce Coleman, Inc. 384: t.l. ©Phil Degginger/Bruce Coleman, Inc.; t.l. ©Sipa-Press; b.r. ©Kraft-Explorer/Science Source/Photo Researchers, Inc. 385: ©Reuters NewMedia Inc./Corbis. 388: ©Phyllis Greenberg/Earth Scenes. 389: t.r. ©Phil Degginger/Bruce Coleman, Inc.; b.r. ©Steve Solum/Bruce Coleman Inc. 391: ©Index Stock Imagery, Inc. 392: ©Darren Bennett/Animals Animals. 394: ©Charles O'Rear/Corbis. 395: t.l. ©Gerald L. French/The PhotoFile; l.c. ©Scott Clemens/Pictor International; b.r. ©Michael T. Sedam/Corbis. 396: l. ©Stefan Schott/Panoramic Images; b.r. ©John Giustina/Bruce Coleman, Inc. 397: ©George Godfrey/Earth Scenes. 398: r. ©Frank S. Balthis; b.l. Courtesy Weyerhaeuser Company. 399: t.r. D.Robert & Lorrin Franz/Corbis; b. ©Peter Weiman/Animals Animals. 402: b.l. ©Douglas Peebles Photography; b.r. Courtesy of Bancroft Library, University of California, Berkeley. 403: t. Courtesy of the Arizona Historical Society/Tucson; b.l. Oliver Upton/Motion Picture and Television Archive. 404: ©Douglas Pebbles/Westlight. 406: t. ©Culver Pictures; c. ©The Granger Collection. b. ©CMCD/PhotoDisc/PictureQuest. 407: r.c. Bishop Museum Archives; t. Bishop Museum Archives. 408: Bishop Museum Archives. 409: t.r. ©Superstock; c.r. ©Andrew Ward/Life File/PhotoDisc/Getty Images. 410: Courtesy of The National Cowboy and Western Heritage Museum. 411: b.r. The Granger Collection; c. ©Underwood Archives, SF. 412: t.l. ©Corbis-Bettmann; b. ©Nawrocki Stock Photos. 413: b.r. ©North Wind Pictures/Colorized by Walter Stuart; c.r. ©Nawrocki Stock Photo. 415: ©Catherine Buchanan/Oakland Museum of California. 416-417: b. © Charlie Manz/Artistic Visuals. 418: ©San Francisco History Center, San Francisco Public Library. 419: ©Bruce Coleman Inc. 419-420: b. J.O. Tucker/National Geographic Society. 420: t.r. ©Tom Meyers. 421: m.l. ©1976 Bob Fitch/Take Stock. 422: t. The Granger Collection; b.r. ©University of Southern California Library. 423: ©Ronnie Kaufman/Corbis Stock Market. 424: ©Tim Davis/Photo Researchers. 425: Courtesy of Gary Soto. 426: ©Brenda Tharp/Photo Researchers. 427: t. ©Index Stock Imagery, Inc.; b.r. ©Roy Bishop/Stock Boston, Inc./PictureQuest. 428: b. ©Mark Newman/Visuals Unlimited; inset, t.l. ©Reuters/Dreamworks Pictures/Timepix; b.r. ©Reuters/Walt Disney Pictures and Pixar Animation Studio Films Handout/Timepix; t.l. ©CMCD/PhotoDisc/Getty Images. 429: t.m. ©Index Stock Imagery, Inc.; t.l. ©Michael Newman/PhotoEdit; b. ©Univac/Imagebank. 430: b.l. ©Bill Varie/Corbis; b.r. Photograph courtesy Worldwide Environmental Products, Inc. 431: m. ©Superstock; t. ©Superstock. 432: ©Index Stock Imagery, Inc. 434: t.r. ©Michael Macintyre/Hutchinson Picture Library; b.l. ©1998 Alon Reininger/Contact Press Images. 436: Courtesy of Ann Hudson and Salmon Corps.

Acknowledgments (continued from page ii)

From **Crazy Horse's Vision** by Joseph Bruchac. Copyright © 2000 by Joseph Bruchac. Lee & Low Books Inc., New York. Used by permission. From **Coolies** by Yin. Copyright © 2001 by Yin. Philomel Books, a division of Penguin Putnam Books, New York. Used by permission. From **The Legend of Freedom Hill** by Linda Jacobs Altman. Copyright © 2000 by Linda Jacobs Altman. Lee & Low Books Inc., New York. Used by permission. "The California Song" from **Songs the Whalemen Sang** by Gail Huntington. Copyright © 1970 Dover Publications Inc. Dover Publications Inc., New York. Used by permission. From **Farmers Pray For Rain But Wind Answers** by Associated Press, from the *Amarillo Daily News*, April 15, 1935. Used by permission. From "To Some Few Hopi Ancestors" by Wendy Rose from **Academic Squaw**. Copyright © 1977 by Wendy Rose. Blue Cloud Press, Marvin, South Dakota. Used by permission. From **Discover! America's Great River Road**, Volume 2, by Pat Middleton. Copyright © 1992 by Pat Middleton. Great River Publishing, Stoddard, Wisconsin. Used by permission. From **Long Walk to Freedom: The Autobiography of Nelson Mandela** by Nelson Mandela. Copyright © 1994 by Nelson Rolihlahla Mandela. Little, Brown and Company, Boston. Used by permission. From **Cry of the Thunderbird: The American Indian's Own Story**, edited by Charles Hamilton. Copyright © 1972 University of Oklahoma Press. Used by permission. "The California Song" from **Songs the Whalemen Sang** by Gail Huntington. Copyright © 1970 Dover Publications Inc. Dover Publications Inc., New York. Used by permission. From **Farmers Pray For Rain But Wind Answers** by Associated Press, from the *Amarillo Daily News*, April 15, 1935. Used by permission. From "To Some Few Hopi Ancestors" by Wendy Rose from **Academic Squaw**. Copyright © 1977 by Wendy Rose. Blue Cloud Press, Marvin, South Dakota. Used by permission. From **Discover! America's Great River Road**, Volume 2, by Pat Middleton. Copyright © 1992 by Pat Middleton. Great River Publishing, Stoddard, Wisconsin. Used by permission. From **Long Walk to Freedom: The Autobiography of Nelson Mandela** by Nelson Mandela. Copyright © 1994 by Nelson Rolihlahla Mandela. Little, Brown and Company, Boston. Used by permission. From **Cry of the Thunderbird: The American Indian's Own Story**, edited by Charles Hamilton. Copyright © 1972 University of Oklahoma Press. Used by permission. From **Storm Blindsides Cape Ann** by Gail McCarthy from the *Gloucester Daily Times*, October 31, 1991. Used by permission. From **Remembering Mount St. Helens** by Shelley Powers. Copyright © 1996–2001 by Burning Bird Enterprises, Inc. The Burning Bird Corporation, and YASD. www.burningbird.com Used by permission. From **Little House on the Prairie** by Laura Ingalls Wilder. Copyright © 1973 HarperCollins Publishers, New York. Used by permission. From **Gary Soto's Biography** by Gary Soto. Copyright © 2001–1996 by Scholastic Inc., New York. www.teacher.scholastic.com/authorsandbooks/authors/soto/bio.html Used by permission.